STRATEGIC

A

# The
# Changing
# Role of
# Information
# in Warfare

Edited by
**ZALMAY M. KHALILZAD**
**JOHN P. WHITE**

Foreword by
ANDREW W. MARSHALL

Prepared for the
United States Air Force

ution unlimited

The effects of new information technologies are all around us. Change is abundant in everything from the computers on our desks to the cell phones in our pockets. For the most part, we welcome these changes and the improvements they herald in our lives. These changes have also affected the global balance of power in favor of the United States.

But along with the blessings and opportunities come dangers. Information that is readily available is available to friend and foe alike; a system that relies on communication can become useless if its ability to communicate is interfered with or destroyed. Because this reliance is so general, attacks on the information infrastructure can have widespread effects, both for the military and for society. And such attacks can come from a variety of sources, some difficult or impossible to identify. This book focuses on the opportunities and vulnerabilities inherent in the increasing reliance on information technology, looking both at its usefulness to the warrior and the need to protect its usefulness for everyone.

While the work was carried out under the auspices of the Strategy and Doctrine program of RAND's Project AIR FORCE, which is sponsored by the U.S. Air Force, this volume draws on the expertise of researchers from across RAND in a variety of related disciplines. The primary audience of this work consists of Air Force leaders and planners, but it should be of interest to others interested in national security issues and information technology.

The *Strategic Appraisal* series is intended to review, for a broad audience, issues bearing on national security and defense planning.

*Strategic Appraisal 1997: Strategy and Defense Planning for the 21st Century,* dealt with the challenges the United States military faces in meeting the changing demands made upon it in a changing world. *Strategic Appraisal 1996* assessed challenges to U.S. interests around the world, focusing on key nations and regions.

## PROJECT AIR FORCE

Project AIR FORCE, a division of RAND, is the Air Force federally funded research and development center (FFRDC) for studies and analyses. It provides the Air Force with independent analyses of policy alternatives affecting the development, employment, combat readiness, and support of current and future aerospace forces. Research is being performed in three programs: Strategy and Doctrine, Force Modernization and Employment, and Resource Management and System Acquisition.

# CONTENTS

Preface . . . . . . . . . . . . . . . . . . . . . . . . . . . . . . . . . . . . . . . . . . . . . . . . iii

Figures . . . . . . . . . . . . . . . . . . . . . . . . . . . . . . . . . . . . . . . . . . . . . . . xiii

Tables . . . . . . . . . . . . . . . . . . . . . . . . . . . . . . . . . . . . . . . . . . . . . . . . . xv

Acknowledgments . . . . . . . . . . . . . . . . . . . . . . . . . . . . . . . . . . . . xvii

Abbreviations . . . . . . . . . . . . . . . . . . . . . . . . . . . . . . . . . . . . . . . . . xix

Foreword
    *Andrew W. Marshall* . . . . . . . . . . . . . . . . . . . . . . . . . . . . . . 1

Chapter One
  INTRODUCTION
    *Zalmay Khalilzad and John White* . . . . . . . . . . . . . . . . . . 7
    Structure of the Book . . . . . . . . . . . . . . . . . . . . . . . . . . . . . . 11
        Information Technology and Society . . . . . . . . . . . . . 11
        U.S. Opportunities and Vulnerabilities . . . . . . . . . . . . 12
        Issues and Lessons for Decisionmakers . . . . . . . . . . . . 13
    References . . . . . . . . . . . . . . . . . . . . . . . . . . . . . . . . . . . . . . 14

PART I:  SOCIETY AND THE INTERNATIONAL SYSTEM . . . . . 17

Chapter Two
  THE AMERICAN MILITARY ENTERPRISE IN THE
  INFORMATION AGE
    *Carl H. Builder* . . . . . . . . . . . . . . . . . . . . . . . . . . . . . . . . . 19
    Introduction:  The Social and Military Perspectives . . . . . 19
    The Roots of Revolution . . . . . . . . . . . . . . . . . . . . . . . . . . 20
    Historical Patterns . . . . . . . . . . . . . . . . . . . . . . . . . . . . . . . 24

Cultural Factors . . . . . . . . . . . . . . . . . . . . . . . . . . . . .    26
What Is the Enterprise? . . . . . . . . . . . . . . . . . . . . . . . .    28
Adapting to the Information Revolution . . . . . . . . . . . . . .    32
Applying New Technologies to Old Enterprises . . . . . . . .    35
The Future Enterprise of the Military . . . . . . . . . . . . . . .    37
Bibliography . . . . . . . . . . . . . . . . . . . . . . . . . . . . . . . .    42

Chapter Three
RIGHT MAKES MIGHT:  FREEDOM AND POWER IN
THE INFORMATION AGE
*David C. Gompert* . . . . . . . . . . . . . . . . . . . . . . . . . . .    45
Introduction . . . . . . . . . . . . . . . . . . . . . . . . . . . . . . . .    45
    Information Technology and World Politics . . . . . . . . .    45
    Implications . . . . . . . . . . . . . . . . . . . . . . . . . . . . . .    48
Information Technology Needs Freedom . . . . . . . . . . . . .    50
    Knowledge and Economic Freedom . . . . . . . . . . . . . .    50
    Knowledge and Political Freedom . . . . . . . . . . . . . . .    55
    Economic Freedom and Political Freedom . . . . . . . . . .    56
National Power Needs Information Technology . . . . . . . .    59
    Information Technology and Military Capabilities . . . .    59
    Freedom as Vulnerability . . . . . . . . . . . . . . . . . . . . .    62
    The Changing Profile of Power . . . . . . . . . . . . . . . . .    65
Powers as Partners . . . . . . . . . . . . . . . . . . . . . . . . . . .    66
    Power, Integration, and Common Success . . . . . . . . . .    66
    Integrating Rising Powers . . . . . . . . . . . . . . . . . . . .    69
    The Future of the Core . . . . . . . . . . . . . . . . . . . . . . .    70
Bibliography . . . . . . . . . . . . . . . . . . . . . . . . . . . . . . . .    73

Chapter Four
NETWORKS, NETWAR, AND INFORMATION-AGE
TERRORISM
*John Arquilla, David Ronfeldt, and Michele Zanini* . . . . . .    75
A New Terrorism (with Old Roots) . . . . . . . . . . . . . . . . .    75
Recent Views About Terrorism . . . . . . . . . . . . . . . . . . . .    78
The Advent of Netwar—Analytical Background . . . . . . . .    80
    Definition of Netwar . . . . . . . . . . . . . . . . . . . . . . . . .    82
    More About Organizational Design . . . . . . . . . . . . . . .    83
    Caveats About the Role of Technology . . . . . . . . . . . . .    87
    Swarming, and the Blurring of Offense and Defense . . .    88
    Networks Versus Hierarchies:  Challenges for
        Counternetwar . . . . . . . . . . . . . . . . . . . . . . . . . . .    89

Middle Eastern Terrorism and Netwar . . . . . . . . . . . . . .    90
  Middle Eastern Terrorist Groups:  Structure and
    Actions . . . . . . . . . . . . . . . . . . . . . . . . . . . . . . . . .    92
  Middle Eastern Terrorist Groups and the Use of
    Information Technology . . . . . . . . . . . . . . . . . . . . .    97
  Summary Comment  . . . . . . . . . . . . . . . . . . . . . . . . . .    100
Terrorist Doctrines—The Rise of a "War Paradigm" . . . . .    101
  The Coercive-Diplomacy Paradigm . . . . . . . . . . . . . .    101
  The War Paradigm . . . . . . . . . . . . . . . . . . . . . . . . . .    102
  The New World Paradigm  . . . . . . . . . . . . . . . . . . . . .    103
  The Paradigms and Netwar . . . . . . . . . . . . . . . . . . . .    104
References  . . . . . . . . . . . . . . . . . . . . . . . . . . . . . . . . . . .    105

Chapter Five
INFORMATION AND WAR:  IS IT A REVOLUTION?
*Jeremy Shapiro* . . . . . . . . . . . . . . . . . . . . . . . . . . . . . . . .    113
Introduction: Al-Khafji . . . . . . . . . . . . . . . . . . . . . . . . . .    113
The Meaning of Revolution . . . . . . . . . . . . . . . . . . . . . . .    114
Possible Revolutions . . . . . . . . . . . . . . . . . . . . . . . . . . . .    117
  Social Revolution . . . . . . . . . . . . . . . . . . . . . . . . . . . .    118
  Political Revolution . . . . . . . . . . . . . . . . . . . . . . . . . .    123
  Military Revolution  . . . . . . . . . . . . . . . . . . . . . . . . . .    129
Evolutionary and Revolutionary Proposals . . . . . . . . . . .    142
Conclusion:  Implications of a False Revolution  . . . . . . . .    146
References  . . . . . . . . . . . . . . . . . . . . . . . . . . . . . . . . . . .    148

PART II:  U.S. OPPORTUNITIES AND VULNERABILITIES . . . .    155

Chapter Six
INFORMATION AND WARFARE:  NEW
OPPORTUNITIES FOR U.S. MILITARY FORCES
*Edward Harshberger and David Ochmanek* . . . . . . . . . . .    157
Information in Warfare: A Simple Taxonomy . . . . . . . . . .    158
  Knowing the Enemy . . . . . . . . . . . . . . . . . . . . . . . . . . .    158
  Knowing Yourself . . . . . . . . . . . . . . . . . . . . . . . . . . . .    159
  Knowing the Ground, Knowing the Weather . . . . . . . .    160
  Controlling Forces . . . . . . . . . . . . . . . . . . . . . . . . . . . .    160
  Speed and Decisiveness . . . . . . . . . . . . . . . . . . . . . . . .    161
  A Two-Sided Game  . . . . . . . . . . . . . . . . . . . . . . . . . . .    162
Future Victory:  New Opportunities . . . . . . . . . . . . . . . . .    162
  Military Advances in Information Technology . . . . . . . .    163

How New Information Capabilities Might Affect
    U.S. Military Operations . . . . . . . . . . . . . . . . . . . . . . .    170
Conclusions . . . . . . . . . . . . . . . . . . . . . . . . . . . . . . . . .    176
References  . . . . . . . . . . . . . . . . . . . . . . . . . . . . . . . . .    178

Chapter Seven
U.S. MILITARY OPPORTUNITIES:  INFORMATION-
WARFARE CONCEPTS OF OPERATION
*Brian Nichiporuk*  . . . . . . . . . . . . . . . . . . . . . . . . . . . .    179
Introduction . . . . . . . . . . . . . . . . . . . . . . . . . . . . . . . . .    179
    What Do We Mean by "Information Warfare"?  . . . . . . .    180
    The Importance of Offensive Information Warfare  . . . .    181
Emerging Asymmetric Strategies  . . . . . . . . . . . . . . . . . .    183
    Increasing Niche Capabilities . . . . . . . . . . . . . . . . . . .    184
    Enemy Strategies That Target Key U.S.
        Vulnerabilities . . . . . . . . . . . . . . . . . . . . . . . . . . . .    188
    Political Constraints on U.S. Force Deployments  . . . . .    190
Developing Operational Concepts for Future Offensive
    Information Warfare  . . . . . . . . . . . . . . . . . . . . . . . . .    191
Information-Based Deterrence . . . . . . . . . . . . . . . . . . . .    193
Preserving Strategic Reach . . . . . . . . . . . . . . . . . . . . . .    198
Counterstrike. . . . . . . . . . . . . . . . . . . . . . . . . . . . . . . .    202
Counter-C4ISR  . . . . . . . . . . . . . . . . . . . . . . . . . . . . . .    207
Comparing the Four CONOPs  . . . . . . . . . . . . . . . . . . . .    211
References  . . . . . . . . . . . . . . . . . . . . . . . . . . . . . . . . .    213

Chapter Eight
THE INFORMATION REVOLUTION AND
PSYCHOLOGICAL EFFECTS
*Stephen T. Hosmer*. . . . . . . . . . . . . . . . . . . . . . . . . . . .    217
Objectives and Instruments of Psychological Effects . . . . .    217
U.S. and Enemy Experience with Psychological Effects . . .    219
    U.S.-Caused Psychological Effects at the Strategic
        Level:  Air Attacks on Enemy Strategic Targets . . . . . .    219
    U.S.-Caused Psychological Effects at the
        Operational and Tactical Levels . . . . . . . . . . . . . . . .    221
    Enemy-Caused Psychological Effects at the
        Strategic Level . . . . . . . . . . . . . . . . . . . . . . . . . . . .    224
    Enemy-Caused Psychological Effects at the
        Operational and Tactical Levels . . . . . . . . . . . . . . . .    230

Advanced Technological Systems and Psychological
    Effects . . . . . . . . . . . . . . . . . . . . . . . . . . . . . . . . . . . . . .    231
  Impact of Advanced Systems on Future War-Fighting
    Capabilities . . . . . . . . . . . . . . . . . . . . . . . . . . . . . . . . .    231
  Implications for Future U.S.-Caused Psychological
    Effects . . . . . . . . . . . . . . . . . . . . . . . . . . . . . . . . . . . . . .    232
  Implications for Future Enemy-Caused
    Psychological Effects . . . . . . . . . . . . . . . . . . . . . . . . . .    236
The Need to Manage Future Psychological Effects . . . . . .    242
  Managing Psychological Effects in a Changing
    Information Environment . . . . . . . . . . . . . . . . . . . . . .    242
  Managing the Psychological Effects of Future
    Military Operations . . . . . . . . . . . . . . . . . . . . . . . . . .    245
Conclusion . . . . . . . . . . . . . . . . . . . . . . . . . . . . . . . . . . . . .    247
References . . . . . . . . . . . . . . . . . . . . . . . . . . . . . . . . . . . . .    248

Chapter Nine
U.S. STRATEGIC VULNERABILITIES: THREATS
AGAINST SOCIETY
*Roger C. Molander, Peter A. Wilson, and Robert H.*
*Anderson*. . . . . . . . . . . . . . . . . . . . . . . . . . . . . . . . . . . . . . . .    253
What Is SIW? . . . . . . . . . . . . . . . . . . . . . . . . . . . . . . . . . . . . .    253
U.S. Strategic Infrastructure Vulnerabilities
    and Threats . . . . . . . . . . . . . . . . . . . . . . . . . . . . . . . . . .    256
  Information and Communications . . . . . . . . . . . . . . . . .    259
  Physical Distribution . . . . . . . . . . . . . . . . . . . . . . . . . . .    260
  Energy . . . . . . . . . . . . . . . . . . . . . . . . . . . . . . . . . . . . . . . .    261
  Banking and Finance . . . . . . . . . . . . . . . . . . . . . . . . . . . .    262
  Vital Human Services . . . . . . . . . . . . . . . . . . . . . . . . . . . .    263
The Need for New Decisionmaking Frameworks . . . . . . .    263
An Evolving Series of Frameworks . . . . . . . . . . . . . . . . . . .    264
An Initial Formulation . . . . . . . . . . . . . . . . . . . . . . . . . . . . .    264
  Key Dimensions of the SIW Environment . . . . . . . . . . .    266
  Key Strategy and Policy Issues . . . . . . . . . . . . . . . . . . . .    267
  Current State of First-Generation SIW . . . . . . . . . . . . .    271
  Alternative First-Generation SIW End States . . . . . . . .    275
  Alternative Action Plans . . . . . . . . . . . . . . . . . . . . . . . . .    277
Conclusions . . . . . . . . . . . . . . . . . . . . . . . . . . . . . . . . . . . . .    280
References . . . . . . . . . . . . . . . . . . . . . . . . . . . . . . . . . . . . .    280

Chapter Ten
    IMPLICATIONS OF INFORMATION VULNERABILITIES
    FOR MILITARY OPERATIONS
    *Glenn C. Buchan* . . . . . . . . . . . . . . . . . . . . . . . . . . .    283
    An Overview of Air Force Operations and Their
        Dependence on Information:  Present
        and Future . . . . . . . . . . . . . . . . . . . . . . . . . . . . .    284
    Disrupting Air Force Operations  . . . . . . . . . . . . . . . . .    287
        Potential Threats . . . . . . . . . . . . . . . . . . . . . . . . .    287
        Potential Vulnerabilities . . . . . . . . . . . . . . . . . . . . .    290
    Direct Impacts of Information Disruption  . . . . . . . . . . .    296
    Operational Implications  . . . . . . . . . . . . . . . . . . . . . .    298
        Major Conflicts  . . . . . . . . . . . . . . . . . . . . . . . . . .    298
        Lesser Operations  . . . . . . . . . . . . . . . . . . . . . . . .    307
    Reducing Vulnerabilities and Coping with Their Effects  . .    313
        Why Intelligence Assessments and Warning Concepts
            Are Largely Irrelevant . . . . . . . . . . . . . . . . . . . . .    313
        How to Defend and Recover . . . . . . . . . . . . . . . . . .    317
    Conclusions  . . . . . . . . . . . . . . . . . . . . . . . . . . . . . .    321
    References  . . . . . . . . . . . . . . . . . . . . . . . . . . . . . . .    322

PART III:  ISSUES, STRATEGIES, AND LESSONS FOR
    DECISIONMAKERS . . . . . . . . . . . . . . . . . . . . . . . . . .    325

Chapter Eleven
    MILITARY ORGANIZATION IN THE INFORMATION
    AGE: LESSONS FROM THE WORLD OF BUSINESS
    *Francis Fukuyama and Abram N. Shulsky* . . . . . . . . . . . .    327
    The Importance of Organization in a Time of
        Revolutionary Change . . . . . . . . . . . . . . . . . . . . . . .    327
    The Effects of the "Information Revolution" on
        Corporate Organization . . . . . . . . . . . . . . . . . . . . .    330
        Flattening:  Creating Shorter Data Paths . . . . . . . . . . .    331
        "Informating"  . . . . . . . . . . . . . . . . . . . . . . . . . . .    335
        Concentrating on "Core Competencies" . . . . . . . . . . .    338
    Implications for the U.S. Armed Forces  . . . . . . . . . . . . .    340
        Organizational Structures  . . . . . . . . . . . . . . . . . . . .    342
        Creating a Learning Institution . . . . . . . . . . . . . . . . .    344
        Personnel Policy:  "Freedom to Fail" . . . . . . . . . . . . .    349
        Personnel Policy:  Distribution of Skills in the
            Organization . . . . . . . . . . . . . . . . . . . . . . . . . . .    352

"Revolution in Business Affairs": Procurement . . . . . . .  353
Organizational Structure Must Reflect Objectives . . . . . . .  357
Exogenous Political Constraints . . . . . . . . . . . . . . . . . . .  358
References . . . . . . . . . . . . . . . . . . . . . . . . . . . . . . . . . . .  359

Chapter Twelve
ARMS CONTROL, EXPORT REGIMES, AND
MULTILATERAL COOPERATION
*Lynn E. Davis* . . . . . . . . . . . . . . . . . . . . . . . . . . . . . . . . .  361
  Past Accomplishments . . . . . . . . . . . . . . . . . . . . . . . . . .  362
    Arms Control . . . . . . . . . . . . . . . . . . . . . . . . . . . . . . . .  362
    Export Control Regimes . . . . . . . . . . . . . . . . . . . . . . . .  364
    Multilateral Cooperation . . . . . . . . . . . . . . . . . . . . . . .  366
  Information Systems and Technologies . . . . . . . . . . . . . .  367
    Arms Control . . . . . . . . . . . . . . . . . . . . . . . . . . . . . . . .  367
    Export Controls . . . . . . . . . . . . . . . . . . . . . . . . . . . . . .  371
    Multilateral Cooperation . . . . . . . . . . . . . . . . . . . . . . .  374
  A Strategy During This Time of Uncertainty . . . . . . . . . . .  375
  References . . . . . . . . . . . . . . . . . . . . . . . . . . . . . . . . . . .  377

Chapter Thirteen
ETHICS AND INFORMATION WARFARE
*John Arquilla* . . . . . . . . . . . . . . . . . . . . . . . . . . . . . . . . . .  379
  Concepts and Definitions . . . . . . . . . . . . . . . . . . . . . . . .  380
    The Concepts of Just War Theory . . . . . . . . . . . . . . . . .  381
    Defining Information Warfare . . . . . . . . . . . . . . . . . . . .  384
  Just War Theory and Information Warfare . . . . . . . . . . . .  386
    Jus ad Bellum . . . . . . . . . . . . . . . . . . . . . . . . . . . . . . . .  387
    Jus in Bello . . . . . . . . . . . . . . . . . . . . . . . . . . . . . . . . . .  388
  Some Guidelines for Policy . . . . . . . . . . . . . . . . . . . . . . .  391
    Policy Toward Going to War . . . . . . . . . . . . . . . . . . . . .  392
    On Just Warfighting . . . . . . . . . . . . . . . . . . . . . . . . . . .  394
  Closing Thoughts . . . . . . . . . . . . . . . . . . . . . . . . . . . . . .  398
  References . . . . . . . . . . . . . . . . . . . . . . . . . . . . . . . . . . .  398

Chapter Fourteen
DEFENSE IN A WIRED WORLD: PROTECTION,
DETERRENCE, AND PREVENTION
*Zalmay Khalilzad* . . . . . . . . . . . . . . . . . . . . . . . . . . . . . .  403
  The Threat . . . . . . . . . . . . . . . . . . . . . . . . . . . . . . . . . . .  406
  The Attacks . . . . . . . . . . . . . . . . . . . . . . . . . . . . . . . . . . .  410

Strategies of Defense: Protection, Deterrence, and
    Prevention................................... 412
    Protection .................................... 413
    Deterrence ................................... 418
    Prevention.................................... 426
Toward a National Strategy for Information-Warfare
    Defense..................................... 433
References ..................................... 434

Chapter Fifteen
CONCLUSION: THE CHANGING ROLE OF
INFORMATION IN WARFARE
*Martin Libicki and Jeremy Shapiro*.................. 437
Trend or Fad? ................................... 438
Perfect Security? ................................ 440
National Policy Issues ............................ 442
Air Force Policy Issues ........................... 447
A Timeless Lesson of Information Warfare ............ 451
References ..................................... 452

4.1   Types of Networks . . . . . . . . . . . . . . . . . . . . . . . . . . .   85
6.1   JSTARS Picture of Moving Mechanized Forces . . . . . .   164
6.2   Effects of Weapon Accuracy on Weapon Needs . . . . .   173
6.3   Operational Impact of Effective Wide-Area
      Surveillance of Moving Ground Forces . . . . . . . . . . .   175
6.4   Armored Vehicle Interdiction: Yesterday
      and Today. . . . . . . . . . . . . . . . . . . . . . . . . . . . . . . .   177
7.1   Adversary Asymmetric Options and Potential
      CONOPs . . . . . . . . . . . . . . . . . . . . . . . . . . . . . . . . . .   192
9.1   Future U.S. Regional Adversaries Might Seek
      Asymmetric Strategies . . . . . . . . . . . . . . . . . . . . . . . .   254
9.2   Two Concepts of SIW . . . . . . . . . . . . . . . . . . . . . . . . .   255
9.3   Designing a First-Generation SIW Strategy and
      Policy Decisionmaking Framework . . . . . . . . . . . . . .   265
10.1  Air Force Combat Operations . . . . . . . . . . . . . . . . . .   285
10.2  Supporting the Forces and Sustaining Operations . . .   286
10.3  Potential Threats to Air Force Information
      Systems . . . . . . . . . . . . . . . . . . . . . . . . . . . . . . . . . .   288
10.4  Potential Computer Vulnerabilities in the AOC . . . . . .   291
10.5  Potential Computer Vulnerabilities in the Support
      and Sustainability Network . . . . . . . . . . . . . . . . . . . .   292
10.6  Some Typical Theater Air Communication Links . . . .   294
10.7  Air Force Systems Rely Heavily on Defense and
      Public Information Infrastructure . . . . . . . . . . . . . . .   295
10.8  GPS Jamming Can Reduce Weapon Accuracy
      Substantially . . . . . . . . . . . . . . . . . . . . . . . . . . . . . .   297
10.9  Potential Effects of Attacks on Information
      Systems . . . . . . . . . . . . . . . . . . . . . . . . . . . . . . . . . .   298

10.10   Arrival Delays Have Little Effect . . . . . . . . . . . . . . . . .    300
10.11   Planning Cycle Delays Have Only Minor Effect . . . . . .    300
10.12   Maintaining Multiple Types of Munitions May
        Reduce the Impact of the Vulnerability of
        Specific Types of Systems  . . . . . . . . . . . . . . . . . . . . .    305
10.13   The Combination of Reduced Force Structure and
        Simplified Weapon Mix Can Substantially
        Increase the Impact of Information
        Vulnerabilities . . . . . . . . . . . . . . . . . . . . . . . . . . . . . .    305

# TABLES

7.1   Comparing the Four CONOPs . . . . . . . . . . . . . . . . . .   211

9.1   From Defining Features to Key Dimensions of the
SIW Environment . . . . . . . . . . . . . . . . . . . . . . . . . . .   267

9.2   Alternative Action Plans . . . . . . . . . . . . . . . . . . . . . .   278

10.1   Summary of Information Vulnerabilities and
Their Impact on the Outcome of Major
Conventional Campaigns . . . . . . . . . . . . . . . . . . . . .   306

10.2   Characteristics of Some Generic Types of Low-
Intensity Conflicts and Lesser Operations—
Implications for Information Sensitivities . . . . . . . . .   308

10.3   Low-Cost Package to Reduce Obvious
Vulnerabilities . . . . . . . . . . . . . . . . . . . . . . . . . . . . .   318

10.4   Supplementary Package to Enhance Security
Against All Levels of Threats Substantially . . . . . . . .   320

14.1   Information-Warfare Actors . . . . . . . . . . . . . . . . . . . .   407

14.2   Information-Warfare Attacks . . . . . . . . . . . . . . . . . . .   411

14.3   Information-Warfare Actors and Strategies . . . . . . . .   433

15.1   Information-Warfare Matrix . . . . . . . . . . . . . . . . . . .   449

# ACKNOWLEDGMENTS

The editors would like to thank Jeremy Shapiro for his research support. Without his diligence, the book would not have been completed. We are indebted to Phyllis Gilmore for enhancing the clarity of the text and shepherding the book though the publication process. Thanks are also due to Dick Neu for his oversight of the review process and to Natalie Crawford for her support of the Strategic Appraisal series.

| | |
|---|---|
| ABCCC | Airborne battlefield command and control center |
| ACC | Air Combat Command |
| ADANS | Airlift Deployment Analysis System |
| AFCERT | Air Force |
| AMC | Air Mobility Command |
| ANO | Abu Nidal Organization |
| AOC | Air Operations Center |
| ASAT | Antisatellite |
| ASTERX | A commercial e-mail system used in CTAPS |
| AT&T | American Telephone and Telegraph |
| ATO | Air Tasking Order |
| AUTODIN | Automatic Digital Network |
| BCE | Before the common era |
| BDA | Battle damage assessment |
| C/A | Course acquisition |
| C2 | Command and control |
| C2IPS | Command and Control Information Processing System |
| C2W | Command-and-control warfare |
| C4ISR | Command, control, communications, computing, intelligence, surveillance, and reconnaissance |
| CAFMS | Computer Assisted Force Management System |
| CDC | Centers for Disease Control |

| | |
|---|---|
| CE | The common era |
| CEO | Chief executive officer |
| CEP | Circular error probable |
| CFE | Conference on Forces in Europe |
| CINC | Commander in chief |
| CNN | Cable News Network |
| CONOP | Concept of operation |
| CONUS | Continental United States |
| COTS | Commercial off-the-shelf |
| CRC | Combat and Recording Center |
| CRE | Combat Reporting Element |
| CSCE | Conference on Security and Cooperation in Europe |
| CTAPS | Contingency Theater Automated Planning System |
| CW | Continuous wave |
| DEC | Digital Equipment Corporation |
| DFLP | Democratic Front for the Liberation of Palestine |
| DMS | Defense Message System |
| DoD | Department of Defense |
| DOT | U.S. Department of Transportation |
| DSB | Defense Science Board |
| EIW | Economic information warfare |
| ELINT | Electronic intelligence |
| EO-IR | Electro-optical infrared |
| EU | European Union |
| EW | Electronic warfare |
| EZLN | Zapatista National Liberation Army |
| FLTSATCOM | Fleet Satellite Communications |
| GAO | U.S. General Accounting Office |
| GCCS | Global Command and Control System |
| GEO | Geosynchronous orbit |
| GIA | Armed Islamic Group |
| GLONASS | A Russian system similar to GPS |

| | |
|---|---|
| GPS | Global Positioning System |
| GVN | Government of South Vietnam |
| HIC | High-intensity conflicts |
| HMS | His Majesty's Ship (a British vessel) |
| HPM | High-power microwave |
| I&C | Information and communications |
| IADS | Integrated air defense system |
| IBM | International Business Machines |
| IBW | Intelligence-based warfare |
| ICBMs | Intercontinental ballistic missiles |
| IG | Islamic Group |
| ILP | Islamic Liberation Party |
| IMINT | Image intelligence |
| IP | Internet Protocol |
| ISR | Intelligence, surveillance, and reconnaissance |
| JDAM | Joint Direct Attack Munition |
| JFACC | Joint Forces Air Component Commander |
| JSTARS | Joint Surveillance and Target Attack Radar System |
| JTIDS | Joint Tactical Information Distribution System |
| KTO | Kuwait Theater of Operations |
| LEO | Low-earth orbit |
| LIC | Low-intensity conflicts |
| MEII | Minimum essential information infrastructure |
| MILSTAR | Military Strategic and Tactical Relay System |
| MOOTW | Military operations other than war |
| MRC | Major regional conflict or contingency |
| MTCR | Missile Technology Control Regime |
| MTW | Major theater war |
| NATO | North Atlantic Treaty Organization |
| NGO | Nongovernmental organization |
| NICON | National Infrastructure Condition |
| NIPC | National Infrastructure Protection Center |

| | |
|---|---|
| NLF | National Liberation Front |
| NVA | North Vietnamese Army |
| OODA | "Observe, orient, decide, act"—a sequence of actions for fighter pilots to react more quickly than the opponent (Chapter Six) |
| OOTW | Operations other than war |
| P | Position code |
| Pan Am | Pan American Airlines |
| PBX | Private branch exchange |
| PCCIP | President's Commission on Critical Infrastructure Protection |
| PFLP | People's Front for the Liberation of Palestine |
| PFLP-GC | People's Front for the Liberation of Palestine–General Command |
| PIJ | Palestinian Islamic Jihad |
| PLF | Palestine Liberation Front |
| PLO | Palestine Liberation Organization |
| PRG | Provisional Revolutionary Government |
| PSN | Public switched network |
| PSYOP | Psychological operations |
| PSYW | Psychological warfare |
| R&D | Research and development |
| Recce | Reconnaissance |
| RMA | Revolution in military affairs |
| S&T | Science and technology |
| SALT | Strategic Arms Limitation Treaty |
| SCADA | Supervisory Control and Data Acquisition systems |
| SFW | Sensor fuzed weapon |
| SIGINT | Signals intelligence |
| SIW | Strategic information warfare |
| SNA | Somalia National Alliance |
| SOCOM | Southern Command |
| SONET | Synchronous optical networks |

| | |
|---|---|
| SPIN | Segmented, polycentric, ideologically integrated network |
| SSBN | Ballistic-missile submarines |
| START | Strategic Arms Reduction Talks |
| TADIL | Tactical Data Information Link |
| TADIL–J | Tactical Data Information Link-JTIDS |
| TARPS | Tactical Aerial Reconnaissance Pod System |
| TCO | Transnational criminal organizations |
| TRADOC | U.S. Army Training and Doctrine Command |
| TW/AA | Tactical warning and attack assessment |
| UAV | Unmanned aerial vehicle |
| UN | United Nations |
| WCCS | Wing command and control system |
| WHO | World Health Organization |
| WMD | Weapons of mass destruction |
| WOC | Wing Operations Center |
| Y2K | Year 2000 |

*Andrew W. Marshall*

This effort to assess how the role of information in warfare is changing seeks to understand many of the remarkable developments under way in information and communications technology, and their potential effects on warfare.  It is because the uncertainties are so substantial in this realm that this effort by Zalmay Khalilzad, John White, and their collaborators is so admirable.  They are attempting to deal with a topic whose complexities and lack of consensus, at present, easily match its importance.  The principal value in such an effort is that it helps to organize our thoughts and to sort out the areas of agreement and disagreement.  Indeed, this volume reveals several important lessons that can be gleaned from the very different and distinct perspectives contained in it:

- Information advances will affect more than just how we fight wars. The nature and purpose of war itself may change. How wars start, how they end, their length, and the nature of the participants may change as shifts in the relative power of states and nonstate entities occur.

- New technologies cut both ways in terms of their effects on national security.  Together, the chapters make clear that advances create new vulnerabilities; new threats create new opportunities.  We should resist the temptation to see the changes documented here either as wholly bad or wholly good. Rather, we need to understand that profound technological changes are inevitably two sided.

- The Department of Defense (DoD) has little control over the pace and direction of the information revolution.  Although in

1

the past DoD played an important role in developing, refining, and implementing new information technologies, today the technological envelope is being pushed largely by the commercial sector. DoD needs to manage a difficult transition from being a pioneer to being a leading user. This transition will require not only keeping abreast of new technological developments but also accepting that technology will no longer be developed exactly to military specifications.

- The increasing capacity to produce, communicate, and use information will have an important effect on every area of national security. Information is everywhere. As a result, we will not be able to understand how these new technologies will change our own jobs unless we understand how they will change the jobs of others. The advent of the information age will require, as never before, that we take a wider perspective and avoid stovepipes that blind us to changes taking place outside our own spheres of direct responsibility.

Considering how the U.S. defense establishment operates today, these lessons are important and not as self-evident as they might first appear. Unfortunately, they provide only the broadest guidance for how to adapt to the whirl of changes we face. As the chapters indicate, any consensus on more detailed instruction escapes us at the moment. In part, this is because changes at the level of information and information systems represent a particular challenge for understanding the future. In a recent work, Robert Axelrod and Michael Cohen provided some relevant insights into the particular complex uncertainties that we face.[1] Axelrod and Cohen refer to systems as "complex" not merely because they are being influenced by many simultaneous factors but also because of how those factors interact with each other.

> [T]here are many systems with lots of moving parts that are nonetheless quite easy to predict—think of the gigantic number of colliding molecules in a perfect gas. By "complexity" we want to indicate something else: that the system consists of many parts

[1]See Michael Cohen and Robert Axelrod, "Complexity and Adaptation in Community Information Systems: Implications for Design," in Toru Ishida, ed., *Community Computing and Support Systems*, Heidelberg: Springer Verlag, 1998.

and/or processes each of which interacts significantly, and perhaps nonlinearly, with some of the others. Ecologies and brains seem to be well described as systems that are complex in this more socialized sense.

What makes prediction especially difficult in these settings is that the forces shaping the future do not act additively, but rather their effects are via nonlinear interactions among systems components. In such worlds events change the probabilities of other events— sometimes dramatically.

Warfare has always been nonlinear and complex in the sense that Axelrod and Cohen describe. Minor events have often produced disproportionate effects on an organization that consists of badly understood machines and unpredictable humans operating in an extraordinarily stressful environment. Despite this continuity, a profound and new message about complexity permeates this volume. As the sensors, networks, and communications systems both allow more information to be obtained about the battlefield, or the surrounding context of military action, and allow the coordination of the actions of separate military platforms and military units, military organizations have become ever more finely balanced on the edge of chaos.

It is very difficult to understand what happens to the functioning of these organizations when parts of these networks or parts of the overall system are disrupted in their functioning or possibly are destroyed. For the moment we do not have an analytic framework to get at such issues, and we certainly do not have adequate models. So the effects of changes in information levels or asymmetries or the effects of information warfare on the performance of military organization are matters of considerable uncertainty.

There is a second set of relevant problems that Axelrod and Cohen also surface. To illustrate the difficulty in foreseeing how the current information revolution may affect international politics, they look at a previous information revolution, namely the printing revolution:

> [T]he printing revolution led in Europe to indirect effects that were often quite different from the immediate effects. Ancient authority was undermined even though good editions of ancient texts became accessible, scientific progress was promoted even though

pseudo-science was popular, religious divisions occurred even though information could be more widely shared, and national languages and states developed even though long range communication was fostered. All this should leave us humble about predicting the effect of the current Information Revolution. We can began to see some of the direct effects, but we need to be aware that the indirect effects might be quite different and much more powerful.

With that as background, let me make some comments on two major issues that arise in nearly all of the chapters. First, as many of the contributions to this volume suggest, there are major vulnerabilities in the computer networks and in the information infrastructures of the United States, our military information systems, and undoubtedly other countries' military establishments. Some analysts have seen in these vulnerabilities new possibilities for strategic attack, launched from almost anywhere in the world, on the economy, national infrastructure, and military preparedness of a state.

History teaches us, however, that the immediate effect is often quite different and generally less important than the indirect effects. Every action creates a reaction; every new weapon spurs the creation of a new defense. The important question, therefore, is what the situation is likely to be 10 or 20 years from now. Will these vulnerabilities persist? Will the attackers keep ahead of the development of defenses?

Experience indicates that the current vulnerabilities may not persist. Little attention has been paid to building defenses until now. The technology is changing rapidly, and information systems continue to evolve as they keep up with these changes. Installing new systems every couple of years takes a lot of energy and attention. In some areas, especially in commercial domains where the interest is high and where the risks are seen more clearly, there has been a greater response to the threat of external intrusions. Certainly, the demand for the services of those who make a business of helping companies defend themselves is increasing at a very rapid rate. I am not in a position to judge how effective these protections are in the best cases, but I believe it is wrong to judge the future by our current state of vulnerability.

Similarly, there is a lot of speculation that the state will weaken as new media and cheaper means of communication empower smaller groups.  While this may be true, the more important question is how much and how fast?  Roger D. Masters, a political philosopher at Dartmouth College, has pointed out that Machiavelli foresaw that the rise of the nation-state was inevitable in the early part of the 16th century.[2]  Nonetheless, it took 200 years for the nation-state to emerge in something like its current form.  Perhaps the state is in decline—given its current preeminence, its most likely direction is certainly downward.  The real question is how long will it take?  Will it decline faster than it ascended?

If one looks more narrowly at warfare in a theater, one can bring similar observations to bear about the uncertainty of change within complex systems.  At this level of warfare, new information technologies are having an effect on almost everything from training to logistics to public relations.  Not only will developments of new sensors, communications, and the capacity to process information allow new levels of coordination of dispersed, widely separated units, but almost all weapon systems will have new capabilities derived from the embedded microprocessors within them.  Weapons and platforms are becoming smarter, and more decisions are being delegated to them.

As the result of such changes, forecasting in this realm is also laced with uncertainty.  Nonetheless, two observations have emerged, both from this volume and from war games that my office has been conducting on warfare in 2020.  First, long-range precision strike weapons coupled to systems of sensors and to command and control systems will fairly soon come to dominate much of warfare.  The critical operational tasks will be destroying or disabling elements of an opponent's forces and supporting systems at a distance.  Defeat will occur due to disintegration of command and control capacities, rather than due to attrition or annihilation.

Second, the information "dimension" increasingly becomes central to the outcome of battles and campaigns.  Therefore, protecting the effective and continuous operation of one's own information systems and being able to degrade, destroy, or disrupt the functioning of the opponent's information systems will become a major focus of

---

[2]Personal communication.

the operational art.  Obtaining early superiority in the information realm will become central to success in future warfare.  It has always been important; it will soon be central.

In essence, however, these are predictions about where the action will be, not about how it will come out.  Information and its associated technologies are destined to become a central focus on the battlefield.  Does that mean that the offense or the defense will dominate?  Will these developments favor states or terrorists?  Will war become an exercise in media spin?  In the face of the uncertainties of the future, and the disagreements of the present, I can only suggest caution and humility in predicting the future.

# Chapter One

# INTRODUCTION

*Zalmay Khalilzad and John White*

> *As we approach the 21st Century, our foes have extended the fields of battle from physical space to cyberspace; from the world's vast bodies of water to the complex workings of our own human bodies. Rather than invading our beaches or launching bombers, these adversaries may attempt cyberattacks against our critical military systems and our economic base.*
>
> —President William J. Clinton, May 22, 1998

> *Computers are changing our lives faster than any other invention in our history. Our society is becoming increasingly dependent on information technologies, which are changing at an amazing rate. ... We must ask whether we are becoming so dependent on communications links and electronic microprocessors that a determined adversary or terrorist could possibly shut down federal operations or damage the economy simply by attacking our computers.*
>
> —Senator Fred Thompson, May 19, 1998

As these quotes imply, the United States and indeed the world is undergoing dramatic changes due in great part to the dramatic transformations brought about by new information technologies. The technical changes include advances in how information is collected, stored, processed, and communicated. While the speed with which these processes have taken place has increased manyfold, the costs for propagating and storing information have decreased dramatically. The implementation of these capabilities has vastly increased our communications and related functions, including large increases in international connectivity. More and more people and nations around the world are acquiring access to the Internet and to space-based communications and reconnaissance capabilities.

These changes have been rapid, and more are on the way. Advanced information technologies will fundamentally alter how people and societies interact, in ways that cannot be predicted. Nations around the world are both adapting to and trying to shape the ongoing developments in information technologies. This interaction between advancing information technologies and society is one of the key phenomena of our era.

One facet of how the world adapts to changes in information technologies will be in the way that conflicts are conducted. If current trends hold, these changes could have a profound effect on our national security, in terms of the threats we face, the way we fight, and how we advance the national interests of the United States.

Of course, the role of information as a key factor in warfare is not new. Nonetheless, the changes in technology and the integration of those changes into weapons, concepts, and organization means that the role of information relative to more-conventional measures of military strength is likely to change in dramatic ways.

Changes in information technology have already affected the global balance of power. The collapse of the Soviet Union, which transformed the international system, was facilitated by these changes. (See Shane, 1994.) The Soviet style of communism and command economy failed in part because it was not compatible with the requirements of the information age. These changes in information technologies have helped strengthen free markets and democratic forces around the world. They have also promoted greater international interdependence, including increased international trade and investment. Some of the consequences of the changes under way are reflected in the weakening of government control over society and the shifting of power away from governments to nongovernmental organizations, small groups, and individuals. The recent consequences identified here may continue, but we do not know whether they will.

The ultimate effects of changes in information technologies on the future of the nation-state and on conflict are far from obvious. History does not offer clear precedents. Earlier changes in information technology—such as the introduction of the printing press, telegraph, telephone, or wireless radio—produced direct and indirect effects that were at times in tension with each other. For example, the printing press initially was seen as a way to ease access to traditional and religious texts, but it soon became a way to spread new and revolutionary documents. (Dewar, 1998.) The changes predicted at the onset of these capabilities were very often wrong as society adapted to them in unexpected ways. There is another uncertainty that is also important and difficult to predict: Different political and cultural systems often use new technologies differently.

An assessment of the situation up to now indicates that, at the international level, the changes in information technologies have benefited the United States and reinforced its military preeminence. Not only did these changes help undermine the only global adversary to U.S. power, they have also aided the rejuvenation of the U.S. economy and strengthened the appeal of the U.S. system of market democracy around the world. The information age has allowed the United States to knit together the political, economic, and military sources of its national power. But such advantage may be transitory.

Militarily, as the Gulf War demonstrated, the United States is in a good position to exploit the advances in military technology, especially changes in information technology, due in great part to the high quality of its personnel and their training. The U.S. military has an unsurpassed ability to integrate complicated technical systems into preexisting forces. This military technological prowess is backed up by a solid civilian technological base. The United States has made large investments in its national information infrastructure and has a well-established market for computers, software, and Internet services. Most other nations depend on our systems and technology.

But there is another side to all of these profound changes. The United States may become increasingly vulnerable to disruption—perhaps catastrophically so—because of its heavy reliance on advanced information systems in both the civilian and military sectors.[1] The increased potential vulnerability to disruption—which

---

[1]Three recent General Accounting Office (GAO) reports document this type of vulnerability at the Department of Defense (DoD) and the Department of State and in the Air Traffic Control network: GAO (1996), GAO (1998b), and GAO (1998a), respectively.

some potentially hostile nations and nonstate actors recognize—is the negative side effect of an otherwise very positive development.

The same techniques that can be used to disrupt and manipulate civilian targets can be used for military purposes. Information attacks may be used to gather critical intelligence (for military or commercial purposes), to reduce military readiness, or to blunt or delay military operations. These developments could greatly complicate the U.S. capability to project power in a timely fashion. At times, such a delay could result in having to accept a *fait accompli* and putting at risk important national security interests. Disruption attacks also can degrade the combat effectiveness of U.S. forces that rely heavily on rapid communications and joint operations. (Bennett, Twomey, and Treverton, forthcoming.)

Adversaries are likely to rely on modern information operations, such as computer hacking or network attacks—in addition to traditional means, such as communication jamming and physical attacks—as an asymmetric strategy to compensate for their own weaknesses and for conventional U.S. military preeminence. They may value information attacks as a new type of guerrilla warfare against U.S. conventional weaponry—but one with a very long reach.

Propelled by numerous press reports of break-ins into DoD and other sensitive computer systems, threats to our information systems have become an important national issue. A recent presidential commission documented the widespread information vulnerability of various critical infrastructures, ranging from the financial system to the air traffic control system.[2] In response to these developments and to the report of the commission, President Clinton recently announced the goal of building "the capability to protect critical infrastructures from intentional acts by 2003." (The White House, 1998, p. 1.[3]) The military threats have also been recognized. Two recent congressional commissions, the Commission on Roles and Missions of the Armed Forces and the National Defense Panel, have

---

[2]The eight infrastructures that the commission identified as both critical and vulnerable were information and communications, electrical power systems, gas and oil transportation and storage, banking and finance, transportation, water supply systems, emergency services, and government services. (PCCIP, 1997.)

[3]The President also appointed a national Coordinator for Security, Infrastructure Protection, and Counter-Terrorism.

enunciated these concerns. The DoD has been working to deal with these threats in numerous ways. The Joint Chiefs have recognized the vulnerability of the military to information attacks and have emphasized the need for "full dimensional protection." (DoD, 1996.)

These changes will continue to affect our lives and our national security, both positively and negatively. Consequently, there is a strong need to increase our understanding of this revolution and its implications. The President's decision and other actions taken by the U.S. government represent important first steps in defending the nation against information attack. Plans for achieving the objectives will have to be developed. This volume is intended to assist in the development of such plans, as well as to assist in understanding the potential opportunities for U.S. military forces and society that derive from information technology.

## STRUCTURE OF THE BOOK

Because emerging information technologies will affect all corners of our lives, their national security implications have many dimensions. This volume will reflect those wide-ranging implications. The book is divided into three parts: Part I analyzes the effects of information technology on society and the international system. Part II focuses on the United States and examines what new opportunities and vulnerabilities these new information technologies will present for the United States. Part III focuses on current issues and lessons that today's U.S. decisionmakers need to understand if they are to function in the world to come.

### Information Technology and Society

Part I begins with the implications of information technologies at the highest level: their effects on society and the international system. The late Carl Builder believed that the most important national security implications of new information technology will come at the societal level. He argued that, while the American military is attempting to use new information technologies to improve what it currently does, societal changes mean that the military's missions, indeed its very reason for existence, will change as society adapts to new technology.

David Gompert also foresees that the most important changes will come at the societal level, but he is much more sanguine about the outcome. For Gompert, information technology requires democracy and free markets to unleash its vast productive and military potential. Countries that choose not to embrace democracy and free markets will therefore lose power relative to open democracies. The world's great powers will therefore be, like the United States, open, free, and united in their opposition to any threats that may arise.

In contrast, John Arquilla, David Ronfeldt, and Michelle Zanini believe that these changes will shift the locus of power away from the nation-state altogether and toward nonstate actors whose nonhierarchical, networked form of organization will allow them to take best advantage of new information technologies. This shift in power from governments to nonstate actors means that the problems of terrorism, transnational criminal organizations, and insurgent groups will grow increasingly difficult to control. They suggest that the U.S. military and government organize themselves around networks to meet this growing threat.

## U.S. Opportunities and Vulnerabilities

Part II explores the many opportunities and vulnerabilities that new information technologies will create for the United States. First, Jeremy Shapiro offers a cautionary note by questioning the idea, often taken for granted, that information technology will revolutionize warfare. He suggests, instead, that the idea of an information-based revolution in warfare actually serves as an attempt to use technology to solve the perennial U.S. problem of lack of political will to accomplish foreign policy objectives.

In contrast, Ted Harshberger and David Ochmanek are quite convinced that new technologies offer a multitude of revolutionary military opportunities for U.S. forces. They describe how recent advances in surveillance, communications, and guidance technologies have allowed U.S. forces to approach Sun Tzu's "acme of skill." They predict that the ability of the U.S. military to use these technologies to achieve "information dominance" will enable the United States to maintain a vast military superiority for the foreseeable future.

Brian Nichiporuk elaborates on these ideas by demonstrating how the United States can use new information technologies and information warfare to counter some prospective enemies' most appealing asymmetric strategies. He presents four concepts of operation for how the United States could, with little expenditure of blood or treasure, effectively preserve its power-projection capability and diminish the utility of enemy weapons of mass destruction.

Steve Hosmer continues this discussion by analyzing how the new technologies will allow the United States to conduct ever more-sophisticated psychological operations. While the United States will gain a substantial capability to influence enemy perceptions and to reduce U.S. casualties, Hosmer warns that the new technologies will also present opportunities for U.S. adversaries to achieve new psychological effects.

Roger Molander, Peter Wilson, and Robert Anderson expand on this discussion of the vulnerabilities that information technology may create for the United States. They analyze how U.S. adversaries might use the tools and techniques of new information systems to hold at risk key national strategic assets, including the financial system, the public switched network, and the transportation system. They call for a new decisionmaking framework to take into account the emerging challenge of "strategic information warfare" in national security and military policy.

Glenn Buchan then takes up the thread of vulnerability at the military operational level. He examines how an increasing military reliance on the systems described by Ochmanek, Harshberger, and Nichiporuk may create dependencies that could be exploited by clever enemies. He analyzes the dependence of Air Force operations on information and information systems and concludes that the risks are manageable but that the military needs to maintain sufficient skilled manpower to continue operating if new information systems fail.

## Issues and Lessons for Decisionmakers

Part III presents some issues and lessons for U.S. decisionmakers that emerge from the preceding chapters. First, Frank Fukuyama and Abe Shulsky draw on lessons from the corporate world about how to adapt organizational structures to new information technology and apply those lessons to military organization. They conclude that, to take full advantage of information technology, the military will need to institutionalize an environment of constant learning, one that includes the freedom to fail without serious consequences. They also stress the need to redistribute skills and authority toward the bottom of the hierarchy and to give more autonomy to lower levels of the military. Finally, they cite the need to solve the debilitating yet seemingly intractable problem of streamlining the procurement system to allow the military to benefit from cutting-edge commercial technology.

Lynn Davis analyzes the role that arms control and nonproliferation regimes might play in managing some of the vulnerabilities mentioned in the preceding chapters. She concludes that it will be very difficult, and perhaps undesirable, to attempt to apply previous arms control and nonproliferation regimes to information technology. While variants of such responses may become necessary in the future, the greater need at present is to establish more effective means for multilateral cooperation to manage cross nationally the new threats posed by emerging information technology.

Zalmay Khalilzad discusses how the United States should undertake to defend itself from information attacks. He notes that, as with nuclear weapons, the United States is unlikely to be able to eliminate its vulnerability to information attacks completely. A successful national defense, therefore, will require strategies that also strive to deter adversaries from using information weapons and to prevent adversaries from developing the capability to produce or use such weapons.

Finally, Martin Libicki and Jeremy Shapiro assess the implications the changes in information technologies hold for the U.S. military, especially the U.S. Air Force.

## REFERENCES

Bennett, Bruce, Christopher P. Twomey, and Gregory Treverton, *Future Warfare Scenarios and Asymmetric Threats*, Santa Monica, Calif.: RAND, MR-1025-OSD, forthcoming.

Dewar, James A., "The Information Age and the Printing Press: Looking Backward to See Ahead," Santa Monica, Calif.: RAND, P-8014, 1998.

DoD—s*ee* U.S. Department of Defense.

GAO—*see* U.S. General Accounting Office.

PCCIP—*see* President's Commission on Critical Infrastructure Protection.

President's Commission on Critical Infrastructure Protection , *Critical Foundations: Protecting America's Infrastructures*, October 1997.

Shane, Scott, *Dismantling Utopia: How Information Ended the Soviet Union*, Chicago: Ivan Dee, 1994.

U.S. Department of Defense, Joint Chiefs of Staff, *Joint Vision 2010*, Washington, D.C., 1996.

U.S. General Accounting Office, *Information Security: Computer Attacks at the Department of Defense Pose Increasing Risks*, Washington, D.C.GAO/AIMD-96-84, May 1996.

U.S. General Accounting Office, *Air Traffic Control: Weak Computer Security Practices Jeopardize Flight Safety*, Washington, D.C., GAO/AIMD-98-155, May 1998a.

U.S. General Accounting Office, *Computer Security: Pervasive, Serious Weaknesses Jeopardize State Department Operations*, Washington, D.C., GAO/AIMD-98-145, May 1998b.

The White House, Office of the Press Secretary, "Protecting America's Critical Infrastructure," Washington, D.C., PDD 63, May 22, 1998.

# Part I

# SOCIETY AND THE INTERNATIONAL SYSTEM

# Chapter Two

# THE AMERICAN MILITARY ENTERPRISE IN THE INFORMATION AGE

*Carl H. Builder*

## INTRODUCTION: THE SOCIAL AND MILITARY PERSPECTIVES

The social and military effects of the ongoing information revolution occupy the thoughts of modern thinkers. From a social standpoint, the true believers hold that the current revolution in computing, telecommunications, and information technologies will profoundly remake our society, our democracy, and our daily lives. From a military perspective, visionaries within the U.S. military see in the new technologies of the information revolution the means to radically increase military effectiveness, reduce casualties, and save money. The purpose of this chapter is to develop an understanding of how these two perspectives, usually considered apart, impinge upon one another.

A nation's military is a reflection and a servant of the society from which it is drawn. If that society undergoes a change as profound as the information revolution, its security requirements will change as well. As a result of these changes, what society asks and expects the military to do to defend the nation, the military's "enterprise," will almost certainly change. If so, the most important consequence of the information revolution for the American military will not be the application of new information technologies to its existing missions, as the military perspective often implies. Rather, the most important effect will be the need for the military to adapt itself to performing new and different missions. The key, then, to understanding how we should apply new information technologies in the military is to unite the social and military perspectives into an understanding of how the American military enterprise will evolve.

## THE ROOTS OF REVOLUTION

No technological development since the release of nuclear energy has so preoccupied the American military as the currently cresting revolution in computing, telecommunications, and information technologies[1]; no part of that revolution has been the subject of more speculation by the military than the idea of information warfare. Those preoccupations are evident in the professional journals of the American military and in the emergent doctrines, organization, and funding of the American armed forces. The fallout from these preoccupations is neither complete nor obvious—because many of the issues remain unresolved and involve large stakes within the American military institutions.

Some see the information revolution as but one component of an ongoing (or forthcoming) revolution in military affairs, in which the information technologies, when combined with new concepts for military operations and their command and control, will usher in a revolution in warfare comparable to that which occurred with blitzkrieg and aircraft carriers in World War II.[2]  Some of these expectations are captured in *Joint Vision 2010*, which sees the information technologies as enabling "full-spectrum dominance" of military operations and "dominant battlespace awareness." (DoD, 1996a.)  Critics see such expectations of transparent battlefields as technological chimeras—futile hopes to eliminate the Clausewitzian friction of war.[3]

Few would dispute the importance of the new information technologies for militaries and warfare, but beyond that point, the

---

[1]Hereinafter called the *information revolution*, recognizing that computers, telecommunications, and the explosive expansion of information access and utilization are inextricably intertwined.

[2]See, for example, Builder (1995), pp. 38 and 39.

[3]Perhaps the best treatment of this subject is found in Watts (1996). Dunlap (1997) cites information superiority or dominance in future conflicts as one of his four myths. One flag officer recently quipped that if he were thrust into the boxing ring with Mike Tyson, information dominance would hardly prevent him from being soundly beaten.

schools of thought divide and fan out on just how important and how pervasive these technologies will become. At the conservative end are those who see the application of the information technologies limited to marginal improvements in existing military operations—in communications, navigation, intelligence, logistics, etc.—as already evident with the introduction of Global Positioning System receivers, laptop computers, and wideband global communications nets. At a somewhat more ambitious level is the so-called "digitization of the battlefield," in which maps and sensors are registered together in a common framework for all who would venture there.[4]

Toward the more expansive end are those who see the "information sphere" becoming the battlefield of the future—where the main battle will not be fought over territory using physical force, but over the minds of the combatants and their access to information. It is this school of thought that now precipitates turbulence within the American military, as it clamors for the attention of leaders who must decide on resource allocations and organizational changes. At the outer fringes of this school of thought, one can hear calls for an independent "information corps" similar to those (still heard) for an independent "space corps," echoing much earlier (and ultimately successful) calls for an independent air corps in the first half of the 20th century. And it is here that one finds the jarring concept of the "information warrior," a new and different breed of military person, like the pioneering aviator before, who boldly lays claim to the future of warfare.

The mainstream American military finds itself torn between (a) gaining for itself the fruits of the information revolution when applied to its traditional concepts of military roles and missions and (b) finding itself riding the back of a tiger that might threaten to overturn those traditional concepts and replace them with a new kind of war and warrior. The balancing act is how to embrace the information technologies without being institutionally undone by them.[5]

---

[4]This perspective is captured in the Army's Force XXI concepts and experiments.

[5]For example, the most effective exploitation of information is achieved through networklike organizations, while the most effective command and control is achieved through the hierarchical organizations so long associated with the military. Marrying the two forms risks one undoing the other, for hierarchical and network organizations

Whether the choice is real or not may be less pertinent than the fact that there are factions within the American military that are willing to make the choice seem real to those in and out of uniform who must decide how the military should be organized and funded.  That such opposing views might surface within the military and be broadcast is certainly not without precedent, but the information revolution has just as certainly made the debate more visible and widely spread.

So, one important fallout of the information revolution is the looming prospect of information warfare—warfare waged with information as a *primary* weapon or target.[6]  Although information warfare as a component of war is not new (as in deception and electronic warfare), the possibility that it might become the *dominant* dimension in future war is new.  That possibility looms now because of the growing dependence on information infrastructures for the most modern means of warfare—such as the use of precision weapons— and for the economic functioning of a modern society and state.

Even those in the American military who believe information warfare is the wave of the future find themselves pulled between complementary interests and concerns:

1. The interests are the potential military advantages of *exploiting* information as a weapon against the entire range of enemy targets—from the minds of the enemy's leadership to the performance of their weapons.

2. The concerns are the potential *vulnerabilities* of the sophisticated U.S. civil and military infrastructures—communications, commercial, logistical, and command—to hostile actions using information as a weapon.

---

tend to be mutually corrosive—the former cutting network links for greater control, the latter bypassing hierarchical levels in the search for more information.

[6]Information warfare is formally defined as

> Actions taken to achieve information superiority by affecting adversary information, information-based processes, information systems, and computer-based networks while defending one's own information, information-based processes, information systems and computer-based networks. (DoD, 1996b.)

That information might be a *primary* weapon or target is evident from Army Field Manual 100-6 (TRADOC, 1996), which declares that "The objective of IW [information warfare] is to attain a significant information advantage that enables the total force to quickly dominate and control the adversary."

The interests are generally contemplated under the heading of *offensive* information warfare, while the concerns are associated with *defensive* information warfare. The interests and concerns are, of course, intertwined: Means devised for offensive purposes might be turned against us, and exposition of our vulnerabilities—if neither corrected nor correctable—might invite the very attacks we hope to avoid. Indeed, there is a line of argument that says information warfare is something that the most developed societies in particular should eschew—that its relative advantages will accrue mostly to the weak and underdeveloped adversary.[7] An opposing argument is that the most developed societies can bring their enormous information resources—from global infrastructures and technological superiority in depth—to bear against an enemy with surprising new effects and reduced risks.

These arguments will not be resolved soon. They will reverberate over the next several decades as the information revolution crests and then subsides in the first half of the 21st century.[8] But to anticipate how these arguments and others might be resolved, they will be illuminated here in four different lights:

1. the historical patterns in 20th-century technological revolutions, particularly as they have affected the American society and interacted with American military cultures

2. the current information revolution—which may break with the historical patterns—because it is fundamentally transforming the relationships between the American society and its institutions, including its military

3. the adaptations—past and prospective—of other American institutions to the information revolution, with the American family, business, government, and education as examples of how the information revolution can or will wreak changes—changes that might foretell what will happen to the American military

---

[7]The reasons being that the capital investments required to wage offensive information warfare within the existing global networks are modest and that the required technology is developing faster in the commercial sector than in the military because of differences in acquisition cycles. (See Dunlap, 1997.)

[8]For more perspectives on the information revolution as a passing wave, see Builder (1990).

4. the historically changing enterprise or focus of American military activities, as a way of anticipating changes even as the institutional roles and missions remain constant.

## HISTORICAL PATTERNS

The contemporary American military response to information warfare—rooted as it is in the information revolution—is not without precedent. In the 20th century, at least three and perhaps four technological revolutions swept through the American military: the mechanization of warfare by means of the internal combustion engine, the release of almost unlimited nuclear energy, the opening of access to space as a new vantage point, and now the information revolution. In each of the first three instances, the American military was transformed in its thinking and eventually in its physical makeup. The fallout from these three revolutions included the ideas of strategic air warfare, nuclear warfare, and even space warfare. We should not be surprised today, therefore, to find a part of the American military captivated by the idea of information warfare.

However, as the idea of information warfare is now embraced by its advocates, it is worth reflecting on the evolution of these transforming ideas as they were incorporated into the American military. First, they took a long time to move into the mainstream of military thought. Although World War II was a mechanized war, horsemanship remained a required skill at West Point two years after the dropping of atomic bombs on Japan. In many segments of the American military, airpower is still seen today as it was in the 1920s—primarily as support for the surface forces, not as an independent national instrument of power.[9] Space operators in the military are still struggling, like the aviators before them, to find their place in the mainstreams of American military institutions.

Second, the ideas were oversold as expectations, at least in the short term. In the mechanization of warfare, strategic bombardment theories were finally vindicated by the advent of the atomic bomb more than by the bombers themselves. Within four decades, many of the theories of nuclear warfare were made irrelevant by the unimagin-

---

[9]See, for example, Correll (1997), in an editorial in *Air Force Magazine*.

able destructiveness of the very arsenals they promoted. And after four decades, space, like prominent high features on the surface of the earth, still remains mostly a place of vantage for navigation, communication, and observation infrastructures instead of an arena for earth-centered conflicts. Space warfare may yet materialize, but it seems more likely to be a 21st-century rather than a 20th-century phenomenon.

All that suggests that the idea of information warfare will take a longer time to mature than its most ardent proponents expect and, in the near term, will probably deliver less than it promises. But there is also something unique about the information revolution compared to the previous technological revolutions in the 20th century, with differences that could break the observable patterns of the past. Unlike the prior technical revolutions in this century, the information revolution is dramatically altering the power relationships between the state and society, not just in America or even the developed world, but throughout the globe. And it is from the state that the military draws its mandate.[10]

While the revolution wrought by the internal combustion engine gave Americans wheels and wings, the relative power of the state to the individual only increased as society looked to the state for the needed roads and airways. Nuclear power and space were, for the most part, state-managed monopolies that did not involve relinquishment of state power to individuals. But the information revolution has unleashed forces—both political and economic—that have significantly eroded the relative power of the state with respect to individuals and all sorts of new nonstate actors. Sovereign powers that states took for granted even two decades ago—such as control over their borders, markets, currency, information, and population movements—have been significantly weakened. (Wriston, 1992.) This is not to say that the state is about to disappear—only that the powers of individuals relative to states, because of their access to information, are presently in ascendancy. Jessica Mathews has put it thusly:

---

[10]That mandate is only 350 years old. The Treaty of Westphalia, in 1648, established that militaries would henceforth be instruments of the state and not mercenary bands or freebooters.

> The most powerful engine of change in the relative decline of states and the rise of nonstate actors is the computer and telecommunications revolution, whose deep political and social consequences have been almost completely ignored. Widely accessible and affordable technology has broken governments' monopoly on the collection and management of large amounts of information and deprived governments of the deference they enjoyed because of it. (Mathews, 1997, p. 51.)

Even the ability of the state to wield military power with the freedom that its elites might prefer has been greatly circumscribed by the information revolution—a fact the American military has come to appreciate throughout the last half of the 20th century when it talks about (a) "the CNN effect," through which military operations are increasingly exposed to news-media examination, (b) the political imperative to hold casualties to a minimum to retain public support,[11] and (c) planning in the face of political constraints on the use of force.[12] These were not significant considerations in the first half of the 20th century, before the information revolution.

## CULTURAL FACTORS

To complicate matters, the American military's responses to new technological revolutions may not be typical of militaries more generally. There is a cultural component of the American military that bears watching, for it may create asymmetries with the militaries of other nations that will be revealed fully only through conflict. Many have observed that Americans have a penchant for quick technical fixes for their problems and have historically been more attracted than most to proposals for bloodless technological solutions for waging war. Between the two world wars, Americans embraced airpower and strategic bombardment with greater alacrity than any other nation except Great Britain, largely on the promise of reducing

---

[11]As when the humanitarian mission in Somalia escalated to partisan involvement in determining political leaderships and began incurring casualties.

[12]Although these constraints were painfully evident to the American military during the Korean and Vietnam conflicts, in which self-imposed sanctuaries thwarted strategic actions, they also emerged during the Gulf War in response to the destruction of the Al Firdos bunker and the devastation of Iraqi forces fleeing Kuwait City at the end of the war.

the casualties associated with stalemated trench warfare.[13] After World War II, no other nation committed itself so quickly or completely to nuclear weapons for its security. Despite a late start in the space race with the Soviet Union, the United States was determined not to be second, even though it tacitly accepted numerical inferiority in many other aspects of military force.

So, there is a dilemma here as well for the American military. On the one hand, there are obvious risks that the American fascination with technical fixes could lead to the selling of a commitment to (and reliance on) information warfare as a less costly, easier way to deal with future national security problems. That is the lesson of our earlier commitments to strategic bombardment and nuclear deterrence for security in the middle of the 20th century. Neither could adequately deliver for the real situations that ultimately arose in the 1940s and 1950s. On the other hand, the natural conservative tendencies of the mainstream of the American military make it reluctant to embrace new technologies at the expense of maintaining adequate stocks of traditional forces. That is the lesson that restive military aviators in the 1920s and space operators in the 1990s learned.

The leaderships of the uniformed American military services find themselves (1) not wanting to disaffect their information and space cadres because of the importance of these fields to present and future military operations and (2) not willing to devote scarce resources or to grant cherished authority that their information and space proponents claim they need, while (3) enduring concerns that these factions—like the aviators before them—may seek independence from their parent services with the help of congressional or Department of Defense sympathizers. The result is a delicate dance between the mainstream military leaderships and their information and space cadres—each knowing that they now need the support of the other, neither wanting to alienate the other, each waiting for the future to reveal that it lies in their favor. In that sense, both sides are relying on political and technological developments outside their direct control to render a favorable verdict.

---

[13]In the event, however, the mechanization of land warfare made stalemates rare; instead of a repeat of the bloody attrition in the trenches, the war for control of the air turned into bloody attrition at 20,000 feet over Europe. On this point, see Meilinger (1997).

## WHAT IS THE ENTERPRISE?

The term *enterprise* is used here in the business sense of the *primary purposeful activity* of an organization. That is a deliberately different idea from the objective, mission, role, or purpose of an institution. *Enterprise* tells us about the activities that preoccupy an organization. For example, many business organizations will claim a constant objective or purpose, such as making a profit for their owners, but their enterprise may change—as in the case of IBM, whose enterprise changed from making office machines (mainly typewriters) to making computers as a result of the information revolution. The American military has had a constant mission of defending the nation's interests, but its enterprise has changed several times, even within the 20th century—from constabulary activities at the far-flung outposts of America's new empire, to mounting expeditionary forces for fighting two world and three regional wars, to ensuring the nation's very survival during the Cold War. The notion of enterprise is used here not to apply business concepts to the military but to highlight possible changes in the primary purposeful activity of the American military as it moves into the 21st century—with a recognition that the military enterprise has not been a constant and may change in the future.

Much of the current focus of the American military on information warfare—offensive or defensive—is on applying the burgeoning information technologies as new tools for what it sees as its traditional mission of fighting and winning the nation's wars. More precisely, as stated in *Joint Vision 2010*, the mission is "to deter conflict—but, should deterrence fail, to fight and win our nation's wars." However, it is increasingly common to hear those in uniform say that the *primary* mission of the American armed forces is and should be to fight and win the nation's wars, particularly as encroaching demands for humanitarian and peacekeeping tasks fall upon those forces. GEN John J. Sheehan, Commander in Chief of the Atlantic Command, recently voiced his skepticism about that common interpretation:

> Any service member, asked to define the mission of the U.S. military, will most likely reply, "to fight and win our nation's wars." But is that really our mission? If so, who decided, and when? Where is it written? (Sheehan, 1997.)

This contemporary emphasis on "fighting and winning the nation's wars" seems to have emerged in the wake of the war in Vietnam, for the very idea of fighting or winning the nation's wars, as the raison d'être of American military forces, would have been an anathema during the height of the Cold War, when the nation's strategy was deterrence and the primary purpose of our military forces was to *avoid* war. Indeed, the cornerstone of nuclear deterrence strategy was laid by Bernard Brodie in his early observation that

> Thus far the chief purpose of our military establishment has been to win wars. From now on its chief purpose must be to avert them. It can have no other useful purpose. (Brodie, 1973, fn. 2, p. 377.)

An additional impetus for recentering the American military mission on "fighting and winning the nation's wars" arises from the growing demands in the wake of the Cold War to use the military for operations short of war—as in the humanitarian operations in Somalia and Rwanda and the peacekeeping operations in Haiti and Bosnia. These seemingly open-ended demands, when exacerbated by budget constraints,[14] are perceived as a threat to resources for traditional forces to fight conventional wars:

> The revised defense strategy puts unprecedented emphasis on Smaller-scale Contingencies and Military Operations Other Than War. That diverts attention and resources from the main requirement, which is to fight and win the nation's wars. It also tends to lessen the priority on Air Force combat airpower, since other services are seen as more relevant to peacekeeping and constabulary functions. (Correll, 1997.)

Not addressed by this lament is whether airpower could be fashioned to be much more relevant than in the past for peacekeeping and

---

[14]It is more common to hear the current budget constraints referred to as budget reductions. But the current budgets for the American military are larger, in real or inflation-adjusted dollars, than those at the height of the Cold War. In 1955, when the United States was urgently preparing for what appeared to many to be imminent thermonuclear war with the Soviet Union, the national defense budget was $242.8 billion in 1995 dollars. In 1995, the number was $271.6 billion. These numbers are taken from the historical tables in U.S. Congress (1995), p. 21. The recent reductions in military budgets are with reference to the so-called "Reagan buildup" of the defense budget, which peaked a little more than a decade ago.

constabulary functions (Builder and Karasik, 1995) and whether peacekeeping and constabulary functions (1) have been the more traditional peacetime roles for the American military throughout most of American history and (2) could become the predominant role for the American military for the first several decades of the 21st century.

Implicit in the contemporary focus on "fighting and winning the nation's wars" is that the mission of the military, however defined, will remain more or less what it has been in the 20th century—at least before and after the Cold War—and the only thing that will change is the way the military goes about this traditional mission. That is to say, the military mission is still fighting and winning the nation's wars, but those wars will now be fought with some new tools and in new ways. Information warfare is one of those new ways, and the information technologies will provide many of the new tools.

The problem with that formulation is that the information technologies are driving much more fundamental changes elsewhere—transforming societies and their institutions, creating new and destroying old enterprises. The American society that created and supported the American military in the 20th century has already been transformed by demography and technology—the two most fundamental drivers of change in the world today. The aspirations, expectations, and values of the American society now emerging are not the same ones that gave birth only a generation ago to the American military of today.

The current military posture—a relatively large, standing, ready military force in peacetime—is still running on the powerful legacies of the Reagan buildup and its vindication in the Gulf War. The creation of that posture almost two decades ago involved a combination of threat, political will, and public support that is no longer evident or easily re-created. Because the political will and public support to *change* the current posture will require initiative and hard choices, deliberate posture change may not manifest itself until the American society is forced to choose between social and defense programs—a choice that seems to be postponed for now by a remarkably healthy national economy. However, that should not mask the possibility that the military posture is riding on its momentum along a path of least political resistance more than it is buoyed by intrinsic public support. Thus, for the American military posture to remain substantially unaltered despite great changes in the society that supports and tasks it is an assumption of heroic proportions.

Is it possible that the American society has been so transformed in the last quarter of the 21st century—during the lifetime of a single military career?  The number of observers who say that it has been transformed by technology and demography is growing rapidly—the collective testimonies of Peter Drucker, Samuel Huntington, Arthur Schlesinger, Walter Wriston, and George Kennan in the September-October 1997 issue of *Foreign Affairs* should be sufficient to raise if not prove the possibility.  Could it be that the enterprise or business of the American military will change as well?  Even here, the observers who think the military enterprise has changed are growing in numbers and stature.  Jessica Mathews, writing in *Foreign Affairs* earlier in 1997, argued that traditional interstate conflict is on a downward course, even as intrastate conflicts are on the rise:

> War will not disappear, but . . . the security threat to states from other states is on a downward course.  Nontraditional threats, however, are rising—terrorism, organized crime, drug trafficking, ethnic conflict, and the combination of rapid population growth, environmental decline, and poverty that breeds economic stagnation, political instability, and, sometimes, state collapse.  The nearly 100 armed conflicts since the end of the Cold War have virtually all been intrastate affairs. (Mathews, 1997.)

Israeli military historian Martin van Creveld argues that traditional interstate wars and the kinds of armed forces required to fight them will slowly disappear, in part because of the proliferation of nuclear weapons—itself one of the many consequences of the information revolution:

> Slowly, unevenly but inexorably nuclear proliferation is causing interstate war and the kind of armed forces by which it is waged to disappear.  The future belongs to wars fought by, and against, organizations that are not states.  Indeed in most parts of the world this form of war has already taken over. . . . Unless some yet to be designed system enables states to reliably defend themselves against nuclear weapons . . . the writing for large-scale, interstate war, as well as the armed forces by which it is waged, is on the wall. (Van Creveld, 1996.)

To be sure, there are many who argue that war is in the very nature of humans[15] and is not about to disappear—even though the modern nation-state as the wager of traditional warfare is only 350 years old. The confusion arises because war, for most in the American military, has come to mean interstate warfare between regular military forces. The possibility that the 20th century may have seen the apex of the powers of the nation-state (and its frequent resort to interstate warfare) is disturbing in its implications for the future enterprise of regular military forces. The argument that information warfare is the wave of the future only adds to those concerns.

Whether the enterprise of the American military is changing or what the new enterprise might be is addressed below. At this point, it is enough to suggest that it *could* be changing—from what thoughtful observers are saying—and that it *may* be something different from, or more than, providing for deterrence or fighting and winning the nation's wars.[16] And if the enterprise of the American military *might* be changing, applying the information technologies to the old enterprise could be a diversion from, rather than an adaptation to, the future.

## ADAPTING TO THE INFORMATION REVOLUTION

In large measure, the outlines of the first half of the 21st century are already quite evident with respect to the two greatest drivers of change:

1. **Demography:** The patterns of population growth and migration are widely appreciated. The number of people of retirement age in 2050 is known today with considerable confidence; it is a matter of counting the number of teenagers today and adjusting for mortality and migration trends.

2. **Information Technologies:** The computational and telecommunications capabilities for 2025 can be projected with confidence, for they are closely tracking the stable trend lines they have been

---

[15]This view is addressed and challenged by Keegan (1993).

[16]As an existence proof, the future enterprise of the American military might be what it has been throughout most of its 220-year history in peacetime, save the 40-year Cold War—keeping the arts and sciences of warfare alive with meager funds while carrying out constabulary duties as assigned.

on for more than two decades[17] and are forecast to follow for at least two more decades with foreseeable developments in laboratories today.

So, the things that are most changing our world as the information revolution crests either have already occurred or have clearly signaled their trajectories for decades to come.

What is less apparent in our future is how our institutions—particularly our government institutions—will adapt to these changes. Nongovernmental institutions have already demonstrated their ability to adapt to the new world that demography and information technologies are creating before our eyes. The American family, as an institution, changed dramatically in the 1950s and 1960s. We may not like those changes, but individuals have a way of adapting quickly when they find themselves in a changed world. They quickly surmise that if they do not change, they will not be able compete, survive, or flourish. Moreover, inertia does not impede individual change to the degree that it does in groups governed by collective or institutional behavior.

Businesses, as institutions, mostly changed or adapted in the 1970s and 1980s. They had to change or be killed by their bottom lines. The business school literature has been rife with theories about how businesses must redefine, reengineer, reinvent, reorganize, or rethink themselves in the new world with its global markets for finance, production, and goods. At the same time, old businesses have collapsed or been transformed, and completely new commercial giants have emerged in businesses that did not exist two decades ago (e.g., Microsoft). Those that have stumbled or fallen, after half a century or more of success, include such familiar names as IBM, Xerox, Sears, DEC, DuPont, and Pan Am. (See Hamel and Prahalad, 1994, p. 6.) Finding the right niche (enterprise) in the market is often more important than being effective or efficient in a shrinking enterprise or the wrong niche. Being effective or efficient takes on importance after the right enterprise has been discovered and engaged.

Even medicine—at least the business side of medicine—has been transformed. How medicine is practiced today through health

---

[17]See, for example, Moravec (1988). Also see Petersen (1994).

maintenance organizations looks completely different from what it did only 10 or 20 years ago. Again, not all of these societal changes are welcomed, but that is the long history of revolutions, and institutions must either adapt or become less relevant to the new world that is now evolving before our eyes. The fall of many traditional business giants is testimony to these imperatives.

Elected government is showing signs of change. It must because it runs up against the ballot box every two, four, or six years. However, internal government fiefdoms, such as the Central Intelligence Agency, the Internal Revenue Service, or the Department of Energy, are more insulated from the ballot box and can afford, therefore, to be slower to change or to wait until change is forced upon them. Eventually, as creatures of elected government, they will be forced to change also, for their constituencies against change are seldom larger than their own employees and supporting contractors. But two government-supported institutional enclaves enjoy large public constituencies and seem likely to resist change: the American educational and military institutions.

The mission of education may be to educate students, but the traditional enterprise (activity) of educational institutions has been to certify the organization and discipline of students in various subjects and at various levels. That enterprise served both agrarian and industrial economies in its demands for people who could be depended upon to plan, organize, produce, and distribute—or in the case of the military, to fight. The relevance of that traditional enterprise in the new information economies is being challenged from two directions: At one end, information elites demand creativity and intelligence more than organization and discipline[18]—where certificates count for less than portfolios or demonstrations of abilities. At the other end, a demographically changed public poses increasing demands for government-supported custody of its youth—where young people need to be usefully or safely occupied or entertained while maturing. Traditional educational institutions, with their focus on conferring certificates, are likely to ignore these encroachments as fringe problems until the center has become less relevant. This would follow the path of the Catholic Church in the wake of the

---

[18]See, for example, Reinhardt (1997).

Renaissance and an earlier information revolution instigated by the printing press.

Just how education and the military will (or will not) adapt to change is likely to be an important determinant of American political history in the first half of the 21st century. These two institutions are the ones to watch, because they are the most isolated from bottom lines or ballot boxes and because their constituencies against change are large, affluent, and vocal. Both pose the possibilities of institutions that will elect to become less relevant rather than change.

## APPLYING NEW TECHNOLOGIES TO OLD ENTERPRISES

The American military may assume that its enterprise (primary purposeful activity) remains unchanged, despite the ravaging effects of the information revolution on the powers of the nation-state and the transformation of entire societies, economies, and enterprises everywhere. If so, the principal effect of the information technologies on the military will be limited to their application in the existing enterprise.

However, the effects of applying the information technologies as new tools in old enterprises has almost everywhere proved disappointing—in business, governance, and education—because the dramatic changes wrought by the information technologies are to be found elsewhere in the societal changes that are producing new values, expectations, aspirations, and enterprises. When businesses automated their old accounting or inventory processes (often within their old enterprises), they found themselves disappointed with the cost savings. Computers introduced into the classroom have had little visible or measurable effect on the traditional enterprise of education.[19] Managers everywhere see the movement of greater amounts of information through computer networks but only modest improvements in productivity. In traditional businesses, the lament is: Where are the savings promised by computers?

By applying the information technologies to its old enterprises—whether that be digitizing the battlefield or preparing to engage in interstate information warfare—the American military could be

---

[19]This tendency is lamented by Oppenheimer (1997).

diverted from the more important and difficult task of anticipating and reshaping itself to undertake new and different enterprises.[20]  It is not the American military that will *determine* its future tasking and hence its new enterprises; that will be done by a new and different society in a new and different world.  The challenge for the American military is to *anticipate* what those new enterprises may be before it is confronted with the tasking.  How well the American military anticipates its next enterprise will determine whether it has adapted, maladapted, or made itself irrelevant in the cresting information revolution.  Digitizing the battlefield may make soldiers more effective or efficient on battlefields as they were understood in the 20th century, but it may add less than expected to the tasks that lie ahead for the American military in the 21st century.

The ability to wage interstate information warfare—offensive or defensive—may or may not be salient to the new world (and enterprise) that is now emerging for the American military.  Offensive information warfare as it is currently conceived may be salient only if being prepared to wage interstate warfare remains the principal enterprise for the American military in the 21st century.  Offensive information warfare directed against an entire society or community may be the province of the military, but that may be rarer than information attacks upon individuals or small groups where the advantage of the military over individuals is less evident.  In offensive information warfare, the differences in capabilities between the military and an individual may be much less than they are in the applications of physical force.[21]

Defensive information warfare may turn out to be the distributed burden of society every bit as much as its military—where all who use the fruits of the information revolution, civilian or military, must look after their own protection.[22]  Where there are state-sponsored

---

[20]A point RAND colleague Nancy Moore made to the author from her studies of the business and management literature.

[21]Applying large amounts of physical force has tended to be a state-run monopoly, but even that now seems to be slipping away.  In the application of information as a weapon, the state may not long enjoy a monopoly, even if it once did with state-controlled radio and television transmitters and printing presses.

[22]This was presaged by the rising burden upon civil societies to look to themselves for protection from criminal violence.  That burden can no longer be carried almost

information attacks upon U.S. infrastructures, it is to be expected that the responses might come from the military, but not necessarily in like kind. Just as state-sponsored terrorism has brought about responses with military strikes, so too state-sponsored information attacks might bring about responses in the form of physical force. Where information attacks come from individuals or nonstate actors, it is not at all clear that the American military would be involved unless its own infrastructures were the target.

So, the involvement of the American military in information warfare beyond what it has been in the 20th century—in signals intelligence, electronic warfare, jamming, spoofing, etc.—is not at all obvious until and unless the enterprise of the military in the 21st century is more thoughtfully discovered and agreed upon.[23] In the meantime, it might be better to have a 20th-century military preparing itself to engage in possible 21st-century enterprises than it is to have a 21st-century military preparing itself to engage in important but infrequent 20th-century enterprises.

## THE FUTURE ENTERPRISE OF THE MILITARY

To anticipate what the future enterprise of the American military may be in the early 21st century, it may be helpful to look at its past enterprises during the 20th century. This century has seen the American military preoccupied with at least six different enterprises at different times, sometimes reverting to an earlier enterprise. At any given time, several of these six enterprises were usually detectable, but only one at a time, dominated the American military as its *primary purposeful activity*. The six enterprises are as follows:

---

entirely by the state, as it was before the information revolution and demography transformed societies and diffused the power of violence into the hands of individuals.

[23]There is a tendency for managers to be impatient with the question of enterprise, so they can get on with the more comfortable questions of effectiveness and efficiency in known enterprises. Peter Schwartz provides a case study of the management of Royal Dutch Shell, in which strategic planners succeeded in getting the managers to slow down and focus on the question of enterprise. The happy result was that Royal Dutch Shell went through the oil crisis much better than its competitors because it was prepared to change its enterprise from oil production to oil brokering. See Schwartz (1991).

1. **Providing constabulary capabilities.** For the first 15 years of the 20th century, the new empire of the United States—from the Caribbean to the Western Pacific—saddled the American military mostly with constabulary duties: putting down rebellions (Philippines), chasing bandits (Mexico), and providing military governance (Dominican Republic). Constabulary duties reappeared as highly visible activities in the 1920s (Veterans' riots, Dominican Republic) and in the 1990s (Los Angeles, Haiti, Bosnia), but they did not once again become the *primary purposeful activity* of the American military that they had been at the beginning of the century.

2. **Mounting an expeditionary force.** The two world wars and the Korean, Vietnam, and Gulf wars preoccupied the American military for only 17 years of the 20th century. Although those periods are remembered most for the fighting of the forces, the preponderance of the military activities were centered on *mounting* the expeditionary forces, not the briefer periods of sometimes intense fighting.[24] Now, in the aftermath of the Cold War—through the Base Force, the Bottom-Up Review, the Commission on Roles and Missions, and the Quadrennial Defense Review—most of the American military would make preparing to mount two expeditionary forces for fighting two major regional contingencies its primary purposeful activity.

3. **Keeping the military arts and sciences alive.** The desperate challenge of keeping the knowledge base and cadres for a *functional* military was the dominant preoccupation of the American military during the 18-year interlude between the two world wars. Any rereading of that historical period provides vivid accounts of the struggle to find enough funds to develop modern weapons sufficient even to practice new doctrines and tactics.[25] Old newsreel footage of field exercises showing trucks marked as "tanks" in lieu of sufficient tanks is a sad testimony to the times.

---

[24]As an extreme example, the Gulf War involved more than six months of deploying substantial forces into the Gulf, while the actual fighting lasted only six weeks or four days, depending upon whether one refers to the air or the ground war. The logistical efforts in supporting our other wars were also prodigious by any measure except the loss of lives.

[25]See, for example, Van Tol (1997).

4. **Providing a deterrent.** For at least 20 years, the American military was dominated by the activities associated with building and deploying its nuclear deterrent forces after the beginning of the Cold War. This continues to be an important activity even today, but it ceased to be the *primary purposeful activity* of the American military after the Vietnam War began in earnest. It was displaced by a series of other enterprises, right down to the present.

5. **Providing a forward defense.** After the Vietnam War, the American military turned its attention back toward the Cold War, but this time the primary purposeful activity was providing a forward defense in Central Europe rather than relying on a nuclear deterrent—which seemed to have dead-ended in a stalemate. The United States had provided a forward defense on the Korean Peninsula since the 1950s, but it was not the primary focus of the American military. However, all of the American military, including the Navy and Air Force, turned its attention to defending forward in Europe as its principal activity for the 15 years from the end of the Vietnam War to the end of the Cold War.

6. **Providing a global presence.** After the end of the Cold War, forward defense melted into a forward presence. The Navy embraced this activity because it was quite close to naval activities under other names; more importantly, this activity supported the force structures for the Navy's most cherished units, the carrier battle groups. The Air Force tentatively tried to adopt this "cash cow" in arguing that air and space forces could provide a "virtual" global presence, because of their speed or omnipresence, but hedged its bet with the development of an "Air Expeditionary Force." The Army, with the politically mandated drawdown of European forces and without sufficient independent means for mobility and a global presence, focused its enterprise on mounting an expeditionary force.

These six enterprises constitute the past, but they do not exhaust the possibilities for the future. At least two other purposeful enterprises have lurked (but never dominated the American military) during the 20th century:

1. **Defending the homeland.** Homeland defense, as an issue and an activity, was evident several times in the 20th century—in the first

half of the century, when the Navy considered itself as the first line of defense and when coastal artillery was in vogue,[26] and again in the second half, when air and missile defenses (including the Strategic Defense Initiative) became salient issues.

2. **Maintaining a mobilization base.** Today, maintaining the mobilization base mostly means keeping the weapon industry alive and healthy. But for the first half of the 20th century, it also meant keeping the training infrastructures and manpower reservoirs. These issues have sometimes been of acute concern, but they have seldom risen to dominate the American military's purposeful activities.

What of the future? As the 20th century closes, it is clear that the enterprise of the American military—its primary purposeful activity—is being prepared to mount an expeditionary force. That the United States has had to do so five times in this century is enough to make that enterprise plausible, and its force-structure demands obviously make it attractive to the military as a peacetime enterprise. But this is largely a self-selected enterprise—one that the nation has never before supported in peacetime for any lengthy period.[27] Competing societal demands for budget resources remain unresolved—although they may be deferred by a healthy economy as we approach the end of the century. The real question is whether that enterprise—attractive though it may be—will be sustained by the American society into the 21st century. If it can be, the applications of the information technologies to the present enterprise may indeed be a pertinent challenge for the American military as the information revolution crests.

Some, including this writer, have argued that the enterprise will change because of the information revolution's transformation of societies and economies and, hence, the nature of conflict—the sub-

---

[26]For a brief period, the Army Air Corps tried to justify the development of its first long-range bombers for coastal defense. (See Builder, 1993, p. 76.)

[27]After the two world wars, the American military was rapidly demobilized. President Eisenhower demobilized more forcibly after the Korean War in favor of providing a deterrent. The demobilization after the Vietnam War and during the Carter administration was reversed by the so-called Reagan buildup, the final Cold War initiative of the 1980s. Whether the American military will once again be demobilized after the Cold War is the other shoe, not yet dropped.

sidence of nation-state warfare with regular forces and the rise of nonstate and intrastate conflicts brought about by the globalization of information and commerce.  If so, the enterprise might shift toward providing constabulary capabilities for a more disorderly world or, alternatively, toward defending the homeland from terrorists, criminals, and rogues, either outside or within our borders.

Another possibility, raised by those looking to a revolution in military affairs instigated in large part by the information revolution, is a return to circumstances similar to the interlude between the two world wars, "largely peaceful decades but also periods of change and debate in military technology and strategy."[28]  If so, the enterprise might be characterized, as it could be in the 1920s and 1930s, by keeping the military arts and sciences alive or even maintaining a mobilization base in the face of rapidly changing technology and concepts of operation.

Of the eight enterprises considered here, the cresting information revolution would not seem to portend a return to the enterprises of providing a deterrent or forward defense as a primary purposeful activity.  Both have their saliency in the collisions of powerful, autonomous nation-states, circumstances that may have reached their apex in the 20th century and the Cold War and that are now ebbing under the onslaughts of the information revolution.  States can be deterred because they have something to lose, but many nonstate actors have little to lose and may, therefore, be very difficult to deter.  Forward defense seems likely only if the survival of the nation-state is ultimately at stake—a prospect that seems unlikely in the absence of another Cold War.  Providing a global presence could become the enterprise of the American military in the 21st century if the United States pursues the role of global policeman, but that role, too, is likely to be eroded rather than enhanced by the effects of the information revolution.

The more important point to be made here is not which enterprise will dominate the American military in the 21st century—something that will remain arguable even after the fact—but whether the extraordinary effects of the ongoing and cresting information revo-

---

[28]This is a view attributed to Andrew Marshall, Director of Net Assessment.  (See Gigot, 1997.)

lution are likely to change the current enterprise of the American military. If the answer is yes, the change in enterprise almost certainly will be the most important consequence of the information revolution for the American military, not the application of the information technologies to its existing enterprise.

In sum, the most important effects of the current information revolution for the American military will probably not be new tools for fighting traditional kinds of wars—the old enterprise or business— but serving a changed society that has new and different expectations, assignments, and support for its military. The challenge the information revolution poses for the American military is not so much *applying the new technology* as *anticipating the new enterprises* that might arise as it is tasked by a society transformed by the information revolution in a politically and economically transformed world.

## BIBLIOGRAPHY

Brodie, Bernard, ed., *The Absolute Weapon*, New York: Harcourt Brace, 1946.

Brodie, Bernard, *War and Politics*, The Macmillan Company, New York, 1973.

Builder, Carl H., *Patterns in American Intellectual Frontiers*, Santa Monica, Calif.: RAND, N-2917-A, August 1990.

_____, *The Icarus Syndrome*, New Brunswick: Transaction Publishers, 1993.

_____, "Looking in All the Wrong Places?" *Armed Forces Journal International*, May 1995.

Builder, Carl H., and Theodore Karasik, *Organizing, Training and Equipping the Air Force for Crises and Lesser Conflicts*, Santa Monica, Calif.: RAND, MR-626-AF, 1995.

Correll, John T., "The Headwinds of Tradition," editorial, *AIR FORCE Magazine*, Vol. 80, No. 10, October 1997, p. 3.

DoD—*see* U.S. Department of Defense.

Dunlap, Charles J., Jr., "21st-Century Land Warfare:  Four Dangerous Myths," *Parameters*, Autumn 1997, pp. 27–37.

Gigot, Paul A., "Cohen Decides Pentagon Needs Fewer Good Men," *Wall Street Journal*, November 14, 1997, p. 18.

Hamel, Gary, and C. K. Prahalad, *Competing for the Future*, Boston: Harvard Business School Press, 1994.

Keegan, John,  *A History of Warfare*, New York:  Alfred A. Knopf, 1993.

Mathews, Jessica, "Power Shift," *Foreign Affairs*, January–February 1997, pp. 50–66.

Meilinger, Phillip S., "The Next Air Campaign," *AIR & SPACE/Smithsonian*, Vol. 12, No. 4, October–November 1997, pp. 46, 47.

Moravec, Hans, *Mind Children:  The Future of Robot and Human Intelligence*, Cambridge, Mass.:  Harvard University Press, 1988.

Oppenheimer, Todd,  "The Computer Delusion," *The Atlantic Monthly*, Vol. 280, No. 1, July 1997, pp. 45–62.

Petersen, John L., *The Road to 2015:  Profiles of the Future*, Corte Madera, Calif.:  Waite Group Press,  1994.

Reinhardt, Andy, "What Matters Is How Smart You Are," *Business Week*, Special Double Issue on Silicon Valley, August 25, 1997, pp. 68–72.

Schwartz, Peter, *The Art of the Long View*, New York:  Doubleday Currency, 1991.

Sheehan, John J., "Building the Right Military for the 21st Century," *Strategic Review*, Vol. 25, No. 3, Summer 1997, pp. 5–13.

TRADOC—*see* U.S. Army Training and Doctrine Command.

U.S. Army Training and Doctrine Command, *Information Operations*, Field Manual 100-6, August 1996.

U.S. Congress, *The Budget of the United States Government for Fiscal Year 1996*, as reported in *The National Review*, December 25, 1995.

U.S. Department of Defense, Joint Chiefs of Staff, *Joint Vision 2010*, Washington, D.C., 1996a.

U.S. Department of Defense, Office of the Chairman of the Joint Chiefs of Staff, *Joint Information Warfare Policy*, Washington, D.C., Chairman of the Joint Chiefs of Staff Instruction 3210.01, January 2, 1996b.

Van Creveld, Martin, "Air Power 2025," in *New Era Security*, RAAF Air Power Studies Centre, June 1996.

Van Tol, Jan M., "Military Innovation and Carrier Aviation: The Relevant History," *Joint Force Quarterly*, No. 16, Summer 1997, pp. 77–87.

Watts, Barry D., *Clausewitzian Friction and Future War*, Washington, D.C.: Institute for National Security Studies, National Defense University, 1996.

Wriston, Walter B., *The Twilight of Sovereignty*, New York: Scribner's, 1992.

# Chapter Three

# RIGHT MAKES MIGHT:  FREEDOM AND POWER IN THE INFORMATION AGE

*David C. Gompert*[1]

## INTRODUCTION

### Information Technology and World Politics

The locomotive of change in the new era of world politics is information technology.  It propels reform and globalization and is increasingly crucial to national power.  It has thus recast the relationship
between politics and power.  In essence, military power now
depends on information technology and thus on the openness, freedom, and global integration that spawn and sustain that technology.
Consequently, the world's great powers will be, like the United
States, free-enterprise nations, ruled by legitimate governments,
motivated by shared interests in the health and security of the global
economy, and at least loosely united against threats to those interests from lesser states and nonstate actors.

National power and standing will remain important, both as facts
and ambitions.  But the great powers will all be within the core political economy and will thus be partners, not rivals, of the United States
and of each other.  Their growing economic integration, unprecedented in kind, will make hegemonic struggles a high-cost, low-gain
diversion from the pursuit of common core interests.  Countries that
remain closed and apart from the core, including those that are hostile to the core and its interests, will find it increasingly difficult to
acquire or develop the information technology necessary to achieve
modern power.  Simply put:  U.S. adversaries will tend to be weak;

---

[1]This paper is a shorter version of Gompert (1998).

U.S. friends will tend to be strong; and strong states will tend to be friendly.

Such a state of affairs could be considered optimistic, even utopian, were it not roughly the situation today:  The military superiority of the United States is, in large part, a consequence of its lead in information technology, which results from its economic and political openness.  Thus, the strongest democracy is the strongest power. The other leading democracies, Japan and the European Union (EU), trail only the United States in most important measures of actual and potential power.[2]  Yet the three are essentially as congenial now as they were when Japan and Europe depended vitally on U.S. protection during the Cold War.

Thus, today's greatest powers are democratic, integrated economically, in harmony, and predisposed to confront common problems jointly.  The view here is that this pattern will hold true generally, increasingly, and perpetually, owing above all to the effects of the information revolution.  The need for and effects of information technology will cause aspiring great powers, historically a source of instability, to gravitate toward the interests and openness of the United States and the democratic core, rather than to challenge them.  Consequently, the multipolar relationship among modern great powers will feature collaboration, common stakes, and compatible purposes, rather than hegemonic struggle, balance of power, and pecking-order politics.  Post–Cold War relations among the United States, Japan, and the EU provide the model for relations among modern great powers generally.

The most important question in the new era is whether China's emerging power and strategy will conform to that template.  The thesis here, applied to that particular question, is that China's paramount ambitions—stability and greatness—require reform, integration, and concert with the established powers.  There is no other way to master the dominant technology, without which China cannot succeed.

---

[2]The EU has the world's second-largest and best concentration of military power and the largest economy.  In addition to being the closest technological rival of the United States, Japan could become a world-class military power within a short time of any (highly unlikely) decision to do so.

Even giant states that reject the core's interests and values, though potentially dangerous, will be chronically undernourished in the technology that counts the most. They will therefore lie outside not only the global economy but also the power structure of world politics. Such outlying states can still carve out military niches, disrupt international security, and defy even the United States in some circumstances. The broad-based military superiority of the United States and other democratic powers will not ensure complete, permanent security. But states that seek self-sufficiency or oppose the core's interests and values will find it much harder than it is for the great democracies to build and use modern military power, which increasingly depends on wider success with information technology. Consequently, the ability of such states to undermine international security will be limited, and the risks facing them will be great should they try. Instead of might making right, we will discover that right—as in open and free—makes might.

The underlying reason for the emerging convergence between democracy and power lies in the *nature* of information technology: It comes directly from and adds directly to human knowledge. Once thought of as a utility in need of regulation—at least in its telecom origins—it has proven to be the best way to tap human potential, especially if unregulated. Older technologies—metal bending, machine propelling, atom splitting—have been conducive to state power, even to coercive state power. But information technology is linked to the inventiveness, freedom, aspirations, and irrepressibility of the citizen. If anything, state power, in its traditional sense, can only retard this technology. The information revolution both liberates and requires liberation. As the U.S. experience shows, the freer the market, the greater the level of performance that information technology delivers.

Information technology has already revolutionized industrial operations. Information technology enables corporations to operate worldwide systems of production, distribution, and finance that form the anatomy of the integrated world economy. Consequently, U.S., European, and Japanese firms are investing wherever their technology has the best match with local labor. Thus, on a global scale, information technology thrives on open markets and boosts efficiency, productivity, and prosperity.

In the military realm, those who master information technology have the potential to multiply the lethality and mobility of their armed forces, such that they can trade in mass for quality and come out way ahead. To a far greater degree than mechanical technologies, information technologies can yield enduring military advantages only if they are flourishing in the economy and society at large. For the most part, the key technologies for the military—microelectronics, data networking, and software—are driven by the volume and requirements of civilian markets. Indeed, after the initial years of the "computer revolution"—the 1950s and 1960s—the military sector, even in the United States, has lagged the rest of the market, in part because it is sluggish, more rigid, and less open than other sectors and in part because it has become a relatively small segment. Only with vibrant private sectors and integration in the world economy will countries, however large and populous, be able to reap the benefits of the information revolution in military affairs and in their larger societies.

## Implications

This reasoning, if right, has a bearing on how to regard the United States and the world's other current and future powers, especially Japan, the EU, and China.[3] The strength of the United States is not a transitory phenomenon of the immediate post–Cold War period but rather a natural result of the U.S. lead in exploiting the information revolution. Japan and Europe also satisfy the conditions of success in information technology—freedom and integration—and have the economic performance and military potential to show for it. Yet there is little danger that they will become America's strategic rivals, despite their size, the absence of a major common adversary, and their reduced security dependence on the United States. There is no hint of interest in a hegemonic challenge—if anything, the greater danger is that they will be free riders. As the stake Japan, the EU, and the United States share in the health and security of the integrated core economy increases, their cooperation ought to deepen. All

---

[3]India could also become a power of this magnitude. But it will not get as much attention in this chapter because it does not appear to be on a collision course with the United States.

three democratic powers have an equity, figuratively and literally, in each other's success.

As for China, its growing investment in and reliance on information technology will intensify pressures for further economic and political liberalization.  If and as the Chinese state yields to these pressures, China will be drawn ever more closely toward—indeed, into—the core of democratic powers and the interests that motivate them.  Alternatively, a stubbornly authoritarian, nationalistic, and self-sufficient China will find it hard to become competitive in the dominant technology, on which both its economic prospects and future military power increasingly depend.  China can become a modern world power or can reject the ideals and oppose the interests of the core, but it cannot do both.

Fear in the United States of China as a powerful, authoritarian, hegemonic challenger ignores the analysis that power requires information technology, information technology requires freedom and integration, and freedom and integration create a community of values and interests.  Obviously, China will not be a replica of Japan or Western Europe.  Neither will it adopt all of America's ways and beliefs.  But as China's mastery of information technology and its power grow, so should its identification with the interests of the core and thus its qualifications and disposition to become a genuine partner of the United States and a creator of regional and global security rather than of insecurity.

While the prospect of partnership among the world's powers, established and rising, offers great hope to the United States and to global security, there are pitfalls and countervailing trends.  Openness produces not only strength but also vulnerability.  Societies that enjoy political and economic openness, rely on the sharing of information, and are integrated into the world economy are inviting targets for states or groups that oppose them.  Democracies might lack the will to pay for military power or the nerve to use it when threatened.  Moreover, by networking communities of interest and bypassing vertical authority, the information revolution is eroding hierarchies of all sorts, including democratic nation-states.  Finally, so rapid and uncontrollable is the spread of information technology, thanks to the integration and enlargement of the global economy, that even closed states can acquire and use it for military purposes.

Granted, these factors will limit the power and security of even the most powerful nation-states. But this chapter's thesis is not that powerful states will be invulnerable or necessarily dominant in world affairs. If anything, the symbolic and operational utility of national power, including that of democratic states, will be less in the information age than it was in the industrial age. But the thesis here is that the most powerful states will be at least loosely aligned behind a common strategic and political outlook and that states, however sizable, lacking that outlook will encounter difficulty creating and using the dominant economic and military technology.

The thought that freedom and integration promote security is not new. Neither is the idea that democracies do not wage war with each other. (Doyle, 1986; Ray, 1995.) The argument that integration engenders common interests, promotes cooperation, and dampens conflict is also familiar, though less widely accepted, mainly because of the contrary example of European interdependence in the decades before World War I (more on that later). The new idea here—adding the spice of information technology to the curry—is that democracies have the inherent potential to be more powerful than other types of states, which was not the case when states could wield industrial power.

For these ideas to be right, several propositions—mere assertions thus far—must be valid. First, competitiveness in information technology depends on economic and political freedom and on integration into the core. Second, military power and other forms of national power depend on broad-based competitiveness in the creation and use of information technology. Third, integration into the core creates shared stakes that eclipse, or at least qualify, power politics and point toward a democratic commonwealth of interests and values. The remainder of this chapter will examine these propositions.

## INFORMATION TECHNOLOGY NEEDS FREEDOM

### Knowledge and Economic Freedom

Success in creating and exploiting information technology depends on economic freedom. The two most important stages in the lives of most information technologies are *invention* and practical *application*. These stages are especially dependent on healthy market forces and financial returns; government infringement, opposition, or control at either end retards the technology.

Creativity and freedom in invention and use have not been this crucial in every industry:  In steelmaking, for example, the economics of gathering ore and coal and of manufacturing are key; in nuclear power, fault-free engineering and operation are what matter most; in consumer products, success depends above all on distribution.  But as we can already see from the explosion of new ideas, products, and services in the decade since the deregulation of the U.S. telecommunications industry, the combination of invention and application—of science and market—provides the combustion for the information revolution.

The prospect of handsome profit in return for high-value innovation is critical in attracting the talent and justifying the risk-taking required in the discovery and design of information technology.  In addition, the development and introduction of new information systems and services require large, efficient, and venturesome capital markets.  Therefore, returns commensurate with value and risk are needed to stimulate both invention and investment.  Such incentives have not been and cannot be well replicated in a state-dominated economy.  Even if vast public resources are garnered and invested in these technologies, a closed system has no way of emulating the extraordinary, continuing growth in valuation, capitalization, and income for reinvestment that has accompanied the expansion of the information technology industry in the capitalist democracies.

State resource allocation, ownership, control, and planning, even if meant to provide the spark of innovation, will more likely extinguish it.  It takes the price mechanism of a free market to keep up with the fast pace at which information technology is able to create new applications and reduce costs.  The information market has a voracious appetite, demanding the next course before it has digested the last.  No sooner does a market segment seem saturated (mainframe computers, for instance) than it transforms itself and demands a better technology on an even greater scale (distributed processing).  Because of flexible design, versatile components, malleable software, and open connectivity standards, new products and services can be created, brought to market, and incorporated with astonishing speed.  Neither producers nor consumers in this market have patience for government regulation.  No major industry has developed a stronger aversion to state interference. The spread of e-mail and the Internet has occurred well beyond the reach, speed, and competence of the state.

Scale is as important as quickness in achieving competitiveness in information technology. Large commercial and consumer markets are needed to generate the revenue required to justify and afford the high research and development costs inherent in this industry. Absent such markets, military and other state needs are much too small to cover these costs. For want of a market, the Soviet Union was unable to compete in information technology despite its seemingly immense defense sector. In contrast, Japan, with a diminutive military sector, has had great success. The U.S. military market now makes up just 2 percent of the demand for information technology in the United States, down from 25 percent in 1975. While U.S. armed forces still require some customized technology, they have come to rely heavily on the broader information market: the public telephone network, common integrated circuits, everyday computers and data networks, and standardized operating systems.

Even as small, open states, such as Taiwan and Hungary, can find niches in the world information technology market, the investing firms' home countries—the United States, Japan, and Western Europe—also stand to benefit from the spreading of their technology. In addition to new markets and the income stream flowing back to headquarters, globalization expands the capabilities, especially the human capital, to which the great economic powers have access and over which they have continuing control, because they generate most new technology. The conventional wisdom that the diffusion of technology leaves the transferring state worse off is mistaken. The export of their own technology has strengthened the information industries of Japan and the United States and thus the countries themselves, given the importance of their information industries.

Economic freedom both furthers and is furthered by participation in the global economy. Such participation requires data communications for dispersed yet integrated operations. It provides pipelines for the latest innovations and applications. Despite the efforts of governments to control technology transfers, there is a growing, free-flowing transnational pool of information technology, not tightly restricted to but concentrated in the integrated core economy, where nearly all advanced value-added production occurs. (Vernon and

Kapstein, 1991.) Countries lacking economic freedom will have difficulty integrating, owing to their exclusion from the world trading
system and to inhibitions on the part of foreign investors. Consequently, their access to the pool of information technology will be
constricted.

In light of their indigenous deficiencies and investor disinterest,
states without free markets will be forced to try to import advanced
technology, legally or otherwise. While this is feasible for some other
technologies—the ones required to make and launch weapons of
mass destruction, for instance—it is not feasible, broadly speaking,
for information technology. Most information products and services
work well only when embedded in a society whose skills and infrastructure are undergoing a larger information revolution. These
technologies are increasingly interdependent, especially as computer
networking expands; parts are of limited utility. What good are
desktop computers without networks and a steady diet of software
upgrades? Information technology is constantly being modified,
enhanced, and overtaken by better ideas, leaving importing states to
engage in an expensive and never-ending game of catch-up.

Of greatest concern, obviously, is that states that shun free markets
might nevertheless be able to acquire particular information technology for military purposes. But, of course, the more ambitious
those purposes, the more technology they need. Since the technology is virtually impossible to partition and control, the more of it
such states acquire, the greater the likelihood that they will end up
weakened or transformed. Economic openness, integration, and
information technology travel together and are a juggernaut of
progress when they do.

The information revolution has figured centrally in the accelerating
expansion of the world's free-market core—spreading ideas, permit-
ting global operations, improving the output of human capital in
much of the developing world, and facilitating the investment that
has extended capitalism's reach over the last two decades. Throughout this process, the enhancement of economic freedom has enabled
emerging nations to attract investors and to acquire, use, and eventually produce information technology.

But is history since 1980 or so a guide to the long-term future? Will
economic freedom remain a prerequisite of national success in per-

petuity, if and as the information *revolution* turns into a more stable information *age?* Or could it be that the need for creative stimulus and freedom in the invention and application of information technology, so evident today, is not a function of the nature of the technology but of its youthfulness?

After all, invention was where the action was early in the industrial age, too. Perhaps, in a less revolutionary future, production methods, industrial management, or distribution will come to dominate the information age, as occurred when the industrial revolution matured. If so, it could be that the edge now held by open-market states in spawning, financing, and applying new ideas could fade as this revolution settles into a more steady state. Conceivably, capitalism's phenomenal success in recent decades—perhaps democracy's too—might be a temporary phenomenon reflecting its peculiar efficacy in *launching* the information revolution.

But recall that economic freedom is critical in both the creation *and use* of information technology. Thus, there is no reason to expect a lessening over time in the importance of free markets in sustaining an edge in information technology. An open economy requires distributed information for its private companies to operate, especially as they themselves become decentralized and more interactive with their suppliers and customers. Large private enterprises have become the most sophisticated users of information technology, demanding the best to enhance their own strategic competitiveness. They provide the essential leading edge in challenging the industry to furnish better hardware, software, networks, and services. In addition, extensive and modern backbone telecommunications, with gateways to the global network, are a requirement of a vibrant private sector. In contrast, closed economic systems lack private enterprises whose appetite for information technology stems from the urge to compete, cut costs, and increase profits. Governments do not express such demands.

Thus, the *nature* of this technology, not just its stage of development, favors open economic systems. The nature of heavy mechanical industry lent itself to state involvement. The nature of atomic power required it. But information technology contradicts the purposes and can weaken the props of state economic power. The main economic uses to which information technology is put—distributing information, decentralizing functions and decisionmaking, creating horizontal links, improving producer-consumer contact, sharpening external awareness and adaptability—correspond with strong market forces. Even if the supply of information technology becomes less dependent on economic freedom over time, the demand will not. Therefore, we should expect capitalist systems to retain their advantage through the information age.

## Knowledge and Political Freedom

Success in creating and exploiting information technology also depends on and fosters political freedom. As we were taught in introductory civics, access to information, via as many media as possible, is a precondition for accountable government and effective democracy. In turn, the free flow of information amplifies democratic demands. Recent research confirms a strong causal link between the availability of communications and the expansion of political freedom in the wake of communism.[4]

Dictators who try to control information freedom, lest it weaken their grip on power, clearly understand the connection (without having read the research). The world's most oppressive states—North Korea, Iraq, Cuba, Libya, Syria, and Serbia—are also those most determined to monopolize and manipulate information. The availability of information technology, whether or not sanctioned by the state, spreads news and opinions about what is happening both inside and outside the country, which for most dictators can only hasten involuntary retirement.

Looked at from the opposite direction, a climate of intellectual and personal freedom is important in encouraging breakthrough ideas, which are especially critical in information technology. True, authoritarian states can cultivate, pamper, and even motivate scientists and engineers whose inventions serve "the cause." But the speed with which the vaunted science and technology establishment of the former Soviet Union collapsed demonstrates the fragility of state-controlled science in the information age.

Intellectuals, including those of science and of letters, demand intellectual freedom. Intellectual freedom, in turn, gives rise to insistence

---

[4]Christopher Kedzie of RAND did work on this in 1996 in the context of what he calls the "dictator's dilemma."

on the right to question the ruler, the ruler's policies, and the very system of government. It is difficult, arguably impossible, for a regime to pigeonhole individual freedom and political freedom for long. Conversely, a state's refusal to embark on genuine political reform will, in due course, become an impediment to the successful creation and use of information technology, thus limiting its economic and military potential.

The prompt and unrestricted use of new information products and services, characteristic of open political systems, increases the expected financial return on both innovation and capital. The digital network, the personal computer, cellular telephony, and the Internet, all of which required hefty investment in the face of market and technical risk, have relied on confidence that the government would not interfere in the market or restrict use. The growth of Web browsers would hardly be as rapid as it is if industry feared that government might crack down on the Web. In addition, the free sharing of ideas, a hallmark of democracy, is important in disseminating and thus making full use of the latest information technology. The fact that the first Chinese magazine about the Internet had to begin underground underscores the contradiction between the urge to spread the technology and the urge to police it.

The link between democracy and information technology is not transitory. Attempts by government to restrict the international diffusion of information technology have been largely futile. Over the past several decades, the industry has eagerly spread its know-how as part of the competition for global markets. So, mastery of these technologies ought, in principle, to be widespread. Yet nearly all of the new information technology generated today still comes from the democracies that account for less than one-fifth of the world's population. And other societies that are beginning to use and produce information technology are, for the most part, also democratic. The pattern is too strong to be accidental.

## Economic Freedom and Political Freedom

Free enterprise breeds political reform and, eventually, accountable government. In Asia, for example, nearly all of the emerging free-market nations are democratizing. Empirical research confirms that marketization, the process of moving from a centrally controlled economy to a free market, provides the conditions necessary for fostering democracy and the means by which the citizenry can establish this system of government. (Ravich, 1996.)

The growing middle classes of the emerging societies demand political rights to go with their economic freedom. Authoritarian regimes have had little success at satisfying, or buying off, the new economic classes with prosperity. Give a person the chance to make money, and he will want more, not less, freedom to use his earnings as he wishes, to go where he pleases, to say what he wants, and to criticize what he dislikes.

With marketization, the government becomes an economic backwater, the guardian and paymaster of uncompetitive state enterprises. As the economic power of the state shrivels, so does its ability to resist pluralist demands and political reform. Its ability to provide public and social service is weakened. As it loses its economic legitimacy, its lack of political legitimacy invites more determined opposition.

Economic freedom, as already noted, goes hand in hand with integration in the international economy, leading to exposure to foreign goods and services, customers and suppliers, management know-how, and liberal political notions. These exposures encourage the challenging of undemocratic government. Attempts to create a dual economy—part open, part not—can work only for a while, since the open part will become noticeably more prosperous, and seditious ideas from abroad will take hold there and seep into the rest of the society. Fidel Castro's misgivings about freeing up part of Cuba's economy, as Cuban reformers advocate, suggest that he has a nose for these risks.

Direct support for dissidents or embryonic democratic institutions is increasingly available both from the governments and nongovernmental organizations of the democratic core, thanks to (what else?) information technology. The penetrability of even self-isolated societies is growing, especially when sophisticated transnational "civil society" groups make it their business to network with the oppressed. Determined despots can combat this porosity only by resorting to more severe oppression and to economic self-isolation.

The price of resisting democratic pressures—deprivation and popular hatred—is rising.

While undemocratic states are capable of instituting capitalism, they are generally less good at it. Even if they condone economic freedom, undemocratic states hardly offer a climate conducive to the individual initiative needed for success in creating and applying information technology. Moreover, the durability of undemocratic free-market states is doubtful. Pinochet's Chile was often mentioned—until Chile became democratic. Singapore is the most commonly cited example, but it is too small and idiosyncratic to support any generalization. Chinese elites admit that political reform—indeed, some recognizable form of democracy—cannot be postponed indefinitely if China's success is to continue. Their forecast that this will occur over many decades—Jiang Zemin recently prescribed democracy for China in 50 years—might underestimate the difficulty of inoculating free enterprise against free politics. Even now, though obscured by China's poor human-rights record, political openness and representative government are spreading at local levels, and the appetite of Chinese citizens for freedom is unlikely to be satisfied by just a taste.

History will settle whether marketization produces democratization—though *recent* history suggests it does. The point is germane but not critical here. Even an undemocratic state that integrates into the core economy, yet remains undemocratic, will come to share the bulk of the *interests* of the great democratic powers even if it does not also subscribe to core *values*. Those already integrated into the core are largely motivated by a set of common economic interests: the security of world energy supplies, the smooth functioning of global markets, the institutionalization of free trade, and common approaches to transnational challenges. A distillate of current U.S. global strategy reveals a preponderant economic motivation, with its concentration on East Asia, Europe, and the Middle East; its relentless drive to open markets; and its willingness to project power to ensure access to petroleum. Although America's closest and best partners have been other democracies, it usually can also count on less savory states that share its material interests. As the world economic core integrates and expands, it acquires collective interests that will animate the behavior of all who participate, be they politically open or not.

## NATIONAL POWER NEEDS INFORMATION TECHNOLOGY

### Information Technology and Military Capabilities

This chapter's second proposition is that military power, and other types of national power, depend increasingly on broad-based competitiveness in the creation and use of the dominant technology.  If this is true, in conjunction with the first proposition, power will come more easily and be more sustainable for states whose economic and political freedoms and integration in the world economy make them more competitive in information technology.

Information technology is becoming the most important factor in military operations and power.  The centrality of information technology in military capabilities is now recognized in the two most definitive recent statements on U.S. defense strategy:  the *Report of the Quadrennial Defense Review* (DoD, 1997a) and *Joint Vision 2010* (DoD, 1997b).  Until recently, the U.S. military was applying information technology to improve at the margin its traditional ways of fighting and managing.  Like many private enterprises before, it is only now beginning to change its ways, the better to realize the new technology's promise.

As military forces and operations exploit the information revolution, the very measures of military power will change.  The sizes of armies, the heaviness of armored forces, raw numbers of combat aircraft and ships, and atomic megatonnage will matter less in the new era.  The performance—accuracy, reliability, lethality—of individual weapons has been enhanced by microelectronics, but their real value will come from networking them together.  Improved data communications can now combine sensors, platforms, weapons, and command into far more potent capabilities than those of high-performance systems used independently.

The ability to use weapons, sensors, platforms, and other military systems in conjunction with one another depends on elegant but rugged command, control, communications, computing, intelligence, surveillance, and reconnaissance (mercifully, "C4ISR").  The side with C4ISR superiority—"information dominance," in the jargon du jour—can track its adversary's every move, see and direct its own forces, and largely determine the course of the conflict.

Information technology is eliminating the inverse relationship between range and accuracy, and thus lethality. Combined with the improved ability to find and follow enemy units, such lethality permits rapid and systematic destruction of the enemy's whole force and war infrastructure. The need to fly manned aircraft into enemy-controlled air space to do this job is declining, as accurate standoff weapons can be used to destroy any target and as unmanned vehicles are developed.

Small, light ground units with large arsenals of affordable precision-strike munitions borne by remote platforms at their command can pack a heavy offensive punch. Using "swarm" tactics, they will be more than a match for much larger but slower enemy forces and permit quicker deployment and reduced logistical demands, all thanks to the improved lethality and connectivity provided by information technology. These capabilities will expand the ability of those possessing them to project power, strike with impunity from any distance and direction, render an adversary defenseless, and achieve decisive victory, all with lower casualties. Tactical operations could be fought from strategic distances. Mechanized aggression could go the way of the cavalry charge.

Information technology has also brought within reach the elusive goal of joint warfare, which provides enormous combat advantages over those who lack it. Instead of waging segregated warfare among ground-, sea-, and air-based components, "jointness" unifies forces to carry out decisive operations. Potentially, any capability from the entire integrated force, depending on priorities, can be brought to bear on any component of the enemy's force, but not vice versa. As options multiply, the adversary's hope of defending its forces and infrastructure fades.

Using private-sector information technology and methods, defense logistics are becoming leaner and quicker. American military leaders and critics still lament the difficulty of restructuring and shrinking their huge support establishment and inventories. But at least they have reached the foothills of this mountain chain. Most other militaries remain far behind, encumbered with calcified support establishments that drain resources and hamper operations as much as support them. Information technology also offers the possibility of streamlining procurement, improving resource management, sharpening training (e.g., with simulations), and enhancing productivity throughout the defense establishment. In sum, both "tooth" and "tail" are undergoing transformation to exploit the information revolution.

Information technology, physically defined—hardware and software, devices and systems—only partly accounts for U.S. military superiority and for the inherent advantages of open societies. The quality of American military personnel, on the rise since the end of the Vietnam War, is an equally towering strength. While quality encompasses a bundle of aptitudes and education, more and more it emphasizes skill in "knowledge" tasks and technologies. An ample supply of high-quality information-oriented people has become a critical ingredient for military excellence, and it is more readily found in free-market economies and open societies (not only the United States) with ubiquitous information technology. A state-dominated system might be able to make, buy, and use this or that weapon system, but it is condemned to make do with inferior personnel and an industrial-age military establishment that will severely limit its power. Democracies are more capable of providing both the "machine" and "man" components of information power in military affairs.

Even though the United States is transforming its forces, structures, and doctrine to exploit information technology, it does not automatically follow that other states must mimic this approach to pose military challenges. North Vietnam, by analogy, understood the weaknesses of U.S. strategy and tactics—not to mention U.S. will—and did just the opposite, fighting on foot underneath the U.S. long-range attacks. In the future, reliance on massed platforms in open territory, skies, and waters will guarantee defeat against information-rich forces, such as those of the United States. But low-intensity conflict, the use of dispersed infantry, and hiding are promising tactics against such forces, and they do not require information technology. Does the prospect of low-tech asymmetric strategies contradict the idea that nations must excel in information technology if they are to avoid being at a military disadvantage?

Fundamentally, no. Bearing in mind that the revolution in military affairs is still in its infancy, as the application of information technology improves, a growing assortment of counterstrategies will fall victim to it.  Military facilities, stationary troops, and exposed tank columns are the easiest but not the only targets that can be detected, locked on, and destroyed by increasingly precise, quick, and affordable data links and munitions of a joint, information-age force.

This does not exclude the possibility that some hostile state will buck the trend, shun the dominant technology, and still present a military challenge.  But any state that aspires to regional or global military power, or that expects to fare well in a military showdown with the United States, will have to incorporate information technology increasingly into its military capabilities.  Other powers that step onto the playing field preferred and dominated by the free-market democracies will be able to advance only by opening themselves up to the pressures for reform and freedom that create modern knowledge-based power.

## Freedom as Vulnerability

Pessimists warn that, traditional military power aside, the information revolution is posing new security problems that could prove more severe for open than for closed societies.  Because the United States and its democratic partners are more economically dependent than other countries on connectivity and computing, they could become more vulnerable to information warfare, even ending the sanctuary from hostile attack that they now enjoy.  Integration in the world economy, with its crisscrossing networks, enlarges the risk.

Threats to the democracies' cyberspace endanger not only the citizens' quality of life but also their resolve.  Americans are ambivalent enough about projecting power as it is.  The prospect of a disruption of the national economy due to attacks on domestic information infrastructure could tilt that ambivalence in a distinctly negative direction, thus emboldening a militarily inferior enemy to challenge U.S. interests.

Moreover, as the United States and other advanced nations become more dependent on information technology in their military systems, they will become more susceptible to information warfare during operations.  The revolution in military affairs places a bull's eye on the C4ISR that is critical to it.  In the extreme, the ability of the United States to project power and to strike at will could be undermined if an otherwise weaker enemy interfered with the links that network U.S. forces, fuse U.S. sensor data, and permit joint warfare. Even if the military establishment secures its own dedicated links and nodes, effective information warfare attacks on the U.S. public telecommunications network, on which nearly all routine military traffic flows, could create havoc in a crisis and cripple a major power-projection campaign.

Given these vulnerabilities, could the economic and political open-ness of the United States and other advanced democracies become more of a strategic liability than an asset as the information revolu-tion unfolds? Probably not. Free-market democracies should be able to fashion sufficient security, resilience, and redundancy into their civil and military information systems to avoid being hobbled by hostile information warriors. Private enterprises, especially large providers and users of information systems and services, are already working to improve security, for their own profit-and-loss reasons. Moreover, we need not have absolute security from cyberspace invasions; a certain tolerance and toughness should be possible for an open society that already experiences blackouts, stock market swings, cable cuts, and traffic jams.

It is even possible that the irregular, unregimented, decentralized, and adaptive patterns of very open societies will make them more able than rigid, closed systems to withstand disruptions. Some vul-nerability will be a fact of life for democracies in the information age. Yet the countries that are superior in the military application of information technology also have a greater potential to conduct offensive information operations. They will hardly be defenseless. Moreover, the democratic powers should not confine themselves to responding in kind to information warfare attacks. If they can find the source—which improved track-back technology will help them do—they can settle scores with their superior conventional military strength.

A more fundamental question is whether we are merely experiencing a bend in the endless, winding road of military power that happens to favor the United States and other democracies. If so, the next turn could benefit despots. With the relentless spread of virtually all technologies, what faith have we that states and nonstate actors hostile to the interests of the democratic core will not get weapons,

perhaps cheap high-tech ones, that neutralize the superior capabilities of the United States and its friends? (See Stavardis, 1997.) After
all, globalization propagates innovation rapidly throughout the
world economy. Arguably, this will flatten out world economic and
technological strength, which could in turn lead to the equalization
of military power, or at least to trouble ahead for any country that
relies mainly on its technological edge for its power.

More specifically, even though the democracies might retain military
superiority based on their edge in information technology, their
ability and will to use their power could be undermined by improved
missiles, mines, and of course chemical and biological weapons in
the hands of hostile states. It would not take a very high forecast of
casualties to deter the United States from taking military action even
against an inferior enemy, especially if no vital U.S. interests were at
stake. Alternatively, if the military role of information technology
were to wane in the next cycle—supplanted, for example, by
weapons of mass destruction or swarms of guerrilla fighters (this
time, Mujahideen instead of Vietcong)—democracies would have no
advantage and perhaps major disadvantages, including the higher
value they place on human life.

Yet these reservations do not negate the essential advantages of military capabilities based on information technology: Such capabilities
are more usable than less precise and less discriminating weapons
and reduce the human role in—though never the responsibility for—
international violence. The information revolution in military affairs
makes the use of force easier, more surgical, more refined, and less
costly in lives and treasure. The combination of accurate long-range
weapons and data networks can improve the ability to project power
over great distance, in any direction, at low risk. Information technology can reduce its possessors' reliance on massing humans on the
battlefield, whether to fire weapons, man sensors, halt an enemy
army, or mount a counteroffensive.

Even if new military technologies find their way into the hands of
rogues, and even if those rogues master their use (which is problematic), their greatest value will be to those who need to project
power without heavy losses. Because of their global interests and
public aversion to casualties, the United States and other democracies of the integrated core stand to benefit the most strategically.

Even as states hostile to the core counter with other capabilities and tactics, the fundamental point is that superior information can provide a transcending advantage—one that the countries strongest in the essential technology will enjoy.

Because open societies hold the lead in guiding and exploiting the information revolution, they also hold a lead in the military application of that revolution. While blind confidence would be foolish, the rise in the relative power of open societies will not be easily reversed. The information revolution is not a *cycle*, but a *threshold* in human advancement. Having been introduced to warfare, the ability to gather, digest, and share information will be crucial from here on—as defining and permanent as metal and fuel are to machines.

## The Changing Profile of Power

Since the end of the Cold War—perhaps earlier—military power has been overtaken by other, "softer" forms of power in world politics. (Nye, 1990.) National power includes economic strength and stability, industrial output, technological output, savings and investment levels, market size, infrastructure, exploitable but renewable resources, education, management competence, and scientific capacity. Every one of these factors correlates positively and increasingly with human knowledge, not commanded by the state but arising from the freedom to create, profit, adapt, and challenge the status quo. Free-market democracies dominate these categories of nonmilitary power and are superior in using information technology and in human talent to achieve their goals. Therefore, the decline in the importance of military power does not reduce either the importance of information technology or the democratic advantage.

There is yet another, subtle but increasingly important aspect of power in the new era: the ability of a system, or society, to sense the need for change and to adapt. The Soviet Union and what became of it illustrate the lack of this power, as well as the consequences. In a world of flux, with the future unpredictable, but surely quite different from the present, the race will be not only to the swift but also to the flexible.

The capacity to adapt has many components: technology, systems, institutions, practices, legitimacy, and of course the freedom to change. In any "complex adaptive system," the ability to assimilate, share, and act on information is indispensable for successful adaptation.[5] This requires excellent internal and external communications, as well as openness. While the intelligence and policymaking organs of the state have a role to play, decentralization and privatization of economic and technological decisionmaking are key, as is the extent of participation in the world economy. Democratic systems, awash with information, in touch with the world, and communicating freely within, tend to adapt well.

Information technology is generally weakening all forms of vertical authority and strengthening networked communities of interest. One of the human institutions being weakened is the nation-state itself. National governments, including democratic ones, are losing some of their functional and constitutional importance. So even as nation-state power is concentrating among the free-market democracies, they too will experience losses to nonstate actors, some of whom could in turn exploit national vulnerabilities. While this is true, the general erosion of state power will affect most the nations in which that power has been dominant. The economies, societies, and technologies of democracies depend relatively little on central government. So states like the United States are less likely to be undermined by information technology than those that rely on control rather than legitimacy and in which economic and technological performance depend on that control.

## POWERS AS PARTNERS

### Power, Integration, and Common Success

The congruence of freedom, knowledge, and power is no guarantee of a peaceful world. But it does point toward greater security insofar as democratic powers are not hostile toward each other and have military superiority over undemocratic states that are hostile to them. At a minimum, the risk of great-power conflict—the world-endangering sort—would be reduced. As the democratic powers

---

[5]The notion of a complex adaptive system has been developed principally at the Santa Fe Institute and RAND, the former more in theory and the latter more in policy application.

become more integrated economically, they will become even less inclined toward confrontation, having little to gain and much to jeopardize, and will become more inclined toward pursuit of their common interests.

Rising powers should come to see the world in essentially the same light. In the information age, they must integrate to rise, and integration reduces conflict and increases collaboration. As national success depends less and less on national power, hegemonic rivalry will be regarded as pointless and damaging to success. The relative standing among the principal nations will become less important in world politics.

The claim that economic integration discourages conflict usually elicits the reminder that the nations of Europe were interdependent prior to the outbreak of World War I. This is true, but the relevance of that history to our future begs examination. An important difference between then and now is that the old European powers engaged each other mainly in commodity trade, whereas today's integration encompasses vital, high-value-added products and services, including information technology. (Vernon and Kapstein, 1991.) Commodity trade can be cut and redirected; dependence on common crucial inputs cannot.

Moreover, a major arena of economic interest among the powers of late-nineteenth-century Europe—colonialism—far from dampening conflict, stoked it. Industrial-age economies depended on the control of raw materials, valuable land, and trade routes. Britain's empire and Germany's continental preeminence were economically important and depended on strength—indeed, on relative strength. Every power's industrial capacity could be seen as a potential threat, not a benefit, to other powers. Hegemony could yield real benefits; consequently, hegemonic rivalry had a certain logic. The low-value trade taking place engendered no sense of common economic fate, let alone common strategic interest. Add the turn of the century's cocky brand of nationalism, and the result was a flammable mix of maneuvering, distrust, and miscalculation that culminated in 1914. In sum, the old European powers were not truly integrated and saw each other's success as a threat to their own. Their trade did not alter that strategic calculus.

No such competition for colonies, land, or resources—not even energy—pits the leading democracies against one another today. In the information age, the existing powers have no interest in conquest, for it leads nowhere they cannot get more directly through investment and cooperation. Globalization, the liquidity of economic assets, and the creation of a single pool of information technology reduce the economic utility of power. How can territorial dominion, let alone aggression, help when the prize is information and ideas?

The United States, Western Europe, and Japan share interests in the health, security, and growth of the core political economy: the unimpeded flow of goods, services, resources, money, information, and know-how throughout the core; the integration of emerging states; the success of new democracies; the security of world energy supplies, which lie mainly beyond the core; the stability of the dangerous regions where most of those energy supplies lie, the Middle East and the former Soviet Union; denial of weapons of mass destruction to hostile states; and the capacity to relieve human crises in failed states. Although each power in the core also has particular interests, these generally do not contradict the common interests. If and as other countries become more open, integrated, and powerful, they should come to identify with these same core interests.

Is hegemony obsolete? The current situation might provide a clue, since one of the powerful democracies in the G-7 is clearly more powerful than the others. Despite a clear opportunity for hegemony, the United States does not seek to dominate others. American triumphalism and its unilateralist lapses are criticized by its closest friends. But there is a huge difference between insensitivity and an attempt, based on superior strength, to exert hegemonic control or to trample the interests of others in pursuit of one's own.

At present, the great democratic powers are functioning as an effective community of trustful partners despite an imbalance of power, as well as responsibility, among them. If, as well, the Chinese understand that joining a community of powers in which the United States is strongest does not mean subjecting China to American hegemony, they need not hesitate to join. Such progress is possible because relative power no longer determines absolute success.

## Integrating Rising Powers

Because of the new link between knowledge and power, no country, whatever its size by traditional measures, will find it possible to develop modern power without being competitive in the creation and use of information technology. Only by allowing economic and political freedom and by participating in the core economy will a state be able to acquire the investment, know-how, and market access needed to take full advantage of what information technology has to offer. A rising power that offers such economic and political freedom will find the governments and firms of the core prepared not only to accept but also to facilitate its integration and success. Thus, in the information age, becoming a great power means becoming part of the core. How will that integration affect the rising power's international outlook and conduct?

The surest, most feasible, and most durable way to get a rising power, such as China, to accept core interests is through the effects of integration. Where have we heard that before? Why believe this will work now with China when its antecedent, détente, failed with the Soviet Union? The Soviet Union was, as we know now, not a rising power at all, but one whose economic system was starting to fail well before the collapse. It had no real hope of integrating into the world economy and was not even trying to do so.

China harbors no interest in transforming the world—its interest is in transforming *itself.* It is eager to integrate and can realistically aspire to a major role in the world economy. Another major difference lies in the effects of information technology. Because of it, integration should affect Chinese internal politics and international behavior in ways détente never could have affected the Soviet Union. To achieve its goals, China must be able to acquire, create, and use information technology. Therefore, China must continue to reform and integrate. As it does, it will come to share the core economic and security interests that motivate cooperation among the United States, Japan, and Europe.

Like the current democratic powers, China will identify with the need for technology, products, money, energy, and information to flow freely throughout the world economy. It should also begin to sympathize with and eventually subscribe to the security concerns of the core democracies, particularly access to world petroleum reserves, for which China's future needs are great. Similarly, threats posed by the spread of weapons of mass destruction have already begun to outweigh whatever economic and political benefits the Chinese might see in trafficking with the likes of Iran. With global trade increasingly vital to China, it will value the security of trade routes and thus the need to resolve territorial disputes peacefully. There are straws in the wind that the Chinese are beginning to identify with these interests—the cutoff of nuclear dealings with Iran and its cooperation with the United States in response to the Asian financial crisis.

There will likely be continued friction between China and the United States and its partners over human rights, trade policy, and regional questions. And one issue, Taiwan, could produce a head-on collision. But the safety net beneath such difficulties, even if Chinese nationalism persists, will be the convergence of China's fundamental economic and strategic interests with those of the United States, Japan, and Europe. Even the Taiwan problem should become more soluble, despite China's growing military power, as China itself changes and as the idea of war between China and the United States begins to look unacceptable to both.

The decoupling of national power and national success, as the industrial age gives way to the information age, makes confrontation between leading powers and the rising power both reckless and pointless. If the leading power is not attached to the status quo, because progress, not power, produces success, the rising power has nothing to assault. The world's leading powers can function in lasting concert rather than in precarious balance, even if their power is out of balance. The dependence of power on information technology and of information technology on openness has created a new possibility.

## The Future of the Core

Thus, great-power relations in the new era need not, and from this standpoint will not, resemble those of the past: ever maneuvering to rebalance power, distrustful of each other because of the maneuvering, and preoccupied with stability yet potentially unstable. Globalization and its prime mover, information technology, are producing a growing commonwealth of responsible great powers, compatible in outlook and ideals and confident enough to welcome change. The last two decades have been encouraging: Relations among the United States, Japan, and Europe are reassuring, and the prospect of China and India joining this stream of progress is good. So the question inevitably arises: Does the information revolution have the strength to convert the entire planet (but for the odd rogue) to openness, responsibility, cooperation, and peace?

Since the end of World War II, the expansion of the core from North America outward has had a pacifying effect: Western Europe and Northeast Asia, two of the world's most dangerous regions in the first half of the 20th century, are now at peace. More recently, Eastern Europe and Southeast Asia, also notorious for violence, have begun to enjoy security as a consequence of their transformation and integration. The locations of conflict since the end of the Cold War have been outside the democratic pale: Somalia, Haiti, Yugoslavia, Kurdistan, Afghanistan, and Central Africa. It is reasonable to believe that the wider the democratic core, the greater the expanse of security.

But globalization might be in for a slowdown. Several regions—the greater Middle East, the former Soviet Union, and Africa—are showing unpromising signs. Ancient feuds persist among states and tribes. Reform is at best uneven. Most governments lack legitimacy. Cynicism and corruption among elites are unabated, if not rising. Human capital is not being developed and used to the fullest. Education and science are weak. For all these reasons, investors are wary, except when it comes to extracting raw materials. With all the options available to firms from the core in search of new locations in which to produce for global markets, now including vast pools of Chinese and Indian talent, they are not likely to choose these regions. If they stay effectively outside the core, these three regions will remain the world's most dangerous.

There is also a possibility that, as the core gets larger, its rate of expansion will slow—the opposite of the acceleration we witnessed from 1980 to the present. The emerging countries of Latin America, Asia, and Europe offer abundant investment opportunities. A flood tide of previously underutilized labor has been matched with capital, production technology, and global market access. China is adding some 10 million workers (former peasants) every year, and India has comparable potential. (Oksenberg, Swaine, and Lynch, 1997.) The competition for investment and technology is fierce. To the extent that further globalization depends on the spread of such investment to the Middle East, the former Soviet Union, and Africa, it will be hard to sustain the pace. Additionally, the financial turmoil and economic sag in East Asia and other emerging markets suggest that the process, more specifically the investments that drive it, might have overreached in recent years. This, too, does not bode well for regions not yet included.

Time will tell whether globalization sweeps in or sweeps past the outlying regions. The purpose here is not to practice futurology with false precision. Rather, it is to underscore that the expansive progress of the last two decades of this century could be hard to sustain. The expectation of a community of powers offered in this chapter is considerably more modest than any claim that the information revolution will soon produce a worldwide commonwealth of democracy, blossoming human talent, prosperity, and peace.

The sobering view of the exclusion of whole regions—nearly half the world—suggests that the core powers, the United States, Japan, and the EU, with China and India in the wings, will have much about which to cooperate. Power will be heavily concentrated in the core, but dangers will persist outside it. The strongest power cannot possibly cope with these dangers by itself—and why should it, when the other powers have similar interests at stake and growing means to help? Japan and the EU must share the burdens, as well as the prerogatives, of leadership with the United States. At the same time, the American policy elite should shed its fondness for unipolarity, not because it is infeasible, but because it is unnecessary and counterproductive to seek. The success, liberty, and happiness of Americans are not ensured by American supremacy but by the creation of a strong U.S. economy and a peaceful, and powerful, community of democracies.

In sum, world politics in the early 21st century could feature a concert of the most powerful nations, characterized by openness, integrating their economies and responding jointly to dangers to shared interests beyond their perimeter, e.g., energy insecurity, weapons of mass destruction, and ethnic conflict. Because they have the power of the information revolution at their disposal, they will be stronger than any adversary and should have the means to enhance world security in general.

> It has been of the world's history hitherto that might makes right. It is for us and for our time to reverse the maxim.—Abraham Lincoln

## BIBLIOGRAPHY

DoD—*See* U.S. Department of Defense.

Doyle, Michael, "Liberalism and World Politics," *American Political Science Review*, Vol. 80, December 1986, pp. 1151–1169.

Gompert, David, "Right Makes Might:  Freedom and Power in the Information," Washington, D.C.:  National Defense University Press, McNair Paper No. 59, 1998.

Nye, Joseph S., *Bound to Lead: The Changing Nature of American Power*, New York: Basic Books, 1990.

Oksenberg, Michel C., Michael D. Swaine, and Daniel C. Lynch, "The Chinese Future," Pacific Council on International Policy and the RAND Center for Asia-Pacific Policy, 1997.

Oksenburg, Michel, and Elizabeth Economy, *Shaping US-China Relations*, New York:  Council on Foreign Relations, 1997.

Ravich, Samantha Fay, *Marketization and Prosperity: Pathways to East Asian Democracy*, dissertation, RAND Graduate School, Santa Monica, Calif.: RAND, RGSD-132, 1996.

Ray, James Lee, *Democracy and International Conflict*, Columbia, S.C.: University of South Carolina Press, 1995.

Stavardis, James (Capt. USN), "The Second Revolution," *Joint Forces Quarterly*, Spring 1997, pp. 8–13.

U.S. Department of Defense, *Report of the Quadrennial Defense Review*, May 1997a.

U.S. Department of Defense, Joint Chiefs of Staff, *Joint Vision 2010*, 1997b.

Vernon, Raymond, and Ethan B. Kapstein, "National Needs, Global Resources," *Daedalus*, Vol. 120, No. 4, Fall 1991, pp. 1–22.

# Chapter Four

# NETWORKS, NETWAR, AND INFORMATION-AGE TERRORISM

*John Arquilla, David Ronfeldt, and Michele Zanini*

The rise of network forms of organization is a key consequence of the ongoing information revolution. Business organizations are being newly energized by networking, and many professional militaries are experimenting with flatter forms of organization. In this chapter, we explore the impact of networks on terrorist capabilities, and consider how this development may be associated with a move away from emphasis on traditional, episodic efforts at coercion to a new view of terror as a form of protracted warfare. Seen in this light, the recent bombings of U.S. embassies in East Africa, along with the retaliatory American missile strikes, may prove to be the opening shots of a war between a leading state and a terror network. We consider both the likely context and the conduct of such a war, and offer some insights that might inform policies aimed at defending against and countering terrorism.

## A NEW TERRORISM (WITH OLD ROOTS)

The age-old phenomenon of terrorism continues to appeal to its perpetrators for three principal reasons. First, it appeals as a weapon of the weak—a shadowy way to wage war by attacking asymmetrically to harm and try to defeat an ostensibly superior force. This has had particular appeal to ethno-nationalists, racist militias, religious fundamentalists, and other minorities who cannot match the military formations and firepower of their "oppressors"—the case, for example, with some radical Middle Eastern Islamist groups vis-à-vis Israel, and, until recently, the Provisional Irish Republican Army vis-à-vis Great Britain.

Second, terrorism has appealed as a way to assert identity and command attention—rather like proclaiming, "I bomb, therefore I am." Terrorism enables a perpetrator to publicize his identity, project it explosively, and touch the nerves of powerful distant leaders. This kind of attraction to violence transcends its instrumental utility. Mainstream revolutionary writings may view violence as a means of struggle, but terrorists often regard violence as an end in itself that generates identity or damages the enemy's identity.

Third, terrorism has sometimes appealed as a way to achieve a new future order by willfully wrecking the present. This is manifest in the religious fervor of some radical Islamists, but examples also lie among millenarian and apocalyptic groups, like Aum Shinrikyo in Japan, who aim to wreak havoc and rend a system asunder so that something new may emerge from the cracks. The substance of the future vision may be only vaguely defined, but its moral worth is clear and appealing to the terrorist.

In the first and second of these motivations or rationales, terrorism may involve retaliation and retribution for past wrongs, whereas the third is also about revelation and rebirth, the coming of a new age. The first is largely strategic; it has a practical tone, and the objectives may be limited and specific. In contrast, the third may engage a transcendental, unconstrained view of how to change the world through terrorism.

Such contrasts do not mean the three are necessarily at odds; blends often occur. Presumptions of weakness (the first rationale) and of willfulness (in the second and third) can lead to peculiar synergies. For example, Aum's members may have known it was weak in a conventional sense, but they believed that they had special knowledge, a unique leader, invincible willpower, and secret ways to strike out.

These classic motivations or rationales will endure in the information age. However, terrorism is not a fixed phenomenon; its perpetrators adapt it to suit their times and situations. What changes is the conduct of terrorism—the operational characteristics built around the motivations and rationales.

This chapter addresses, often in a deliberately speculative manner, changes in organization, doctrine, strategy, and technology that, taken together, speak to the emergence of a "new terrorism" attuned to the information age. Our principal hypotheses are as follows:

- **Organization.** Terrorists will continue moving from hierarchical toward information-age network designs. Within groups, "great man" leaderships will give way to flatter decentralized designs. More effort will go into building arrays of transnationally inter-netted groups than into building stand-alone groups.

- **Doctrine and strategy.** Terrorists will likely gain new capabilities for lethal acts. Some terrorist groups are likely to move to a "war paradigm" that focuses on attacking U.S. military forces and assets. But where terrorists suppose that "information opera-tions" may be as useful as traditional commando-style opera-tions for achieving their goals, systemic *disruption* may become as much an objective as target *destruction*. Difficulties in coping with the new terrorism will mount if terrorists move beyond iso-lated acts toward a new approach to doctrine and strategy that emphasizes campaigns based on swarming.

- **Technology.** Terrorists are likely to increasingly use advanced information technologies for offensive and defensive purposes, as well as to support their organizational structures. Despite widespread speculation about terrorists using cyberspace war-fare techniques to take "the Net" down, they may often have stronger reasons for wanting to keep it up (e.g., to spread their message and communicate with one another).

In short, terrorism is evolving in a direction we call *netwar*. Thus, after briefly reviewing terrorist trends, we outline the concept of net-war and its relevance for understanding information-age terrorism. In particular, we elaborate on the above points about organization, doctrine, and strategy, and briefly discuss how recent developments in the nature and behavior of Middle Eastern terrorist groups can be interpreted as early signs of a move toward netwar-type terrorism.

Given the prospect of a netwar-oriented shift in which some terror-ists pursue a war paradigm, we then focus on the implications such a development may have for the U.S. military. We use these insights to consider defensive antiterrorist measures, as well as proactive coun-terterrorist strategies. We propose that a key to coping with information-age terrorism will be the creation of interorganizational networks within the U.S. military and government, partly on the grounds that it takes networks to fight networks.

## RECENT VIEWS ABOUT TERRORISM

Terrorism remains a distinct phenomenon while reflecting broader trends in irregular warfare. The latter has been on the rise around the world since before the end of the Cold War. Ethnic and religious conflicts, recently in evidence in areas of Africa, the Balkans, and the Caucasus, for awhile in Central America, and seemingly forever in the Middle East, attest to the brutality that increasingly attends this kind of warfare. These are not conflicts between regular, professional armed forces dedicated to warrior creeds and Geneva Conventions. Instead, even where regular forces play roles, these conflicts often revolve around the strategies and tactics of thuggish paramilitary gangs and local warlords. Some leaders may have some professional training; but the foot soldiers are often people who, for one reason or another, get caught in a fray and learn on the job. Adolescents and children with high-powered weaponry are taking part in growing numbers. In many of these conflicts, savage acts are increasingly committed without anyone taking credit—it may not even be clear which side is responsible. The press releases of the protagonists sound high-minded and self-legitimizing, but the reality at the local level is often about clan rivalries and criminal ventures (e.g., looting, smuggling, or protection rackets).[1]

Thus, irregular warfare has become endemic and vicious around the world. A decade or so ago, terrorism was a rather distinct entry on the spectrum of conflict, with its own unique attributes. Today, it seems increasingly connected with these broader trends in irregular warfare, especially as waged by nonstate actors. As Martin Van Creveld warns:

> In today's world, the main threat to many states, including specifically the U.S., no longer comes from other states. Instead, it comes from small groups and other organizations which are not states. Either we make the necessary changes and face them today, or what is commonly known as the modern world will lose all sense of security and will dwell in perpetual fear. (Van Creveld, 1996, p. 58.)

Meanwhile, for the past several years, terrorism experts have broadly concurred that this phenomenon will persist, if not get worse. Gen-

---

[1]For an illuminating take on irregular warfare that emphasizes the challenges to the Red Cross, see Ignatieff (1997).

eral agreement that terrorism may worsen parses into different scenarios. For example, Walter Laqueur warns that religious motivations could lead to "superviolence," with millenarian visions of a coming apocalypse driving "postmodern" terrorism. Fred Iklé worries that increased violence may be used by terrorists to usher in a new totalitarian age based on Leninist ideals. Bruce Hoffman raises the prospect that religiously motivated terrorists may escalate their violence in order to wreak sufficient havoc to undermine the world political system and replace it with a chaos that is particularly detrimental to the United States—a basically nihilist strategy. (See Laqueur, 1996; Iklé, 1997; Hoffman, 1994 and 1998; Kaplan, 1994.)

The preponderance of U.S. conventional power may continue to motivate some state and nonstate adversaries to opt for terror as an asymmetric response. Technological advances and underground trafficking may make weapons of mass destruction (WMD—nuclear, chemical, biological weapons) ever easier for terrorists to acquire. (See Campbell, 1996.) Terrorists' shifts toward looser, less hierarchical organizational structures, and their growing use of advanced communications technologies for command, control, and coordination, may further empower small terrorist groups and individuals who want to mount operations from a distance.

There is also agreement about an emergence of two tiers of terror: one characterized by hard-core professionals, the other by amateur cut-outs. (Hoffman and Carr, 1997.) The deniability gained by terrorists operating through willing amateurs, coupled with the increasing accessibility of ever more destructive weaponry, has also led many experts to concur that terrorists will be attracted to engaging in more lethal destruction, with increased targeting of information and communications infrastructures.[2]

Some specialists also suggest that "information" will become a key target—both the conduits of information infrastructures and the content of information, particularly the media. (See Littleton, 1995, and Nacos, 1994.) While these target-sets may involve little lethal activity, they offer additional theaters of operations for terrorists. Laqueur in particular foresees that, "If the new terrorism directs its energies toward information warfare, its destructive power will be

---

[2]See, for instance, Shubik (1997) and Hoffman (1998).

exponentially greater than any it wielded in the past—greater even than it would be with biological and chemical weapons." (Laqueur, 1996, p. 35.) New planning and scenario-building is needed to help think through how to defend against this form of terrorism.[3]

Such dire predictions have galvanized a variety of responses, which range from urging the creation of international control regimes over the tools of terror (such as WMD materials and advanced encryption capabilities), to the use of coercive diplomacy against state sponsors of terror. Increasingly, the liberal use of military force against terrorists has also been recommended. Caleb Carr in particular espoused this theme, sparking a heated debate (Carr, 1997).[4] Today, many leading works on combating terrorism blend notions of control mechanisms, international regimes, and the use of force.[5]

Against this background, experts have begun to recognize the growing role of networks—of networked organizational designs and related doctrines, strategies, and technologies—among the practitioners of terrorism. The growth of these networks is related to the spread of advanced information technologies that allow dispersed groups, and individuals, to conspire and coordinate across considerable distances. Recent U.S. efforts to investigate and attack the bin Laden network (named for the central influence of Osama bin Laden) attest to this. The rise of networks is likely to reshape terrorism in the information age, and lead to the adoption of netwar—a kind of information-age conflict that will be waged principally by nonstate actors. Our contribution to this volume is to present the concept of netwar and show how terrorism is being affected by it.

## THE ADVENT OF NETWAR—ANALYTICAL BACKGROUND[6]

The information revolution is altering the nature of conflict across the spectrum. Of the many reasons for this, we call attention to two

---

[3]For more on this issue, see Molander, Riddile, and Wilson (1996) and Molander, Wilson, Mussington, and Mesic (1998).

[4]This theme was advocated early by Rivers (1986). For more on the debate, see Hoffman and Carr (1997).

[5]See, for instance, Netanyahu (1996) and Kerry (1997).

[6]This analytical background is drawn from Arquilla and Ronfeldt (1996) and Ronfeldt, Arquilla, Fuller, and Fuller (forthcoming). Also see Arquilla and Ronfeldt (1997).

in particular. First, the information revolution is favoring and strengthening network forms of organization, often giving them an advantage over hierarchical forms. The rise of networks means that power is migrating to nonstate actors, who are able to organize into sprawling multi-organizational networks (especially all-channel networks, in which every node is connected to every other node) more readily than can traditional, hierarchical, state actors. Non-state-actor networks are thought to be more flexible and responsive than hierarchies in reacting to outside developments, and to be better than hierarchies at using information to improve decisionmaking.[7]

Second, as the information revolution deepens, conflicts will increasingly depend on information and communications matters. More than ever before, conflicts will revolve around "knowledge" and the use of "soft power."[8] Adversaries will emphasize "information operations" and "perception management"—that is, media-oriented measures that aim to attract rather than coerce, and that affect how secure a society, a military, or other actor feels about its knowledge of itself and of its adversaries. Psychological disruption may become as important a goal as physical destruction.

Thus, major transformations are coming in the nature of adversaries, in the type of threats they may pose, and in how conflicts can be waged. Information-age threats are likely to be more diffuse, dispersed, multidimensional, and ambiguous than more traditional threats. Metaphorically, future conflicts may resemble the Oriental game of *Go* more than the Western game of chess. The conflict spectrum will be molded from end to end by these dynamics:

- *Cyberwar*—a concept that refers to information-oriented military warfare—is becoming an important entry at the military end of the spectrum, where the language has normally been about high-intensity conflicts.

- *Netwar* figures increasingly at the societal end of the spectrum, where the language has normally been about low-intensity con-

---

[7]For background on this issue, see Heckscher (1995).

[8]The concept of soft power was introduced by Nye (1990) and further elaborated in Nye and Owens (1996).

flict, operations other than war, and nonmilitary modes of conflict and crime. [9]

Whereas cyberwar usually pits formal military forces against each other, netwar is more likely to involve nonstate, paramilitary, and irregular forces—as in the case of terrorism. Both concepts are consistent with the views of analysts such as Van Creveld, who believe that a "transformation of war" is under way. (Van Creveld, 1991.) Neither concept is just about technology; both refer to *comprehensive* approaches to conflict—comprehensive in that they mix organizational, doctrinal, strategic, tactical, and technological innovations, for offense and defense.

## Definition of Netwar

To be more precise, *netwar* refers to an emerging mode of conflict and crime at societal levels, involving measures short of traditional war, in which the protagonists use network forms of organization and related doctrines, strategies, and technologies attuned to the information age. These protagonists are likely to consist of dispersed small groups who communicate, coordinate, and conduct their campaigns in an internetted manner, without a precise central command. Thus, information-age netwar differs from modes of conflict and crime in which the protagonists prefer formal, stand-alone, hierarchical organizations, doctrines, and strategies, as in past efforts, for example, to build centralized movements along Marxist lines.

The term is meant to call attention to the prospect that network-based conflict and crime will become major phenomena in the decades ahead. Various actors across the spectrum of conflict and crime are already evolving in this direction. To give a string of examples, netwar is about the Middle East's Hamas more than the Palestine Liberation Organization (PLO), Mexico's Zapatistas more than Cuba's Fidelistas, and the American Christian Patriot movement more than the Ku Klux Klan. It is also about the Asian Triads more than the Sicilian Mafia, and Chicago's Gangsta Disciples more than the Al Capone Gang.

---

[9]For more on information-age conflict, netwar, and cyberwar, see Arquilla and Ronfeldt (1993), Arquilla and Ronfeldt (1996), and Arquilla and Ronfeldt (1997).

This spectrum includes familiar adversaries who are modifying their structures and strategies to take advantage of networked designs, such as transnational terrorist groups, black-market proliferators of WMD, transnational crime syndicates, fundamentalist and ethno-nationalist movements, intellectual property and high-sea pirates, and smugglers of black-market goods or migrants. Some urban gangs, back-country militias, and militant single-issue groups in the United States are also developing netwar-like attributes. In addition, there is a new generation of radicals and activists who are just beginning to create information-age ideologies, in which identities and loyalties may shift from the nation-state to the transnational level of global civil society. New kinds of actors, such as anarchistic and nihilistic leagues of computer-hacking "cyboteurs," may also partake of netwar.

Many—if not most—netwar actors will be nonstate. Some may be agents of a state, but others may try to turn states into *their* agents. Moreover, a netwar actor may be both subnational and transnational in scope. Odd hybrids and symbioses are likely. Furthermore, some actors (e.g., violent terrorist and criminal organizations) may threaten U.S. and other nations' interests, but other netwar actors (e.g., peaceful social activists) may not. Some may aim at destruction, others at disruption. Again, many variations are possible.

The full spectrum of netwar proponents may thus seem broad and odd at first glance. But there is an underlying pattern that cuts across all variations: *the use of network forms of organization, doctrine, strategy, and technology attuned to the information age.*

## More About Organizational Design

The notion of an organizational structure qualitatively different from traditional hierarchical designs is not recent; for example, in the early 1960s Burns and Stalker referred to the *organic* form as "a network structure of control, authority, and communication," with "lateral rather than vertical direction of communication." In organic structure,

> omniscience [is] no longer imputed to the head of the concern; knowledge about the technical or commercial nature of the here and now task may be located anywhere in the network; [with] this

location becoming the ad hoc centre of control authority and communication. (Burns and Stalker, 1961, p. 121.)

In the business world, virtual or networked organizations are being
heralded as effective alternatives to bureaucracies—as in the case of
Eastman Chemical Company and the Shell-Sarnia Plant—because of
their inherent flexibility, adaptiveness, and ability to capitalize on the
talents of all members of the organization.[10]

What has long been emerging in the business world is now becoming
apparent in the organizational structures of netwar actors. In an
archetypal netwar, the protagonists are likely to amount to a set of
diverse, dispersed "nodes" who share a set of ideas and interests and
who are arrayed to act in a fully internetted "all-channel" manner.
Networks come in basically three types (or topologies) (see Figure
4.1):[11]

- The *chain* network, as in a smuggling chain where people, goods,
  or information move along a line of separated contacts, and
  where end-to-end communication must travel through the
  intermediate nodes.

- The *star*, hub, or wheel network, as in a franchise or a cartel
  structure where a set of actors is tied to a central node or actor,
  and must go through that node to communicate and coordinate.

- The *all-channel* network, as in a collaborative network of militant small groups where every group is connected to every other.

Each node in the diagrams of Figure 4.1 may be to an individual, a
group, an institution, part of a group or institution, or even a state.
The nodes may be large or small, tightly or loosely coupled, and in-
clusive or exclusive in membership. They may be segmentary or
specialized—that is, they may look alike and engage in similar activities, or they may undertake a division of labor based on specialization. The boundaries of the network may be well defined, or blurred
and porous in relation to the outside environment. All such variations are possible.

---

[10]See, for instance, Lipnack and Stamps (1994), pp. 51–78, and Heckscher (1995), p.
45.

[11]Adapted from Evan (1972).

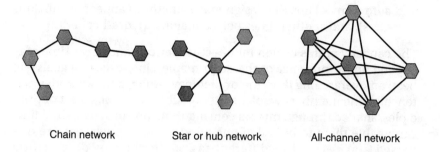

Chain network          Star or hub network          All-channel network

**Figure 4.1—Types of Networks**

Each type may be suited to different conditions and purposes, and all three may be found among netwar-related adversaries—e.g., the chain in smuggling operations, the star at the core of terrorist and criminal syndicates, and the all-channel type among militant groups that are highly internetted and decentralized.  There may also be hybrids.  For example, a netwar actor may have an all-channel council at its core, but use stars and chains for tactical operations. There may also be hybrids of network and hierarchical forms of organization, and hierarchies may exist inside particular nodes in a network.  Some actors may have a hierarchical organization overall, but use networks for tactical operations; other actors may have an all-channel network design, but use hierarchical teams for tactical operations.  Again, many configurations are possible, and it may be difficult for an analyst to discern exactly what type of networking characterizes a particular actor.

Of the three network types, the all-channel has been the most difficult to organize and sustain historically, partly because it may require dense communications.  However, it gives the network form the most potential for collaborative undertakings, and it is the type that is gaining strength from the information revolution.  Pictorially, an all-channel netwar actor resembles a geodesic "Bucky ball" (named for Buckminster Fuller); it does not resemble a pyramid.  The design is flat.  Ideally, there is no single, central leadership, command, or headquarters—no precise heart or head that can be targeted.  The network as a whole (but not necessarily each node) has little to no hierarchy, and there may be multiple leaders.  Decision-making and operations are decentralized, allowing for local initiative and autonomy.  Thus the design may sometimes appear acephalous (headless), and at other times polycephalous (Hydra-headed).[12]

The capacity of this design for effective performance over time may depend on the presence of shared principles, interests, and goals—at best, an overarching doctrine or ideology—that spans all nodes and to which the members wholeheartedly subscribe.  Such a set of principles, shaped through mutual consultation and consensus-building, can enable them to be "all of one mind," even though they are dispersed and devoted to different tasks.  It can provide a central ideational, strategic, and operational coherence that allows for tactical decentralization.  It can set boundaries and provide guidelines for decisions and actions so that the members do not have to resort to a hierarchy—"they know what they have to do."[13]

The network design may depend on having an infrastructure for the dense communication of functional information.  All nodes are not necessarily in constant communication, which may not make sense for a secretive, conspiratorial actor.  But when communication is needed, the network's members must be able to disseminate information promptly and as broadly as desired within the network and to outside audiences.

In many respects, then, the archetypal netwar design corresponds to what earlier analysts called a "segmented, polycentric, ideologically integrated network" (SPIN)[14]:

---

[12]The structure may also be cellular, although the presence of cells does not necessarily mean a network exists.  A hierarchy can also be cellular, as is the case with some subversive organizations.  A key difference between cells and nodes is that the former are designed to minimize information flows for security reasons (usually only the head of the cell reports to the leadership), while nodes in principle can easily establish connections with other parts of the network (so that communications and coordination can occur horizontally).

[13]The quotation is from a doctrinal statement by Louis Beam about "leaderless resistance," which has strongly influenced right-wing white-power groups in the United States. (See Beam, 1992.)

[14]See Gerlach (1987), p. 115, based on Gerlach and Hine (1970). This SPIN concept, a precursor of the netwar concept, was proposed by Luther Gerlach and Virginia Hine in the 1960s to depict U.S. social movements.  It anticipates many points about network forms of organization that are now coming into focus in the analysis of not only social movements but also some terrorist, criminal, ethno-nationalist, and fundamentalist organizations.

By segmentary I mean that it is cellular, composed of many different groups.... By polycentric I mean that it has many different leaders or centers of direction.... By networked I mean that the segments and the leaders are integrated into reticulated systems or networks through various structural, personal, and ideological ties. Networks are usually unbounded and expanding.... This acronym [SPIN] helps us picture this organization as a fluid, dynamic, expanding one, spinning out into mainstream society.

## Caveats About the Role of Technology

To realize its potential, a fully interconnected network requires a capacity for constant, dense information and communications flows, more so than do other forms of organization (e.g., hierarchies). This capacity is afforded by the latest information and communications technologies—cellular telephones, fax machines, electronic mail (e-mail), World Wide Web (WWW) sites, and computer conferencing. Moreover, netwar agents are poised to benefit from future increases in the speed of communication, dramatic reductions in the costs of communication, increases in bandwidth, vastly expanded connectivity, and integration of communication with computing technologies. (See Heydenbrand, 1989.) Such technologies are highly advantageous for a netwar actor whose constituents are geographically dispersed.

However, caveats are in order. First, the new technologies, however enabling for organizational networking, may not be the only crucial technologies for a netwar actor. Old means of communications such as human couriers, and mixes of old and new systems, may suffice. Second, netwar is not simply a function of the Internet; it does not take place only in cyberspace or the infosphere. Some key *battles* may occur there, but a *war's* overall conduct and outcome will normally depend mostly on what happens in the real world. Even in information-age conflicts, what happens in the real world is generally more important than what happens in the virtual worlds of cyberspace or the infosphere. (See Kneisel, 1996.[15]) Netwar is not Internet war.

---

[15]Kneisel analyzes the largest vote ever taken about the creation of a new Usenet newsgroup—a vote to prevent the creation of a group that was ostensibly about white-

## Swarming, and the Blurring of Offense and Defense

This distinctive, often ad-hoc design has unusual strengths, for both offense and defense. On the offense, networks are known for being adaptable, flexible, and versatile vis-à-vis opportunities and challenges. This may be particularly the case where a set of actors can engage in *swarming*. Little analytic attention has been given to swarming, yet it may be a key mode of conflict in the information age. The cutting edge for this possibility is found among netwar protagonists.[16]

Swarming occurs when the dispersed nodes of a network of small (and perhaps some large) forces converge on a target from multiple directions. The overall aim is the *sustainable pulsing* of force or fire. Once in motion, swarm networks must be able to coalesce rapidly and stealthily on a target, then dissever and redisperse, immediately ready to recombine for a new pulse. In other words, information-age attacks may come in "swarms" rather than the more traditional "waves."

In terms of defensive potential, well-constructed networks tend to be redundant and diverse, making them robust and resilient in the face of adversity. Where they have a capacity for interoperability and shun centralized command and control, network designs can be difficult to crack and defeat as a whole. In particular, they may defy counterleadership targeting—attackers can find and confront only portions of the network. Moreover, the deniability built into a network may allow it to simply absorb a number of attacks on distributed nodes, leading the attacker to believe the network has been harmed when, in fact, it remains viable, and is seeking new opportunities for tactical surprise.

The difficulties of dealing with netwar actors deepen when the lines between offense and defense are blurred, or blended. When *blurring* is the case, it may be difficult to distinguish between attacking and defending actions, particularly when an actor goes on the offense in the name of self-defense. The *blending* of offense and defense will

---

power music. He concludes that "The *war* against contemporary fascism will be won in the 'real world' off the net; but *battles* against fascist netwar are fought and won on the Internet." His title is testimony to the spreading usage of the term *netwar*.

[16]Swarm networks are discussed in Kelly (1994). Also see Arquilla and Ronfeldt (1997).

often mix the strategic and tactical levels of operations. For example, guerrillas on the defensive strategically may go on the offense tactically; the war of the *mujahideen* in Afghanistan provides a modern example.

The blurring of offense and defense reflects another feature of netwar: It tends to defy and cut across standard boundaries, jurisdictions, and distinctions between state and society, public and private, war and peace, war and crime, civilian and military, police and military, and legal and illegal. A government has difficulty assigning responsibility to a single agency—military, police, or intelligence—to respond.

Thus, the spread of netwar adds to the challenges facing the nation-state in the information age. Nation-state ideals of sovereignty and authority are traditionally linked to a bureaucratic rationality in which issues and problems can be neatly divided, and specific offices can be charged with taking care of specific problems. In netwar, things are rarely so clear. A protagonist is likely to operate in the cracks and gray areas of society, striking where lines of authority crisscross and the operational paradigms of politicians, officials, soldiers, police officers, and related actors get fuzzy and clash.

## Networks Versus Hierarchies:  Challenges for Counternetwar

Against this background, we are led to a set of three policy-oriented propositions about the information revolution and its implications for netwar and *counternetwar*.[17]

*Hierarchies have a difficult time fighting networks.* There are examples across the conflict spectrum. Some of the best are found in the failings of governments to defeat transnational criminal cartels engaged in drug smuggling, as in Colombia. The persistence of religious revivalist movements, as in Algeria, in the face of unremitting state opposition, shows the robustness of the network form. The Zapatista movement in Mexico, with its legions of supporters and sympathizers among local and transnational nongovernmental organizations, shows that social netwar can put a democratizing

---

[17]Also see Berger (1998) for additional thinking and analysis about such propositions.

autocracy on the defensive and pressure it to continue adopting reforms.

*It takes networks to fight networks.* Governments that would defend against netwar may have to adopt organizational designs and strategies like those of their adversaries. This does not mean mirroring the adversary, but rather learning to draw on the same design principles of network forms in the information age. These principles depend to some extent upon technological innovation, but mainly on a willingness to innovate organizationally and doctrinally, and by building new mechanisms for interagency and multijurisdictional cooperation.

*Whoever masters the network form first and best will gain major advantages.* In these early decades of the information age, adversaries who have adopted networking (be they criminals, terrorists, or peaceful social activists) are enjoying an increase in their power relative to state agencies.

Counternetwar may thus require effective interagency approaches, which by their nature involve networked structures. The challenge will be to blend hierarchies and networks skillfully, while retaining enough core authority to encourage and enforce adherence to networked processes. By creating effective hybrids, governments may better confront the new threats and challenges emerging in the information age, whether generated by terrorists, militias, criminals, or other actors.[18] The U.S. Counterterrorist Center, based at the Central Intelligence Agency (CIA), is a good example of a promising effort to establish a functional interagency network, although its success may depend increasingly on the strength of links with the military services and other institutions that fall outside the realm of the intelligence community. (Loeb, 1998.[19])

## MIDDLE EASTERN TERRORISM AND NETWAR

Terrorism seems to be evolving in the direction of violent netwar. Islamic fundamentalist organizations like Hamas and the bin Laden network consist of groups organized in loosely interconnected, semi-

---

[18]For elaboration, see Arquilla and Ronfeldt (1997), Chapter Nineteen.

[19]For a broader discussion of interagency cooperation in countering terrorism, see Carter, Deutch, and Zelikow (1998).

independent cells that have no single commanding hierarchy.[20] Hamas exemplifies the shift away from a hierarchically oriented movement based on a "great leader" (like the PLO and Yasser Arafat).[21]

The netwar concept is consistent with patterns and trends in the Middle East, where the newer and more active terrorist groups appear to be adopting decentralized, flexible network structures. The rise of networked arrangements in terrorist organizations is part of a wider move away from formally organized, state-sponsored groups to privately financed, loose networks of individuals and sub-groups that may have strategic guidance but enjoy tactical independence. Related to these shifts is the fact that terrorist groups are taking advantage of information technology to coordinate the activities of dispersed members. Such technology may be employed by terrorists not only to wage information warfare, but also to support their own networked organizations.[22]

While a comprehensive empirical analysis of the relationship between (a) the structure of terrorist organizations and (b) group activity or strength is beyond the scope of this chapter,[23] a cursory examination of such a relationship among Middle Eastern groups offers some evidence to support the claim that terrorists are prepar-

---

[20]Analogously, right-wing militias and extremist groups in the United States also rely on a doctrine of "leaderless resistance" propounded by Aryan nationalist Louis Beam. (See Beam, 1992, and Stern, 1996.) Meanwhile, as part of a broader trend toward netwar, transnational criminal organizations have been shifting away from centralized "Dons" to more networked structures. (See Williams, 1994, and Williams, 1998.) As noted earlier, social activist movements long ago began to evolve "segmented, polycephalous, integrated networks." For a discussion of a social netwar in which human-rights and other peaceful activist groups supported an insurgent group in Mexico, see Ronfeldt and Martinez (1997).

[21]It is important to differentiate our notions of information-age networking from earlier ideas about terror as consisting of a network in which all nodes revolved around a Soviet core (Sterling, 1981). This view has generally been regarded as unsupported by available evidence (see Combs, 1997, pp. 99–119). However, there were a few early studies that did give credit to the possibility of the rise of terror networks that were bound more by loose ties to general strategic goals than by Soviet control (see especially Friedman, 1985).

[22]For good general background, see Whine (1998).

[23]We assume that group activity is a proxy for group strength. Group activity can be measured more easily than group strength, and is expected to be significantly correlated with strength. The relationship may not be perfect, but it is deemed to be sufficiently strong for our purposes.

ing to wage netwar. The Middle East was selected for analysis mainly because terrorist groups based in this region have been active in targeting U.S. government facilities and interests, as in the bombings of the Khobar Towers and, most recently, the American embassies in Kenya and Tanzania.

## Middle Eastern Terrorist Groups: Structure and Actions

Terrorist groups in the Middle East have diverse origins, ideologies, and organizational structures, but can be roughly categorized into traditional and new-generation groups. Traditional groups date back to the late 1960s and early 1970s, and the majority of these were (and some still are) formally or informally linked to the PLO. Typically, they are also relatively bureaucratic and maintain a nationalist or Marxist agenda. In contrast, most new-generation groups arose in the 1980s and 1990s, have more fluid organizational forms, and rely on Islam as a basis for their radical ideology.

The traditional, more-bureaucratic groups have survived to this day partly through support from states such as Syria, Libya, and Iran. The groups retain an ability to train and prepare for terrorist missions; however, their involvement in actual operations has been limited in recent years, partly because of successful counterterrorism campaigns by Israeli and Western agencies. In contrast, the newer and less hierarchical groups, such as Hamas, the Palestinian Islamic Jihad (PIJ), Hizbullah, Algeria's Armed Islamic Group (GIA), the Egyptian Islamic Group (IG), and Osama bin Laden's Arab Afghans, have become the most active organizations in and around the Middle East.

*The traditional groups.* Traditional terrorist groups in the Middle East include the Abu Nidal Organization, the Popular Front for the Liberation of Palestine (PFLP), and three PFLP-related splinters—the PFLP-General Command, the Palestine Liberation Front (PLF), and the Democratic Front for the Liberation of Palestine (DFLP).

Abu Nidal was an integral part of the PLO until it became independent in 1974. It has a bureaucratic structure composed of various functional committees. (U.S. Department of State [DoS], for 1996.) The activism it displayed in the 1970s and 1980s has lessened considerably, owing to a lessening of support from state sponsors and to effective counterterrorist campaigns by Israeli and Western intelligence services. (Loeb, 1998; and Murray and Ward, 1996.) The very existence of the organization has recently been put into question, given uncertainty as to the whereabouts and fate of Abu Nidal, the leader of the group. (Ibrahim, 1998.)

The PFLP was founded in 1967 by George Habash as a PLO-affiliated organization. It has traditionally embraced a Marxist ideology, and remains an important PLO faction. However, in recent years it has suffered considerable losses from Israeli counterterrorist strikes. (Murray and Ward, 1996.) The PFLP-General Command split from the PFLP in 1968, and in turn experienced a schism in the mid-1970s. This splinter group, which called itself the PLF, is composed of three subgroups, and has not been involved in high-profile acts since the 1985 hijacking of the Italian cruise ship *Achille Lauro*. (DoS, for 1996, and Murray and Ward, 1996.) The PFLP was subjected to another split in 1969, which resulted in the Democratic Front for the Libera- tion of Palestine. The DFLP resembles a small army more than a ter- rorist group—its operatives are organized in battalions, backed by intelligence and special forces. (Murray and Ward, 1996.) DFLP strikes have become less frequent since the 1970s, and since the late 1980s it has limited its attacks to Israeli targets near borders. (DoS, for 1995, 1996, 1997.)

What seems evident here is that this old generation of traditional, hierarchical, bureaucratic groups is on the wane. The reasons are varied, but the point remains—their way of waging terrorism is not likely to make a comeback, and is being superseded by a new way that is more attuned to the organizational, doctrinal, and technologi- cal imperatives of the information age.

*The most active groups and their organization.* The new generation of Middle Eastern groups has been active both in and outside the region in recent years. In Israel and the occupied territories, Hamas, and to a lesser extent the Palestinian Islamic Jihad, have shown their strength over the last four years with a series of suicide bombings that have killed more than 100 people and injured several more.[24]

---

[24]For instance, in 1997 Hamas operatives set off three suicide bombs in crowded public places in Tel Aviv and Jerusalem. On March 21, a Hamas satchel bomb exploded at a Tel Aviv cafe, killing three persons and injuring 48; on July 30, two Hamas suicide bombers blew themselves up in a Jerusalem market, killing 16 persons and wounding 178; on September 4, three suicide bombers attacked a Jerusalem

Exploiting a strong presence in Lebanon, the Shi'ite Hizbullah organization has also staged a number of attacks against Israeli Defense Forces troops and Israeli cities in Galilee. (See Israeli Foreign Ministry, 1996.)

The al-Gama'a al-Islamiya, or IG, is the most active Islamic extremist group in Egypt. In November 1997 IG carried out an attack on Hatshepsut's Temple in Luxor, killing 58 tourists and 4 Egyptians. The group has also claimed responsibility for the bombing of the Egyptian embassy in Islamabad, Pakistan, which left 16 dead and 60 injured. (See DoS, for 1995, 1996, 1997.) In Algeria, the GIA has been behind the most violent, lethal attacks in Algeria's protracted civil war. Approximately 70,000 Algerians have lost their lives since the domestic terrorist campaign began in 1992. (DoS, for 1997.)

Recently, the loosely organized group of Arab Afghans—radical Islamic fighters from several North African and Middle Eastern countries who forged ties while resisting the Soviet occupation of Afghanistan[25]—has come to the fore as an active terrorist outfit. One of the leaders and founders of the Arab Afghan movement, Osama bin Laden, a Saudi entrepreneur who bases his activities in Afghanistan (Gertz, 1996), is suspected of sending operatives to Yemen to bomb a hotel used by U.S. soldiers on their way to Somalia in 1992, plotting to assassinate President Clinton in the Philippines in 1994 and Egyptian President Hosni Mubarak in 1995, and of having a role in the Riyadh and Khobar blasts in Saudi Arabia that resulted in the deaths of 24 Americans in 1995 and 1996. (Weiner, 1998, and Zuckerman, 1998.) U.S. officials have pointed to bin Laden as the mastermind behind the U.S. embassy bombings in Kenya and Tanzania, which claimed the lives of more than 260 people, including 12 Americans. (Constable, 1998.)

To varying degrees, these groups share the principles of the networked organization—relatively flat hierarchies, decentralization and delegation of decisionmaking authority, and loose lateral ties

---

pedestrian mall, killing at least five persons (in addition to the suicide bombers), and injuring at least 181. The Palestinian Islamic Jihad has claimed responsibility (along with Hamas) for a bomb that killed 20 and injured 75 others in March 1996, and in 1995 it carried out five bombings that killed 29 persons and wounded 107. (See DoS, for 1995, 1996, 1997.)

[25]"Arab Afghans Said to Launch Worldwide Terrorist War" (1995).

among dispersed groups and individuals.[26] For instance, Hamas is loosely structured, with some elements working openly through mosques and social service institutions to recruit members, raise funds, organize activities, and distribute propaganda. Palestinian security sources indicate that there are ten or more Hamas splinter groups and factions with no centralized operational leadership.[27] The Palestine Islamic Jihad is a series of loosely affiliated factions, rather than a cohesive group.[28] The pro-Iranian Hizbullah acts as an umbrella organization of radical Shi'ite groups, and in many respects is a hybrid of hierarchical and network arrangements; Although the formal structure is highly bureaucratic, interactions among members are volatile and do not follow rigid lines of control. (Ranstorp, 1994) According to the U.S. Department of State, Egypt's Islamic Group is a decentralized organization that operates without a single operational leader (DoS, for 1996), while the GIA is notorious for the lack of centralized authority.[29]

Unlike traditional terrorist organizations, Arab Afghans are part of a complex network of relatively autonomous groups that are financed from private sources forming "a kind of international terrorists' Internet." (Ottaway, 1996.) The most notorious element of the network is Osama bin Laden, who uses his wealth and organizational skills to support and direct a multinational alliance of Islamic extremists. At the heart of this alliance is his own inner core group, known as Al-Qaeda ("The Base"), which sometimes conducts mis-

---

[26]We distinguish between deliberate and factional decentralization. Factional decentralization—prevalent in older groups—occurs when subgroups separate themselves from the central leadership because of differences in tactics or approach. Deliberate or operational decentralization is what distinguishes netwar agents from others, since delegation of authority in this case occurs because of the distinct advantages this organizational arrangement brings, and not because of lack of consensus. We expect both influences on decentralization to continue, but newer groups will tend to decentralize authority even in the absence of political disagreements.

[27]"Gaza Strip, West Bank: Dahlan on Relations with Israel, Terrorism" (1997).

[28]The leader of the PIJ's most powerful faction, Fathi Shaqaqi, was assassinated in October 1995 in Malta, allegedly by the Israeli Mossad. Shaqaqi's killing followed the assassination of Hani Abed, another PIJ leader killed in 1994 in Gaza. Reports that the group has been considerably weakened as a result of Israeli counterleadership operations are balanced by the strength demonstrated by the PIJ in its recent terrorist activity. See "Islamic Group Vows Revenge for Slaying of Its Leader" (1995).

[29]"Algeria: Infighting Among Proliferating 'Wings' of Armed Groups" (1997).

sions on its own, but more often in conjunction with other groups or elements in the alliance. The goal of the alliance is opposition on a global scale to perceived threats to Islam, as indicated by bin Laden's 1996 declaration of a holy war against the United States and the West. In the document, bin Laden specifies that such a holy war will be fought by irregular, light, highly mobile forces using guerrilla tactics.[30]

Even though bin Laden finances Arab Afghan activities and directs some operations, he apparently does not play a direct command and control role over all operatives. Rather, he is a key figure in the coordination and support of several dispersed activities.[31] For instance, bin Laden founded the "World Islamic Front for Jihad Against Jews and Crusaders."[32] And yet most of the groups that participate in this front (including Egypt's Islamic Group) remain independent, although the organizational barriers between them are fluid.[33]

From a netwar perspective, an interesting feature of bin Laden's Arab Afghan movement is its ability to relocate operations swiftly from one geographic area to another in response to changing circumstances and needs. Arab Afghans have participated in operations conducted by Algeria's GIA and Egypt's IG. Reports in 1997 also indicated that Arab Afghans transferred training operations to Somalia, where they joined the Islamic Liberation Party.[34] The same reports suggest that the Arab Afghan movement has considered sending fighters to Sinkiang Uighur province in western China, to

---

[30]"Saudi Arabia: Bin-Laden Calls for 'Guerrilla Warfare' Against US Forces" (1996).

[31]It is important to avoid equating the bin Laden network solely with bin Laden. He represents a key node in the Arab Afghan terror network, but there should be no illusions about the likely effect on the network of actions taken to neutralize him. The network conducts many operations without his involvement, leadership, or financing—and will continue to be able to do so should he be killed or captured.

[32]"Militants Say There Will Be More Attacks Against U.S." (1998).

[33]For instance, there have been reports of a recent inflow of Arab Afghans into Egypt's IG to reinforce the latter's operations. See Murray and Ward (1996) and "The CIA on Bin Laden" (1998).

[34]This move was also influenced by the Taliban's decision to curb Arab Afghan activities in the territory under its control as a result of U.S. pressure. See "Arab Afghans Reportedly Transfer Operations to Somalia" (1997)

wage a holy war against the Chinese regime.[35] This group's ability to move and act quickly (and, to some extent, to swarm) once opportunities emerge hampers counterterrorist efforts to predict its actions and monitor its activities. The fact that Arab Afghan operatives were able to strike the U.S. embassies in Kenya and Tanzania substantiates the claim that members of this network have the mobility and speed to operate over considerable distances.

Although the organizational arrangements in these groups do not match all the basic features of the network ideal,[36] they stand in contrast to more traditional groups. Another feature that distinguishes the newer generation of terrorist groups is their adoption of information technology.

## Middle Eastern Terrorist Groups and the Use of Information Technology

Information technology is an enabling factor for networked groups; terrorists aiming to wage netwar may adopt it not only as a weapon, but also to help coordinate and support their activities. Before exploring how Middle Eastern terrorist groups have embraced the new technology, we posit three hypotheses that relate the rise of information technology to organization for netwar:

- The greater the degree of organizational networking in a terrorist group, the higher the likelihood that information technology is used to support the network's decisionmaking.

- Recent advances in information technology facilitate networked terrorist organizations because information flows are becoming quicker, cheaper, more secure, and more versatile.

- As terrorist groups learn to use information technology for decisionmaking and other organizational purposes, they will be likely

---

[35]"Afghanistan, China: Report on Bin-Laden Possibly Moving to China" (1997).

[36]While it is possible to discern a general trend toward an organizational structure that displays several features of a network, we expect to observe substantial differences (and many hierarchy/network hybrids) in how organizations make their specific design choices. Different network designs depend on contingent factors, such as personalities, organizational history, operational requirements, and other influences such as state sponsorship and ideology.

to use the same technology as an offensive weapon to destroy or disrupt.

Middle Eastern terrorist groups provide examples of information technology being used for a wide variety of purposes. As discussed below, there is some evidence to support the claim that the most active groups—and therefore the most decentralized groups—have embraced information technology to coordinate activities and disseminate propaganda and ideology.[37] At the same time, the technical assets and know-how gained by terrorist groups as they seek to form into multi-organizational networks can be used for offensive purposes—an Internet connection can be used for both coordination and disruption. The anecdotes provided here are consistent with the rise in the Middle East of what has been termed *techno-terrorism*, or the use by terrorists of satellite communications, e-mail, and the WWW.[38]

Arab Afghans appear to have widely adopted information technology. According to reporters who visited bin Laden's headquarters in a remote mountainous area of Afghanistan, the terrorist financier has computers, communications equipment, and a large number of disks for data storage.[39] Egyptian "Afghan" computer experts are said to have helped devise a communication network that relies on the WWW, e-mail, and electronic bulletin boards so that the extremists can exchange information without running a major risk of being intercepted by counterterrorism officials.[40]

Hamas is another major group that uses the Internet to share operational information. Hamas activists in the United States use chat

---

[37]Assessing the strength of the relationship between organizational structure and use of information technology is difficult to establish. Alternative explanations may exist as to why newer groups would embrace information technology, such as age of the group (one could speculate that newer terrorist groups have on average younger members, who are more familiar with computers) or the amount of funding (a richer group could afford more electronic gadgetry). While it is empirically impossible to refute these points, much in organization theory supports our hypothesis that there is a direct relationship between a higher need for information technology and the use of network structures.

[38]"Saudi Arabia: French Analysis of Islamic Threat" (1997).

[39]"Afghanistan, Saudi Arabia: Editor's Journey to Meet Bin-Laden Described" (1996).

[40]"Arab Afghans Said to Launch Worldwide Terrorist War" (1995).

rooms to plan operations and activities.[41]  Operatives use e-mail to coordinate activities across Gaza, the West Bank, and Lebanon. Hamas has realized that information can be passed securely over the Internet because it is next to impossible for counterterrorism intelligence to monitor accurately the flow and content of Internet traffic. Israeli security officials have difficulty in tracing Hamas messages and decoding their content.[42]

A recent counterterrorist operation uncovered several GIA bases in Italy; each was found to include computers and diskettes with instructions for the construction of bombs.[43]  It has been reported that the GIA uses floppy disks and computers to store and process instructions and other information for its members, who are dispersed in Algeria and Europe.[44]  Furthermore, the Internet is used as a propaganda tool by Hizbullah, which manages three Web sites— one for the central press office (at www.hizbollah.org), another to describe its attacks on Israeli targets (at www.moqawama.org), and the last for news and information (at www.almanar.com.lb).[45]

The presence of Middle Eastern terrorist organizations on the Internet is suspected in the case of the Islamic Gateway, a WWW site that contains information on a number of Islamic activist organizations based in the United Kingdom.  British Islamic activists use the WWW to broadcast their news and attract funding; they are also turning to the Internet as an organizational and communication tool.[46]  While the vast majority of Islamic activist groups represented in the Islamic Gateway are legitimate, one group—the Global Jihad Fund—makes no secret of its militant goals.[47]  The appeal of the Islamic Gateway for militant groups may be enhanced by a representative's claim, in an Internet Newsnet article in August 1996, that the Gateway's Inter-

---

[41]"Israel: U.S. Hamas Activists Use Internet to Send Attack Threats" (1996).

[42]"Israel: Hamas Using Internet to Relay Operational Messages" (1998).

[43]"Italy: Security Alters Following Algerian Extremists' Arrests" (1996).

[44]"Italy, Vatican City: Daily Claims GIA 'Strategist' Based in Milan" (1996).

[45]"Hizbullah TV Summary 18 February 1998" (1998). Also see "Developments in Mideast Media: January–May 1998" (1998).

[46]"Islamists on Internet" (1996).

[47]"Islamic Activism Online" (1997).

net Service Provider (ISP) can give "CIA-proof" protection against electronic surveillance.[48]

## Summary Comment

This review of patterns and trends in the Middle East substantiates our speculations that the new terrorism is evolving in the direction of netwar, along the following lines[49] :

- An increasing number of terrorist groups are adopting networked forms of organization and relying on information technology to support such structures.

- Newer groups (those established in the 1980s and 1990s) are more networked than traditional groups.

- A positive correlation is emerging between the degree of activity of a group and the degree to which it adopts a networked structure.[50]

- Information technology is as likely to be used for organizational support as for offensive warfare.

- The likelihood that young recruits will be familiar with information technology implies that terrorist groups will be increasingly

---

[48]The Muslim Parliament has recently added an Internet Relay Chat (IRC) link and a "Muslims only" List-Serve (automatic e-mail delivery service). See "Islamic Activism Online" (1997).

[49]Similar propositions may apply to varieties of netwar other than the new terrorism.

[50]We make a qualification here. There appears to be a significant positive association between the degree to which a group is active and the degree to which a group is decentralized and networked. But we cannot be confident about the causality of this relationship or its direction (i.e., whether activity and strength affect networking, or vice-versa). A host of confounding factors may affect both the way groups decide to organize and their relative success at operations. For instance, the age of a group may be an important predictor of a group's success—newer groups are likely to be more popular; popular groups are more likely to enlist new operatives; and groups that have a large number of operatives are likely to be more active, regardless of organizational structure. Another important caveat is related to the fact that it is difficult to rank groups precisely in terms of the degree to which they are networked, because no terrorist organization is thought to represent either a hierarchical or network ideal-type. While the conceptual division between newer-generation and traditional groups is appropriate for our scope here, an analytical "degree of networking" scale would have to be devised for more empirical research.

networked and more computer-friendly in the future than they are today.

## TERRORIST DOCTRINES—THE RISE OF A "WAR PARADIGM"

The evolution of terrorism in the direction of netwar will create new difficulties for counterterrorism.  The types of challenges, and their severity, will depend on the kinds of doctrines that terrorists develop and employ.  Some doctrinal effects will occur at the operational level, as in the relative emphasis placed on disruptive information operations as distinct from destructive combat operations.  However, at a deeper level, the direction in which terrorist netwar evolves will depend upon the choices terrorists make as to the overall doctrinal paradigms that shape their goals and strategies.

At least three terrorist paradigms are worth considering:  terror as coercive diplomacy, terror as war, and terror as the harbinger of a "new world."  These three engage, in varying ways, distinct rationales for terrorism—as a weapon of the weak, as a way to assert identity, and as a way to break through to a new world—discussed earlier in this chapter.  While there has been much debate about the overall success or failure of terrorism,[51] the paradigm under which a terrorist operates may have a great deal to do with the likelihood of success.  Coercion, for example, implies distinctive threats or uses of force, whereas norms of "war" often imply maximizing destruction.

### The Coercive-Diplomacy Paradigm

The first paradigm is that of coercive diplomacy.  From its earliest days, terrorism has often sought to persuade others, by means of symbolic violence, either to do something, stop doing something, or undo what has been done.  These are the basic forms of coercive diplomacy (see George and Simons, 1994), and they appear in terrorism as far back as the Jewish Sicarii Zealots who sought independence from Rome in the first century CE, up through the

---

[51]See, for instance, Gutteridge (1986), Hoffman and Carr (1997), and Combs (1997).

Palestinians' often violent acts in pursuit of their independence today.

The fact that terrorist coercion includes violent acts does not make it a form of war—the violence is exemplary, designed to encourage what Alexander George calls "forceful persuasion," or "coercive diplomacy as an alternative to war." (George, 1991.) In this light, terrorism may be viewed as designed to achieve specific goals, and the level of violence is limited, or proportional, to the ends being pursued. Under this paradigm, terrorism was once thought to lack a "demand" for WMD, as such tools would provide means vastly disproportionate to the ends of terror. This view was first elucidated over 20 years ago by Brian Jenkins—though there was some dissent expressed by scholars such as Thomas Schelling—and continued to hold sway until a few years ago. (Jenkins, 1977; Schelling, 1982; and Garrity and Maaranen, 1992.)

## The War Paradigm

Caleb Carr, surveying the history of the failures of coercive terrorism and the recent trends toward increasing destructiveness and deniability, has elucidated what we call a "war paradigm." (Carr, 1996.) This paradigm, which builds on ideas first considered by Jenkins (1974), holds that terrorist acts arise when weaker parties cannot challenge an adversary directly and thus turn to asymmetric methods. A war paradigm implies taking a strategic, campaign-oriented view of violence that makes no specific call for concessions from, or other demands upon, the opponent. Instead, the strategic aim is to inflict damage, in the context of what the terrorists view as an ongoing war. In theory, this paradigm, unlike the coercive diplomacy one, does not seek a proportional relationship between the level of force employed and the aims sought. When the goal is to inflict damage generally, and the terrorist group has no desire or need to claim credit, there is an attenuation of the need for proportionality—the worse the damage, the better. Thus, the use of WMD can be far more easily contemplated than in a frame of reference governed by notions of coercive diplomacy.

A terrorist war paradigm may be undertaken by terrorists acting on their own behalf or in service to a nation-state. In the future, as the information age brings the further empowerment of nonstate and transnational actors, "stateless" versions of the terrorist war paradigm may spread. At the same time, however, states will remain important players in the war paradigm; they may cultivate their own terrorist-style commandos, or seek cut-outs and proxies from among nonstate terrorist groups.

Ambiguity regarding a sponsor's identity may prove a key element of the war paradigm. While the use of proxies provides an insulating layer between a state sponsor and its target, these proxies, if captured, may prove more susceptible to interrogation and investigative techniques designed to winkle out the identity of the sponsor. On the other hand, while home-grown commando-style terrorists may be less forthcoming with information if caught, their own identities, which may be hard to conceal, may provide undeniable evidence of state sponsorship. These risks for states who think about engaging in or supporting terrorism may provide yet more reason for the war paradigm to increasingly become the province of nonstate terrorists—or those with only the most tenuous linkages to particular states.

Exemplars of the war paradigm today are the wealthy Saudi jihadist, Osama bin Laden, and the Arab Afghans that he associates with. As previously mentioned, bin Laden has explicitly called for war-like terrorism against the United States, and especially against U.S. military forces stationed in Saudi Arabia. President Clinton's statement that American retaliation for the U.S. embassy bombings in East Africa represented the first shots in a protracted war on terrorism suggests that the notion of adopting a war paradigm to counter terror has gained currency.

## The New World Paradigm

A third terrorist paradigm aims at achieving the birth of what might be called a "new world." It may be driven by religious mania, a desire for totalitarian control, or an impulse toward ultimate chaos.[52] Aum Shinrikyo would be a recent example. The paradigm harks back to the dynamics of millennialist movements that arose in past epochs of

---

[52]For a discussion of these motives, see Laqueur (1996), Iklé (1997), and Hoffman (1998), respectively.

social upheaval, when *prophetae* attracted adherents from the margins of other social movements and led small groups to pursue salvation by seeking a final, violent cataclysm.[53]

This paradigm is likely to seek the vast disruption of political, social, and economic order. Accomplishing this goal may involve lethal destruction, even a heightened willingness to use WMD. Religious terrorists may desire destruction for its own sake, or for some form of "cleansing." But the ultimate aim is not so much the destruction of society as a rebirth after a period of chaotic disruption.

## The Paradigms and Netwar

All three paradigms offer room for netwar. Moreover, all three paradigms allow the rise of "cybotage"—acts of disruption and destruction against information infrastructures by terrorists who learn the skills of cyberterror, as well as by disaffected individuals with technical skills who are drawn into the terrorist milieu. However, we note that terrorist netwar may also be a battle of ideas—and to wage this form of conflict some terrorists may want the Net *up*, not down.

Many experts argue that terrorism is moving toward ever more-lethal, destructive acts. Our netwar perspective accepts this, but also holds that some terrorist netwars will stress disruption over destruction. Networked terrorists will no doubt continue to destroy things and kill people, but their principal strategy may move toward the nonlethal end of the spectrum, where command and control nodes and vulnerable information infrastructures provide rich sets of targets.

Indeed, terrorism has long been about "information"—from the fact that trainees for suicide bombings are kept from listening to international media, through the ways that terrorists seek to create disasters that will consume the front pages, to the related debates about countermeasures that would limit freedom of the press, increase public surveillance and intelligence gathering, and heighten security over information and communications systems. Terrorist tactics focus attention on the importance of information and communications for

---

[53]See, for instance, Barkun (1974) and Cohn (1961).

the functioning of democratic institutions; debates about how terror-ist threats undermine democratic practices may revolve around free-dom of information issues.

While netwar may be waged by terrorist groups operating with any of the three paradigms, the rise of networked groups whose objective is to wage war may be the one most relevant to and dangerous from the standpoint of the military. Indeed, if terrorists perceive themselves as warriors, they may be inclined to target enemy military assets or interests.

## REFERENCES

"Afghanistan, China: Report on Bin-Laden Possibly Moving to China," *Paris al-Watan al-'Arabi*, Foreign Broadcast Information Service, NES-97-102, May 23, 1997, pp. 19–20.

"Afghanistan, Saudi Arabia: Editor's Journey to Meet Bin-Laden Described," *London al-Quds al-'Arabi*, Foreign Broadcast Infor-mation Service, TOT-97-003-L, November 27, 1996, p. 4.

"Algeria: Infighting Among Proliferating 'Wings' of Armed Groups," *London al-Sharq al-Aswat*, Foreign Broadcast Information Service, TOT-97-021-L, February 24, 1997, p. 4.

"Arab Afghans Reportedly Transfer Operations to Somalia," *Cairo al-Arabi*, Foreign Broadcast Information Service, TOT-97-073, March 10, 1997, p. 1.

"Arab Afghans Said to Launch Worldwide Terrorist War," *Paris al-Watan al-'Arabi*, Foreign Broadcast Information Service, TOT-96-010-L, December 1, 1995, pp. 22–24.

Arquilla, John, and David Ronfeldt, "Cyberwar is Coming!" *Compar-ative Strategy*, Vol. 12, No. 2, Summer 1993, pp. 141–165.

_____, *The Advent of Netwar*, Santa Monica, Calif.: RAND, MR-678-OSD, 1996.

_____, eds., *In Athena's Camp: Preparing for Conflict in the Informa-tion Age*, Santa Monica, Calif.: RAND, MR-880-OSD/RC, 1997.

Barkun, Michael, *Disaster and the Millennium*, New Haven: Yale University Press, 1974.

Beam, Louis, *The Seditionist*, Issue 12, February 1992.

Berger, Alexander, "Organizational Innovation and Redesign in the Information Age: The Drug War, Netwar, and Other Low-End Conflict," Master's Thesis, Monterey, Calif.: Naval Postgraduate School, 1998.

Burns, T., and G. M. Stalker, *The Management of Innovation*, London: Tavistock, 1961.

Campbell, J. Kenneth, "Weapon of Mass Destruction Terrorism," Master's thesis, Monterey, Calif.: Naval Postgraduate School, 1996.

Carr, Caleb, "Terrorism as Warfare," *World Policy Journal*, Vol. 13, No. 4, Winter 1996–1997, pp. 1–12.

Carter, Ashton, John Deutch, and Philip Zelikow, "Catastrophic Terrorism," *Foreign Affairs*, Vol. 77, No. 6, November/December 1998, pp. 80–94.

"The CIA on Bin Laden," *Foreign Report*, No. 2510, August 27, 1998, pp. 2–3.

Cohn, Norman, *The Pursuit of the Millennium: Revolutionary Messianism in Medieval and Reformation Europe and Its Bearing on Modern Totalitarian Movements*, New York: Harper Torch Books, 1961.

Combs, Cindy C., *Terrorism in the Twenty-First Century*, New York: Prentice-Hall, 1997.

Constable, Pamela, "bin Laden 'Is Our Guest, So We Must Protect Him'," *Washington Post*, August 21, 1998.

"Developments in Mideast Media: January–May 1998," Foreign Broadcast Information Service, May 11, 1998.

DoS—*see* U.S. Department of State.

Evan, William M., "An Organization-Set Model of Interorganizational Relations," in Matthew Tuite, Roger Chisholm, and Michael Radnor, eds., *Interorganizational Decisionmaking*, Chicago: Aldine Publishing Company, 1972.

Friedman, Thomas L., "Loose-Linked Network of Terror: Separate Acts, Ideological Bonds," *Terrorism*, Vol. 8, No. 1, Winter 1985, pp. 36–49.

Garrity, Patrick, and Steven Maaranen, *Nuclear Weapons in a Changing World*, New York: Plenum Press, 1992.

"Gaza Strip, West Bank: Dahlan on Relations with Israel, Terrorism," *Tel Aviv Yedi'ot Aharonot*, Foreign Broadcast Information Service, TOT-97-022-L, February 28, 1997, p. 18.

George, Alexander, *Forceful Persuasion: Coercive Diplomacy as an Alternative to War*, Washington, D.C.: United States Institute of Peace Press, 1991.

George, Alexander, and William Simons, *The Limits of Coercive Diplomacy*, Boulder: Westview Press, 1994.

Gerlach, Luther P., "Protest Movements and the Construction of Risk," in B. B. Johnson and V. T. Covello, eds., *The Social and Cultural Construction of Risk*, D. Boston: Reidel Publishing Co., 1987, p. 115.

Gerlach, Luther P., and Virginia Hine, *People, Power, Change: Movements of Social Transformation*, New York: The Bobbs-Merrill Co., 1970.

Gertz, William, "Saudi Financier Tied to Attacks," *Washington Times*, October 23, 1996.

Gutteridge, William, ed., *Contemporary Terrorism*, England: Facts on File, Oxford, 1986.

Heckscher, Charles, "Defining the Post-Bureaucratic Type," in Charles Heckscher and Anne Donnelon, eds., *The Post-Bureaucratic Organization*, Thousand Oaks, Calif.: Sage, 1995.

Heydenbrand, Wolf V., "New Organizational Forms," *Work and Occupations*, No. 3, Vol. 16, August 1989, pp. 323–357.

"Hizbullah TV Summary 18 February 1998," *Al-Manar Television World Wide Webcast*, Foreign Broadcast Information Service, NES-98-050, February 19, 1998.

Hoffman, Bruce, *Inside Terrorism*, Columbia University Press, New York, 1998.

_____, *Responding to Terrorism Across the Technological Spectrum*, Santa Monica, Calif.: RAND, P-7874, 1994.

Hoffman, Bruce, and Caleb Carr, "Terrorism: Who Is Fighting Whom?" *World Policy Journal*, Vol. 14, No. 1, Spring 1997, pp. 97–104.

Ibrahim, Youssef M., "Egyptians Hold Terrorist Chief, Official Asserts," *New York Times*, August 26, 1998.

Ignatieff, Michael, "Unarmed Warriors," *The New Yorker*, March 24, 1997, pp. 56–71.

Iklé, Fred, "The Problem of the Next Lenin," *The National Interest*, Vol. 47, Spring 1997, pp. 9–19.

"Islamic Activism Online," Foreign Broadcast Information Service, Foreign Media Note—02JAN97, January 3, 1997.

"Islamic Group Vows Revenge for Slaying of Its Leader," *New York Times*, October 30, 1995, p. 9.

"Islamists on Internet," Foreign Broadcast Information Service, Foreign Media Note—065EP96, September 9, 1996.

"Israel: Hamas Using Internet to Relay Operational Messages," *Tel Aviv Ha'aretz*, Foreign Broadcast Information Service, TOT-98-034, February 3, 1998, p. 1.

"Israel: U.S. Hamas Activists Use Internet to Send Attack Threats," *Tel Aviv IDF Radio*, Foreign Broadcast Information Service, TOT-97-001-L, 0500 GMT October 13, 1996.

Israeli Foreign Ministry, "Hizbullah," April 11, 1996. Available on the Internet at *http://www.israel-mfa.gov.il.*

"Italy, Vatican City: Daily Claims GIA 'Strategist' Based in Milan," *Milan Corriere della Sera*, Foreign Broadcast Information Service, TOT-97-004-L, December 5, 1996, p. 9.

"Italy: Security Alters Following Algerian Extremists' Arrests," *Milan Il Giornale*, Foreign Broadcast Information Service, TOT-97-002-L, November 12, 1996, p. 10.

Jenkins, Brian, *International Terrorism: A New Kind of Warfare,* Santa Monica, Calif.: RAND, P-5261, 1974.

_____, *The Potential for Nuclear Terrorism,* Santa Monica, Calif.: RAND, P-5876, 1977.

Kaplan, Robert, "The Coming Anarchy," *Atlantic Monthly,* February 1994, pp. 44–76.

Kelly, Kevin, *Out of Control: The Rise of Neo-Biological Civilization,* A William Patrick Book, New York: Addison-Wesley Publishing Company, 1994.

Kerry, John (Senator), *The New War,* Simon & Schuster, New York, 1997.

Kneisel, Paul, "Netwar: The Battle Over Rec.Music.White-Power," *ANTIFA INFO-BULLETIN,* Research Supplement, June 12, 1996, unpaginated ASCII text available on the Internet.

Laqueur, Walter, "Postmodern Terrorism," *Foreign Affairs,* Vol. 75, No. 5, September/October 1996, pp. 24–36.

Lipnack, Jessica, and Jeffrey Stamps, *The Age of the Network,* New York: Wiley & Sons, 1994.

Littleton, Matthew, "Information Age Terrorism," master's thesis, Monterey, Calif.: Naval Postgraduate School, 1995.

Loeb, Vernon, "Where the CIA Wages Its New World War," *Washington Post,* September 9, 1998.

"Militants Say There Will Be More Attacks Against U.S.," *European Stars and Stripes,* August 20, 1998.

Molander, Roger, Andrew Riddile, and Peter Wilson, *Strategic Information Warfare: A New Face of War,* Santa Monica, Calif.: RAND, MR-661-OSD, 1996.

Molander, Roger, Peter Wilson, David Mussington, and Richard Mesic, *Strategic Information Warfare Rising,* Santa Monica, Calif.: RAND, 1998.

Murray, John, and Richard H. Ward, eds., *Extremist Groups,* Chicago: University of Illinois, Office of International Criminal Justice, 1996.

Nacos, Brigitte, *Terrorism and the Media,* Columbia University Press, New York, 1994.

Netanyahu, Benjamin, *Winning the War Against Terrorism,* New York: Simon and Schuster, 1996.

Nye, Joseph S., *Bound to Lead: The Changing Nature of American Power,* New York: Basic Books, 1990.

Nye, Joseph S., and William A. Owens, "America's Information Edge," *Foreign Affairs,* Vol. 75, No. 2, March/April 1996.

Ottaway, David B., "US Considers Slugging It Out With International Terrorism," *Washington Post,* October 17, 1996, p. 25.

Ranstorp, Magnus, "Hizbullah's Command Leadership: Its Structure, Decision-Making and Relationship with Iranian Clergy and Institutions," *Terrorism and Political Violence,* Vol. 6, No. 3, Autumn 1994, p. 304.

Rivers, Gayle, *The War Against the Terrorists: How to Fight and Win,* New York: Stein and Day, 1986.

Ronfeldt, David, and Armando Martinez, "A Comment on the Zapatista 'Netwar'," in Arquilla and Ronfeldt (1997), pp. 369–391.

Ronfeldt, David, John Arquilla, Graham Fuller, and Melissa Fuller, *The Zapatista "Social Netwar" in Mexico,* Santa Monica, Calif.: RAND, MR-994-A, forthcoming.

"Saudi Arabia: Bin-Laden Calls for 'Guerrilla Warfare' Against US Forces," *Beirut Al-Diyar,* Foreign Broadcast Information Service, NES-96-180, September 12, 1996.

"Saudi Arabia: French Analysis of Islamic Threat," *Paris al-Watan al-'Arabi,* Foreign Broadcast Information Service, NES-97-082, April 11, 1997, pp. 4–8.

Schelling, Thomas, "Thinking about Nuclear Terrorism," *International Security,* Vol. 6, No. 4, Spring 1982, pp. 68–75.

Shubik, Martin, "Terrorism, Technology, and the Socioeconomics of Death," *Comparative Strategy,* Vol. 16, No. 4, October–December 1997, pp. 399–414.

Sterling, Claire, *The Terror Network*, New York:  Holt, Rinehart & Winston, 1981.

Stern, Kenneth, *A Force upon the Plain:  The American Militia Movement and the Politics of Hate*, New York:  Simon and Schuster, 1996.

U.S. Department of State, Office of the Coordinator for Counterterrorism, *Patterns of Global Terrorism*, annual editions for the years 1995–1997.

Van Creveld, Martin, *The Transformation of War*, New York:  Free Press, 1991.

Van Creveld, Martin, "In Wake of Terrorism, Modern Armies Prove to Be Dinosaurs of Defense," *New Perspectives Quarterly*, Vol. 13, No. 4, Fall 1996, p. 58.

Weiner, Tim, "U.S. Sees bin Laden as Ringleader of Terrorist Network," *New York Times*, August 21, 1998.

Whine, Michael, "Islamist Organisations on the Internet," draft circulated on the Internet, April 1998 *(www.ict.org.il/articles)*.

Williams, Phil, "Transnational Criminal Organizations and International Security," *Survival*, Vol. 36, No. 1, Spring 1994, pp. 96–113.

_____, "The Nature of Drug-Trafficking Networks," *Current History*, April 1998, pp. 154–159.

Zuckerman, M. J., "Bin Laden Indicted for Bid to Kill Clinton," *USA Today*, August 26, 1998.

# Chapter Five

# INFORMATION AND WAR: IS IT A REVOLUTION?

*Jeremy Shapiro*

## INTRODUCTION: AL-KHAFJI

On January 29, 1991, an Iraqi probing attack crossed the Saudi-Kuwait border and occupied the deserted town of Al-Khafji, Saudi Arabia. As coalition ground forces battled to retake the town, the Iraqi high command ordered large reinforcements into the battle. On January 30, an experimental Joint Surveillance and Target Attack Radar System (JSTARS) aircraft and various unmanned aerial reconnaissance vehicles detected the nighttime movement toward Al-Khafji of two Iraqi divisions some 50 miles behind enemy lines. This information was passed to Airborne Warning and Control System aircraft, which rapidly redirected coalition aircraft to attack the formations (Department of Defense [DoD], 1992, pp. 131–132; Keaney and Cohen, 1993, pp. 19–21 and 246–247). Throughout that night, a variety of aircraft dispatched from all over the theater used JSTARS targeting information and precision-guided weapons to effectively destroy the two divisions on the move. From that point forward, the Iraqis understood that they could not move their forces, even at night, without risking annihilation.

For many observers, the most novel, and most important, aspect of this encounter was the role of information. Many of the weapons and systems used had existed for a long time but had never been so effectively networked together and used to such devastating effect. This dramatic result was possible because precise information about the targets was successfully acquired and rapidly transmitted to those who could use it. In essence, information unavailable or unusable a generation ago had decisively affected the outcome of an important battle. For those who see Al-Khafji as the prototype of a new type of warfare, this battle, though not typical of the Gulf War as a whole, stands out as the harbinger of a coming revolution in military affairs enabled by information technology.

As a result, various executive and congressional committees have been set up to analyze the effect of the coming information revolution on warfare, and the military services have created a variety of information-warfare laboratories and organizations.[1] Articles, jargon, and Web sites devoted to the revolution proliferate at a rate possible only in an information age.[2] Information technology is said to herald revolutionary changes in everything from the sources of economic wealth to the very nature of combat.

As all of this diverse activity implies, the world is clearly changing in dramatic ways. However, not all changes are revolutions. For the word *revolution* to have meaning, at least in a defense policy sense, it must imply a degree of change that requires radical adaptations in current modes of strategies, doctrines, and forms of organization. This chapter explores whether the current changes constitute a revolution according to that stipulation and what such a revolution would mean. After a survey of the variety of currently proposed revolutions, we assess whether a revolution in warfare has actually occurred. The chapter will argue that current strategies, doctrines, and organizations can incorporate the current changes with only evolutionary adaptations. We should beware of proposals for radical reform, as the next revolution has not yet appeared.

## THE MEANING OF REVOLUTION

Revolutions are difficult to identify. History offers few examples of contemporary observers who correctly assessed an ongoing revolu-

---

[1] A few examples include the Defense Science Board's (DSB's) Task Force on Information Warfare, which produced a report on defense against information warfare (DSB, 1996); the General Accounting Office's (GAO's) report on computer security (GAO, 1996); and the President's Commission on Critical Infrastructure Protection's (PCCIP's) report on infrastructure vulnerability (PCCIP, 1997). Key doctrinal statements include those by the Training and Doctrine Command (TRADOC, 1996); Widnall and Fogleman (1996), and Joint Staff (1996).

[2] Some of the most cited works on the subject include Libicki (1995), Schwartau (1994), Toffler and Toffler (1993), Nye and Owens (1996), and Arquilla and Ronfeldt (1996).

tion, but many examples of false prophets.[3]  However, because such revolutions offer tremendous rewards to nations that can accurately anticipate them and tremendous costs to those that miss the wave of the future, the pressure to catch the wave can prove irresistible.  This pressure reflects the many historical instances of disasters befalling nations and groups that have failed to adapt themselves effectively to new technological possibilities.  The catastrophic defeat of the French Army in 1940, for example, is typically attributed to its leaders' failure to fully comprehend the revolutionary implications of the new technologies of tanks, airplanes, and radios for the modern battlefield (see Stolfi, 1970, and Alexander, 1990).

Equally important, however, and much less understood, no nation or military can afford the disruptions and upheavals caused by excessively frequent reorganizations.  False revolutions also impose a severe cost in terms of wasted effort, chaotic disruption of routine, and inappropriate innovations.  In Britain during the interwar period, for example, the idea that strategic bombing had revolutionized warfare helped promote the idea that a large land army and fighter aircraft were unnecessary, so Britain channeled scarce resources into a heavy bomber fleet, with nearly disastrous consequences (see Bond and Murray, 1988).[4]  Complete reorganizations, in particular, impose large costs and should not be made prematurely. As Eliot Cohen (1994) has pointed out, the creation of a corps of "information warriors" today, as some people advocate, might make as much sense as a corps of internal combustion warriors would have at the beginning of the 20th century.[5]  Inappropriate or even premature adaptations can be as wasteful and as detrimental to effectiveness as a failure to innovate.

This potential for "overinnovation" explains why the use of the word *revolution* has important policy implications.  Evolutionary change implies the type of almost reflexive adaptation and flexibility that,

---

[3]For a large compendium of false prophesies, including many predicting military revolution, see Cerf and Navasky (1984).  Our perception of the record of such prophesies is skewed by retrospective writings, which tend to focus on the few prophesies that were correct and to ignore the multitude that were mistaken.

[4]Another frequently cited example of a misidentified revolution is the U.S. Army's move to a nuclear mission in the 1950s.  See Bacevich (1986).

[5]A cautious advocate of this position is Libicki (1994).  Cohen's comment appears in a review of Libicki's book.

however difficult, militaries can and should do most every day. Revolutions, in contrast, are infrequent cataclysmic events that require revisiting all the old assumptions that pass unnoticed in daily life.  Declaring a revolution opens the field to proposals for wholesale transformations in doctrine, equipment, and even personnel.  Indeed, such transformations are a necessary condition of a revolution in military affairs.  For this reason, historians seeking to categorizes past innovations as revolutionary often look for major, permanent changes in organizational structure as an indication of revolution.  If evolutionary adaptation of the type seen continually in large organizations could meet the requirements of a revolution, the word *revolution* would have no practical meaning.

Similarly, revolutionary changes typically need to be identified and responded to by those outside the mainstream of the organization in question.  Insiders concerned with the day-to-day strains of getting the job done often lose sight of the big picture or become so accustomed, even attached emotionally or professionally, to the current modes of operation that they refuse to contemplate dramatic change.

Military professionals derive much of their authority on warfare from their experience.  If revolutionary advances in information technology have rendered that experience less relevant to the changes needed to adapt to new technology, outsiders' views will be given greater weight.  Use of the word *revolution*, therefore, implies greater scope and necessity for outsiders to delve into the internal workings of military organizations and recommend or even force changes against entrenched cultures that have become dangerously outmoded.

Military professionals who choose to use the word *revolution* to characterize the current changes in warfare need to understand that they are inviting, even impelling, civilian intervention in issues usually left to the military.  In the end, the acceptance of the idea that we are in the midst of a revolution will force civilian and military policymakers to insist upon radical adaptations in military organization, doctrine, and even culture.  These adaptations will be difficult, costly, and largely irreversible.  For this reason, if no other, the question of revolution is no mere academic debate but rather a policy issue of the highest order.

## POSSIBLE REVOLUTIONS

The idea that information is crucial to success in warfare is a truism that dates back at least to the ancient Chinese writings of Sun Tzu (see Sun Tzu, trans. Griffith, 1963).[6] No leap of intellectual imagination has suddenly led us to believe that new technologies have enhanced the importance of information in warfare. Rather, the topic has attracted new attention now because certain concrete events have focused attention on the role of information in national security and provided a peek at the potential of new technologies to transform our lives. Many events have contributed to this perception, but three developments stand out and form the basis for most views on how information technology will revolutionize warfare. They provide the evidentiary touchstones, the starting points for extrapolations that, in their extreme, lead to revolutionary change. As such, an understanding of these developments is central to understanding the validity of the idea that information technology is revolutionizing warfare. These developments are the growth of instantaneous, worldwide media coverage ("the CNN [Cable News Network] effect"); the results of the Persian Gulf War; and, most recently, the dramatic expansion of the Internet.

The sole universal that links these events and therefore pervades all accounts of the coming revolution in warfare is that the changes to come flow from what are essentially new and better machines or systems based on information technology. Politics, strategy, and organization will shape the revolution that many analysts predict, perhaps even determining who benefits and who loses from the advance of information technology, but technology enables that revolution. This simple observation means that most characterizations of the future role of information in warfare begin by predicting how certain technologies are already revolutionizing our lives and then theorize and even prescribe how warfare might or should look in the new, technologically enabled world to come. However, depending on which of these concrete events any particular author has in mind as the most salient to the change that is occurring, he will tend to see a very different type of revolutionary change.

---

[6]Sun Tzu's writings are usually dated from the 5th or 6th century BCE. The Sun Tzu dictum most often applied to this subject is: "Know your enemy and know yourself; in a hundred battles you will never be in peril."

One can divine three basic types of revolutions in this body of work, roughly corresponding to the three developments that have sparked the idea of an information-based revolution in warfare. The accounts that begin with the Internet tend to see information technology triggering a societal revolution equivalent in historical importance to the industrial or agricultural revolution. Those that start with the CNN effect usually see a political revolution ushering in a new era and kind of democracy. Finally, the third type begins with the Persian Gulf War or the Internet and sees another in a series of military revolutions reshaping the battlefield of the future.[7]

## Social Revolution

The most radical theorists believe that the information revolution will completely transform society, generating a social upheaval akin to that caused by the industrial revolution. Old forms of political and commercial organization, social control, and wealth will be swept aside by this upheaval, making way for radically new forms. In the process, the old forms, goals, and methods of warfare would be completely transformed. War would be fought by new actors with new means for new ends and, as a result, would barely resemble the industrial-age interstate wars to which we have become so accustomed. The prediction of such a revolution leaves the field wide open for speculation on both the nature of society and the nature of warfare after the upheaval. Consequently, arguments of this type are the most future oriented, the most varied, and the most difficult to substantiate. They are important, nonetheless, both because they have already had considerable influence and because they imply the long-term strategies that will succeed in the new world (see Dinardo and Hughes, 1995, p. 2).

The most common of these views, whose best known exponents are Heidi and Alvin Toffler, extrapolates from the idea that territory, population, and natural resources are becoming less important relative to human capital and the possession of information. Taking this process to its logical conclusion, these theorists see information soon

---

[7]This correspondence is not intended to be perfect. Of course, most authors are aware of and incorporate all these important developments into their work, as well as many others. Nonetheless, they tend to view one of these as more salient and more revolutionary in its effects than the others.

becoming the key source of wealth and power, equivalent to steel, coal, and oil in the industrial age or fertile land in the agricultural age. This change will eventually amount to a social revolution whose scope is equivalent to only two previous such transformations: the agricultural and industrial revolutions. A "Third Wave" society will, as previous social revolutions did, create utterly new types of war. In particular, wars will no longer be fought to seize territory or industrial resources; instead, the object of conflict becomes the new strategic asset: information. Information-age warfare, therefore, is conceived as warfare that has as its object control over information as a source of wealth and power.[8]

John Arquilla and David Ronfeldt view the coming transformation in somewhat different, though related, terms. These authors extrapolate from the idea that instantaneous, global communications and rapid, cheap transportation are creating less hierarchical, more flexible commercial organizations to a similar transformation of society and warfare. For them, information technology transforms society by enabling and favoring the creation of smaller, nimbler, more flexible forms of organization of all types. With the coming of high-speed, global communication networks, these "networked" organizations will possess advantages over more-traditional hierarchical forms of organization.

Arquilla and Ronfeldt see these new organizations as leaderless collections of dispersed, interconnected nodes capable of rapid, autonomous, self-organizing responses to any potential challenge. Their lack of a central control node, as well as their physical dispersion and numerous interconnections, makes these organizations very difficult to destroy or even to degrade. At the same time, new communication technologies will allow these organizations to coordinate action successfully over vast distances.

By contrast, hierarchical organizations will be vulnerable to disabling attacks on critical control nodes that will render these organizations' physical capability useless. They will be incapable of rapid, flexible response, since all actions will require information to filter up to the top and be evaluated and decisions to filter back down to lower lev-

---

[8]This idea is primarily from Toffler and Toffler (1993). Other examples include Dearth and Williams (1996) and Schwartau (1994).

els. In an age in which speed and flexibility determine success, hierarchical organizations—such as large corporations, nation-states, and their traditional military organizations—will inevitably suffer in the competition with networked organizations that can better capitalize on emerging technologies (Arquilla and Ronfeldt, 1996).[9]

Acceptance of the idea that a social revolution is in the offing would require a wholesale reconstruction of the traditional military. Because networked organizations are required to meet the challenge of other networked organizations or because warfare over information resources needs to be fought differently than warfare over land or industrial resources, military organizations would need to be flattened and redirected.[10] In the end, they would barely resemble the industrial-age militaries we have today

**The Internet Metaphor.** These arguments rest on what might usefully be called the "Internet metaphor." Arguments that predict social revolutions frequently analogize from a few basic characteristics of the Internet and then logically extrapolate these features until they culminate in a radical reordering of society. The Internet has at least 70 million users worldwide as of this writing; by some accounts, Internet traffic has been doubling every six months. This rapid growth represents the first fulfillment of the revolutionary promise of computer technology on a truly mass scale and, as such, naturally forms the basis for a lot of speculation about how technology will shape the future.[11]

There are three elements of the Internet most commonly used in this fashion. The first element is the lack of central control over the system. The Internet is a wildly dispersed network of networks, with virtually no centralized control over its content or its users, almost an electronic Wild West. The Internet's strength, vitality, and robustness derive from this organizational style, which can best be described as creative anarchy. However, the system's reputation for

---

[9]For a fictional view of the logical extreme of this idea, see Stephenson (1993).

[10]See, in this volume, Arquilla, Ronfeldt, and Zanini (Chapter Four) and Shulsky and Fukuyama (Chapter Eleven).

[11]The Tofflers' ideas on an "information revolution" certainly date from well before the popular use of the Internet. (See Toffler, 1980.) However, these ideas only began to reach a widespread audience after the Internet analogy connected their ideas to people's daily lives.

security flaws also stems from this organization. Because no one can regulate systems or enforce security standards in such an environment, there can always be rogue users and exploitable security flaws that allow entrée into the system. Inadequately trained personnel and badly designed or implemented software anywhere on the network potentially threaten everyone. From a security standpoint, this means that there is no opportunity to monitor the system collectively and implement systemwide security measures. Local administrators must implement almost all security measures, and everything that comes from beyond the local "firewall," including commercial software, must be regarded as a potential risk.

The second element is cheap, remote access from anywhere in the world. This means that virtually anyone can have access from anywhere with very small startup costs using commercially available technology. It also means that those who use the system may be able to remain anonymous and unidentifiable. Indeed, done with enough subtlety and skill, this type of system often allows attacks or intrusions to go unnoticed.

The final and perhaps most important element of the Internet metaphor is interconnectivity. The Internet connects everyone to everyone else in a variety of redundant and, for most people, incomprehensible ways. Interconnectivity means that the network can provide any information anywhere in real time. It allows knowledge to become a key resource because it can be rapidly transmitted and used most efficiently. Interconnectivity also creates the notion that the network can spread security problems, such as viruses, and that small, unforeseeable disturbances can cause catastrophic systemwide failures. Although the link between accidental systemic failures and deliberately induced ones is weak, several recent accidents in heavily interconnected infrastructures have given prominence to the idea that these systems exist in a precariously balanced state. The idea is that if, for example, a software error in an AT&T switching station in New York can disable the largest long-distance network in the United States for several hours, imagine what malicious actors with intent to disrupt could do to such systems.[12]

---

[12]On January 15, 1990, a software error in a program running at a New York switching station cascaded throughout the AT&T network, effectively shutting down more than half the long-distance network for approximately 10 hours. See Sims (1990).

Together, these elements form the basis for a new human society, based in cyberspace with all of the strengths and weaknesses attributed to the Internet. Because these arguments about social revolution build on the Internet metaphor, they present seductive images that rest on a foundation of conventional wisdom about how technology is currently affecting our lives. Arguments that predict societal revolutions are thus quite compelling and have gained a wide audience within the national security community and in the popular imagination (see Bunker, 1995, and Dinardo and Hughes, 1995).[13] Moreover, such arguments are not directly open to refutation, since they make few empirical claims about the present. If this is a revolution, it is one that has, at yet, shown only its faintest outlines.

**Evidence for a Social Revolution.** Our persistent tendency to believe ourselves in the midst of a social revolution, combined with their historical rarity, should inspire a sense of caution in accepting such faint outlines. The changes caused by the Internet and other information technologies are indeed profound. The standard, however, for a social revolution must be much higher. The invention of the telephone and the airplane early in this century, and later the television, engendered dramatic changes in daily life, but no social revolution, according to these theorists. As the Tofflers emphasize and other social-revolution theorists predict, a social revolution requires a shift in the sources of national wealth and power, not merely in the minutiae of daily life.

The evidence, however, that such a shift is even beginning to occur has not as yet appeared, despite a persistent search. If information technology is creating a new, superior system for creating wealth, we should be able to detect that influence in the contribution it makes to productivity. Past social revolutions have been marked, indeed defined, by dramatic productivity improvements engendered by new technologies. The agricultural revolution saw rapid expansion in the productivity of food production through the use of the new techniques of farming and husbandry (as opposed to hunting and gathering). The industrial revolution saw rapid productivity increases in

---

[13]Daniel Gouré (1996) claims that the Tofflers have had great influence on the Air Force Staff and with GEN Gordon Sullivan, former Chief of Staff of the Army, among others. The DSB and PCCIP reports also use "Tofflerian" logic.

the production of industrial goods through the application of steam and electrical power, as well as modern management and production techniques. The prediction of an information-based social revolution has sparked a widespread search for the effects of information technology on productivity. We would expect it to have had a dramatic influence on productivity statistics. As yet, however, repeated efforts have not yielded any evidence that information technology has produced even slight productivity gains, much less the huge gains necessary to justify the prediction of a social revolution. This finding has been so surprising to devotees of the Third Wave that it has been labeled the "productivity paradox." The debate over the productivity paradox continues, but so far the only prediction of the social-revolution school has turned out to be manifestly false.[14]

## Political Revolution

A second family of arguments believes that information technology will change warfare through its influence on politics. The technological impetus of this change is the spread of new media and communication methods, including instantaneous, global television broadcasting, direct broadcast satellites, fax machines, cellular telephones, and networked computers. The popular impressions that world leaders use CNN as their primary source of information, are forced to respond quickly to live televised developments, and use the medium to communicate with each other have promoted the idea of the CNN effect that sharply limits political leaders' freedom of action. This effect is often seen as the leading edge of a fundamental change in the conduct of national security affairs and military operations caused by new media technologies. Today, a host of other real-time news organizations has joined CNN in using live satellite broadcasting, the Internet, and powerful video imagery to ensure that even complex political events and military operations are covered immediately and globally. Such coverage, however, does not guarantee or even increase accuracy.

For many commentators on this subject, these new technologies mean that governments no longer have the ability to control the flow

---

[14]The evidence for and against the productivity paradox is well-summarized in Biddle (1997).

of information to their publics and to their soldiers, both in peacetime and in wartime. Concurrently, new techniques that allow manipulation of video images and sound recordings have created an even greater technical ability for potential opponents to conduct sophisticated psychological operations (Cooper, 1996). The inability to control information flows has been widely cited as playing an essential role in the downfall of the communist regimes in Eastern Europe and the Soviet Union (see Shane, 1994).[15] Perception management, the vogue term for psychological operations or propaganda directed at the public, already holds considerable sway in U.S. politics, where, according to the most cynical observers, the image is the reality (De Caro, 1996, p. 204).

Many observers worry that potential U.S. foes will combine this new potential for perception management with certain asymmetric strategies that rely on weapons of mass destruction or other means to attack psychologically significant targets. These attacks, though only of marginal use in destroying the U.S. capability to wage war, might, through their effect on public opinion, destroy the will of the United States to wage war. In this way, weaker adversaries secure victory, in some sense, without even engaging the bulk of U.S. military strength.[16]

Recent U.S. experience in Somalia, Haiti, and Bosnia demonstrated to many that U.S. politicians now feel that the public perception of the operation may matter more than the correlation of forces on the ground (De Caro, 1996, pp. 208–209). The United States can usually outmatch any opponent in combat power, but the battle for the hearts and minds of the public appears to be a more balanced fight. In Somalia, the most cited example of this phenomenon, public horror of the images of human suffering caused by state collapse is said to have pushed the United States to intervene. Then, public anger and despair over televised casualties pulled them back out again, securing victory for an opponent clearly outclassed in physical terms.

Although many dispute this interpretation of the events in Somalia, the U.S. military is already keenly aware both that it will have little ability to control the flow of information to and from the theater and

---

[15]On a similar note, see Pool (1983).

[16]One such scenario is presented in Dunlap (1996).

that the media will monitor the soldiers' every action.[17] In a media-intense environment, politicians and the public have become very unforgiving of even minor mistakes and transgressions. Events with minor operational effects, such as the killing of a Somali youth for stealing a soldier's sunglasses or the dramatic rescue of a downed F-16 pilot in Bosnia, often have disproportionately large effects on public opinion and therefore policy and outcomes. As a result, even the most minute aspect of military operations must now be planned with a sensitivity to the public perception of the fight.

The Gulf War demonstrated this process when an attack on a communications bunker in Baghdad that was also being used as an air-raid shelter for the families of Iraqi officials resulted in 300 deaths. Pictures of a smoking bunker and civilian deaths had an immediate effect back home. U.S. political authorities did not allow any bombing of Baghdad for days; even when bombing resumed, they restricted it to a handful of high-priority targets (see Freedman and Karsky, 1991, p. 39). An awareness of this change permeates all aspects of military operations and has forced the military to concentrate not just on performing its mission but also on shaping the perception of that mission and its outcome (see Larson, 1996). For commanders, this means a much greater attention to nonmilitary factors that can impinge upon the mission (see Sciolino, 1998).

An appreciation of the potential power of public information led the North Atlantic Treaty Organization and the U.S. Army in Bosnia to establish a joint information bureau at the inception of the operation to coordinate their responses to breaking events and counter disinformation that they believed would hinder their ability to do their job. According to one observer, this bureau and its director are "central to the functioning of the command group, providing daily advice to the division commander and operating in close partnership with the operations, intelligence, and civic affairs elements." (Allard, 1996.)

At the same time, because these technologies are seen as critical for the economic competitiveness of nations, they also have diminished the government's incentive to limit information flows. Government may have the power to limit the CNN effect, but any government that

---

[17]For the U.S. Army's view, see TRADOC (1996), pp. 1-2 through 1-4.

denies its citizens free and unimpeded use of the new media technologies will, according to this argument, fall behind in the economic competition among nations.[18] As more liberal regimes outproduce and outinvent the countries that limit information flows, oppressive governments will be forced either to allow access to these technologies or to assume a policy of autarkic poverty on the model of North Korea.

These technological changes will revolutionize politics not only because they will force authoritarian regimes to liberalize, but also because they transform how democratic governments are able to formulate policy and wage war. The political revolution most often seen as profoundly affecting warfare was the French Revolution. The ideology of nationalism that revolution unleashed made states orders of magnitude more capable and resilient in war. Before the French revolution, the Alsatian peasant cared little whether his taxes were extorted by Berlin or Paris. Afterward, it became the issue that defined his existence. Nationalism means that the entire populace, not just the elite, identifies its interests with those of the government. Consequently, the government can mobilize the entire capacity of the society for a prolonged war, and even if the regular army is defeated, the people will continue to resist through irregular means.[19]

The inability of the government to control the information flow gives enemies a means to undermine that identity of interests. New techniques that allow manipulation of video images and sound recordings and therefore allow conduct of sophisticated psychological operations provide another resource for undermining that identity of interests between the government and the wider populace. Indeed, some believe that the real war in the information age will be for the hearts and minds of the populace or the fears and insecurities of the troops (Adams, 1996; Cooper, 1996; Nichiporuk and Builder, 1995;

---

[18]See the chapter by David Gompert, Chapter Three in this volume.

[19]For Clausewitz' commentary on the revolutionary impact of this political change on warfare, see Clausewitz (1976), p. 592. A theorist who roots such changes in social revolutions would see the French Revolution and the resulting changes in warfare as simply a reflection of the agricultural revolution that created a surplus workforce ready for military use.

and Stein, 1996).[20] As a result, governments can no longer count on the substantial resources and resilience that come from popular mobilizations. The absence of that popular backing would severely limit a government's ability to wage war. In essence, conventional military power will be rendered useless if potential foes win the propaganda battle.

In the Gulf War, the Bush administration made great efforts to ensure that the public perceived the conflict in terms that sustained the U.S. commitment, an effort bolstered by a residual capability to control the flow of information from the theater. This perception management campaign succeeded, but just barely. U.S. public support for the war remained tepid until the beginning of the war, and a Senate resolution in support of the deployment passed by just five votes. If this shallow support had been combined with military reversals, the war effort would have been quite difficult to sustain politically (see Larson, 1996).

This new, relatively cheap tool of warfare may similarly enable non-state actors to become real players on the international scene and to challenge state actors on crucial issues through clever perception management that undermines a government's greatest strength: the support of its populace and its military.[21] Because of its low cost, criminal organizations, nongovernmental organizations, and antigovernment insurgents can engage in sophisticated psychological operations as easily as traditional state-sponsored militaries can.

Warfare in this new political environment consists largely of the battle to shape the political context of the war and the meaning of victory. According to Brian Nichiporuk and Carl Builder, even when war does involve combat, it will resemble improvisational theater. Everyone, that is to say the public, will be watching closely at all times. Because of the audience's interactive participation, the play will be hard to script, and little events may totally change future scenes in unpredictable ways. In such circumstances, "to be made the villain in the play is almost certainly to be made the loser." (Nichiporuk and Builder, 1995, p. 61.) Since most potential U.S.

---

[20]For a review of how similar psychological operations have worked historically, see Hosmer (1996).

[21]See Matthews (1997) for an example of this viewpoint.

conflicts are likely to skirt the edge of national interest, the ability to influence such perceptions may mean the difference between victory and defeat.

In such an environment, the military is unlikely to maintain complete control over even the most low-level aspects of combat. Micromanagement by political authorities would become necessary, indeed inescapable, if the ultimate outcome of the fight were determined not so much by the performance of the military actors but by the political repercussions of the battle.

**The More Things Change.** The idea that new media and communication technologies have changed the calculus of foreign-policy decisionmaking is a natural one. While such arguments are reasonable and have a basis in current experience, they make two questionable assumptions when predicting revolutionary changes. First, they assume that such media challenges to political authority are entirely new. In fact, they have been recurring features of political debates since at least the invention of the printing press in the 15th century (see Dewar, 1998). Indeed, the current debate about the role of journalism in forcing the hands of political authorities neatly mirrors a similar debate that took place around the time of the Spanish-American War in 1898. Newspaper magnates, particularly William Randolph Hearst and Joseph Pulitzer, were widely blamed for having forced the U.S. government to intervene in the Cuban Revolution. Hearst is even reported to have boasted to one of his sketch artists sent to the cover the war, who complained that there was no war to sketch, "you furnish the pictures and I'll furnish the war." This story (denied by Hearst) led to that war being referred to as "Mr. Hearst's War." More-recent historians, however, have questioned the degree to which Hearst's newspaper, or any newspaper, was actually responsible for the war.[22]

Second, such accounts assume that current trends will continue along their present lines. History rarely moves in such straight lines; rather, each push in one direction generates a reaction in the opposite direction. Although this observation seems obvious, accounts of the future often fail to anticipate how present trends may be interrupted or reversed. This is frequently due to an underestimation of

---

[22]See, for example, Brown (1967).

the capacity of politicians, scientists, or soldiers to respond to challenges that new technologies present and to maintain the world in something approximating its current form. The capability of powerful actors to resist, slow down, or adapt to technological and other historical trends has often surprised contemporary observers. It will do so again.

In a 1996 book, Johanna Neuman demonstrated how relaxing these two assumptions can provide a very different look at the CNN effect. She documented how statesmen have had to deal many times before with new technologies that pundits predicted would destroy their ability to make foreign policy or control the political process (Neuman, 1996). In each instance, from the penny press to the radio and beyond, the politicians quickly learned how to control or master the new media and turn it to their advantage. While each new wave of information technology certainly changed politics, such waves rarely produced wholesale revolutions. Those with an interest in the status quo were able to bend technology, at least to some degree, to preserve their maneuvering room. Certainly, the presence of instantaneous, global media and the loss of control over information have had effects that go beyond those of previous innovations, particularly in their ability to force leaders to make decisions extremely quickly, without time for adequate reflection or consultation. Nonetheless, any account that sees this change as effecting a profound transformation in politics must, based on the historical record, pay due homage to the remarkable ability of politicians and the political system to adapt to and even master a changing technological environment.

## Military Revolution

Probably the most ink on this subject has been spilled in an effort to describe how information technology will directly revolutionize military affairs. In this context, *military revolution* refers to changes in the weapons used to fight battles; the targets they attack; the systems that provide command and control, logistical, and intelligence support for the weapons; and the organizations that use the weapons and systems. In contrast to the previous two types of revolution, this one sees information technology as providing new means to an old end: victory in conflicts between traditional military organizations.

This application of information technology to the problem of warfare does not claim to redefine the meaning of victory or to change the actors involved in any essential way. Rather, it promises to improve dramatically the capability of militaries to apply combat power.

In this way, the "information-based revolution in military affairs" appears as only the latest in a series of technological or social changes that have profoundly remade warfare. Andrew Krepinevich has identified 10 such revolutions in modern times, from the advent of pikemen in the 14th century to the nuclear revolution in the latter half of the 20th (Krepinevich, 1994).[23] Such revolutions have had a tendency to create sudden, dramatic changes in the relative combat power of military organizations. Indeed, one harbinger of a military revolution is an unexpected or extremely lopsided victory. Commonly cited examples of this phenomenon include the Battle of Königratz in 1866, where the use of railroads and telegraphs allowed the Prussians nearly to wipe out the Austro-Hungarian army; the Battle of France in 1940, where the German combination of tanks, airplanes, and radios defeated the French Army in six weeks; and, of course, the Persian Gulf War of 1991.

In current writing on the military revolution, the key technologies that are transforming warfare are usually identified as information technologies—although how specifically such technologies will affect military affairs is an issue of great dispute. For many, the idea of a global or national information infrastructure has created a new medium for battle: "cyberspace," akin to air, land, sea, or space.[24] In a conscious analogy to air warfare, this type of information warfare often involves securing information superiority or "information dominance"[25] in the new medium. Information dominance means that your side has the ability to collect, communicate, and protect information without disruption, while the other side does not. It enables the possessor to seize air dominance easily and, from there, to move on to relatively unimpeded land operations. This implies

---

[23]For a similar but distinct typology, see Murray (1997).

[24]For an example, see Widnall and Fogleman (1996). For the original conceptualization of cyberspace as a separate medium for human interaction, see Gibson (1984).

[25]Two examples of this idea include TRADOC (1996), p. iv, passim, and Joint Staff (1996), p. I-3.

that the new dependence of society and the military on information systems has made information the new center of gravity, the central, most critical node in any nation's ability to wage war. The battle for the information realm will be the first, most important battle, victory in which will virtually ensure victory in the other realms.[26] Building on this new realm for battle, many accounts of this type divide the effect of information-age warfare into two types: the strategic and the operational.[27]

**Strategic Information Warfare.** In strategic information warfare, the battleground is the information infrastructure upon which modern societies have become so dependent, including the electric power grid, the financial system, the air traffic control system, and a variety of sensitive computer systems.[28] Strategic information warfare draws its inspiration from the Internet and makes widespread use of the Internet metaphor. The interconnectivity of these systems renders them vulnerable to systemic disruptions. The ability to access these systems from abroad makes them susceptible to attacks whose origin is difficult to identify. Indeed, done with enough subtlety and skill, it might, according to some accounts, become difficult even to know one is under attack until it is too late. In most accounts, this type of warfare represents a particular vulnerability for the United States, largely because it has the most sophisticated information infrastructure and has become the most reliant upon it. In contrast, typical U.S. opponents are often poorer, less-advanced nations whose information infrastructures contribute little to their war-making capacity.

Although the information infrastructure that strategic information-warfare theorists worry about encompasses much more than just the

---

[26]Examples of authors making this point are Mahnken (1995–1996) and Szafranski and Libicki (1996).

[27]Endorsing this division (without using the term *operational*) is Molander, Riddile, and Wilson (1996). This division is quite common; however, the labeling of the two types varies greatly. The Joint Staff uses *information warfare* to refer to strategic information warfare and *command-and-control warfare* to refer to the operational aspects. (See Joint Staff, 1996.) Army doctrine reverses this notion and conceives of *information warfare* as too narrowly focused on the battlefield. They use *information operations* to encompass both strategic and operational considerations. (See TRADOC, 1996.)

[28]See PCCIP (1997) for a broad identification of the infrastructures involved.

Internet, that network is so closely associated with this infrastructure that, for many, they are essentially equivalent terms. As a result, the dangers and pitfalls of the Internet, outlined above, form the basis for most of the hypothesized threats to the information infrastructure.[29] Frequent reports of computer accidents, computer crime, and possible "infoterrorism" have fixed in the public mind that remote access capability, the lack of central control, and interconnectivity mean that the Internet and computers in general are irremediably insecure.[30] Many of these reports are sensationalist or simply wrong, but a lack of general technical understanding of how computers and modern networks work has created an environment ripe for rumor and speculation.[31]

In the midst of this hype, there have been some real and serious incidents of computer security lapses with potential national security implications. The most troubling attack detected (and publicized) thus far occurred at the Air Force's command and control research facility at Rome Laboratory, New York. During March and April 1994, attackers gained control of Rome's operational network; copied sensitive, though not classified, information; and could have brought down the network and destroyed the information that it contained (although they chose not to). Air Force officials believe that at least one of the hackers may have been working for a foreign country, with the intent of either obtaining military research data or installing malicious code in software that would act as a logic bomb and, perhaps years later, disable sensitive systems.[32]

The message that the national security community has received is that both the military and society are reliant on information infrastructure and that they are vulnerable. The DoD has a vast informa-

---

[29]Definitions of the *Global Information Infrastructure* or the *Information Superhighway* always include the Internet as an important, often primary, component but generally also include other currently more critical components, such as proprietary computer networks and systems, public switched networks (such as the phone system), and the financial system, among others.

[30]For a compendium of such reports, see Schwartau (1994).

[31]Some hoaxes, such as the "Good Times Virus," which purports to be spreading a virus directly via e-mail, have so implanted themselves in the public consciousness that they are difficult to root out. For a compendium of virus and other computer hoaxes, see Rosenberger (1999).

[32]GAO (1996), pp. 18–28, details this and other, less severe attacks on DoD computers.

tion infrastructure, including 2.1 million computers, 10,000 local networks, 100 long-distance networks, 200 command centers, and 16 central computer-processing facilities (GAO, 1996, p. 10). In field testing, the Defense Information Systems Agency has determined that at least 65 percent of DoD unclassified computers are vulnerable to software attack (DSB, 1996, Sec. 2). Moreover, about 90 percent of the critical information needed for the planning and execution of military operations runs over commercial links, including the Internet, implying that the military depends upon infrastructure beyond its control (Casciano, 1996).[33]

Although strategic information warfare is clearly a possibility, the popular success of the Internet and the consequent extension of the Internet metaphor to the information infrastructure as a whole has caused the threat to be blown out of proportion. The Internet is a system with an open architecture specifically designed to facilitate exchange of information and easy access, with little attention, as yet, given to problems of security. Its decentralized, explosive growth, its large public profile, and its ethic of free exchange have reinforced these security problems. The Internet was not designed as a critical infrastructure whose continuous operation was essential to national security or even as a commercial system whose robustness was critical for corporate survival. Most elements of the wider information infrastructure (the electric power grid, the telephone system, various financial networks, etc.) were so designed. Although this does not imply that these systems are invulnerable, it does imply that we are unlikely to reveal their vulnerabilities by a comparison to the Internet.

**Operational Information Warfare.** The operational level of information warfare involves exploiting the battlefield applications of new information technologies, partially demonstrated at Al-Khafji, to create what ADM William Owens, former Vice Chairman of the Joint Chiefs of Staff, calls "a system of systems." This system would give the commander nearly complete knowledge of the battlefield. It consists of a suite of full-time sensors, data fusers, and interpreters in combination with instantaneous command, control, and communication systems; precise navigation; and electronic warfare, among

---

[33]TRADOC (1996), p. I-7, claims that 95 percent of peacetime military communications travel over the civilian public switched network.

others, which together create a "synergistic" increase in combat power that constitutes an information-based revolution in military affairs.

A critical element of this concept is the ability to use the information that the system of systems has gathered, processed, and disseminated. Thus, beyond information technologies, this revolution is enabled by the introduction and spread of precision-guided weaponry that can exploit the new information and serve as the blunt edge of the system of systems. Nonetheless, for these theorists, this is an information-based revolution because, with the eventual widespread availability of precision-guided weapons, the ability to achieve efficient information processes (and to stop the opponent from doing the same) becomes the key element of skill that differentiates military organizations.

Thus, information systems for command, control, and communication become so essential to combat operations that warfare becomes, conceptually, a contest between these systems rather than between strike systems, with information systems themselves as the most critical targets. In stark contrast to strategic information warfare, the operational level of information warfare distinctly favors an American military establishment that is further along and better positioned to take advantage of military applications of information technology. Indeed, for some, this advantage is the key to enabling a second "American century," as Henry Luce called the 20th century in 1950 (Nye and Owens, 1996; Friedman and Friedman, 1997).

Although many of these ideas about the future of warfare predate the Gulf War, they undoubtedly owe their current ascendance to its results. The Persian Gulf War shocked many observers not so much because of its outcome as because of the lopsided nature of the victory and the astonishingly few casualties on the coalition side.[34] As

---

[34]Stephen Biddle (1996) notes that the coalition suffered only 240 deaths out of an attacking force of 795,000 for a loss rate of less than 1 in 3,000, one-tenth the Israeli loss rate in the 1967 Six-Day war, one-twentieth of the Germans' in Poland and France in 1939–1940, and one-thousandth of the U.S. Marines' in the invasion of Tarawa in 1943.

mentioned, such unanticipated, lopsided victories have often been signals that revolutionary changes in warfare have occurred.[35]

In the wake of this victory, technology emerged as the popular hero of the conflict, although no single technology could claim credit for the victory. However, as Tomahawk missiles, laser-guided bombs, and extremely accurate tank rounds rained down on a nearly inert enemy, one key feature that struck many observers as novel and even revolutionary was the use of, and need for, information by the U.S.-led coalition forces to achieve this effect. If, as the popular saying goes, "anything that can be seen, can be killed," the process of seeing, identifying, and communicating information becomes the key skill element in military effectiveness.

During the war, large problems remained in coordinating large-scale operations and creating a reconnaissance-strike complex that could rapidly disseminate critical information to the appropriate shooters.[36] Nonetheless, the perception remains that the war demonstrated that the necessary technology exists or will soon exist to enable the completion of the revolution.

Since the Gulf War, the U.S. military has advanced quite far both in conceptualizing and applying new information technologies to operations. The new operational concepts promoted in the recent Quadrennial Defense Review demonstrate both their origins in the perceived lessons of the Persian Gulf War and the faith that new applications of information technologies either will, or already have, rectified any shortcomings revealed in that conflict (DoD, 1997). In the process, these concepts also reveal how much the U.S. military has come to believe that information technology can transform warfare. The concepts of "Dominant Maneuver," "Precision Strike," and even "Focused Logistics" all rest heavily on the perceived lessons of the Gulf War and demand ever more timely, accurate information to succeed. This, in turn, drives the search for ever more-powerful and

---

[35]The lopsided German victories over France in both 1870 and 1940 have often been attributed to the German's adoption of new technologies, particularly railroads and tanks, respectively, which the French either ignored or misused. See Krepinevich (1994).

[36]See Watts (1996) for a description of how coordination of forces was far from perfect during the Gulf War; see also Keaney and Cohen (1993), pp. 235–251. For an analysis of the role of information in the Persian Gulf War, see Campen (1992).

more-secure information systems. According to this vision, information technologies in the form of command and control systems, navigation, intelligence collection, surveillance, and reconnaissance provided the backbone for the coalition's dominance in the Gulf War and provide the basis for the hope of even greater success in the future.

**You Say You Want a Revolution?**  Before we allow these views to completely transform the force, however, it is worth examining the idea of a military revolution in more detail. There are two radically different, though perhaps complementary, ways to view a military revolution. Historians typically take a long view and see a military revolution as an observable breaking point between two recognizably different types of warfare. Before, for example, the "artillery revolution" of the 16th century, warfare largely consisted of long sieges of strategic fortresses. Afterward, war mostly meant fighting on open plains between massed armies, since fortresses were virtually useless in the face of artillery. This view of military revolutions tends to downplay the role of human agency in the making of a revolution. Such revolutions stem from exogenous forces, which were bound, sooner or later, to spark a fundamental shift in the methods of war. Technological, demographic, or social changes in this sense "push" the revolution into being.

Although the intellectual spark that reveals the possibility of a revolution gives a temporary, and possibly large, advantage to one side, that advantage is usually short-lived as the new method of fighting is copied by one's rivals.[37] After this period of emulation, the main thing that has changed is warfare itself. Any lasting effect on the relative power of states depends less on the intervening events than on the inherent geographical, social, or cultural advantages that particular states (or nonstate actors) possess in adopting the revolution. For example, the aircraft-carrier revolution of the interwar period most favored, in the long run, not the country that invented the technology (Britain) or the country that first melded that technology into a operational concept (Japan—although that country gained great temporary advantages) but the country whose large industrial base and population allowed it to produce expensive carriers and air-

---

[37]Krepinevich (1994) notes that such advantages are growing ever more fleeting.

planes rapidly and in large quantities—as well as the highly trained pilots to man them (the United States). (See Murray and Millett, 1996).

The second view is the strategist's view. The strategist is more concerned with the problems of the here and now and, as a result, sees a revolution as consisting of essentially clever, new solutions to previously insoluble geostrategic problems. These solutions usually, but not necessarily, use new technologies. In any case, the impetus is not some new exogenous technological or social reality but rather a particular nation's strategic problems. From this perspective, *blitzkrieg* was a revolution brought about by the German strategic imperative to avoid a long, drawn-out war on two fronts. Such strategic challenges "pull" the revolution together from the existing technological and social environment. Here, the roles of individual countries and thinkers loom large and can determine who sees the greatest advantage from an emerging revolution. In this story, *blitzkrieg* arose in Germany rather than in other countries not primarily because of superior intellectual ability or organizational capacity, but rather because *blitzkrieg* offered a solution to the Germans' pressing strategic problem.[38] Other countries did not develop *blitzkrieg*, in part because they did not have the same strategic problem. After the success of this new type of warfare had been demonstrated, opponents did not exactly emulate it but rather sought ways to counter it. When that problem had been solved, warfare soon "settled" into the tank battles of the second phase of World War II, resembling neither *blitzkrieg* nor the type of warfare that had preceded it.

These views of military revolutions do not strictly contradict each other. They can be reconciled by an understanding that sees the short-run motor of the strategist's revolution determining the path if not the ultimate outcome of the historian's revolution. However, in their details, these two views see very different revolutions and very different implications of any military revolution. The strategist's revolution is made; the historian's happens. In the World War II case, from the strategist's perspective, the revolution was *blitzkrieg*.

---

[38]Similarly, the Schlieffen plan of World War I to capture Paris in six weeks represents a failed attempt to solve that same problem.

From the historian's, it was the introduction of the tank and its associated technology to warfare that ultimately resulted not in *blitzkrieg*, which was premised on a surprise strike against the enemy's rear, but in the type of massed armored warfare that characterized the latter part of World War II. The strategist's revolution benefited the country that had to solve the two-front problem; the historian's benefited countries with the industrial and technological capability to produce good-quality tanks and airplanes in large numbers.

Indeed, a strategic "revolution" for which an effective counter is quickly found may not register at all on the historian's radar screen. Some might argue that the nuclear revolution, which in its early years gave the United States a substantial strategic advantage, effectively left warfare unchanged when proliferation and mutually assured destruction eventually negated that advantage. Nuclear weapons have radically altered the calculus involved in the decision to go to war, but as of yet, they have not greatly changed how we wage war.

The currently proposed information-based revolution in military affairs has been the most self-conscious military revolution in history, yet most commentators have largely passed over the question of whether they see themselves as creating a strategist's revolution or predicting an historian's. While both types of revolution have analytical validity in retrospect, the utility of the historian's viewpoint to inform the current debate is very limited. While contemporaries can and must *create* military revolutions in the strategic sense, their ability to *predict* military revolutions in the historic sense is virtually nonexistent. The record of contemporaries in understanding the historian's revolutions taking place around them is dismal and unlikely to improve.[39] This apparent myopia results largely because the paths that such revolutions take depend on the strategic problems and historical contingencies of the moment, not on the technological and geographic absolutes that ultimately determine the historian's revolutions. These revolutions only seem clear in retrospect.

The strategist's view is much more helpful for understanding the contemporary scene, because it concentrates our analysis on the geostrategic problems that are driving the creation of a military revo-

---

[39]See footnote 3.

lution. In the current situation, moreover, the strategist's view focuses our attention on some of the puzzling aspects of the currently proposed military revolution. Previous military revolutions have usually been spurred by military organizations with either recent failures or pressing geostrategic problems and vulnerabilities. These problems have generated extraordinary efforts both within and beyond the military that eventually result in revolutionary solutions. These innovations often come from champions outside the military. Only very rarely have militaries on the top of the heap, fresh off a dramatic victory like that in the Gulf War, been the source of such dramatic change. Nonetheless, the U.S. military is clearly on the forefront of the currently hypothesized revolution. To its credit, the U.S. defense establishment is consciously trying to upset this historic tendency by moving forward with revolutionary innovation despite its demonstrated superiority.

Such a "revolution by the strong" has historical precedents, but it is relatively rare and also a bit illogical. Revolutions, in contrast to the more mundane process of evolutionary innovation, upset the status quo in a consequential way. Evolutionary innovation allows you to do somewhat better what you already do; revolutionary change has the potential to make useless everything that went before it. When Admiral Jackie Fisher introduced the all–big gun battleship, the HMS *Dreadnought*, into the British fleet in 1907, it made every existing capital ship virtually obsolete. Although the world's strongest naval power introduced this innovation, that power suffered a relative loss of superiority when other nations emulated the *Dreadnought*.[40] Perhaps such ships were inevitable, in which case the British did well to get them first. Nonetheless, upsets to the status quo, whatever their source, present opportunities for those on the bottom to improve their relative positions and dangers for those on top to lose ground. The United States as the sole superpower and possessor of the world's most effective military would appear to have little to gain and much to lose, from a relative perspective, from any changes in the bases of power that its own revolutionary innovations might initiate.

This risk is often justified as a defensive measure. As with the *Dreadnought* revolution, this argument goes, the U.S. military must

---

[40]See Massie (1991), pp. 467–490, especially pp. 473, 485–489.

understand the revolution before an opponent grasps it and achieves a quantum leap in military power that would threaten U.S. superiority. This is a legitimate concern, but it highlights the confusion between the strategist's and the historian's views of military revolution. The idea that there is a single wave of technological change looming "out there" that will wash over all nations in roughly the same way corresponds to the historian's view. While useful in retrospect, it obscures the strategist's point that each country will adopt and even create new technologies in such a way as to attempt to solve its own geostrategic problems. Thus, if the United States wishes to avoid any nasty technological surprises, it must understand not only the nature of emerging technology but also how specific nations will apply that technology to their own particular geostrategic problems. Because technology does not dictate the path of the revolution, there is no race to reach some technological plateau before the other guy. Rather, the military must try to anticipate and counter other nations' potentially revolutionary innovations. This is a worthy goal, indeed a duty, for military planners, but it is not the path to military revolution. To propel the strategist's revolution, there must be a geostrategic problem to solve.

What geostrategic problems impel the U.S. military to embrace the idea that a revolution is necessary? They are not the problems of national defense, strictly speaking, but rather the problem of maintaining military leadership on the cheap. To maintain its status as the world's leading military power, the U.S. military cannot simply outmatch its opponents but rather must provide a capability to project power across vast distances and completely dominate its opponents in their own backyards. The military must further do so within the dictates of fairly strict limitations on the amount of time, blood, and treasure that can be spent to secure American leadership. According to Secretary of Defense William Cohen,

> [w]e don't want to engage in a fair fight, a contemporary war of attrition. We want to dominate across the full spectrum of conflict, so that if we ever do have to fight, we will win on our terms. (Cohen, 1997.)

To be successful in the long term, a strategy of military dominance requires victories of such a magnitude that they deter most challenges. There are simply not enough resources to do the job if all of the potential challengers decide to become active.  The American military strategist is seized with the geostrategic problem of providing military leadership with a limited budget, within a limited time, and with the approval of an extremely casualty-sensitive public. According to Joseph Nye and William Owens, "battlefield awareness cannot reduce the risk of casualties to zero, but it can keep that risk low enough to maintain the American public's support for the use of force." (Nye and Owens, 1996, p. 25.)  The revolutionary technologies and systems proposed as part of the ongoing (or forthcoming) military revolution do not offer the strategist the ability to accomplish tasks he cannot accomplish today.  Rather, they allow him to do so convincingly and within the confines of ever-diminishing resources and ever-increasing sensitivity to human losses, military and civilian.

The question remains, however, whether such a geostrategic problem, somewhat different in character than those in the past, can serve as the impetus for a military revolution according to the strategist's definition.  This particular geostrategic problem is, in part, socially and internally generated rather than a fact of geography or international politics, such as the two-front problem that confronted the German military in the first half of this century.  There is a tendency to view information technology, and technology in general, through the lens of American political needs.  The U.S. political system currently demands rapid victories, a less costly military, and an extreme sensitivity to casualties in many circumstances.  Naturally, this leads U.S. planners to attempt to solve those political problems through technology.  While this is appropriate, even essential, it does not reflect a fundamental change in the nature of warfare or national security, as its proponents often claim.  Rather, it reflects a change in the circumstances and manner in which the United States is willing to buy and use force.

The problematic aspect of this approach becomes apparent when the very success of these technologies and techniques creates ever-increasing demands on the military.  Nye and Owens (1996) assume that there is some level of casualties that the American people will accept for any given military operation.  However, as we have seen, that number evolves over time, depending in part on experience.  If the military manages to come up with a solution for its geostrategic problem through a clever application of military technologies, it may simply generate new pressures to further reduce the time, treasure, and blood spent to secure military goals. President Clinton was said to have asked before the intervention in Haiti what the casualty figures had been for recent U.S. military ventures in Panama, Grenada, and the Gulf, stating that he thought the public would tolerate the average (see Sapolsky and Shapiro, 1996).

The logical extrapolation of this thinking will quickly bring the military to a place in which technology will cease to provide answers to an increasingly difficult geostrategic problem. As Nye and Owens (1996) acknowledge, technology cannot provide a bloodless war. Eventually, technological solutions may cease to be able to provide an answer to the country's need for ever more-overwhelming victories at an ever-diminishing cost. In this sense, while this process may end up adding many new and effective information technologies to the military's arsenal, it is unlikely to succeed in being a revolutionary solution to the U.S. geostrategic problem.

## EVOLUTIONARY AND REVOLUTIONARY PROPOSALS

The battle over the use of the word *revolution* is often mischaracterized as a fight between those who favor change and those who favor stasis. Rejecting the idea of revolution does not mean that the U.S. military can or should stand still in the face of the whirl of changes going on around it. Even in the short term, change is necessary and inevitable. Revolution, however, is not. The distinction rests in which type of change is required, not in whether change takes place. An evolutionary response begins with existing doctrine, organizations, and systems and effects incremental changes to them as the new environment requires. A revolutionary response starts with the assumption that world has changed in some fundamental way that renders old structures irrelevant. It thus wipes them out and starts anew.

Current U.S. military efforts to deal with the changes brought about by information technology almost all fall into the evolutionary category. Rather than making wholesale reorganizations, the U.S. military has tended to graft these new ideas and new technologies onto old forms of organization and doctrine. An example is the U.S. Army's Force XXI digital experiment. This experimental force is theoretically capable of greatly increasing combat capability by providing individual soldiers and vehicles with enhanced battlefield aware-ness through a mobile computer network linked to a wide variety of sensors (see Hanna, 1997). Although this force incorporates a host of new technologies, it is built on existing weapons and vehicles and anticipates few major changes in the hierarchical organization, doc-trine, or size of the Army. The Army would remain a heavy force based on a combined-arms division as the unit of maneuver. Despite the use of the latest information technology for the creation of this force and frequent recourse to the rhetoric of revolution, this is clearly an evolutionary change.

Advocates of revolution tend to criticize U.S. military responses to new technology specifically on these terms. Military responses, according to revolution theorists, focus too often on how to improve current operations within the current context rather than on under-standing that new operations are required or that revolutionary developments have changed the context.[41] According to Andrew Krepinevich, an advocate of a major restructuring of U.S. forces, "The need for a transformation strategy [for the American military] . . . is being stimulated by a growing awareness that the world is likely entering into a period of military revolution." (Krepinevich, 1997.)

In contrast to the evolutionary approach of the military, the propos-als for change coming from advocates of social, political, or military revolutions recommend much more drastic measures that strike deep at the heart of the military doctrine, strategy, and organization. Such proposals are radical in design, usually (though not always) stem from outside the military, and justify their radical nature by the premise that some form of revolution is in the offing. Thus, despite their radical nature, each of these proposals is quite serious and has numerous supporters.

Proponents of a social revolution generally feel that the military should restructure, in a manner similar to that of corporations, to take advantage of the sources of power in the information age.[42] Arquilla and Ronfeldt (1997a), for example, argue that, given the ascendance of networked forms of organization in the new world to

---

[41]For example, see Nichiporuk and Builder (1995), p. 81, and Stein (1996).

[42]See Fukuyama and Shulsky, Chapter Eleven in this volume, for a discussion of the influence of the business literature on military restructuring.

come, the military should consider flattening its hierarchy by eliminating all levels between regional commander in chief and platoon. The resulting small maneuver units would operate independently but would be able to communicate and coordinate with each other and call on fire from assets owned by any service. They further advocate that this reorganization should be accompanied by a move to a swarm doctrine, whereby small units act independently toward a common goal (Arquilla and Ronfeldt, 1997a).

The theorists who have taken the idea of political revolution to heart advocate a reorientation of U.S. military forces that is in some ways even more radical. New information weapons will allow us to influence directly the perception and decisions of the enemy, implying the need for armed forces organizationally and doctrinally capable of waging a battle of words and image rather than of steel. The aim of military power, therefore, according to Richard Szafranski, is "to cause the enemy to choose not to fight by exercising reflexive influence . . . over the products of the adversary's neocortex." (Szafranski, 1997.)

The implications for doctrine and force structure of Szafranski's insight are vast. First, Szafranski recommends that the core element of the national security effort be shifted away from the development of destructive weapon platforms toward improving the intelligence-gathering and information-dissemination capabilities that count most in what is essentially a strategic-level psychological operation. Second, the residual force element of the military would consist of small, elite special forces units, in combination with air and space forces, capable of rapid, precise applications of force in support of the information campaign but incapable of large-scale warfare on the traditional model.[43]

The proposals for military restructuring by advocates of a military revolution are the least radical but are nonetheless quite far reaching. From outside the military, George and Meredith Friedman contend that precision-guided munitions and distant missile fires have rendered the tank, the airplane, and the aircraft carrier obsolete. These older technologies, in their view, have become "senile," which

---

[43]Szafranski (1997), pp. 395–416, especially pp. 405–412. Similar ideas are found in Stein (1996) and De Caro (1996)

is to say that incremental improvements serve only to protect the weapon, while diminishing its capability to carry out its original mission. The future will be revolutionized by long-distance, even intercontinental, precision-guided missile fires, an idea that implies a radical reorientation of military doctrine, organization, and weapon development. This notion leads them to advocate abandoning development of next-generation planes, tanks, and ships in favor of achieving the revolution (Friedman and Friedman, 1997).

From a more mainstream military source, ADM William Owens, former Vice Chairman of the Joint Chiefs of Staff, comes the idea of the "system of systems" discussed earlier. At first blush, this proposal might appear as just an evolutionary change in the capacity of command, control, communications, computing, intelligence, surveillance, and reconnaissance systems. However, its revolutionary nature resides in the profound challenge it offers to the Clausewitzian view of warfare that has guided American military doctrine since the Vietnam War.[44]

A central tenet of Clausewitzian thought is the idea of friction. For Clausewitz, friction is the force that makes the apparently simple tasks in war so difficult. The multiple interacting parts of any battle, the fragile psychology of human decisionmakers, and the danger and stakes involved in war create a situation that is ruled by chance, in which perfect or even good information is impossible and in which the commander must use intuition, achieve genius, and take risks to prevail. Owens (1996) believes, however, that advances in information technology will be revolutionary because they will allow the U.S. military to greatly reduce the role of friction and to achieve "dominant battlespace knowledge," or nearly complete situational awareness of the battlefield.[45]

If new technology can truly provide for this level of knowledge, the need for military commanders to take risks, an element that Clausewitz emphasized was critical for managing friction, become far less important than mastery of technology. U.S. military doctrine

---

[44] Carl Von Clausewitz, a Prussian military theorist, wrote his definitive work in 1832. See Clausewitz (1976).

[45] See Owens (1996), Nye and Owens (1996), Brown (1996) (citing others), and Widnall and Fogleman (1996) for examples. For Clausewitz's statement of the importance of friction, see Clausewitz (1976), pp. 100–102, 119–122.

still emphasizes the need for risk-taking behavior, specifically to counter the Clausewitzian uncertainty inherent in battle.[46] At the same time, however, new U.S. military doctrine has already begun to reflect the possibility that such qualities are no longer critical for success:

> In the past, leveraging a knowledge advantage to decisively achieve a desired end state has been largely an intuitive process. Truly exceptional commanders have almost always possessed this trait; less successful commanders often have not. Information technologies now hold a potential for making this grasp of the battlespace, and the inherent opportunities it affords, more accessible to every leader. (TRADOC, 1996, p. 1-10.)

The "system of systems" is thus revolutionary because it would reshape U.S. doctrine to de-emphasize many of the qualities that have historically been valued in a soldier. Commanders would no longer be encouraged to use intuition or take risks because "dominant battlespace knowledge" would render such attributes unnecessary or even dangerous. A radically different military and a very different style of fighting would certainly result.

Although all of these proposals are a long way from implementation, they all gain credence every time military professionals and analysts proclaim a revolution. One of the principal challenges for militaries in responding to change is to preserve the elements that were developed through hard experience and that can be adapted to the new environment. Those who too easily succumb to the temptation to label all changes revolutionary risk failing in this challenge and leave the field to those who would ignore the lessons of the past in the quest for the promise of the future.

## CONCLUSION: IMPLICATIONS OF A FALSE REVOLUTION

The word *revolution* is often bandied about with a reckless abandon that does little to enhance policymaking. We see, in addition to the information revolution and the revolution in military affairs, a wide variety of epoch-making events ranging from the "revolution in acquisition affairs" to the "revolution in military medical affairs."

---

[46]See, for example, TRADOC (1997), pp. 8-4 and 8-5.

Revolutions appear so omnipresent and common that they overwhelm their audience and become meaningless. This chapter has attempted to restore some of the meaning, and one hopes, some caution, to the use of the word *revolution* by highlighting the implications of declaring specific social, political, or technological changes revolutionary.

First, identification of a revolutionary change gives license to question all of the old assumptions about how to organize, equip, and use military forces. Essentially, wholesale, irreversible transformations in doctrine, equipment, and personnel are required by the possibility that we will be left behind by a revolution in military affairs.

Second, the use of the word *revolution* gives greater scope for outsiders to impose changes on the military. Military officers, rooted in their day-to-day routine and professionally and culturally attached to the current force structure, are often seen as incapable of implementing truly revolutionary change. In times of revolutionary changes, civilians have both greater scope and greater justification for imposing their views. Military expertise is discounted because it is seen as reflecting the experience of a bygone age.

The possibility that information technology will revolutionize warfare, through its effects on society, politics, or the military, cannot be definitively denied. Such revolutions, despite our best efforts, tend to come as surprises. Nonetheless, as this chapter has shown, there is substantial reason to doubt that any of these proposed revolutions are currently taking place. The current situation fails to satisfy the first and most important test of a social revolution: that it alter the sources of productivity improvements and therefore national economic strength. The political revolution idea is based on an inappropriate extrapolation of current trends and an ahistorical appreciation of the capacity of politicians and soldiers to adapt to new media technologies. Finally, the concept of a military revolution finds it roots in the political and social idiosyncrasies of the American polity, rather than in a truly geostrategic problem, the source of any strategist's military revolution. In short, these revolutions seem a weak foundation on which to rest proposals for the wholesale transformation of the U.S. armed forces, the most powerful military instrument in the history of the world.

# REFERENCES

Adams, James, "The Role of the Media," in Campen, Dearth, and Goodden (1996), pp. 107–118.

Alexander, Martin S., "The Fall of France, 1940," *Journal of Strategic Studies*, Vol. 13, No. 1, March 1990, pp. 10–44.

Allard, Kenneth, "Information Operations in Bosnia:  A Preliminary Assessment," Washington, D.C.:  National Defense University, Strategic Forum 91, November 1996.

Arquilla, John, and David F. Ronfeldt, *The Advent of Netwar*, Santa Monica, Calif.:  RAND, MR-789-OSD, 1996.

_____, "Looking Ahead:  Preparing for Information-Age Conflict," in Arquilla and Ronfeldt (1997b), 1997a, pp. 463–473.

Arquilla, John, and David Ronfeldt, eds., *In Athena's Camp:  Preparing for Conflict in the Information Age*, Santa Monica, Calif.: RAND, MR-880-OSD/RC, 1997b.

Bacevich, Andrew J., *The Pentomic Era:  The US Army between Korea and Vietnam*, Washington, D.C.:  National Defense University Press, 1986.

Biddle, Stephen, "Victory Misunderstood:  What the Gulf War Tells Us about the Future of Conflict," *International Security*, Vol. 21, No. 2, Fall 1996, p. 142.

Biddle, Stephen, "Assessing Theories of Future Warfare," paper presented to the 1997 Annual Meeting of the American Political Science Association, August 29, 1997, pp. 24–33.

Bond, Brian, and Williamson Murray, "British Armed Forces, 1918–1939," in Millett and Murrray (1988), pp. 112–113.

Brown, Charles H., *The Correspondent's War*, New York:  Charles Scribner's Sons, 1967.

_____, "The RMA:  The Information Dimension," in Campen, Dearth, and Goodden (1996).

Bunker, Robert J., "The Tofflerian Paradox," *Military Review,* Vol. 75, No. 3, May/June 1995, pp. 199–202.

Campen, Alan D., ed., *The First Information War: The Story of Communications, Computers and Intelligence Systems,* Fairfax, Va.: AFCEA International Press, 1992.

Campen, Alan D., Douglas H. Dearth, and R. Thomas Goodden, eds., *Cyberwar: Security, Strategy, and Conflict in the Information Age,* Fairfax, Va.: AFCEA International Press, 1996.

Casciano, Major General John P., "Information Warfare," speech to Aerospace Education Foundation Forum, Los Angeles, October 18, 1996.

Cerf, Christopher, and Victor Navasky, *The Experts Speak,* New York: Pantheon Books, 1984.

Clausewitz, Carl von, *On War,* Princeton, N.J.: Princeton University Press, 1976.

Cohen, Eliot A., "Defense Book Reviews," *Foreign Affairs,* Vol. 73, No. 5, July/August 1994.

Cohen, William S., Secretary of Defense, quoted in Philip Shenon, "Troop Cuts Likely to Be Main Result of Major Review," *New York Times,* April 29, 1997, p. A1.

Cooper, Jeffrey R., "Another View of Information Warfare," in Schwartzstein (1996), p. 120.

De Caro, Chuck, "Softwar," in Campen, Dearth, and Goodden (1996), pp. 204ff.

Dearth, Douglas, and Charles Williams, "Information Age/Information War," in Campen, Dearth, and Goodden (1996)

Defense Science Board, "Report of the Defense Science Board Task Force on Information Warfare—Defense," November 1996.

Dewar, James A., *The Information Age and the Printing Press: Looking Backward to See Ahead,"* Santa Monica, CA: RAND, P-8014, 1998.

Dinardo, R. L., and Daniel J. Hughes, "Some Cautionary Thoughts on Information Warfare," *Airpower Journal*, Winter 1995, p. 2.

DoD—*see* U.S. Department of Defense.

DSB—*see* Defense Science Board.

Dunlap, Charles, "How We Lost the High-Tech War of 2007," *The Weekly Standard*, January 29, 1996.

Freedman, Lawrence, and Efraim Karsky, "How Kuwait Was Won: Strategy in the Gulf War," *International Security*, Vol. 16, Fall 1991, p. 39.

Friedman, George, and Meredith Friedman, *The Future of War: Power, Technology and American World Dominance in the 21st Century*, New York: St Martin's Press, 1997.

GAO—*see* U.S. General Accounting Office.

Gibson, William, *Neuromancer*, New York: Ace Books, 1984.

Gouré, Daniel, "The Impact of the Information Revolution on Strategy and Doctrine," in Schwartzstein (1996), p. 230.

Hanna, Mark, "Task Force XXI: The Army's Digital Experiment," Washington, D.C.: National Defense University, Strategic Forum 119, July 1997.

Hosmer, Stephen T., *Psychological Effects of U.S. Air Operations in Four Wars, 1941–1991: Lessons for U.S. Commanders*, Santa Monica, Calif.: RAND, MR-576-AF, 1996.

Joint Staff, *Joint Doctrine for Command and Control Warfare*, Joint Publication 3-13.1, February 7, 1996.

Keaney, Thomas A., and Eliot A. Cohen, *Gulf War Air Power Survey: Summary Report (GWAPS)*, Washington, D.C.: U.S. Government Printing Office, 1993.

Krepinevich, Andrew F., "From Cavalry to Computer: The Pattern of Military Revolutions," *The National Interest*, Fall 1994, pp. 30–42.

_____, "Transforming the American Military," speech to the George Bush School of Government and Public Service at the Texas A&M

University, 1 September 1997.  Last accessed on January 27, 1999 at **http://www.csbahome.com/Publications/bush%20speech.htm**

Larson, Eric V., *Casualties and Consensus:  The Historical Role of Casualties in Domestic Support for U.S. Military Operations*, Santa Monica, Calif.:  RAND, MR-726-RC, 1996.

Libicki, Martin C., *The Mesh and the Net:  Speculations on Armed Conflict in a Time of Free Silicon*, Washington, D.C.:   U.S. Government Printing Office, 1994.

\_\_\_\_\_, *What Is Information Warfare?* Washington, D.C.:  National Defense University, 1995.

Mahnken, Thomas G., "War in the Information Age," *Joint Forces Quarterly*, Winter 1995–1996, pp. 39–43

Massie, Robert K., *Dreadnought:  Britain, Germany and the Coming of the Great War*, New York:  Random House, 1991.

Matthews, Jessica, "Power Shift," *Foreign Affairs*, January–February 1997, pp. 50–66.

Millett, Allan R., and Williamson Murrray, *Military Effectiveness*, Vol. II, Boston:  Unwin Hyman, 1988.

Molander, Roger C., Andrew S. Riddile, and Peter Wilson. *Strategic Information Warfare:  A New Face of War*, Santa Monica, Calif.: RAND, MR-661-OSD, 1996.

Murray, Williamson, "Thinking about Revolutions in Military Affairs," *Joint Forces Quarterly*, Summer 1997, pp. 60–76.

Murray, Williamson, and Allan R. Millett, editors, *Military innovation in the Interwar Period*, New York:  Cambridge University Press, 1996.

Neuman, Johanna, *Lights, Camera, War: Is Media Technology Driving International Politics?* New York: St. Martin's Press, 1996.

Nichiporuk, Brian, and Carl H. Builder, *Information Technologies and the Future of Land Warfare*, Santa Monica, Calif.:  RAND, MR-560-A, 1995.

Nye, Joseph S., Jr., and William A. Owens, "America's Information Edge," *Foreign Affairs*, Vol. 75, No. 2, March/April 1996, pp. 20–36.

Owens, William A., "Foreword" in Schwartzstein (1996), p. xi

Pool, Ithiel de Sola, *Technologies of Freedom*, Cambridge: Belknap Press, 1983.

PCCIP—*see* President's Commission on Critical Infrastructure Protection.

President's Commission on Critical Infrastructure Protection, *Critical Foundations: Protecting America's Infrastructures*, October 1997.

Rosenberger, Rob, Computer Virus Myths Home Page. Last accessed September 2, 1997 at **http://www.kumite.com/myths**

Sapolsky, Harvey M., and Jeremy Shapiro, "Casualties, Technology, and America's Future Wars," *Parameters*, Summer 1996, pp. 119–127.

Schwartau, Winn, *Information Warfare: Chaos on the Electronic Superhighway*, New York: Thunder's Mouth Press, 1994.

Schwartzstein, Stuart J. D., *The Information Revolution and National Security: Dimensions and Directions*, Washington, D.C.: CSIS, 1996.

Sciolino, Elaine, "War Theater: The New Face of Battle Wears Greasepaint," *New York Times*, February 22, 1998, Sec. 4, p. 1.

Shane, Scott, *Dismantling Utopia: How Information Ended the Soviet Union*, Chicago: Ivan Dee, 1994.

Sims, Calvin, "Computer Failure Disrupts AT&T Long Distance," *New York Times*, January 15, 1990, p. 1.

Stein, George, "Information Warfare," in Campen, Dearth, and Goodden (1996), pp. 175–184.

Stephenson, Neal, *Snow Crash*, New York: Bantam Books, 1993.

Stolfi, R. H. S., "Equipment for Victory in 1940," *History*, Vol. 55, 1970, pp. 1–20.

Sun Tzu, *The Art of War*, trans. Samuel B. Griffith, Oxford: Clarendon Press, 1963.

Szafranski, Richard, "Neocortical Warfare? The Acme of Skill," in Arquilla and Ronfeldt (1997b), 1997, p. 405.

Szafranski, Richard, and Martin C. Libicki, ". . . Or Go Down in Flame? Toward an Airpower Manifesto for the Twenty-First Century," *Airpower Journal*, Fall 1996, pp. 65–79.

Toffler, Alvin, and Heidi Toffler, *War and Anti-War: Survival at the Dawn of the 21st Century*, Boston: Little, Brown, 1993.

Toffler, Alvin, *The Third Wave*, New York: Morrow, 1980.

TRADOC—*see* U.S. Army Training and Doctrine Command.

U.S. Army Training and Doctrine Command, FM 100-6 *Information Operations*, August 1996.

_____, FM 100-5 *Operations*, Final Draft, August 5, 1997.

U.S. Department of Defense, *Conduct of the Persian Gulf War*, Washington, D.C.: U.S. Government Printing Office, 1992.

_____, *Report of the Quadrennial Defense Review*, May 1997.

U.S. General Accounting Office, *Information Security: Computer Attacks at the Department of Defense Pose Increasing Risks*, GAO/AIMD-96-84, May 1996.

Watts, Barry D., *Clausewitzian Friction and Future War*, Washington, D.C.: Institute for National Strategic Studies, National Defense University, McNair Paper 52, 1996.

Widnall, Sheila, and Richard Fogleman, "Cornerstones of Information Warfare," U.S. Air Force White Paper, ca. 1996. Last accessed January 27, 1999 at **http://www.af.mil/lib/corner.html**

# Part II

# U.S. OPPORTUNITIES AND VULNERABILITIES

# Chapter Six

# INFORMATION AND WARFARE:  NEW OPPORTUNITIES FOR U.S. MILITARY FORCES

*Edward Harshberger and David Ochmanek*

> Know your enemy, know yourself; your victory will never be endangered.  Know the ground, know the weather; your victory will then be total.
>
> *—Sun Tzu (trans. Griffith, 1963, p. 129.)*

Any complex undertaking in which the actions of a large number of people must be coordinated will be information intensive.  Think of the production of a complex piece of machinery, the construction of a large building, or the operation of a transportation network.  The participants in such activities must know their roles, must be informed of the status of other aspects of the project, and must be able to adjust their activities in reaction to unforeseen events.  Someone must also be able to oversee the process, make decisions, and communicate those decisions to others involved.  All of this activity creates demands for the generation and communication of information.

The same holds true for warfare:  Successfully conducting any aspect of a major military operation demands that the participants be informed about their objective, the means at their disposal for achieving it, the enemy's capabilities and activities, relevant environmental conditions, the status of the unfolding operation, and a host of other factors, many of which can change at a moment's notice.  No wonder those who provide communications to military commands and units have encountered an almost limitless demand for bandwidth.

In this chapter, we offer a framework that identifies the major "information" dimensions of large-scale military operations. We then apply this framework to current and emerging information capabilities available to U.S. military forces. In this way, we assess the degree to which the growing capability to gather, process, interpret, and disseminate information might offer opportunities to improve the effectiveness of U.S. military operations.

## INFORMATION IN WARFARE: A SIMPLE TAXONOMY

Writing in the 4th century BCE, the Chinese scholar Sun Tzu clearly recognized the centrality of accurate and timely information to the military commander. In his pithy way, Sun Tzu also pointed to several of the most important dimensions of warfare in which information plays a decisive role. First among these is knowing your enemy.

### Knowing the Enemy

A commander wants to know a host of things about the forces arrayed against him—their size, the number and types of equipment available to them, their location, their readiness for battle, the extent of their logistics base, the intentions of the enemy commander, and more. The more accurate one's picture of the enemy in all of these dimensions, the better one can prepare operational plans, array one's own forces and assets, and anticipate the course of future events.

It is in the nature of warfare that knowledge of the enemy is almost always highly imperfect. Clausewitz certainly believed this. He observed that a "great part of the information obtained in war is contradictory, a still greater part is false, and by far the greatest part is of a doubtful character." (trans. Graham, 1968, p. 162.) Clausewitz likened the result to seeing through a "fog" or "twilight." This "difficulty of seeing things correctly," he concluded, "is one of the greatest sources of friction in war." (trans. Graham, 1968, p. 163.)

One way to judge the enduring validity of Clausewitz's observations is to consider the quality of the information available to the leaders of the coalition's forces during the Gulf War. Arguably, no military force has ever had a clearer picture of its enemy: In five months of buildup and six weeks of combat, coalition forces brought to bear against the Iraqis an unprecedented set of reconnaissance capabilities, including airborne and space-based imaging sensors, electronic signal collectors, and human intelligence assets. Moreover, these reconnaissance assets were able to operate with relative impunity around; above; and, in some cases, within Iraqi territory and airspace.

Nonetheless, it became clear after the war that coalition analysts and leaders had formed a picture of their adversary that was, in some important ways, far from perfect. The coalition had miscalculated the strength of the Iraqi ground forces facing them, had vastly underestimated Iraq's capacity to produce weapons of mass destruction, was unable to find and target mobile surface-to-surface missiles that bedeviled them, and had underestimated Saddam Hussein's ability to maintain himself in power. If this flawed picture is as good as any commander has ever had, one can begin to grasp the vast uncertainties that have faced military commanders throughout history.

## Knowing Yourself

As important as knowing the enemy is the need for accurate information on the capabilities, limitations, and location of one's own forces. It is not immediately obvious why gaining such information should be difficult. After all, the enemy is working to conceal his actions from you, but your own forces have no such motivation. Nevertheless, the fog of war also affects the picture that commanders have of their own forces.

Commanders at the highest levels have often found it difficult to maintain a clear picture of operations that may be taking place hundreds of miles away. The younger Moltke, trying to direct the German advance through France in August and September 1914, became less and less confident in the ability of his forces to carry out the ambitious encirclement maneuver called for in the Schlieffen Plan. In the end, he ordered a sudden withdrawal based primarily on the observations of a junior staff officer dispatched to the front to assess the situation—a decision whose merits are still the subject of historical debate.

Misconceptions about one's own forces and their status also arise at lower levels. One of the most problematic of these is the difficulty of knowing the exact location of other friendly units during the heat of battle. In situations where friendly and enemy forces are mingled, it becomes very difficult to bring effective fire support to bear on the enemy without risking friendly casualties. U.S. air and ground forces have devised elaborate procedures for controlling fires in close proximity to friendly troops. These have included creating lines of demarcation governing friendly fires, equipping aircraft and vehicles with special transponders, and placing special markings on friendly vehicles. In spite of these and other measures, no foolproof means has yet been found to preclude "blue-on-blue" engagements.[1]

## Knowing the Ground, Knowing the Weather

Knowledge of the terrain has always been a top priority for military forces. Indeed, one of the first challenges commanders and their staffs encounter in wartime has often been the need to get decent maps of the area of operations. In the mid-1960s, when the United States first began to commit combat forces to Vietnam, oil company road maps were for some time the best maps available to many units. Of course, even when good maps were produced, tactical comman- ders in Vietnam often found themselves operating in unfamiliar and unfavorable terrain.

Airmen, too, need timely and accurate information about the envi- ronment. Only since the Gulf War has the U.S. Air Force begun to field munitions that can be delivered with precision in all types of weather. Prior to that, knowing what the weather was in the target area was essential to the success of the mission. No one wanted to run the risks of flying through heavy air defenses only to find that the target was obscured by clouds or fog. Likewise, air crews want to have confidence that the weather at their recovery bases will be ade- quate for safe landings when they return from a sortie.

## Controlling Forces

Another vital dimension of warfare in which information plays a critical role is control—the ability to direct the activities of forces in

---

[1]It is thought that some of the casualties inflicted on friendly ground forces in the Gulf War were from allied fires.

the field. It is said that no plan survives first contact with the enemy. Once the battle is joined, it is essential that commanders be able to adjust the focus of their forces' efforts, exploiting opportunities and limiting vulnerabilities as the tactical situation dictates.

Because exercising control over engaged forces is so important, limitations on the mechanisms of control have been a determining factor shaping the organization of military forces and tactics they employ. Before long-distance communications, a commander's span of control was limited to the subordinates who could directly hear his voice. Modern communications allow control over much greater distances. Nonetheless, even given modern communications, a single commander can only exercise close control over a finite number of other soldiers during a fast-moving battle. And while radios, digitized messages, electronic maps, and symbology have improved upon the human voice in many ways, none of these enhancements has done much to expand the cognitive capacity of the individual tactical commander.

## Speed and Decisiveness

Having good information and control systems is one thing. Acting on them is another. Generally, the closer one is to the tactical battle, the more demanding are the timelines. For ground units involved in a firefight or air crews in an aerial engagement, seconds count. During a battle or a campaign, operational-level commanders may have only a few hours in which to make decisions about the allocation of forces available to them. In both cases, the value of information about the enemy can be quite fleeting.

This intimate relationship between information and action is nicely summarized by John Boyd's "OODA loop." Boyd—a fighter pilot of great skill—believed that success in warfare is heavily dependent upon the ability to act more quickly than one's opponent can react. He identified four activities to be accomplished in sequence: *"observe, orient, decide, act"* (OODA). In war, the side that can get these right and do them more quickly will generally come out on top, whether at the engagement, tactical, or operational level. Clearly, capabilities that enhance one's ability to acquire, process, and disseminate information quickly and effectively have the potential to improve performance in every aspect of the OODA loop.

## A Two-Sided Game

The OODA loop highlights the fact that warfare at all levels is a two-sided game. That is, even as one is trying to form a clearer picture of the enemy, one's own forces, and the environment or is trying to control one's own forces, the enemy is at the same time working to counter these efforts. This fact renders even the most simple of tasks difficult to execute in the presence of the enemy.

A competent commander will always actively try to keep his opponent guessing about the force he is facing. Eisenhower, for example, used a variety of deceptive measures, including the creation of an entire phantom corps under a real commander (Patton), to convince Hitler that the allied invasion of Europe would take place near Calais, rather than in Normandy.

In maneuver warfare, especially, denying the enemy an accurate picture of the battlefield is critical. Knowing where the gaps are in the enemy's forces can allow a fast-moving attacker to concentrate his forces and to exploit those gaps. Conversely, knowing where one's opponent is about to strike can enable the defender to concentrate forces (or fires) in anticipation of the attack. And a commander who cannot know with confidence where his opponent might attack must either be prepared to give ground or must spread his forces across the battlefield in an attempt to hedge against surprise. As Sun Tzu (trans. Griffith, 1963, p. 98) also observed, an enemy who prepares to fight everywhere is weak everywhere. In general, as forces gain improved capabilities to observe each other, the value of deception and speed of maneuver increases.

## FUTURE VICTORY: NEW OPPORTUNITIES

Discussions of the recent, rapid advances in military information capabilities often slip into the realm and vernacular of science fiction. Terms like "virtual battlespace" and "cyberwar" appear and disappear from the literature, to be replaced by others like "net-centric warfare." All of this churn and froth leads to skepticism on the part of military professionals, as well it should. After all, we have as yet little experience with using modern, computer-based information systems in battle conditions, and it is sometimes difficult to know just how such systems will perform and how they might affect the conduct of military operations.

Yet, some conclusions can be drawn. Advances in information technology are undoubtedly real and (at least in some instances) of obvious benefit. The National Defense Panel, which Congress commissioned in 1997 to evaluate the work of the Pentagon's Quadrennial Defense Review, stated in its report that U.S. forces "are on the cusp of a military revolution stimulated by rapid advances in information and information-related technologies." Many other observers accept this proposition, but what might such a revolution mean, and where might it manifest itself, in more concrete terms? The continuing challenge for military planners is to place these new information technologies and capabilities into a logical construct with ties to current and past military thought and operations. The following subsection attempts to aid in that task by exploring how new capabilities to acquire, process, and disseminate information apply to each "information" dimension of warfare.

## Military Advances in Information Technology

**Know Your Enemy.** Some of the most dramatic changes in the capabilities of U.S. forces to gather, evaluate, and disseminate information involve increased knowledge of the enemy. In general, we can break these capabilities into two broad areas:

- Ubiquitous, near real-time surveillance sensors using multiple phenomena

- Processors and communication systems that enable fusion, transfer, and display of information from these sensors.

In combination, these new capabilities have fundamentally altered the state of knowledge that U.S. commanders have about the location and disposition of enemy forces. Improved information capabilities can also provide commanders with vital clues about an enemy's *intent*. Such information has been rare in the past, but, when attained, often critically important.

As a nation, we have become accustomed to seeing startlingly clear satellite pictures of military forces in distant parts of the world. Spaceborne sensors have steadily improved since the 1960s, and today they can provide nearly constant coverage of many of the military activities of potential opponents. While not perfect—a fact underscored by the difficulties in locating and assessing Iraq's efforts to produce weapons of mass destruction—our ability to observe and assess the overall military capabilities and activities of potential adversaries is vastly greater than it was just a few decades ago.

However, even more-dramatic changes are occurring at the operational level of war. Among the most striking images from the Gulf War are depictions of moving enemy ground forces, at points far from the Saudi border, as they advanced toward Khafji or fled from Kuwait City. A snapshot of such a display is shown in Figure 6.1, with each square representing a moving vehicle.

This knowledge of the situation on the ground, covering thousands of square kilometers and delivered in "real time," arises from new sensors, such as the moving target indicator radar aboard the Joint Surveillance Target Attack Radar System (JSTARS). By exploiting breakthroughs in radar technology and signal processing, the JSTARS aircraft is able to detect and locate moving vehicles with some preci-

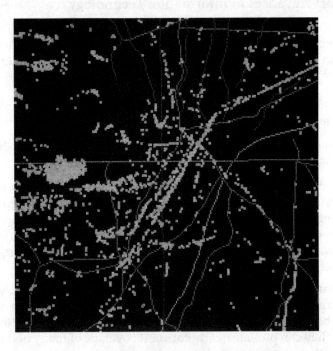

**Figure 6.1—JSTARS Picture of Moving
Mechanized Forces**

sion. This picture can be enhanced by integrating information from other sensors, such as synthetic aperture radars (on board JSTARS) or other imaging sensors that can be carried by smaller unmanned aerial vehicles (UAVs). Because of these types of systems, our knowledge of enemy movements beyond the horizon of friendly ground forces is orders of magnitude more accurate, timely, and reliable than ever before.

Even so, such information would count for little if it could not be placed in the hands of commanders and forces in the field. Moreover, commanders also want to know which units are where and what their strength and intentions are. Building this fuller picture and putting it in the right place require the capability to communicate large quantities of information over great distances, coupled with the capability to bring multiple sources of information together coherently.

And the types of information available are many. The Predator UAV, first used in Bosnia, sends back a real-time video feed from optical sensors. Rivet Joint and other aircraft gather information on radar, radio, and other emissions of enemy forces, the analysis of which can help identify unit and equipment type and location. Of course, reporting by human sources also remains essential. To deal with this massive flow of disparate types of data, U.S. forces are aided by the same kinds of information processing and display technologies that are revolutionizing the workplace. Our military forces can tap into the same digital satellite communication systems that carry civilian traffic every day and can augment these capabilities with secure military systems, such as the Military Strategical and Tactical Relay System and the Global Broadcast System. In the theater, specialized and common digital communications systems, such as the Joint Tactical Information Distribution System, can bring together most— if not all—of these information sources coherently on common displays in multiple command centers.

The net result of the mix of these systems is a dramatically improved picture of the operational battlefield for military leaders and staffs at many levels of command. This knowledge reduces the likelihood of surprise at the operational and tactical levels, increases the commander's decision timelines, and moves U.S. commanders closer to an understanding of enemy intent, a critical step toward thwarting that intent and enforcing our own.

**Know Yourself.** Throughout history, as the scale and geographic scope of military operations have grown, one of the greatest roadblocks to effective operations has been uncertainty about the disposition of one's own forces. The first dimension of this is simple location: A long-standing joke notes that one of the most dangerous things in the military is "a second lieutenant with a map." In a stressful, unfamiliar, and changing environment, forces can simply get lost. This has led to catastrophic consequences in the past, among them failure to support other forces effectively when those forces come under fire; exposure of a unit's flanks to attack; and at times, losses due to "friendly fire."

The potential sources of this problem have been many—poor maps, different coordinate systems, and individual incompetence, to name a few. One technology has transformed this problem: the Global Positioning System (GPS). GPS is based upon a constellation of satellites, each of which continuously broadcasts a time signal. By receiving and analyzing the minute differences in the arrival times of these time signals, a simple, portable GPS receiver (some of which are now commercially available) can determine its position to within tens of meters anywhere in the world.

Enhanced knowledge of position, coupled with improved means of communication, can dramatically change the nature of ground forces' operations. When creating operational plans, higher-level U.S. commanders can effectively monitor and coordinate the location and movement of all of their forces. This capability has the potential to reduce substantially the possibility of casualties by "friendly fire"—a development that will be furthered by improved Identification Friend or Foe capabilities for both air and ground forces.

The second key element of information regarding one's own force disposition is knowledge of the state of supply and logistics. The availability of supplies (or lack thereof) has determined the outcome of many battles. For the United States, this issue takes on overwhelming importance as one realizes the distance at which U.S. forces tend to fight and the massive amounts of supplies that must be provided to sustain high-intensity operations. Here, commercial technologies and practices are helping to increase the efficiency and effectiveness with which U.S. forces are supplied. For example, the same bar-coding and worldwide database technologies that Federal

Express and the United Parcel Service have pioneered to automate their tracking and delivery systems are becoming commonplace in military depots, flight lines, and loading docks. These and other approaches are moving U.S. forces toward the logisticians' holy grail of "total asset visibility"—real-time knowledge of the position and destination of all critical supplies.

A third way in which information-related capabilities can assist commanders is in the ability to control and direct one's forces. Here, each of the capabilities discussed above plays a role. Sensors, processing, and communications combine to provide at least the beginnings of what is often termed a "common operating picture" for commanders across the theater, at multiple levels of command, and across multiple military branches. This, in itself, is an important step toward control—history is replete with instances when different views of reality led to miscommunication between commanders.

Increasingly secure, wide-area communications will continue to improve the likelihood that commands will reach their destinations. The advent of modern communication systems has another effect: garbled or incomplete information is being replaced by standardized message sets with less chance for confusion or ambiguity upon reception. The combination of these capabilities makes it far more likely than ever before that a U.S. commander's orders will be communicated to the correct subordinates and understood when received.

**Know the Ground, Know the Weather.** In a time when commercial aircraft fly in almost any weather and roads are (generally) quickly cleared during snowstorms, it is often easy to forget the dramatic effects that weather and terrain continue to have on military operations. For a mechanized ground force, the difference between the rate of mechanized advance on an open plain and that through a swamp can be the difference between success and failure. Coordination of an infantry assault in driving rain is qualitatively different from the same maneuver in good weather.

So it is not surprising that timely and accurate information on the operating environment remains at the top of the list of U.S. military commanders' needs. For this reason, the U.S. defense establishment maintains global weather observation and forecasting networks, augmenting the capability of civilian weather satellites with military systems that focus on areas of greatest interest. All four military services participate in this activity, and high-quality weather information is available to forces worldwide, 24 hours a day.

Beyond predicting the weather, U.S. forces are, to an increasing extent, doing something about it. Obviously, we cannot (yet) control the weather, but new systems are enabling some military forces to operate more effectively in spite of adverse weather conditions. Since the dawn of military aviation, effective reconnaissance and attack operations have depended on clear weather: Air crews had to be able to see their targets to photograph or attack them effectively. Even the laser-guided bombs that proved so accurate in Operation Desert Storm, Bosnia, and elsewhere can only be delivered through fairly clear skies. Today, however, U.S. forces are beginning to field a new generation of munitions that are guided to their targets by the use of GPS signals. These low-cost munitions will be nearly as accurate as laser-guided weapons, and they can be used in all kinds of weather. By eliminating the need to point a laser at the target, this guidance technique will also enable aircraft to attack targets at longer ranges. As sensors and processors become smaller, cheaper, and more capable, increasing numbers of munitions will be fielded that will find and home in on their targets autonomously. Radar sensors on satellites and aircraft are also enabling U.S. forces to conduct reconnaissance of enemy forces and targets at night and through clouds.

U.S. forces are also benefiting from enhanced knowledge of terrain. The U.S. Defense Mapping Agency has, for the past two decades, been engaged in developing digital information on land surfaces throughout the world. Digital information includes digital versions of standard maps (allowing such information to be used on computer displays), digital wide-area photography, and Digitized Terrain Elevation Data—vertical profiles of terrain features. Used in combination, these sources of topographic information are allowing U.S. forces to "know the terrain" by creating three-dimensional imagery for use in mission planning, mission rehearsal, and training systems. During operations in Bosnia, for example, Air Force and Navy pilots used this information loaded into simulators at their bases or on their ships to "fly" simulated missions over difficult and unknown terrain many times before flying an actual mission. The result has been a higher mission success rate and fewer bombs that miss their targets.

**Know When Victory Is Endangered.** The preceding pages paint a rosy picture regarding the rapidly increasing amount and quality of information available to U.S. warfighters. We are, in fact, on (or even beyond) the cusp of a revolution. But just like political revolutions, technical revolutions can be dangerous to those involved: by building and relying on new systems and concepts, we inevitably create new concerns and potential vulnerabilities. In this respect, we should not forget that warfare is a two-sided affair, and that challenges to U.S. "information dominance" in war can come from many directions.

In particular, as U.S. commanders adjust their forces, training, and operations to take advantage of increased knowledge and better communications, the impact of losing these capabilities can become more serious. Attempts by an adversary to deny the U.S. timely and accurate information can take many forms. Most straightforward are those that might be termed traditional approaches: electronic jamming, physical destruction of sensors and control means, deception, and disinformation. Some aspects of new U.S. capabilities do, in fact, appear susceptible to these means: For example, GPS signals are quite weak and can be jammed under some circumstances, and satellite communications generally rely on relatively few ground stations.

However, a more ominous aspect of new information systems is their susceptibility to more subtle attacks. The amount of computer-based information, the automation that handling this information requires, and the increased connectivity of systems means that a capable opponent might attempt to use the U.S. information and information systems as weapons, by inserting computer viruses or false information into U.S. information networks. The effects of such attacks could be manifested at all levels of warfare, from strategic to tactical.[2]

For the present and near future, the United States appears to have a distinct advantage in almost all areas of this two-sided struggle for

_____

[2]See, for example, Molander, Riddile, and Wilson (1996).

information dominance.[3]  In the area of traditional means, the United States' conventional military capabilities stand alone—even in 1991, the systematic destruction, jamming, and spoofing of Iraq's surveillance and control systems was an unquestioned success.  And development and reliance on computer and communication systems have paid a dividend in terms of knowledge of system vulnerabilities and the means to exploit and reduce these.  As knowledge of advanced information systems spreads, however, it will become increasingly difficult to maintain this lopsided advantage.

## How New Information Capabilities Might Affect U.S. Military Operations

**Tactical-Level Effects.**  At the tactical level, information is critical for assuring that systems that are meant to attack the enemy have targets to shoot at; that when they shoot, they do so accurately; and that what they are shooting at is, in fact, what they think it is.  A fighter pilot may see a "blip" on his radar scope.  This blip constitutes a datum—a piece of evidence to be used for reasoning or inference. The pilot may use other data—the location and form of the blip, its direction and velocity, responses to electronic interrogation—to help inform his or her judgment about whether the source of the blip is a mountain, a cloud, an electronic anomaly on the scope, or an aircraft—friendly or enemy.  Some of these data can be used to guide a weapon to the target if the pilot decides to attack the source of the blip. All of this takes place at the engagement and tactical levels.

Information is also a key to survivability on the battlefield.  Just as information is needed to locate, identify, and engage targets, it is also useful in helping combatants determine whether or not they are someone else's target.  It is thought that the crews of most of the aircraft lost in combat are not aware that they have been engaged by the enemy until the final seconds of the engagement.  In the airmen's lexicon, these victims had inadequate "situational awareness," which has been shown in training to be at least as important as major aircraft performance parameters in determining the results of air-to-air

---

[3]Of course, the growing role of advanced information systems in the United States economy may be creating vulnerabilities that adversaries can exploit.  See Molander, Riddile, and Wilson (1996).

combat. The importance of maintaining situational awareness has been a major factor in the design and equipping of combat aircraft, leading to the development of radar warning receivers, longer-range radars, and "bubble" canopies.

For all these reasons, information (or the lack thereof) at the tactical level can have powerful effects that can determine outcomes at higher levels of operations. Consider the modern battlefield: Even during major battles, at any given time, most of the firepower systems available to each side are idle. In the case of shorter-range, "direct fire" systems, such as infantrymen's rifles and tank guns, this is often because each side has striven to avoid putting many of his assets within reach of firepower. In the case of longer-range systems, such as missiles and aircraft, however, the problem may be that the other side has been able to conceal for a time the assets that might be most lucrative to attack. Most fighter pilots completed their tours of duty in World War II, Korea, Vietnam, and other wars without shooting down any enemy aircraft. This is not because of any lack of vigor on their part. Rather, it is either because direct encounters with the enemy were uncommon (Korea and Vietnam) or because the probability of shooting down the enemy given an encounter was quite low (all three wars). Today, with modern and highly lethal air-to-air missiles, the latter problem is being resolved. What is needed to get the most out of a force is to provide it with targets. This, in turn, requires timely and accurate information on the enemy's forces and assets. Where are the enemy's forces? Can we reliably distinguish them from background noise and from friendly, neutral, and civilian assets? Can we get this information to our "shooters" in a timely fashion?

Richard Simpkin, the British armor officer and military theorist, proclaimed in 1985 that modern armed forces had entered an era in which firepower would be increasingly dominant on the battlefield. This development, he observed, was based chiefly on information: "It is really the acquisition, processing, and dissemination of information that lies [sic] at the root of the speed and accuracy with which fire can now be applied." (Simpkin, 1985, p. 169.) As battlefields become ever less densely populated, the value of this sort of information, along with the ability to get it to those who most need it, grows exponentially.

All this implies that improved capabilities to acquire, process, and transmit information have the potential to transform warfare at the tactical level. One clear effect of information systems, such as GPS and detailed mapping, is increased accuracy in the delivery of weapons. These enhancements are being incorporated into weapon-delivery platforms (e.g., aircraft and missiles) and the weapons themselves (e.g., bombs and submunitions). An example is the Joint Direct Attack Munition (JDAM), currently in development for the Air Force, Navy, and Marines. An aircraft equipped with a GPS-linked navigation system downloads GPS target coordinates into the JDAM, which, when released, uses a simple inertial navigation system to fly to the target. Using this method, JDAM can achieve accuracies on the order of 30 to 50 feet, in contrast to unguided weapons, whose accuracies have been on the order of hundreds of feet under operational conditions. The practical effect of increased accuracy is that far fewer weapons (and therefore far fewer aircraft sorties) are needed to achieve desired levels of damage against a target. Shown below in Figure 6.2 is an example of how improvements in accuracy can increase the effectiveness of a force. It shows the number of 1,000 lb. bombs required to achieve a certain probability of destroying a highway bridge. Such calculations make the leverage that high accuracy can generate abundantly clear. Far fewer sorties (and hence less time and fewer losses) are required to accomplish a given task.

Moving targets, such as mechanized ground forces, present a very different target set from fixed points, such as bridges. Nonetheless, information technologies are improving the capabilities of individual weapons in this mission area as well. An example is the recently fielded Sensor Fuzed Weapon (SFW). SFW consists of a dispenser that releases 40 guided submunitions in a pattern. Each submunition, or "Skeet," is equipped with its own infrared seeker, enabling it to locate and fire an explosively forged fragment at vehicles that are warm enough to present a detectable infrared "signature."

SFW capabilities are best understood in contrast with previous generations of air-delivered antiarmor munitions, such as the Rockeye. Rockeye submunitions lack the individual seekers found on the SFW Skeet. This means that each submunition falls ballistically after it is dispensed, happening upon an enemy vehicle only by chance. The

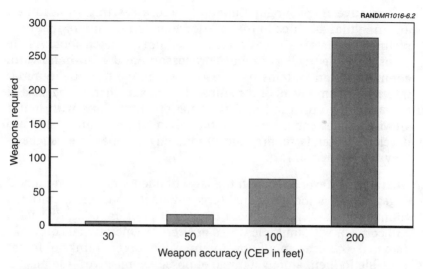

NOTE: In this calculation, a 1,000 pound bomb was used against a 500- by 22-ft Warren through-truss bridge. Sufficient weapons were used to achieve a 90 percent damage expectancy.

**Figure 6.2—Effects of Weapon Accuracy on Weapon Needs**

difference in weapon effectiveness is startling. In operational tests, single SFWs released over a column of armored vehicles have regularly damaged several of these vehicles. By contrast, it would require dozens of Rockeye dispensers to achieve similar effects. Over the course of several days' operations and hundreds of sorties, the impact of these new weapons is enormous: They have the potential to change the conduct of entire campaigns.

The Navy's Cooperative Engagement Capability is another example of how new information systems are enabling solutions to important tactical problems. During hostilities, sea-skimming cruise missiles (such as Harpoon and Exocet) pose a constant threat to naval forces on the surface. Such missiles have an interesting feature: Their radar signature is at its lowest when viewed head-on; thus, the ship under attack has the worst view of the missile attacking it. The practical effect is that the reaction timelines of the defending ship (that is, the time from detection of the incoming missile until the missile reaches the ship) can be alarmingly short.

Cooperative Engagement Capability addresses this situation by ensuring that all ships in the task force have a common, real-time picture of threats to the entire task force from all dimensions. All the ships have dentical computer processors, and high-bandwidth communication systems pass real-time, fire-control-quality radar information among all of the ships. This means that, in the case of the attacking cruise missile, information from ships with better viewing angles can be used by the defender or by other ships to develop a better, faster fire-control solution and, one hopes, successfully defend the ship.

**Operational-Level Effects.** If the level of fidelity needed for tactical engagements is the individual target or small unit, the operational commander is concerned with the activities of brigades, divisions, and corps or with multiple wings of aircraft. Operational commanders make choices about how to apportion larger chunks of forces available to them among a range of possible objectives—defensive, offensive, and reserve—and geographically as well: When and where should one concentrate one's forces and prepare to give battle or, alternatively, to disperse and avoid battle? What are the enemy's centers of gravity, and how can one best attack them? At this level, a different kind of information is needed. Here, commanders need to be able to appraise the overall situation within the theater of operations and make timely decisions about how and where to make the best use of forces available. Once those choices have been made, the decisions must be translated quickly into directives that can be readily grasped and acted upon by the forces.

At this level, the effects of wide-area surveillance capabilities that such systems as JSTARS provide are readily apparent. One major effect of these capabilities is to reduce the possibility of operational surprise by a large-scale ground attack. By monitoring vehicular movement hundreds of kilometers inside enemy territory, JSTARS and similar sensors can allow national leaders to reinforce U.S. and allied military postures in threatened regions prior to an attack and can allow commanders to position their forces with greater confidence.

In addition to this warning function, JSTARS has the capability to control joint forces as well. When combined with accurate weapons and munitions, the targeting and control capabilities provided by

JSTARS can allow U.S. forces to destroy an enemy force while it is attempting to maneuver for an engagement.  By directing attack assets to their targets, JSTARS increases the likelihood that an aircraft sortie or missile will be effective, even when attacking fleeting targets, such as moving vehicles.  In the past, without deep surveillance and communications, U.S. aircraft would be assigned to "kill boxes" or would fly route reconnaissance sorties, often with little likelihood of encountering enemy vehicles.  JSTARS and other sensors and control platforms can dramatically improve this performance.

Figure 6.3 depicts the effect of these improvements in surveillance and control.  Calculations in this figure are based upon a large enemy attacking force (roughly 12 divisions, or 9,600 armored fighting vehicles) advancing on two main axes and opposed by a variety of U.S. firepower resources, including ground-launched missiles, attack helicopters, and fixed wing aircraft.[4]  The depth of the enemy ground

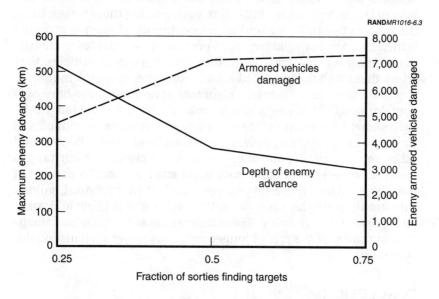

Figure 6.3—Operational Impact of Effective Wide-Area
Surveillance of Moving Ground Forces

---

[4]For a more complete exploration of the effectiveness and implications of modern surveillance, control, and attack capabilities, see Ochmanek et al. (1998).

force's advance (plotted against the left-hand scale) and the number of enemy armored vehicles damaged (plotted against the right-hand scale) are estimated as a function of the fraction of sorties finding valid moving vehicles as targets. By ensuring that far fewer sorties are wasted, we can expect dramatic differences between what we have experienced in the recent past and what we can expect in the future. And, as noted above, because new reconnaissance, engagement, and munition systems are increasingly effective at night and in poor weather, their effects will be further multiplied. In the very near future, enemy mechanized forces in most types of terrain will have no sanctuary from observation and attack from long-range reconnaissance and firepower assets.

In combination, these factors can have dramatic effects. Figure 6.4 contrasts the capabilities of two equal-sized forces of aircraft in attacks on moving armored vehicles over the first 10 days of a notional war. The bar on the left shows an estimate of the effectiveness of U.S. forces in the 1970s. It is assumed that these forces, using the human eye to locate and engage columns of moving armored vehicles, encounter valid targets 25 percent of the time (an optimistic assumption for that era). Once they find a group of vehicles, they attack them with the unguided Mk-20 "Rockeye" anti-tank munition. Under these circumstances, it might take several sorties to have high confidence of destroying a single tank. By contrast, the bar on the right shows an estimate of the same number of sorties equipped and supported with systems now reaching the field. Here, JSTARS and other sensors allow controllers to direct aircrews to their targets more effectively (we assume successful engagements 75 percent of the time). When those targets are attacked by advanced, guided submunitions (in this case, the SFW), each sortie is likely to destroy multiple armored vehicles. These differences argue for a fundamental reappraisal of the role of longer-range firepower systems in joint operations.

## CONCLUSIONS

With respect to prospective theater conflicts, the armed forces of the United States (and, by extension, the forces of allies who fight alongside them) have entered an era in which they can expect to have a substantial margin of superiority over their enemies in terms of their

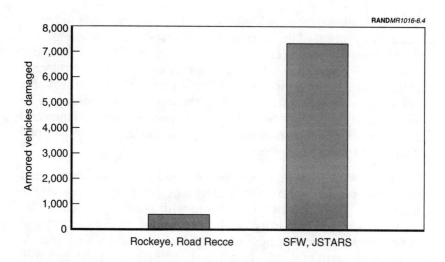

**Figure 6.4—Armored Vehicle Interdiction:  Yesterday and Today**

ability to "see" and understand what is happening on the battlefield. How long this era lasts will depend as much on our ability to deny future adversaries access to comparable information as it will on the development of further enhancements to our own forces' information gathering, processing, and dissemination capabilities.  But the value of this one-sided "information dominance" cannot be overstated.  Together with sound generalship, realistic training, and the ability to gain and exploit air superiority, information dominance was key to the allies' victory in Operation Desert Storm.

The value of new information-related capabilities will be especially pronounced at the engagement, tactical, and operational levels of war.  At the engagement level, the ability to put more information and processing capability into "smart" munitions will make individual shooters—especially long-range shooters that engage targets beyond line of sight—increasingly effective.  Smaller, more accurate munitions will have greater effectiveness than the larger ones they replace, allowing each delivery platform to do more per unit of time.

At the tactical level, forces with current and accurate information should have heightened situational awareness and, hence, should experience fewer unpleasant surprises.  It should also be possible to reduce further the risk of "friendly fire" engagements.

At the operational-level, information will make it possible to have a greater proportion of the force engaged against valuable enemy targets. Longer-range fires can be focused on the most lucrative targets. In defensive operations, forces can be concentrated where they are needed, rather then being spread thinly across the battlefield as a hedge against operational surprise. Ultimately, commanders may be able, in many situations, to "cover" the terrain with surveillance and fires. On the offensive, ground-force commanders can choose optimal points at which to concentrate.

Clausewitz wrote that friction is inherent and pervasive in war—that executing even fairly simple tasks can be exceedingly difficult on the battlefield. The difficulty in knowing with confidence where the enemy is and what he intends, the capabilities and limitations of one's own forces, and a host of other variables has always been a major component of this friction in war. And clever adversaries will, from time to time, find ways to outwit and confuse their enemies even in the face of sophisticated surveillance means. But there is no denying that the conduct of engagements, battles, and campaigns is changing dramatically with the advent of new information systems. Mastering these new capabilities will become an increasingly crucial component of the art of war.

## REFERENCES

Clausewitz, Carl Von, *On War*, trans. Col. J. J. Graham, Penguin Classics, 1968, p. 162.

Molander, Roger C., Andrew S. Riddile, and Peter A. Wilson, *Strategic Information Warfare: A New Face of War*, Santa Monica, Calif.: RAND, MR-661-AF, 1996.

Ochmanek, David A., Edward R. Harshberger, David E. Thaler, and Glenn Kent, *To Find, and Not to Yield: How Advances in Information and Firepower Can Transform Theater Warfare*, Santa Monica, Calif.: RAND, MR-958-AF, 1998.

Simpkin, Richard, *Race to the Swift*, London: Brassey's Defence Publishers, 1985, p. 169.

Sun Tzu, *The Art of War*, trans. Samuel B. Griffith, Oxford University Press, 1963.

# Chapter Seven

# U.S. MILITARY OPPORTUNITIES: INFORMATION-WARFARE CONCEPTS OF OPERATION

*Brian Nichiporuk*

## INTRODUCTION

Information warfare is often seen as a new threat; a tool for adversaries to use against the U.S. homeland or U.S. forces. Numerous stories about break-ins at Pentagon computers, disabled satellites, and downed phone networks have focused the attention of the public and the national security community on the need for information-warfare defense. The possibility that these new information-warfare tools could threaten America's ability to project power or to realize its national interests is real and deserves analytical attention and public awareness. However, information warfare creates more than just vulnerability—it may also mean many new opportunities for the U.S military. New information-warfare tools and techniques hold the potential for the United States to achieve its national security objectives using cheaper, more efficient, and less lethal methods.

Although these potential opportunities are a frequent topic of research and discussion within the defense analysis community, they have not received much attention beyond very specialized pockets of that community. This topic garners little outside attention, largely because the literature on information-warfare opportunities falls into one of two distinct categories: (1) broad policy and strategic-implications work and (2) highly technical feasibility studies. Research in the former is often too general to be of specific use to military planners. Research in the latter is often highly classified and compartmentalized. This chapter seeks to bridge the gap between the two by providing an operational-level view of how a set of offensive information-warfare concepts of operation (CONOPs) could expand the U.S. Air Force's capabilities to fight future wars (in the

2010–2015 time frame).  It seeks to answer the question:  How might the Air Force expand its doctrinal thinking about the systematic use of offensive information warfare to improve performance?[1]

## What Do We Mean by "Information Warfare"?

One of the major features of information-warfare research is the pot-pourri of different definitions for the term *information warfare*. Without engaging in that debate, this chapter will simply define information warfare as the process of protecting one's own sources of battlefield information and, at the same time, seeking to deny, degrade, corrupt, or destroy the enemy's sources of battlefield information.  This is taken to include six preexisting subareas that have only recently been grouped together under the heading of information warfare:  operational security, electronic warfare (EW), psychological operations (PSYOPs), deception, physical attack on information processes, and information attack on information processes.[2]  Since operational security is all about defensive information warfare, it is not as important to us here as the other five subareas. Therefore, offensive information warfare consists of the aggregation of EW, PSYOPs, deception, physical attack, and information attack.

EW encompasses the traditional concepts of jamming and spoofing radars and radio communication links.  The Air Force's now-retired EF-111 aircraft and the Navy's EA-6B aircraft are good examples of traditional EW platforms.  PSYOPs are all about using information dissemination to weaken the enemy's morale and, ultimately, to break his will to resist.  Classical PSYOP techniques include the air dropping of propaganda leaflets and using airborne loudspeakers that broadcast demands for surrender to enemy troops.  Deception involves the employment of physical or electronic means to camou-flage one's own force posture in theater.  Deploying dummy aircraft on the tarmac of a major air base or broadcasting radio situation reports in the clear from "phantom" or nonexistent units are two

---

[1]The author would like to thank RAND colleagues Alan Vick, Martin Libicki, Jeremy Shapiro, and Zalmay Khalilzad for their insightful comments on earlier drafts of this chapter.

[2]This grouping is derived from Fig. 8 in Hutcherson (1994), p. 22, as well as Joint Staff (1996), Ch. 2.

instances of deception that have been used in the past.[3]  Physical attack is simply the act of physically damaging or destroying an adversary's means of collecting, processing, and organizing information.  This includes means as diverse as using aircraft to deliver dumb iron bombs to destroy a corps-level command bunker and using a high-powered ground-based laser to cripple an enemy communications satellite permanently.  Finally, information attack involves the use of computer technology to electronically shut down, degrade, corrupt, or destroy an enemy's information systems in theater. Viruses, logic bombs, and sniffers are but three of the "information munitions" that experts in this area commonly discuss.

Many authors tend to equate offensive information warfare with information attack.  However, for a true appreciation of the breadth of offensive information warfare, it is really necessary to consider all five elements.  Indeed, as we shall see later, a rich mix of all five gives the best chance for success in the information campaign.

## The Importance of Offensive Information Warfare

Offensive information warfare is not a "new" way of attacking one's adversary.  To be sure, some of the current tools and technologies in this area are novel, but the goals of offensive information warfare today bear striking resemblance to those of the "military deception" campaigns of wars past.  In short, while the means for offensive information warfare have changed, the ends have remained similar to those of yesterday.

Broadly speaking, the goals of an offensive information-warfare campaign are to deny, corrupt, degrade, or destroy the enemy's sources of information on the battlefield.  Doing so successfully, while maintaining the operational security of your own information sources, is the key to achieving "information superiority"—that is, the ability to see the battlefield while your opponent cannot.[4]  In

---

[3]Deception may appear to be a purely defensive tool at first glance; however, deception operations have been used throughout history as integral parts of information campaigns that were heavily offensive.  Therefore, in this analysis, deception will be considered to be part of offensive information warfare.

[4]For an overview of how important information superiority in general will be to the United States in future conflicts, see Joint Chiefs of Staff (1996).

today's era of smart weapons and compressed decision cycles, there can be little doubt that the acquisition of information superiority in conventional warfare goes a long way toward achieving final victory.

History provides multiple examples of previous uses of "old-fashioned" offensive information warfare.[5] In the Revolutionary War, American agents supposedly inserted forged documents into British diplomatic pouches as a way of convincing the British that George Washington's army was far larger than it actually was. During World War I, the U.S. Army in France executed an important deception operation called the "Belfort Ruse" before a major attack on St. Mihiel. The Western Allies in World War II accomplished what was perhaps one of the largest "information warfare" successes in history when they fabricated the Calais invasion force in 1944, fooling some German leaders (including Hitler) into believing that the invasion of Northwest Europe would come at Calais, which is well to the north of the actual Allied landing sites in Normandy.[6] All of these historical examples involved the types of tactics that a 1990s defense analyst would place in the category of offensive information warfare.

Despite the fact that information-warfare campaigns have occurred before, it is now possible to say with confidence that information-warfare campaigns are a relatively more important part of conventional wars than they have been in the past. The increased importance of information-warfare campaigns to the United States in general and the Air Force in particular is due to a combination of technological, doctrinal, and force-structure factors. First, the growth in information technologies is making offensive information warfare a more potent instrument against enemy militaries. As such, offensive information warfare offers new possibilities and options to the regional commanders in chief (CINCs) when they prepare their war plans. As part of a recognition of these new options, U.S. military doctrine is moving away from the platform-centric warfare of the Cold War toward a new concept of network-centric warfare. (Cebrowski and Garstka, 1998.) In network-centric warfare, information superiority is an essential ingredient of success. Finally,

---

[5]The historical examples provided here are drawn from Hutcherson (1994), pp. 23–24.

[6]For a succinct account of the Allied deception campaign before D-Day in 1944, see Ambrose (1994), pp. 80–83.

America's shrinking conventional force structure demands innovative solutions to emerging problems. As the number of U.S. wings, divisions, and combatant ships declines, U.S. commanders will increasingly rely upon advanced information technology and computer savvy soldiers to gain the upper hand against adversaries in conventional warfare.

In recognition of this fact, this chapter will develop and elaborate four CONOPs that rely on offensive information warfare. Each CONOP is designed to counter some of the new (and not so new) asymmetric strategies that U.S. opponents are likely to use in future regional conflicts. The first section therefore discusses how the use of such strategies by regional adversaries could make the tasks of the Air Force more difficult. A rich literature on asymmetric strategies already exists, so the discussion here will be heavily derivative. Nonetheless, to set the stage for the proposed CONOPs, this section will lay out the types of asymmetric strategies posing the greatest threat to the United States. The second section presents and evaluates four offensive information-warfare CONOPs that appear to be promising countermeasures to this menu of asymmetric options. The chapter concludes with a third section that evaluates the utility of each of the CONOPs presented.

## EMERGING ASYMMETRIC STRATEGIES

The lopsided American victory in Desert Storm featured a clear display of the vast margin of superiority the U.S. Air Force holds over any conceivable adversary. Most analysts agree therefore that, in future wars, hostile regional powers will use asymmetric options to counter the U.S. advantage in air power. To organize our thinking about the contributions that offensive information warfare–oriented CONOPs could make toward defeating these asymmetric strategies, we need to begin by listing and categorizing the different strategies. As was noted earlier, a rich literature on asymmetric strategies has developed over the past few years.[7] The work on asymmetric strategies has revealed three types of enemy options the United States needs to be concerned about:

---

[7]Two examples of this literature are unpublished manuscripts by Marcy Agmon et al. and by Kenneth Watman of RAND.

- increasing capabilities in selected niche areas
- enemy strategies that target key U.S. vulnerabilities
- creation of political constraints that hinder U.S. force deployments.

## Increasing Niche Capabilities

Regional powers could achieve significant niche capabilities in a number of areas. However, the two that present the greatest cause for alarm are surely the acquisition of weapons of mass destruction (WMD) and improvements in command, control, communications, computing, intelligence, surveillance, and reconnaissance (C4ISR) networks.

**Enhanced WMD Inventories and Delivery Systems.** Several regional powers have stockpiles of biological and chemical weapons, along with the means to deliver them. Making this already difficult problem even more complicated, some regional powers may soon come into possession of what can be termed a mature small nuclear arsenal. This would be an arsenal of at least five or six secure and deliverable nuclear weapons supported by a reliable command and control and early-warning network.

The possession of a mature arsenal of nuclear, chemical, or biological weapons by a hostile regional power could restrict air power's freedom of action. It would be relatively easy for the leadership of that regional power to interpret many types of air strikes that U.S. Air Force planners would regard as strictly "conventional"—such as attacks on air defenses, command and control systems, or mobile missile launchers—as attempts to destroy, or at least degrade, its modest nuclear deterrent.

It is difficult to predict the reactions of small leadership groups in closed states, such as Iran, Iraq, and North Korea, to U.S. air operations that threaten their deterrent. Clearly, if the enemy leadership comes to perceive a U.S. conventional air campaign as part of a thinly veiled counterforce plan, the risk that the adversary will escalate to nuclear use increases.[8] The adversary's homeland might evolve into a kind of sanctuary in which large masses of U.S. combat

---

[8]For a discussion of related issues, see Wilkening and Watman (1995).

aircraft and cruise missiles could not operate freely because of concerns about escalation to WMD.[9] We will see later on that offensive information-warfare tools, working in concert with small packets of strike aircraft, could be a mechanism for both regaining some operational freedom and reducing the risks of escalation in a sanctuary-type environment. Offensive information-warfare tools can achieve this purpose because they can temporarily degrade or disrupt elements of an adversary's early-warning and air-defense systems without permanently destroying them. This reduces the chances that a U.S. air-defense suppression campaign will be interpreted as veiled counterforce.

The emergence of a homeland sanctuary in wartime would have concrete implications for Air Force planners and operators. Specifically, the enemy's leadership, national command and control, and internal security networks would all become harder to target. Supply and communications for enemy ground forces could not be disrupted on a regular basis, and a large chunk of the enemy's industrial warmaking capacity (including electric power generation and telecommunications capacity) would be essentially off limits to the orthodox offensive use of air power.

U.S. leaders could choose not to let the enemy establish a homeland airspace sanctuary. If the U.S. leadership is not highly risk averse, it could deal with WMD in other ways besides offensive information warfare. The United States could, for example, threaten massive nuclear retaliation for any adversary use of WMD and then proceed to carry out an air campaign against the enemy homeland under the assumption that the threat of escalation dominance by the superior U.S. nuclear arsenal cancels out the enemy's nuclear capability. Another option would be to mount a conventional counterforce campaign aimed at destroying the enemy's WMD before they could be employed. A future U.S. president could well select either of these approaches. However, in the event that the national leadership is highly risk averse in a future major theater war (MTW), it behooves the Air Force to plan to deal with scenarios in which much of an enemy's homeland is off limits to sustained aerial attack.

---

[9]This sanctuary concept was first proposed by RAND colleague Alan Vick in internal discussions in late 1996.

**Improved C4ISR Capabilities.** The information revolution that is now sweeping the world will create more opportunities for regional powers to access advanced space-based communications and reconnaissance systems. Much of this increased opportunity will result from having relatively easy access to multinational commercial assets; some will come from being granted access to dedicated military satellites owned by major powers that could become hostile to U.S. interests (e.g., China, Russia, India); and yet a smaller amount will be due to the development and exploitation of indigenous capabilities.

The proliferation of space-based military and commercial capabilities for both imagery and communications will offer tremendous opportunities for regional powers to increase their capabilities, bringing them closer to those of the United States. The greatest concern in terms of space-based imagery is the proliferation of foreign systems with resolutions equal to or below 5 m. This threshold is critical because 5 m is the level at which one can discern large, soft military targets—such as ports, air bases, and defense ministry buildings—in a theater with enough accuracy to target them specifically using cruise or ballistic missiles, especially if these weapons are Global Positioning System (GPS)–guided.[10] By 2002, France, Israel, India, and Russia will have deployed commercial or military systems capable of 5-m accuracy. (Air Force Space Command, 1996, p. 24; Stoney, 1997.) However, the available evidence suggests that no midsized regional power will be able to build its own spaceborne imagery satellites by 2010.

Growth in communication satellites will be more explosive than for imagery systems. There are plans for a whole host of new commercial space communication systems in both low earth (LEO) and geosynchronous orbits. (Keffer, 1996.) Some of the planned geosynchronous systems will exploit the Ka-band and will use cross-links between satellites to minimize the need for ground stations. Experts predict that, by the end of this decade, there will be two or three new global Ka-band geosynchronous systems and at least one or two "Big

---

[10]See Air Force Space Command (1996), p. 24. Recent RAND analysis has made some quantitative assessments concerning the impact of GPS guidance upon the cruise and ballistic missile accuracies likely to be achieved by the militaries of hostile regional powers. See Pace et al. (1995), especially pp. 45–91.

LEO" global constellations. Some of these systems will bring massive capacity increases into the world market. As an example, the Hughes Spaceways Ka-band geosynchronous system is projected to have a capacity of 88 Gb/s. This can be compared to the current total Department of Defense requirement for satellite-communication capacity, which is a mere 12 Gb/s. (U.S. Space Command, 1997, p. 4-14.) At least five such Ka-band systems have been planned for the near future.

Important advances are also occurring in transoceanic fiber-optic technology. Satellite communications may be the optimal solution for mobile military users, but fiber-optic connectivity is probably the most efficient communication option for fixed military users in rear areas. Research into such areas as wave division multiplexing promises to produce per-fiber capacities of up to 160 Gb/s.[11] The number of transoceanic fiber-optic lines is increasing as well, with many large new projects, such as the FLAG line from England to Japan, now entering service.

The upshot of this proliferation of highly capable commercial imagery and satellite and terrestrial communications is that it will be easier in the future for hostile regional powers to have access to the type of C4ISR architectures that only the most advanced militaries could access a few years ago. This applies for both voice and data transmissions. The sheer number of available redundant commercial routes and links will make it almost impossible for the United States to deny service to the adversary on a large scale for a long period of time—because too many communication "choke points" would need to be destroyed, disrupted, or corrupted. However, large-scale service denial for short periods during a theater campaign may still be possible, and such denials would indeed have military significance.

Increased access to overhead imagery will allow regional powers to monitor U.S. and allied force deployments both into and within a theater with greater fidelity than was possible before. The greatest military impact of this new capability is the availability of accurate and timely targeting data to aid in the planning of rapid ballistic- and

---

[11]For an overview of technological developments in the field of undersea fiber-optic lines, see Submarine Systems International (1997).

cruise-missile strikes against air bases, port facilities, and logistics stockpiles being used by U.S. forces in the region.[12] Increased access to highly capable communication systems will lend regional powers the potential for much more timely control of their forces in theater. Decision cycles for these militaries could decrease dramatically. Furthermore, the ability to access large, new international communication networks could facilitate a regional power's offensive information warfare against the Department of Defense's worldwide command and control systems.

## Enemy Strategies That Target Key U.S. Vulnerabilities

Another asymmetric option available to regional adversaries of the United States is the use of strategies that threaten key U.S. vulnerabilities and centers of gravity. Such strategies and tactics would be most effective in conjunction with the improved capabilities discussed above, but they could also pose a threat if used on their own. Three strategy types merit consideration: short-warning attacks, antiaccess operations, and deep-strike operations. Each will be covered briefly below.

**Short-Warning Attacks.** The first strategy that could be used would be a so-called standing-start attack, in which the U.S. intelligence community has little warning of an impending attack. Such an attack would take place before any major U.S. deployment to the region had begun.

A short-warning attack would force the Air Force either to fight with major early disadvantages or to take time to build up its strength in the theater, thus letting the regional adversary make some initial territorial gains. This would be a difficult decision to make. If the National Command Authorities elected to commit combat aircraft immediately to battle against a standing-start attack, the Air Force might have to operate initially without its normal complement of critical enabling assets, such as tankers, the Airborne Warning and Control System, the Joint Surveillance and Target Attack Radar System, jamming aircraft, and dedicated air-defense suppression aircraft. In such a situation, the Air Force also could find itself at a heavy numerical disadvantage in early air-to-air engagements.

---

[12]See Stillion and Orletsky (unpublished manuscript), Ch. 2 and 3.

The upshot is that the Air Force could suffer significant losses in the early phase of a standing-start attack, especially if the opponent possessed advanced surface-to-air missile systems. Risks would also be involved if the National Command Authorities chose to delay their response until U.S. forces were fully deployed. Serious political implications could result from the territorial losses that a local U.S. ally would almost certainly suffer in a delayed-response scenario. While most conceivable short-warning attack scenarios would not result in an ultimate U.S. defeat, they would almost certainly all extract a greater price in terms of blood and treasure.

**Antiaccess Operations.**    Perhaps the cardinal mistake the Iraqis made during Desert Shield and Desert Storm was the six months of unhindered deployment and buildup time they gave to coalition forces before the January 1991 commencement of hostilities. During the height of a deployment of U.S. forces into a theater during an MTW contingency, future regional adversaries will have greater opportunities to avoid the error the Iraqis made and to mount strike operations designed to hinder U.S. access to critical points in the battlespace. This would likely be done through the use of missiles, unmanned aerial vehicles (UAVs), mines, and aircraft to damage and/or shut down both aerial and sea ports of debarkation in the region so as to cut down the throughput capacity of such facilities.[13]

Although the Air Force is attempting to diminish the threat of antiaccess operations by shaping itself into an expeditionary force with enhanced force-protection capabilities, the realm of offensive information warfare should also offer possibilities for mitigating the antiaccess threat.

**Deep-Strike Operations.**    The final threat in the area of strategies and tactics has to do with deep-strike operations that a regional adversary could mount during the counteroffensive stage of an MTW, the phase during which U.S. forces would be fully assembled in theater and attempting to roll back any initial gains that the adversary had made. During this phase of an MTW, the logistical demands of major ground and air offensive operations will compel the United States to amass large stockpiles of fuel, ammunition, and spare parts throughout the rear areas of the theater. Major scripted offensive operations

---

[13]Stillion and Orletsky (unpublished manuscript), Ch. 2 and 3.

would also force U.S. air bases in the region to operate at a high tempo, possibly with little room for slack.  These realities would create tempting targets for an adversary's remaining cruise and theater ballistic missiles.  While the aforementioned antiaccess operations would concentrate on disrupting and delaying a U.S. deployment into theater, the goal of deep-strike operations would be to slow down and prolong a U.S. counteroffensive so as to keep U.S. forces off balance and to inflict greater casualties, possibly breaking down the U.S. national will to continue the campaign.  Likely targets for adversary cruise and ballistic missiles in the deep-strike campaign would include ammunition and fuel storage sites throughout the theater, air bases, the theater air operations center, early-warning radars, anti–tactical ballistic missile batteries, ports, troop concentrations, and headquarters.

## Political Constraints on U.S. Force Deployments

Not all of the troubling asymmetric options available to a regional adversary involve military means.  Indeed, some of the most potent options may be political and diplomatic.  There are a variety of diplomatic tactics available to a smart regional adversary for the purpose of complicating U.S. military deployments.  The goal of such tactics would be to intimidate potential or existing U.S. allies to back out of political coalitions or at least to deny the use of their air bases to U.S. forces.  The blunt approach for an adversary would be to attempt direct coercion against a U.S. ally by threatening that ally's cities with WMD attacks from theater-range delivery vehicles.  More nuanced political strategies could include furnishing support to opposition groups in allied countries and encouraging them to foment civil unrest during a crisis.  An alternative approach for regional adversaries would be to emphasize carrots over sticks by promising substantial political and/or economic rewards to their neighbors for keeping U.S. air power off their soil.

Denial of U.S. access to theater bases would most likely force the Air Force to adopt a standoff approach to combat—that is, conducting air operations from bases outside the immediate theater.  The Joint Forces Air Component Commander (JFACC) would face a number of penalties as a result of the need to pursue a standoff CONOP, including lower sortie rates for strike and counterair operations, greater demands on the tanker fleet, reduced chances of rescuing downed aircrews, increased pressure on heavy bombers and cruise missiles to hit deep fixed targets because of a lack of alternative delivery vehicles, a substantial degradation in the capability to hold critical mobile targets at risk, increased difficulty in supporting U.S. and allied ground forces, increased aircrew fatigue, and greater maintenance turnaround times.

A recent RAND study examined the operational effects of using a standoff strategy in response to an adversary's employment of chemical or biological weapons against close-in air bases. The study found that a 600-mile standoff range in Southwest Asia reduces the Air Force's sortie rate by approximately 25 percent; in Northeast Asia, a 500-mile standoff range reduces the sortie rate by roughly 30 percent.[14] Such reductions could result in a substantially longer and bloodier conflict than would otherwise be necessary.

## DEVELOPING OPERATIONAL CONCEPTS FOR FUTURE OFFENSIVE INFORMATION WARFARE

Now that we have identified the major asymmetric options available to regional adversaries, we can begin to think about the role of offensive information warfare in improving U.S. chances of dealing successfully with such challenges. Figure 7.1 maps each of the asymmetric options outlined above to a CONOP using offensive information warfare that provides a possible way to negate the enemy's strategy. The following subsections will discuss each of the potential offensive information-warfare CONOPs in detail. Here, we will only provide a preview.

Short-warning attacks can perhaps best be dealt with through effective regional deterrence strategies. The "information-based deterrence" CONOP attempts to expand upon previous notions of deterrence by using an array of information technologies to affect an opponent's perception of the overall political and military situation in his region during peacetime or during a crisis.

---

[14]Chow et al. (unpublished manuscript), pp. 66–78.

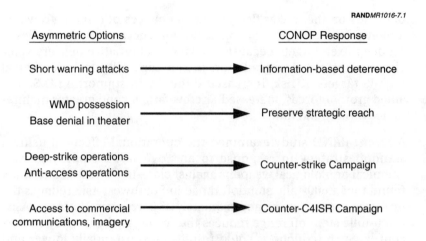

Figure 7.1—Adversary Asymmetric Options and Potential U.S. CONOPs

WMD possession and base denial are grouped together because both strategies have to do with an adversary striving to decrease the Air Force's freedom and capability to operate over his homeland on a sustained basis.  We attempt to address these through a CONOP entitled "preserve strategic reach," which seeks to use offensive information warfare to suppress enemy air defenses to facilitate conventional strategic air attacks upon selected targets in the enemy homeland.

Next, there is the risk that the enemy may mount antiaccess and deep-strike operations.  Both these asymmetric options involve the use of relatively new technologies (e.g., GPS-based targeting) to strike at U.S. and allied rear areas.  The "counterstrike campaign" CONOP is a possible remedy.  Counterstrike also uses a variety of offensive information-warfare tools, this time to disrupt an enemy's strike-planning and execution functions.

Finally, the increasing ability of regional powers to exploit spaceborne communications and imagery assets is mapped against a CONOP called the "counter-C4ISR campaign."  Counter-C4ISR uses a variety of offensive information-warfare tools to disrupt an enemy's ability to collect and process information gained from overhead assets.

## Information-Based Deterrence

The overarching goal of the information-based deterrence CONOP is successfully manipulating the attitude of a potential adversary during peacetime or a crisis to prevent him from ever attacking an ally. Such efforts have been made in the past, but technological growth is creating opportunities to increase the power of information campaigns aimed at either long- or short-term deterrence.

Information-based deterrence strives to sow doubt in the mind of a potential adversary about the likely outcome of his aggression. This can be done in three ways: turning international opinion against the aggressor, altering his perception of the military correlation of forces in theater, and fostering instability in his country. Information-based deterrence does not require a pure strategy; it can include a combination of two or three options, depending on the circumstances. Although these three mechanisms could also be used during wartime itself as a means of coercing an enemy, history demonstrates that wartime coercion is much more difficult than is deterrence. Therefore, the U.S. military would have a better chance of success with these mechanisms using them within the context of a deterrence effort.

Three cautions are important when discussing perception-shaping strategies against other states. First, in recent times, technology has often outpaced international norms and standards. We still do not have a clear sense of which types of perception-shaping activities will be construed as legitimate peacetime behavior and which as *casus belli* by international organizations and institutions. Therefore, to reduce the risk of inadvertent escalation, it will be necessary to rethink our doctrine for perception shaping periodically in accordance with developing international norms and standards.

Second, perception-shaping activities carry a constant threat of "blowback": Operations designed to manage the opponent's perceptions may end up distorting our own perceptions to an equal or even greater extent. For example, while it may be advantageous to convince the enemy that U.S. forces are more capable than they actually are, it would be less helpful to convince oneself of that fiction. Yet, because of the need for consistency and secrecy to accomplish perception-shaping objectives, these two effects are, in practice, not completely separable.

Third, deterrence of any sort relies on convincing the adversary not to act. While our actions can affect the adversary's calculus, we must always be prepared for deterrence to fail. For our purposes, this reality means that information-based deterrence is not the complete solution for short-warning attacks. Other means must be developed to cope with the possible failure of information-based deterrence.

**Turning International Opinion Against the Aggressor.** A major U.S. strength lies in its ability to create wide coalitions against potential enemies that can isolate opponents from external support, both material and moral. Such coalitions reinforce U.S. combat power, reduce enemy access to critical supplies, and provide a greater legitimacy for U.S. action—a legitimacy that solidifies domestic U.S. support for deterrence actions and war, if that becomes necessary. Repeatedly, U.S. leaders have stressed that U.S. forces will only engage in a multilateral context. An increased likelihood of such a coalition will therefore have a deterrent effect on potential foes.

Creating and maintaining such coalitions require that international opinion views U.S. foes as aggressors with little regard for international law or human rights. Optimally, such a coalition would be sustained by a continuous and long-standing information campaign. However, new conflicts and enemies can arise, and U.S. leaders must be prepared to cut such coalitions nearly from whole cloth. Particularly in the case of a short-warning attack, prospective foes will take great care to hide their intentions until shortly before hostilities break out. Preventing and responding to short-warning attack therefore may necessitate a rapid-reaction information campaign that is prepared to foster the appropriate climate of international opinion.

In the short period before the outbreak of hostilities, a rapid-reaction information campaign has two basic parts. First, television and radio broadcasts of accurate information from U.S. sources should show enemy intent and preparations for attack. Second, the information campaign should include television and radio broadcasts that demonstrate both U.S. friendly intent and allied military prowess. These broadcasts should go to enemies and prospective allies, as well as to domestic audiences.

Both before and after hostilities break out, short-warning attacks often provide ready material for images that will outrage and inflame international opinion against the aggressor.  Such attacks will typically require such preparations as the loading and unloading of trains, massing of supplies and forces, and shock attacks by rapidly moving forces.  Capturing these preparations and attacks on video or satellite imagery will demonstrate the enemy's aggressive intent, give the lie to any pretext they might have established for invasion, and serve to catalyze international opinion and support for a broad coalition to oppose aggression.  There is some historical precedent for the use of simple images as a tool for marshaling international opinion against an aggressor.  During the Cuban Missile Crisis, for example, aerial reconnaissance photos of Soviet missile sites in Cuba helped strengthen the U.S. position at the United Nations.

Increasingly, the independent media can be counted on to capture and broadcast this information.  However, some countries still maintain fairly effective control over even foreign media outlets operating in their territory.  To avoid leaving such things to the intrepid action of individual reporters, information deterrence could be aided by a rapid-reaction information force that can quickly establish video surveillance of potentially hostile territory.  UAVs equipped with video equipment and command planes capable of gathering, editing, and instantaneously disseminating that coverage are the essential features of such a force.  If the risks of such aircraft being shot down or identified over enemy territory are too great, one could even use satellite imagery to provide evidence of mass graves, burned-out villages, etc.  At the same time, U.S. leaders would need to work hard to counter enemy propaganda campaigns by tirelessly presenting the major elements of the true situation on a wide spectrum of information outlets (Internet, television, radio, etc.).  Video coverage of the battle area will help expose any enemy attempt to portray U.S. actions in a deceptive light.  Great effort needs to be expended to provide counterevidence for the inevitable enemy pro-propaganda campaign.  Good video images can make ruses—such as the Iraqi attempt to portray a U.S. attack on a military target as an attack on a facility that served solely as a baby-milk factory—nearly impossible.

It is critical that such a campaign maintain a consistency of message and purpose throughout its broadcasts.  This kind of campaign should make no effort whatsoever to deceive or manipulate the international media, concentrating instead on the simple goal of using modern technology to highlight the hard physical evidence of a rogue state's aggressive intentions. Deceptive techniques are unnecessary and counterproductive in this context. In an age of numerous media outlets and largely unconstrained information flows, it makes little sense to risk American credibility as an honest international citizen by manufacturing video images.

**Altering the Enemy's Perception of the Correlation of Forces.** When leaders of the various ex-Yugoslavian factions met at Dayton, Ohio, to divide zones of control in Bosnia, the U.S. military provided satellite imagery to assist in the demarcation of borders. To the shock of the participants, the imagery demonstrated a knowledge of terrain and force dispositions far in excess of what the participants had previously believed possible. Indeed, the imagery showed a three-dimensional picture of the contested areas that demonstrated a more detailed knowledge of the participants' own forces than the parties themselves possessed. All sides now understood that the U.S. military could see virtually anything on the battlefield; the implicit threat was that it could destroy anything it could see.[15]

While such knowledge was useful in negotiating the peace, it might be even more useful in deterring a future MTW. The U.S. military, particularly the Air Force, excels at simulation, which it uses to train its troops in conditions as realistic as possible. These simulations can similarly be used to demonstrate U.S. combat power, without actually employing it. Indeed, in the summer of 1998, NATO carried out simulated air raids over Kosovo as a deterrent to further Serb repression in that province. Realistic simulations have a tremendous capacity to impress an enemy's population, frighten his soldiers, and radically alter the enemy's assessment of U.S. military power. Such simulations would include images of U.S. military equipment operating, simulated attacks on significant military targets, and broadcasts of past U.S. combat successes. While these simulations and replays will certainly give insight on actual U.S. combat capabilities, they need not always reflect actual U.S. capabilities or intentions. As noted, if a simulation is realistic enough, it will create such a strong image in the mind of the adversary that it will

---

[15]For accounts of this episode, see Watters (1996); Libicki (1997), Ch. 3; and Nye and Owens (1996), p. 32.

irrevocably alter his perception of the correlation of forces, regardless of actual U.S. capabilities.

**Fostering Instability.** Every society contains divisions simmering below an often calm exterior. Nondemocratic societies, especially, contain latent tensions that, if exploited, can severely limit a country's ability to engage in offensive military action. Offensive information warfare offers many new covert means to exploit those tensions because it increases the opportunity to communicate directly with constituent parts of the adversary's society. As the information revolution increases the number and types of communication channels within any society, the opportunities to introduce false data into communication links between constituent parts of the society also increase.

It should be noted that fostering instability is the riskiest of the three methods of information deterrence. It should only be used against nations that pose a particularly grave military threat. It is also the most difficult method to implement as it requires a detailed understanding of the target society and the cultural context in which such action will be received. Inappropriate or clumsy efforts to foster instability may well create unity in an otherwise divisive polity by providing evidence of an external threat to the nation. The United States should not attempt this type of tactic unless it possesses an experienced cadre of intelligence analysts who have proven themselves to have an extremely high degree of cultural understanding and sophistication with respect to the target state.

Nonetheless, by exploiting cleavages among the government, the population, and the military (the so-called Clausewitzian trinity), it could sometimes be possible to convince the adversary leadership that its hold on power is fragile and that it thus cannot afford any type of military contest, let alone one with the United States. There are many ways such an approach could be pursued. False messages inserted into national communication networks could be used to create mistrust between the civilian and military leaderships by spreading rumors of military coup plots or planned purges against the officer corps. Support to nongovernmental organizations operating on the Internet could be used to spread popular disenchantment with government policies and to foster public protests against the regime. The United States could also use media organizations in the target country and its neighbors as a lever to influence public opinion in the adversary state and turn that opinion against its own government's policies. Finally, the low-technology approach should not be forgotten: Leaflets dropped from U.S. aircraft were extremely effective during the Gulf War in convincing Iraqi troops to surrender. (Hosmer, 1996.)

Some nations will be far less vulnerable to such measures than others by virtue of their closed political systems. However, as time goes on and as international connectivity increases, there will be fewer and fewer nondemocratic nations that can be sanguine about their ability to insulate themselves against the effects of a well-coordinated information strategy exploiting the mass media, the Internet, and proprietary communication networks.

## Preserving Strategic Reach

The prospect of facing regional adversaries with mature nuclear arsenals raises questions about how much freedom the Air Force will have to conduct parallel warfare against the enemy homeland without substantially increasing the risk of escalation. The prospect of having local allies deny the U.S. Air Force the use of bases in the theater means that it may be prohibitively expensive and dangerous to employ air assets over the enemy's territory for the reasons outlined above.

The "preserving strategic reach" CONOP is intended as a response to these emerging challenges. The chief mechanism of preserving strategic reach is the periodic use of offensive information-warfare means to degrade the enemy's integrated air defense system (IADS).[16] The significant degradation of the enemy IADS would allow the U.S. Air Force to operate over enemy territory in reasonable safety and, given well-chosen targets, with much less fear of nuclear escalation. As with information-based deterrence, however, preserving strategic reach may not be the final solution to these problems. Using offensive information warfare will not eliminate the possibility of escalation and will not completely make up for the loss of theater bases. Nonetheless, it represents an important part of the response to these relatively new challenges.

---

[16]An IADS includes surface-to-air missiles, anti-aircraft artillery, air-superiority fighters, and the communication and sensor infrastructure that connects them.

More-conventional operations to suppress enemy air defenses that use physical attacks, such as those mounted by F-16s equipped with High-Speed Anti-Radiation Missiles, contain a risk of escalation when used against an adversary with WMD. The adversary leadership may not be able to distinguish such an operation from an attempt to destroy nuclear warning and command and control systems in preparation for a counterforce attack designed to eliminate the adversary's nuclear deterrent. Such operations also require putting friendly forces at risk and are particularly difficult and dangerous to launch from a standoff posture. Offensive information-warfare operations contain a much smaller risk of escalation because they need not involve physical attacks on command and control systems and because they can be done covertly. They do not put friendly forces at risk and are not affected by the loss of theater bases, because they can be launched just as easily from outside the theater.

Any IADS contains information systems and information-based processes that are essential for its operations and that are lucrative targets for offensive information warfare. Schematically, an IADS consists of one or a few air defense headquarters connected by communication links to sensors, such as early-warning radars, EW sensors, or aircraft like those for the Airborne Warning and Control System. Each headquarters also communicates with and controls a variety of antiaircraft weapons, such as fire-control radars, missile launchers, and air-superiority fighters.

Without physical destruction, offensive information warfare can attack an IADS at three points. First, offensive information warfare can attack the system's sensors, either degrading their ability to gather information or feeding them false data. Second, offensive information warfare can degrade or plant false information in the communication links between headquarters and the sensors or shooters. Third, offensive information warfare can degrade or deceive the information processes that compile the sensor information, interpret it for human decisionmakers, and assign particular weapons to targets.

The centralized nature of this system implies that the air headquarters is a critical chokepoint, the disabling of which will render the entire system useless without the need to disable every sensor and weapon. This point should not be taken too far, however. An IADS can be configured to work in several modes from centralized to fully autonomous. The characteristics of these systems in each different mode should be well understood because information munitions that prove effective against an IADS operating in centralized mode may be ineffective against the same set of surface-to-air missile batteries and sensors operating in autonomous mode. Indeed, in autonomous mode, the local air-defense headquarters may not even be that significant to the overall function of the system.

The decision about which part of the system to attack therefore depends on the reason for using offensive information warfare to bring down the IADS. If escalation to WMD is a concern, the emphasis should be on allowing the enemy to believe that the IADS is still functioning even as one has severely degraded its effectiveness. While attacks on sensors and communications can be useful under such circumstances, attacks on the information processes themselves are probably most useful under such circumstances because errors in such processes are difficult to trace, badly understood, and widely expected in the normal course of operation. Such processes can be degraded by means of various information munitions (viruses, worms, logic bombs, etc.) prepositioned or inserted into the enemy air-defense computers. This degradation could cause the IADS to fail to assign targets, assign targets to inappropriate weapons, lose orders to weapons, misinterpret sensor data, or mistarget surface-to-air missile batteries. If cleverly applied, these weapons can go undetected, and any errors in IADS information processes will be attributed to operational errors. The key difficulty in such an attack is timing. The information munitions must "go off" only just before the air strike, or the degradation in the IADS is likely to be detected and corrected. Timing such information munitions is a tricky problem. Viruses and worms travel at an unpredictable rate, and logic bombs are difficult to trigger remotely. One must also keep in mind that some threat air-defense systems will contain bounds-checking features that ensure the system does not malfunction in certain drastic ways (such as assigning targets to inappropriate weapons); these bounds-checking features could present clues that an information attack was in progress to an alert and well-trained air-defense commander.

If the offensive information-warfare attack is meant to allow the United States to operate from a standoff posture, the information attack need not be so unobtrusive in its methods.  In this case, the most lucrative targets are the extremities of the system:  the sensors and the antiaircraft weapons.  Offensive information warfare would attempt to disable the sensors or weapons temporarily in particular nodes of the IADS in closely timed coordination with strike missions routed to pass through the resulting geographic gaps.  Such temporary effects could be achieved by overloading sensors with false data, jamming communications via EW, inserting false data into communication streams, or conducting perception-shaping campaigns via broadcast or leaflets that threatened operators who turned on their radars or acquired allied targets.

Two caveats are in order.  First, as we have already seen, timing is crucial for realizing the full potential of the preserving strategic reach CONOP.  Precise timing of effects will be difficult to achieve and will require Air Force planners with considerable skill.  Second, there is the issue of reliable damage assessment for offensive information-warfare attacks against IADS.  How do you know if your attack has done its job and if it is safe for manned aircraft to fly through the area?  This information-warfare battle damage assessment (BDA) problem could become larger the more frequently this particular CONOP is used.  A cunning enemy, once he sees a pattern developing, may set traps by intentionally shutting down the radars in an air-defense sector during an offensive information-warfare attack and then luring American aircraft into an ambush.  Once again, the only solution here is to support research into technologies that might make information-warfare BDA a more accurate science.

Preserving strategic reach should only be used if the following three conditions are met.  First, U.S. policymakers need to have made a clear decision that other approaches to reducing the significance of the adversary's WMD have less potential.  These other approaches include deterrence through the threat of massive retaliation; deterrence through the threat of escalation dominance; and a conventional counterforce campaign aimed at destroying WMD ordnance, delivery vehicles, and storage sites through the use of precision-guided munitions.  In many cases, the other approaches could be more appropriate to the situation at hand than the cautious strategy embodied in preserving strategic reach.

Second, it will be critical for other components of the unified geographic command to be fully aware of the JFACC's concept of offensive information warfare and also to be prepared to coordinate actions if necessary. The importance of sharing information across organizational boundaries must not be underestimated when planning for offensive information warfare.

Lastly, national-level authorities must be made aware of the risks of enemy retaliation against the U.S. National Information Infrastructure in response to U.S. offensive information-warfare attacks against enemy IADS. These authorities should take appropriate precautionary measures. Addressing these vulnerabilities, detailed in other chapters in this volume, would give the United States more freedom of action to use offensive information warfare in MTWs.

## Counterstrike

The purpose of the counterstrike CONOP is to keep the enemy from mounting antiaccess operations against U.S. power-projection capabilities and deep-strike operations designed to target U.S. logistics bases critical for sustaining U.S. air operations. Offensive information-warfare operations provide a new capability in this regard because they offer an opportunity to attack the enemy's rear areas and affect his capacity for antiaccess and deep-strike operations even before U.S. forces have deployed in strength to the theater. Through remote attacks on the enemy's planning and assessment processes, offensive information warfare denies him the use of a homeland sanctuary from the very beginning of the deployment.

It should also be noted, however, that offensive information warfare in this context is intended to be used in conjunction with conventional attacks on enemy strike assets. Offensive information warfare will enhance the effectiveness of conventional counterstrike operations, especially early in the battle, before all forces have deployed, but it will not replace those traditional missions.

At the most basic level, offensive information warfare is useful for this purpose because strike operations are highly information intensive. Successful strike operations require detailed planning, careful coordination, and reliable data on target locations. When viewed as an information process, strike operations can be seen as iterative, with three stages: planning, execution, and BDA. Offensive information warfare will aim to disrupt or defeat all three stages of that process. For this purpose, the United States would deploy an information-warfare squadron to the theater to support the JFACC. This squadron would also have access to numerous information-warfare centers based in the continental United States that can provide analysis and expertise, such as the Army's Land Information Warfare Activity or the Air Force Information Warfare Center.

**Strike Planning.** Strike planning is the process of allocating and coordinating scarce attack assets (cruise missiles, ballistic missiles, strike aircraft) to inflict the greatest possible damage on the target's operational capacity. To be employed efficiently, such a planning process will need to have access to mountains of data on U.S. capabilities, force-deployment plans, orders of battle, air defenses, and target locations. Planners will also need more prosaic data, such as terrain and navigation information and weather reports.

Offensive information-warfare operations can deny or corrupt all these data sources by attacking information systems. The adversary will use a variety of information systems to collect, process, and disseminate the data. Most of the imagery, weather, and navigation data necessary to pinpoint fixed U.S. targets will be collected from commercial satellites, as well as from such open sources as commercial maps and media outlets. Terrestrial and satellite communications will be used to disseminate raw data to planners, strike plans to the assigned units, and mission plans to the individual shooters. Finally, the creation of any complex strike plan will involve software to evaluate the mountain of data involved, produce mission plans, and transfer data to weapon systems.

There are many methods for denying and corrupting the data. Some are quite conventional, such as limiting access to critical facilities, camouflaging ship and aircraft movements, or periodically moving high-value assets and air defenses. Other methods are more novel and potentially more effective. Physical destruction or electronic jamming of critical junctures in the strike-planning process—satellites, satellite downlink stations, and mission-planning centers—will be particularly effective. Information munitions could also be implanted in the enemy's strike-planning system to render it inoperable at critical moments.

We should keep in mind that planners are adaptive and will find workarounds to the problems of missing data, downed systems, and destroyed communication links. A more subtle method, then, might be to corrupt the mission-planning process, thus causing the enemy to squander scarce strike resources. This can be done primarily by introducing false data on U.S. and allied force disposition, terrain, and even weather data into the enemy's striking-planning process. There are many potential points of access, the most promising being via falsified, corrupted, or hijacked satellite downlinks. Since the enemy may collect some targeting data on large, fixed targets long before a strike, another option is to implant errors in the enemy's mission-planning hardware or software to cause subtle errors in the strike-planning process.

**Strike Execution.** Strike execution is the process of carrying out the strike plan. For information systems, strike execution depends primarily on a dense system of communication links and navigational aids. This includes communication links—from command and control units to aircraft and missile launchers—used to make changes in the mission plan or report intelligence gained from the mission, communications between aircraft used to synchronize the attack, and navigational data acquired from satellite systems, such as GPS or GLONASS.[17]

Once again, each of these links is potentially vulnerable to destruction or disruption. Most vulnerable are the navigational systems. Without this type of navigational data, enemy cruise missiles and even strike aircraft will be far less accurate. U.S. forces can easily turn off or jam GPS and can jam GLONASS in local areas. Of course, this may also adversely affect the U.S. capacity to operate. Even if access to GPS were limited to U.S. and allied forces, the enemy might well be able to jam U.S. access to GPS in retaliation. Any degradation of satellite navigation systems must always be assessed in a relative perspective. Given that there is a good possibility that the loss of GPS would affect U.S. forces more than it would enemy forces, a more effective measure might be to introduce errors into the GPS or GLONASS signal at critical periods during strike execution. Alternatively, the United States could use information munitions to attack the information processes that load targeting and navigational data into enemy cruise missiles and strike aircraft. Both attacks

_____
[17]GPS is a U.S. satellite navigation system. GLONASS is a similar Russian system.

could introduce navigational errors that should cause strike aircraft to attack erroneous targets or cause cruise missiles to collide with terrain features.

Similarly, the United States could hope to introduce false data into communication links between strike assets and command and control centers or between the strike aircraft themselves. Such false data could generate false targets or give false target updates to strike assets already in the air. Unfortunately, the growing use and sophistication of encryption techniques makes such insertion increasingly difficult, so jamming these links may soon become the only option. Nonetheless, aircraft or cruise missiles that are unable to receive information from their command and control centers will be unable to adjust their mission plans to reflect real-time changes in target disposition and will be unable to function as forward sensors.

New offensive information warfare or related methods may also soon be available for destroying the platforms themselves. One can well imagine having the technology available to generate bogus electronic signals that would prevent arming or prematurely activate warheads on inbound cruise missiles and fighter aircraft. Another interesting possibility is the use of high-altitude electromagnetic pulse weapons based on airborne platforms to disable navigation, flight control, target acquisition, and fire-control systems on inbound aircraft and cruise missiles, rendering them all but useless as offensive weapons or causing them to crash.

**Battle Damage Assessment.** BDA, the least examined part of the strike process, is critical for a successful overall strike plan. Given the scarcity and price of sophisticated strike assets, it is vital to know which defensive systems have been disabled and which targets have been destroyed in order to allocate strike assets efficiently and safely. BDA has several information sources, including the strike asset itself; open-source media outlets; human intelligence agents; and remote-sensing platforms, such as satellites, UAVs, and surveillance aircraft.

Once again, all of these data sources can potentially be degraded or destroyed by offensive information-warfare operations. Although jamming and physical destruction of communications and satellite downlinks will be very useful measures in this regard, BDA also presents ample opportunity for deception. False damage signatures may fool strike aircraft into thinking they have hit their target. Careful camouflage can fool satellite imagery into believing that targets have been destroyed or, conversely, remain unharmed.

Perhaps the most promising method of complicating the enemy's BDA process is by tainting open sources. In the future, much BDA may be done through the media or through human agents reporting openly available information from within the target zone via e-mail, cell phones, etc. The problem of open-source BDA of strike operations will no doubt persist and, indeed, may increase as more of the population gains access to cell phones and Internet e-mail. Offensive information-warfare operations can turn this intelligence drain into an asset by planting false information on battle damage into open sources. False damage reports and even false video images of bomb damage (or, conversely, of false images of still-operating facilities) can greatly complicate enemy planning. In contrast to information deterrence, if this activity damages the credibility of the media and human agents as sources of BDA, so much the better. It is again important to be aware of the risk of blowback: Special BDA spoofing efforts against the enemy may well fool some planners and operators on the U.S. side who are not familiar with these programs.

**The Utility of Counterstrike.** The importance of counterstrike will vary with the current phase of conflict. Pentagon planners have divided MTWs into three phases: halt, stabilize (or "buildup and pound"), and rollback. The counterstrike CONOP would be the most useful during the halt phase of a stressful MTW, in which the enemy has physical forward momentum on the ground and a numerical advantage in the air. Normal U.S. air and missile defenses may not be fully deployed, creating opportunities for the opposing side to mount deep-strike and antiaccess attacks against American and allied rear areas.

The usefulness of counterstrike drops steeply as one enters the buildup-and-pound and counterattack phases of an MTW. During the last two phases, the Air Force will presumably have established a comfortable level of air superiority; anti–tactical ballistic missile systems, such as Theater High-Altitude Area Defense and Patriot, will be fully deployed throughout the battlespace; and dispersal and decoy arrangements will be in place at the Air Force's main operating bases. In such an environment, counterstrike would probably be unnecessary, and it would be far better to devote offensive information-warfare resources to other purposes.

## Counter-C4ISR

The "counter-C4ISR campaign" CONOP involves using a mix of offensive information-warfare tools and techniques to attack adversary sensors and communication assets across the board at critical "transition points" during a campaign. The goal of the counter-C4ISR campaign is to reduce enemy's battlespace awareness at key junctures by degrading his ability to collect and process information from space, airborne, and ground-based C4ISR assets.

Earlier in this chapter, it was noted that the size and capacity of global commercial satellite and terrestrial communication networks is increasing at a rapid rate. By the 2010–2015 time frame, there will be so many redundant communication paths and links in existence that it will be impractical to achieve large, sustained reductions in the enemy's C4ISR capacity across the board from the tactical level up through national-level command and control. In fact, available evidence suggests that the United States was not even able to achieve this goal completely against Iraq during Operation Desert Storm. However, this reality does not render counter-C4ISR futile. Instead, it suggests that U.S. operations should focus on degrading key choke points of the enemy's C4ISR system at critical moments in the campaign, rather than on an attempt to destroy all enemy communications.

Increased access to commercial space-based imagery, communication, and navigation systems will greatly enhance the enemy's C4ISR capacity but may also make those systems more vulnerable to offensive information warfare. Use of space-based systems will introduce choke points into the enemy's C4ISR system. Satellites themselves become critical nodes that, if disabled, would drastically reduce enemy C4ISR capacity. Commercial communication satellites require downlink stations and locally dense communication networks that are also vulnerable to physical and information attack. Imaging satellites also require downlink stations and an imagery analysis center to read, interpret, and disseminate the information gleaned from satellites. Reception of GPS navigation, while more dispersed, will often require differential GPS transmitters to achieve needed accuracy. A well-timed attack that disables or degrades these systems may well leave the enemy worse off, especially for short but critical periods of time, than if he had never grown accustomed to their significant advantages over terrestrial communications, surveillance, and navigation.

Counter-C4ISR involves many of the same means and mechanisms as the two previous CONOPs, "preserving strategic reach" and "counterstrike." There is a fundamental difference in their goals, however. Counter-C4ISR is designed to have a decisive effect on the outcome of a campaign, while the other CONOPs would have more-limited objectives. Counter-C4ISR is a potential war winner; preserving strategic reach and counterstrike are not. This distinction means that, even more than the other CONOPs presented, counter-C4ISR requires tight integration with the regional CINC's overall campaign plan. Indeed, counter-C4ISR will depend for its success on careful synchronization with more-conventional attack assets. This implies placing responsibility for the C4ISR campaign firmly in the hands of the JFACC, rather than creating a special information-warfare component commander, so that the principle of centralized control with decentralized execution can be maintained. Creating a special information-warfare component command may sound appealing at first blush, but would probably be unwise, because it would only add another layer of command and control that could slow down U.S. and allied decision cycles. Enemy forces will use C4ISR systems to anticipate U.S. force movements and order force movements in response. They will use satellite reconnaissance to show large force movements or attack preparations, such as the movement of large amounts of supplies and weapon platforms. They will use commercial communication satellites, as well as dedicated terrestrial communications, to receive human intelligence on such movements and to order counterpreparations and strike missions against massing U.S. forces and supplies. They will use satellite navigation to provide targeting information to cruise missiles and strike aircraft on the position of key U.S. forces and supplies. Finally, they will use advanced software and computer systems to program targeting information into cruise missiles. Again, the intent of counter-C4ISR is to deny the enemy these sources of information and information processes, not always or everywhere, but just at the critical moments and places where they are most needed.

This implies that the leading edge of the rollback phase offensive will be a coordinated offensive information-warfare attack on these information systems, including physical attacks. The exact nature of that attack would depend on the CINC's overall campaign plan. As an example, however, it will be helpful to consider how the CINC might have attempted to achieve a surprise flanking attack, such as U.S. forces accomplished during Desert Storm, despite the presence of a sophisticated enemy C4ISR system.

The first, and probably most difficult, task would be to allow the large force movement necessary to accomplish such a flanking maneuver to go undetected. This would require first jamming or disabling any commercial imagery satellites capable of providing images of the staging area. As these systems will be assets of neutral nations, this may require a certain delicacy of approach. One possibility is non-lethal attacks from ground-based antisatellite (ASAT) lasers that could only temporarily blind a satellite. A less-controversial method would be precision weapon attacks on the enemy's imagery analysis centers or the satellite's communication links with enemy command centers.

Unless such movements take place in trackless deserts, they are also likely to be detected by enemy agents on the ground. This unpleasant reality implies that the movement must be accompanied by efforts to cut off the enemy's external communications. The means to accomplish this task include local jamming of commercial communication satellites from mobile transponders, precision-guided weapon attacks on satellite communication downlink stations, and information munitions implanted in key communication switches that control communications with the downlink station. Once again, the enemy is likely to be able to reconstitute these systems in the space of days or even hours, so timing is critical.

Although counter-C4ISR may not be able to prevent for a sufficient period enemy detection of a movement of the same scope as the famous Desert Storm "left hook," it can also help in stymieing enemy responses. First, attacks on communication links will make it difficult for enemy commanders to receive satellite imagery and targeting data or to give and receive orders to respond to U.S. movements. Second, as with the counterstrike CONOP, the United States can hope to deny, degrade, or corrupt enemy access to satellite navigational aids and information processes that control enemy targeting systems. U.S. forces on the move, once detected, will present tempting targets for enemy cruise missiles. If their navigational and targeting systems can be degraded at the critical moment, however, they will present little danger to U.S. forces.

Over the long term, counter-C4ISR would benefit operationally from the deployment of space weaponry. Such systems as space-based co-orbital jammers, lasers, and obscurants would increase the chances of success for this CONOP. However, the price in terms of arms-race risks and military opportunity costs could be steep, and it is not clear that the price would be worth paying.

There are tangible arms-race risks to consider when thinking about the deployment of space-based ASAT weaponry. Other nations with significant scientific, industrial, and technical wherewithal could respond by deploying their own such systems to threaten U.S. satellites. The result of this could be a net negative for the United States, since the U.S. military's main advantage in future wars will come from its superior ability to collect, process, and act upon large amounts of data in very compressed time cycles. Conflicts in space resulting in the destruction or degradation of U.S. communication or imagery satellites would hurt American military capability more than they would a regional adversary's, even if the United States inflicted more damage on enemy space capabilities than it suffered itself. Furthermore, the deployment of space-based ASAT systems could invite adversaries to use asymmetric options to negate U.S. space capabilities-options that could include terrorist acts against U.S. commercial and military satellite ground stations worldwide. Another possibility would be retaliatory jamming against U.S.-owned satellites, including the GPS navigation satellites.

All in all, the operational advantages afforded to the Air Force in terms of being able to better execute the counter-C4ISR campaign look to be outweighed by the many potential disadvantages created by space-based ASAT deployments. The counter-C4ISR campaign will still likely be effective with only ground-based ASAT assets and would even have some use if employed without any ASAT weaponry at all. However, it would be wise for the United States to continue a research and development program into space-based ASAT technologies and also to be prepared to deploy an operational system if another nation shows signs of getting ready unilaterally to place an ASAT system in space.

## COMPARING THE FOUR CONOPs

Table 7.1 is a crude attempt to summarize the strengths and weaknesses of the four CONOPs that have been presented.  Our four offensive information-warfare CONOPs are listed vertically along the column at the far left.  Each of the four is then assessed against five metrics:  the risk of escalation that the CONOP carries with it, the ability of the CONOP to remain relevant as the revolution in information technology continues, the usefulness of the CONOP against medium-sized powers (such as North Korea and Iraq), the usefulness of the CONOP against larger powers (such as Russia), and the potential of the CONOP to be militarily decisive in and of itself.

First, in terms of escalation risk, none of the CONOPs described presents an extreme escalation risk.  Information-based deterrence, because it will take place before any hostilities have broken out, may contain some escalation risks, especially if it involves fostering instability in the target state.  If the offensive information-warfare campaign is discovered and if that campaign is considered tantamount to an act of aggression, it may provoke an adversary to conventional retaliation.  Because international norms on how to treat information attacks are still evolving, it is difficult to say how any adversary might react to this provocation.  Indeed, some Russian writings, for example, declare that Russia would interpret an offen-

### Table 7.1

### Comparing the Four CONOPs

| | Escalation Risk | Long-Term Relevance | Against Medium Powers | Against Large Powers | Military Decisive-ness |
|---|---|---|---|---|---|
| Information-based deterrence | Medium | Yes | Yes | Yes | Yes |
| Preserving strategic reach | Low | Yes | Yes | Yes | No |
| Counterstrike | Low | Yes | Yes | Maybe | Maybe |
| Counter-C4ISR | Medium | Maybe | Yes | Maybe | Maybe |

sive information-warfare campaign against its homeland as being tantamount to physical attack. While this is probably hyperbole, it does point out the need to be especially careful in using offensive information warfare against states that perceive themselves to be in a position of ever-increasing weakness. Preserving strategic reach was specifically designed to minimize escalation risk. Counter-C4ISR, however, presents some risk of nuclear escalation, if the enemy has built a small nuclear arsenal. Because this CONOP involves overt attacks on the enemy's command and control networks and because these networks will likely also be used for control of the nuclear arsenal, there is some risk that the enemy will regard these CONOPs as preparatory to a counterforce first strike and respond by escalation. Preserving strategic reach was specifically intended to solve this problem.

As for long-term relevance, all the CONOPs except counter-C4ISR should remain viable options for the foreseeable future. Counter-C4ISR may become obsolete if international connectivity continues to increase at its current exponential rate. Under such circumstances, the density of the enemy's communication and surveillance networks will limit the number of choke points in the system and, consequently, the possibility of seriously degrading the system even for short periods of time. Counterstrike could lose some of its relevance if the sophistication and proliferation of digital signature technology reach a point where even regional powers could prevent the insertion of false information into the strike-planning and execution processes.

All of the CONOPs will have utility against medium-sized powers. Indeed, they were designed with such powers in mind. Against larger powers, the utility of counterstrike and counter-C4ISR will greatly diminish. Information deterrence does not depend on the size of the adversary, while preserving strategic reach can still be used to allow U.S. air assets to operate safely over particular areas of a larger adversary. However, the size and density of the communication networks of a large power would make it extremely difficult to create even the short communications blackout required for counter-C4ISR without taking drastic steps, such as the use of a high-altitude nuclear burst for electromagnetic pulse effects. Counterstrike may not be an efficient use of resources against an adversary who has very large numbers of cruise missiles and fighter aircraft available during the halt phase. Against such an adversary, it may be better to combine passive defenses with offensive counterair operations to deal with the threat of antiaccess and deep-strike attacks.

Finally, we arrive at military decisiveness. Only information-based deterrence has the potential to be militarily decisive, because it can dissuade an adversary from even starting a conflict. Preserving strategic reach is certainly not decisive, because its whole purpose is distraction, not decisiveness. Counter-C4ISR could be decisive under certain circumstances but not in others. Ultimately, counter-C4ISR creates the conditions under which other means of warfare press decisive operations against the opponent; counter-C4ISR is an enabler of decisive operations rather than a component of them. Counterstrike falls into the same category. The only scenario in which counterstrike could become decisive would be against an adversary who staked all his hopes on deep-strike and antiaccess operations against U.S. rear areas during the halt phase and had no backup plan in case those attacks failed. In such a scenario, counterstrike could act to fend off those attacks and thus implicitly compel the adversary to sue for peace. In virtually all other instances, counterstrike does not offer an opportunity for a decisive outcome in and of itself.

## REFERENCES

Agmon, Marcy, et al., *Thwarting the Superpower: How the Smart Adversary Might Use Political Weapons to Offset U.S. Military Power*, Santa Monica, Calif.: RAND, unpublished manuscript.

Air Force Space Command, "Space Capabilities Integration," briefing slides, July 12, 1996.

Ambrose, Stephen E., *D-Day, June 6, 1944: The Climactic Battle of World War II*, New York: Simon & Schuster, 1994.

Cebrowski, Vice Admiral Arthur K., and John J. Garstka, "Network-Centric Warfare: Its Origin and Future," *Naval Proceedings*, January 1998, pp. 28–35.

Chow, Brian, et al., *Air Force Operations in a Chemical and Biological Environment*, Santa Monica, Calif.: RAND, unpublished manuscript.

Hosmer, Stephen T., *Psychological Effects of U.S. Air Operations in Four Wars 1941–1991: Lessons for U.S. Commanders*, Santa Monica, Calif.: RAND, MR-576-AF, 1996.

Hutcherson, Norman B., *Command and Control Warfare: Putting Another Tool in the War-Fighter's Data Base*, Maxwell AFB, Ala.: Air University Press, September 1994.

Joint Chiefs of Staff, *Joint Vision 2010*, Washington, D.C., July 1996

Joint Staff, *Joint Doctrine for Command and Control Warfare*, Joint Publication 3-13.1, February 7, 1996.

Keffer, John W., "Trends in Commercial Satellite Communications Systems and Implications for MILSATCOM," briefing slides, November 20, 1996.

Libicki, Martin, *Defending Cyberspace and Other Metaphors*, Washington, D.C.: NDU Books, 1997.

Nye, Joseph, and William Owens, "The Information Edge," *Foreign Affairs*, Vol. 75, No. 2, March/April 1996.

Pace, Scott, et al., *The Global Positioning System: Assessing National Policies*, Santa Monica, Calif.: RAND, MR-614-OSTP, 1995.

Stillion, John, and David Orletsky, *Airbase Vulnerability to Conventional Cruise and Ballistic Missile Attack: Technology, Scenarios, and USAF Responses*, Santa Monica, Calif.: RAND, unpublished manuscript.

Stoney, William, "Land Imaging Satellites Planned to Be Operating in the Year 2000," data sheet, Mitretek, July 22, 1997.

Submarine Systems International, Inc., "Global Undersea Networks for Government Applications," briefing slides, July 1997.

U.S. Space Command, "Department of Defense Advanced Satellite Communications Capstone Requirements Document," June 23, 1997.

Watman, Kenneth, *Asymmetric Strategies for MRCs*, Santa Monica, Calif.: RAND, unpublished manuscript.

Watters, Ethan, "Virtual War and Peace," *Wired*, 4.03, March 1996, p. 49.

Wilkening, Dean, and Kenneth Watman, *Nuclear Deterrence in a Regional Context*, Santa Monica, Calif.:  RAND, MR-500-A/AF, 1995.

# Chapter Eight

# THE INFORMATION REVOLUTION AND PSYCHOLOGICAL EFFECTS

*Stephen T. Hosmer*

The advanced military and civilian technological systems that are anticipated to flow from the ongoing information revolution will require that the psychological dimension of warfare receive increased priority in the preparation, planning, and conduct of future U.S. military operations. The improved military capabilities arising from these advanced systems will have the potential to produce significant psychological and physical effects and will present new opportunities and risks for both the United States and its adversaries. Advanced technological systems will not only help shape the environment of future conflict but will also magnify the importance of the psychological battle to conflict outcome.

To gain insight into the potential impact of the information revolution on the psychological dimension of future conflict, it is useful to review the principal psychological effects that are sought in war, the instruments used to produce them, and the past U.S. and enemy experience with such effects.[1]

## OBJECTIVES AND INSTRUMENTS OF PSYCHOLOGICAL EFFECTS

In most conflicts, each belligerent conducts a psychological battle to affect the perceptions of leaders, military forces, and civilian populations so as to induce them to act in a manner favorable to its particu-

---

[1]The author would like to thank Glenn A. Kent, Martin Libicki, David A. Ochmanek, and Alan J. Vick for their comments on a previous version of this chapter.

lar side.  At the strategic level, the fundamental objectives of the psychological battle are to increase the fighting spirit of friendly populations, weaken domestic and international support to the enemy's war effort, and persuade the government of the enemy side to cease hostilities on terms acceptable to the friendly side.  At the operational and tactical levels, the objectives typically are to erode the fighting will and capability of enemy deployed forces and to induce their surrender, desertion, and defection; to deceive enemy leaders about friendly operations; to bolster the motivation and morale of friendly troops; and to win or coerce support from local populations.

The contending sides employ various instruments to generate these psychological effects, including combat operations; shows of force; military demonstrations and exercises; psychological operations (PSYOP); print and broadcast media; public diplomacy; public affairs; and, in the case of some U.S. opponents, overt and covert political operations and terrorist attacks.  Of these various instruments, experience shows that, in wartime, combat operations produce by far the most important effects.  Indeed, the psychological effects that combat operations produce often determine the cost and outcome of conflicts.

Significant advantageous psychological effects can accrue to a contending side even when its combat operations "fail" to achieve assigned objectives.  One example was the effect of the 1968 Tet offensive on U.S. attitudes toward the Vietnam War.  Even though the communist attacks on South Vietnamese urban areas failed to gain their immediate military and political objectives—the Viet Cong units participating in the attacks were unable to foment the popular uprisings they had hoped for, suffered enormous losses, and could not hold a single South Vietnamese town or city—the Tet offensive severely undermined the confidence of the U.S. government and public about the prospects for a U.S. military victory in Vietnam.  The offensive brought about a basic change in U.S. political-military strategy:  The Johnson administration imposed ceilings on further U.S. troop deployments to Southeast Asia and de-escalated the air campaign against North Vietnam.  (See Davidson, 1988, pp. 483–572.)

# U.S. AND ENEMY EXPERIENCE WITH PSYCHOLOGICAL EFFECTS

## U.S.-Caused Psychological Effects at the Strategic Level: Air Attacks on Enemy Strategic Targets

The U.S. instrument of choice for producing strategic effects has been the air attack. During World War II and the Korean, Vietnam, and Persian Gulf conflicts, the United States conducted air attacks against strategic targets located within the enemy heartland to degrade both the enemy's physical capacity to wage war and his will to do so. A major psychological objective common to these strategic attacks was to convince enemy leaders that they could expect to pay a heavy price for their continued refusal to agree to allied peace terms.

In addition, the United States also attempted to use strategic air attacks to demoralize and frighten enemy civilian populations and thereby deny labor to an enemy's war industry (a primary objective of Allied bombing in World War II); foment indigenous opposition to an enemy government's war policies; and, in the case of Iraq, prompt an enemy government's overthrow by a coup or popular uprising.[2] These objectives also became the focus of the U.S. leaflet drops and radio broadcasts that were directed at enemy heartland audiences in the course of these conflicts.

U.S. hopes that strategic bombing would motivate enemy civilian populations to act against their governments and thereby accelerate war termination were largely unrealized. Even in the face of at times highly destructive air attacks, the vast majority of enemy civilians in Germany, Japan, North Korea, and North Vietnam remained willing to accord their national leaders at least passive support or were deterred from taking antigovernment acts by the tight surveillance maintained by their governments' ubiquitous security and intelligence services. An apparent exception to this pattern was the Shia and Kurd uprisings that broke out in southern and northern Iraq at the end of the Gulf War. These popular uprisings, in part, were

---

[2]During the early phases of World War II and the Vietnam War, another important objective of such attacks was to bolster the morale of allied forces and domestic populations.

undoubtedly a consequence of the Coalition air campaign, which contributed importantly to the rout of the Iraqi ground forces in the Kuwait Theater of Operations (KTO). However, most of the uprisings occurred after the Iraqi-Coalition cease-fire was already in place, and none received military support from the United States. (Hosmer, 1996, pp. 59–60.)

U.S. attempts to influence enemy leaders to terminate wars by threatening an ever-increasing destruction of military and military-related civilian strategic targets have proven more successful, having helped to bring about the Japanese surrender, the Korean cease-fire, and the short-lived Vietnam peace agreement. In the case of Japan, the firebombing of Japanese cities and the destruction of Hiroshima and Nagasaki by atomic weapons contributed importantly to Emperor Hirohito's decision to instruct his cabinet to accept U.S. peace terms. The intensive conventional bombing of communist rear areas in Korea and the Eisenhower administration's threat to use nuclear weapons also were instrumental in inducing China and North Korea to end the Korean conflict. The U.S. B-52 bombing of Hanoi and Haiphong in December 1972 helped prompt the North Vietnamese to conclude the 1973 Paris Peace Agreements, which brought the U.S. combat involvement in Vietnam to a close.[3]

Air attacks against strategic targets also helped speed conflict termination in the former Yugoslavia. Following the mortaring of a market in Sarajevo that killed 37 people on August 28, 1995, the United

---

[3]The decisions of these various enemies to conclude war termination agreements were also influenced by other factors. The increasingly tight U.S. naval blockade, the Soviet entry into the war in Manchuria, and the realization that Japanese forces would be unable to prevent a successful U.S. invasion of the homeland also contributed importantly to the Japanese surrender decision. The death of Stalin in spring 1953 and the political thaw in the former Soviet Union's relations with the West that followed his demise also helped to pave the way for the Korean Truce in July 1953. The failure of North Vietnam's 1972 Easter offensive and the realization that communist forces would be unable to conquer South Vietnam so long as U.S. airpower remained over the battlefield also helped to shape Hanoi's decision to sign the 1973 Paris Peace Agreements. Hanoi also calculated that the American public and congressional opposition to the war had reached a point where it would be politically impossible for the United States to reenter the conflict once its forces had been withdrawn. Thus, Hanoi believed that the United States would probably not attempt militarily to enforce the crucial peace terms—such as those prohibiting the infiltration of troops and non-replacement supplies from the North—that the communists intended to violate. (See Hosmer, 1996, pp. 9–42.)

States and its NATO allies used air attacks against Bosnian-Serb command and control centers, air-defense facilities, bridges, and other strategic targets to persuade the Bosnian Serb leaders to order their forces to pull their heavy weapons out of the Sarajevo weapons' exclusion zone and to cease firing on Bosnian-Muslim positions within the city. These NATO air attacks—and the prospect that further attacks might follow—also helped to encourage the Bosnian Serb leaders to agree to a general cease-fire and to enter into the negotiating process that led to the Dayton Accords.

However, an analysis of these successful uses of bombing as a coercive instrument also shows that air attacks and the threat of air attacks have produced decisive psychological effects only when certain other military pressures and conditions were also present. Experience demonstrates that enemy leaders have been persuaded to negotiate the termination of wars on terms acceptable to the United States apparently only when those leaders also perceived that they

- faced defeat or stalemate on the battlefield
- were unlikely to get better peace terms if they prolonged the fighting
- had no prospect of mounting an effective defense or riposte to the strategic attacks
- were convinced that the cost of the damage from the strategic air attacks or threatened attacks was likely to outweigh significantly the cost of the concessions the United States was demanding.

To force an unconditional enemy capitulation, experience suggests than an additional prerequisite may also be needed: that the leader or leaders who started the war would first have been removed from power. (Hosmer, 1996, p. 74.)

## U.S.-Caused Psychological Effects at the Operational and Tactical Levels

**PSYOP Messages.** At the operational and tactical levels, the United States has relied on surrender appeals and other PSYOP messages disseminated by radio and loudspeaker broadcasts and leaflet drops to undermine the resistance of enemy deployed forces. In combat situations, U.S. PSYOP messages typically have sought to weaken the motivation and morale of the individual enemy soldier and to persuade him to desert, defect, or surrender.

During the course of World War II and the large and small wars involving U.S. forces that have followed, many tens of thousands of enemy prisoners have claimed to have been influenced to some extent by U.S. PSYOP messages.[4] Throughout all these wars, the most effective U.S. leaflet has been the "safe conduct pass," which instructed enemy troops on how to surrender and assured them of good treatment once they were in allied hands. PSYOP appeals and instructions have also played an important role in U.S. counterinsurgency and peacekeeping operations, by helping to win the support and cooperation of local civilian populations.

While PSYOP messages have helped to encourage and facilitate enemy surrenders and desertions, they have not been the primary cause of catastrophic collapse of enemy resistance or of large-scale surrender and desertion of enemy deployed troops. Indeed, the number of enemy surrenders and deserters in past wars does not correlate directly with either the intensity or the quality of the U.S. PSYOP campaigns in those conflicts. (Hosmer, 1996, pp. 180–181.) Instead, history shows that it has been U.S. combat operations that have produced the most decisive psychological effects on enemy deployed forces.

**Attacks on Enemy Deployed Forces**. A comparative analysis of psychological effects in the Korean, Vietnam, and Gulf wars disclosed three conditions that consistently produced a catastrophic disintegration of enemy resistance and large-scale surrenders and desertions among enemy forces. These were when friendly military operations (1) subjected enemy forces to sustained, effective air and artillery attacks for a period of several weeks or more; (2) deprived enemy troops of adequate food; and (3) exploited the loss of enemy morale caused by such attacks and deprivation with timely ground operations. The analysis further suggested that, when these conditions were absent, catastrophic disintegration and large-scale surrenders and desertions were also absent.

---

[4]One U.S. Army historian puts the number of enemy prisoners claiming to have been influenced by U.S. battlefield propaganda at "literally hundreds of thousands." (See Sandler, 1996, p. 1.)

During the Korean War, enemy forces surrendered en masse and showed other signs of collapse on two separate occasions: The first, involving North Korean forces, occurred in fall 1950; the second, involving Chinese troops, occurred in spring 1951. In both instances, enemy forces had been on the offensive for several months and had suffered heavy casualties in their repeated attempts to drive the United Nations (UN) defenders from Korea. According to the testimony of North Korean and Chinese prisoners and deserters, the principal causes of the deterioration in morale that preceded each collapse were the weeks of intensive air and artillery attacks the troops experienced and the severe hunger they suffered because of the aerial interdiction of their food resupply. (Hosmer, 1996, pp. 91–139.)

In the case of the Gulf War, the reality and threat posed by round-the-clock Coalition air attacks decisively reduced the morale of Iraqi troops, whose fighting spirit had already faltered. Iraqi prisoners of war of all ranks cited the Coalition's 38-day air campaign and the supply deprivation it caused as the key reasons for their low morale and failure to resist Coalition ground forces. No fewer than 160,000 of the Iraqi troops—some 40 percent of those originally deployed in the KTO—had already deserted by the start of the Coalition ground attack on February 24, 1991, and most of those that remained were prepared to flee or surrender after offering little or no resistance. The absence of much serious fighting by the Iraqis is reflected by the fact that, of the more than 62,000 Iraqi troops captured by U.S. forces, only about 640 required treatment in Central Command medical facilities.[5] Instead of the many thousands of U.S. fatalities that most observers predicted for the ground campaign, the actual number of U.S. Army and Marine personnel that were killed as a result of hostile action during the 100-hour ground fighting was only 63.[6]

In contrast to the Gulf, the enemy forces in Vietnam were rarely exposed to sustained air, artillery, or other military attack. Because

[5]All told, over 85,000 Iraqis surrendered to Coalition forces. (See Hosmer, 1996, pp. 153–154.)

[6]This does not include the 28 U.S. military personnel killed in the February 25, 1991, Scud attack on the U.S. barracks in Dhahran, Saudi Arabia. Before the fighting began, General Schwarzkopf estimated that American casualties could go as high as 20,000, with about one-third of those killed. (Moore, 1991.)

communist commanders largely held the initiative for determining the time and place of battle, the Viet Cong and North Vietnamese Army (NVA) forces were able, for the most part, to control their own combat exposure and casualties. Most engagements were short-lived, and most communist units fought only a few times a year, often only once or twice every six months. Since U.S. and South Vietnamese forces did not, as a rule, pursue retreating enemy troops, communist units that had been mauled by friendly air attacks and defeated in battle were invariably able to withdraw to rear areas, where they could rest, refit, and rebuild their morale under the protective cover of Vietnam's triple-canopied rain forests. The abundance of food sources throughout South Vietnam allowed communist troops to enjoy adequate food rations nearly all the time.

As a result of these combat conditions, U.S. and Government of South Vietnam forces never caused a catastrophic break in communist morale or an en masse surrender of a large-sized enemy main-force unit. Even though the U.S. and Government of South Vietnam mounted massive PSYOP campaigns—involving billions of leaflets and tens of thousands of hours of aero broadcasts—to induce enemy defections and surrenders, the number of main-force prisoners and defectors that came into allied hands was minuscule compared with the number of enemy troops engaged and killed during the conflict. (Hosmer, 1996, pp. 125–129.)

## Enemy-Caused Psychological Effects at the Strategic Level

**Generating U.S. Combat Casualties.** Lacking the capability to attack the U.S. homeland or the military prowess to defeat U.S. forces decisively on the battlefield, America's enemies have sought to create strategic psychological effects by protracting the fighting and maximizing U.S. casualties. In essence, America's adversaries have made U.S. deployed forces their strategic target, calculating that lengthening casualty lists would cause the American public to turn against a continued U.S. combat involvement and force the U.S. government to settle conflicts on terms advantageous to the adversaries. Such calculations have shaped the battlefield strategy of each major adversary the United States has faced from World War II on.

When Japan initiated hostilities against the United States in 1941, its strategic plan assumed that a stubborn defense of the perimeter that

Japanese forces planned to capture in the Pacific and Southeast Asia eventually would undermine the American public's determination to support a prolonged war.  According to the U.S. Strategic Bombing Survey, the Japanese leaders calculated that:

> The weakness of the United States as a democracy would make it impossible for her to continue all-out offensive action in the face of the losses which would be imposed by fanatically resisting Japanese soldiers, sailors, and airmen, and the elimination of its Allies.  The United States in consequence would compromise and allow Japan to retain a substantial portion of her initial territorial gains.  (U.S. Strategic Bombing Survey, 1976a, p. 2.)

As late as summer 1945, hard-line Japanese military leaders hoped that they could still inflict sufficient casualties on any U.S. forces landing on the Japanese homeland to "improve their chances of a negotiated peace." (U.S. Strategic Bombing Survey, 1976b, p. 12.)

The enemy strategy in both the Korean and Vietnam wars was also to generate U.S. casualties so as to undermine U.S. public support for a continued U.S. involvement in those wars.  The Chinese strategy in the Korean War was guided by Mao Zedong's belief that "the masses in the United States had nothing to gain by fighting in Korea.  He could accentuate popular disaffection by killing American troops. . . ."  Mao eventually concluded that as many as "several 100,000" American casualties might be needed to destroy the U.S. will to fight. (See Hunt, 1992.)  The Vietnamese communist leaders also emphasized the importance of generating U.S. casualties to intensify the "contradictions" between the American public and its government and produce other decisive psychological effects.  The North Vietnamese leaders were convinced that, just as the Viet Minh's war against the French had been won in Paris, their struggle to liberate South Vietnam would be won in Washington.

Mounting U.S. casualties in both Korea and Vietnam did eventually reduce U.S. domestic support for those conflicts.  Concerns about the pernicious effects of casualties on U.S. domestic attitudes caused U.S. decisionmakers in both conflicts to order major changes in U.S. war-fighting strategy so as to hold down U.S. losses.  In the case of Korea, U.S. forces were ordered to cease major offensive operations, assume an "active defense," and build up the capabilities of South Korean forces to assume more of the fighting.  In Vietnam, U.S.

leaders adopted a policy of "Vietnamization," which forced South Vietnamese units to take on an increasing share of the ground fighting. At the same time, U.S. forces were ordered to avoid casualties while they were being progressively withdrawn from the conflict. (Hosmer, 1987, pp. 66–74.)

Saddam Hussein's willingness to risk a possible military confrontation with the United States over Kuwait rested in part on his belief that Iraq could impose unacceptable casualties on U.S. forces in the event the confrontation escalated to open warfare. In his meeting with American Ambassador April Glaspie before he invaded Kuwait, Saddam asserted that America was "a society which cannot accept 10,000 dead in one battle."[7] He reiterated this view in a December 20, 1990, interview with German television when he rejected the suggestion that his insistence on retaining Kuwait was suicidal: "We are sure if President Bush pushes things toward war . . . once 5000 of his troops die, he will not be able to continue the war."[8]

Whenever possible, U.S. adversaries in smaller-scale contingencies have also sought to use U.S. casualties to turn U.S. public opinion against U.S. interventions. Such was the case with the Muslim terrorists who planned and conducted the October 1983 truck bombing of the U.S. Marine barracks at the Beirut International Airport, an action that forced the eventual withdrawal of U.S. troops from Lebanon.[9] This also became the strategy of General Mohammed Aideed and the Somalia National Alliance (SNA) in July 1993 when they made a "calculated decision to kill American sol-

---

[7]See "Excerpts from Iraqi Transcripts of Meeting with U.S. Envoy," 1990.

[8]In an August 16 open letter to President Bush, Saddam intimated that U.S. casualties in the Gulf region would turn the American electorate against the president, warning that the president would fall off his "seat" after the defeat of his "brute force." See Foreign Broadcast Information Service (1991), p. 2, and Foreign Broadcast Information Service (1990), p. 2.

[9]As Geoffrey Kemp, who served on the National Security Council staff at the time of the bombing, points out:

> From the U.S. perspective, the bombing of the Marines meant that it was not a question of whether we would leave but when. The domestic pressure in the U.S. to pull the Marines out coincided with the Defense Department's long-standing wish to redeploy the troops back to ships. It was clear to the President's domestic advisers that when Congress returned in January from the long Christmas recess (which begins in early November), grass roots support for keeping the Marines in Lebanon would be zero. (Kemp, 1991, pp. 139–140.)

diers" so as to undermine U.S. domestic support for the U.S. involvement in Somalia. (Richburg, 1993.) According to Ambassador Robert Oakley and John Hirsch, there is little doubt that Aideed and the other SNA "militia leaders had studied not only Operation Desert Storm but Vietnam and Lebanon to understand the domestic political impact of American casualties." (Hirsch and Oakley, 1995, n. 19, pp. 121–122.) The number of U.S. casualties climbed precipitously in the Mogadishu firefight of October 3–4, 1993, which cost U.S. forces the loss of some 18 killed and 73 wounded. These losses forced a fundamental change in U.S. policy toward Somalia and the eventual withdrawal of U.S. troops. (Hirsch and Oakley, 1995, pp. 122–125.)

**Deception and Propaganda.** Adversaries have also employed propaganda and deception in an attempt to undermine U.S. domestic and international support for U.S. military involvements. The principal aims of this strategic propaganda have been to convince U.S. and foreign audiences that (1) the adversary was fighting a "just" war; (2) the U.S. could not win, as the adversary would never give up; and (3) the U.S. methods of warfare and war objectives were "unjust."

One classic example of such deceptive propaganda was the worldwide media campaign mounted by the Soviet Union, China, and North Korea that charged the United States with conducting "germ warfare" during the Korean War. Communist officials claimed that U.S. airmen and artillerymen had delivered bacteria-infected insects and shellfish into North Korea. To build a case for these charges, the communists created faked "exhibits" of U.S. germ warfare paraphernalia, inaugurated a massive inoculation program in their rear areas of Korea, and by torture and threats, forced captured U.S. pilots to "'confess' on film, on tape, and in press interviews that they had indeed been part of a huge United States germ warfare conspiracy." (Blair, 1987, p. 966.) As evaluated by one historian,

> This wholly fabricated propaganda attack, supported by communist-manipulated "demonstrations" all over the world, was astonishingly successful; Washington's slow-footed and righteous denials were not. (Blair, 1987, p. 966.)

The Vietnam War also provided numerous examples of enemy deception and propaganda aimed at eroding U.S. domestic and international support for the U.S. war effort. Despite the fact that an estimated one million NVA soldiers infiltrated into South Vietnam during the course of the war, Hanoi consistently denied that it had any troops fighting in the South.[10]  Furthermore, to mask its dominant role and ultimate objectives in the conflict, Hanoi created two South Vietnamese front groups, the National Liberation Front (NLF) and the Provisional Revolutionary Government (PRG), which Hanoi proclaimed to be "the sole genuine representative of the southern people." Both the NLF and the PRG were abruptly cast aside after the 1975 takeover.  To mollify international and South Vietnamese domestic concerns, Hanoi also claimed during the war that it had no intention of rapidly annexing or communizing South Vietnam.  As one disillusioned former member of the PRG cabinet wrote, these assurances were

> discarded like trash within months of [the 1975] victory.  By then, it was clear that there was no further need for subterfuge—either toward the Western media or antiwar movements, or toward the Southern revolution itself. (Truong Nhu Tang, 1985, p. 284.)

Adversaries have also exploited any injury to civilians or other collateral damage stemming from U.S. bombing so as to build sympathy for their cause, to incite U.S. domestic and international opposition to continued U.S. air strikes, and to constrict the targets of future U.S. air attacks.  The North Vietnamese proved particularly adept at exploiting the propaganda value of errant bombing during the Rolling Thunder and Linebacker I and II air campaigns against North Vietnam.  For example, the Hanoi leaders used allegations about bomb damage to the Red River dikes both to extract greater war effort from the North Vietnamese population and to discredit U.S. bombing in the eyes of the U.S. and international publics.  Even though the bulk of the damage to the dikes resulted from a lack of proper maintenance (the dikes were off-limits to U.S. air attacks), the North Vietnamese population and foreign media were told that the United States was bombing the dikes intentionally, to flood the entire Red River delta.[11]  Baghdad propagandists employed similar

---

[10]For an estimate of NVA infiltration into South Vietnam, see Pike (1986), p. 47.

[11]Foreign media and other visitors to North Vietnam were provided tours to the same "damaged" dike over a period of several years. (Parks, 1983.)

methods in an attempt to discredit and constrain the U.S. bombing campaign during the Gulf War.[12]

In recent smaller-scale contingencies, local leaders have also employed PSYOP media to incite their populations to make war on their neighbors and UN peacekeepers.  Leaders of the several former Yugoslav republics used television, radio, and print media to promote ethnic hatred and mobilize their publics to take up arms to advance or defend communal political and territorial interests. Indeed, some observers believe the media became the "main instruments in stirring up and managing" the conflict in the former Yugoslavia.[13]  Similarly, broadcasts from the government-controlled Rwanda Radio did much to foster the 1994 genocide in Rwanda by deliberately fomenting ethnic hatred among the Hutus and inciting the mass killings of Tutsis.  After the Hutu government had been routed by Tutsi forces, a mobile radio still under the control of former Hutu government officials precipitated the massive flight of Hutu refugees into Tanzania and Zaire by assuring them that they faced "certain slaughter" if they fell under Tutsi control.  (Adelman and Suhrke, 1996, p. 38; also see Burkhalter, 1994.)

Hostile radio broadcasts also helped to undermine the U.S. and UN intervention in Somalia.  To counter U.S. and UN attempts to marginalize him politically, Aideed successfully used his radio station in Mogadishu to rally support for his continued leadership and to foment anti-U.S. and anti-UN sentiment among his countrymen. (Hirsch and Oakley, 1995, pp. 116–117.)  Along with protesting the U.S. and UN interference in Somalia's internal politics, Aideed's radio broadcasts also attacked the motives of the U.S. intervention,

---

[12]After a planned U.S. air strike on the Al Firdos bunker unintentionally killed several hundred Iraqi civilians, further U.S. air strikes on Baghdad were sharply reduced. American intelligence had identified the Al Firdos bunker to be an Iraqi military communications site, and the U.S. air planners had no idea that the bunker was also being used as a civilian air raid shelter.

[13]As one observer put it:

> The function of the war propaganda disseminated by the conflicting parties has been, by turn, to mobilize and intimidate, glorify and demonize, and justify and accuse, bearing out the assumption that the media bears a large part of the responsibility for the outbreak and tragic course of the war in the former Yugoslavia.

For this quote and a discussion of this and other roles the media play, see Simic (1994), pp. 40–47.

accusing the United States of planning to steal Somalia's mineral resources. As proof of this nefarious U.S. intent, which many Somalis apparently believed, the radio cited the abundance of the earth-moving and other engineering equipment that had accompanied U.S. forces into Somalia.

## Enemy-Caused Psychological Effects at the Operational and Tactical Levels

As with U.S. PSYOP, America's enemies have also attempted through radio and loudspeaker broadcasts and leaflets to persuade U.S. fighting personnel to desert, defect, or surrender. While enemy PSYOP has no doubt facilitated and even prompted the surrender of U.S. troops on occasion, enemy attempts to induce U.S. forces to defect or desert have met with little, if any, success.[14] Whether for this or other reasons, the volume of enemy PSYOP directed at U.S. forces has been small in comparison to the effort adversaries have devoted to maintaining the fighting will of their own troops and populations.

**Morale Building and Maintenance.** Enemy combat leaders have used both negative and positive psychological measures to prevent the defections, desertions, and surrenders that U.S. PSYOP has attempted to induce. One measure virtually all U.S. adversaries have used has been to inculcate a fear of capture in their personnel. Enemy troops routinely have been told that they would be tortured and killed if they fell into U.S. hands. German, North Vietnamese, and Iraqi troops, among others, were further warned that their families would be held hostage for their actions and would be severely punished if the troops defected or surrendered. Enemy officers and cadres also have attempted to keep close watch over their troops to prevent them from reading leaflets or listening to allied radio broadcasts and to deter them from attempting to surrender or desert.[15]

---

[14]In the course of his comprehensive study of U.S. Army tactical psychological operations, Stanley Sandler could "find no documented evidence of a single U.S. soldier who has defected to the enemy in time of war as a result of enemy propaganda." (See Sandler, 1996, pp. 2–3.)

[15]During the Gulf War, the Iraqis stationed "death squads" behind their lines to apprehend and punish would-be deserters. In some Iraqi divisions, a few deserters were publicly executed as an object lesson to others.

Along with emphasizing the threat of sanctions, enemy officers and noncommissioned officers have also devoted considerable time and effort to building and maintaining unit morale. This was particularly true during the Korean and Vietnam wars, when communist cadres gave close attention to troop indoctrination and to the evaluation and bolstering of morale so that their men might enter battle with the proper fighting spirit. "Criticism and self-criticism" sessions were conducted regularly at various echelons in all units to ferret out and correct the poor morale of individual fighters. (Hosmer, 1996, pp. 95, 131.)

Finally, enemy leaders have also invested substantial effort in maintaining the motivation and morale of their civilian populations and in mobilizing domestic support for their countries' war efforts. Typically, enemy leaders have used their broadcast and print media to extol the righteousness of their country's cause, the heroism of their fighting men, and the certainty of their eventual victory, while demonizing both the motives and behavior of their adversaries. It will, of course, not escape notice that U.S. and allied leaders have employed similar themes in their attempts to bolster home-front morale and war support.

## ADVANCED TECHNOLOGICAL SYSTEMS AND PSYCHOLOGICAL EFFECTS

### Impact of Advanced Systems on Future War-Fighting Capabilities

Improvements in data acquisition, processing, storage, switching, and transmission technologies, along with accelerating progress in such areas as miniaturization and new material technologies, will produce advanced technological systems that will have important implications for future warfare. Among other consequences, these advanced technological systems will increase significantly the battlefield effectiveness of

- **finders**, by increasing their capacity to see the battlefield, identify targets, and distinguish enemy from friendly forces

- **controllers**, by decreasing their reaction time, improving their decisionmaking, and increasing their span of control

- **shooters**, by increasing their survivability, lethality, and precision.

Because combat operations produce the greatest psychological effects, the relative capabilities of enemy and friendly finders, controllers, and shooters will help to determine the extent to which the United States or its adversaries gain the psychological advantage in future conflicts. These capabilities are likely to be particularly relevant to U.S. operations that are aimed at striking strategic targets and demoralizing deployed forces and to enemy operations that are aimed at generating U.S. battlefield casualties.

## Implications for Future U.S.-Caused Psychological Effects

**Attacks on Enemy Strategic Targets.** Improvements in intelligence sensors and platforms, penetrating aircraft, standoff weapon systems, and precision munitions should progressively increase U.S. capabilities to identify and strike high-value targets deep in an enemy's heartland.

The availability of long-endurance unmanned aerial vehicles (UAVs), for example, should make it possible to maintain persistent surveillance over an enemy's capital city and place at risk otherwise hard-to-locate mobile targets, possibly including enemy leaders. Given that most enemy leaders are likely to attach high value to their personal survival, the round-the-clock threat of sudden aerial attack might increase the incentives of some would-be adversaries to avoid conflict with the United States. So, too, continued improvements in deep-penetrating munitions may increase enemy leaders' sense of vulnerability, by reducing their confidence that heavily reinforced bunkers might afford them protection from U.S. aerial attack.

Advances in stealth, UAV, and standoff weapon technologies will also allow the United States to attack enemy strategic targets with minimal U.S. aircrew losses. Similarly, improvements in intelligence-collection technologies, precision weapon delivery, nonlethal munitions, and electronic and other capabilities to disrupt and destroy enemy computer-dependent systems and command, control, communications, and intelligence should permit the United

States to degrade an enemy's war-fighting capacity and disrupt its economy without causing significant civilian casualties.[16]

The capability to mount effective attacks against targets deep in an enemy's heartland with minimum losses to civilians and U.S. personnel will undoubtedly prove demoralizing to enemy leaders, in part because the leaders will recognize that such attacks can be continued virtually indefinitely without imposing any appreciable compensating cost on the United States. Even so, without the added pressure of actual or prospective reverses on the battlefield, attacks on enemy strategic targets will probably not, in themselves, suffice to secure U.S. war aims.

**Attacks on Enemy Deployed Forces.** There is the prospect that advanced technological systems will increase significantly the psychological effects of U.S. military operations on the motivation and morale of enemy deployed forces. The impact will be greatest in combat situations in which U.S. finders can readily locate enemy targets in any weather and time of day and in which U.S. shooters can promptly kill the targets U.S. controllers designate for attack. Such a capability should be severely demoralizing to enemy forces because they would perceive they faced the following prospects:

- If we fly, we die.
- If we fire, we die.
- If we communicate, we die.
- If we radiate, we die.
- If we move with our vehicles, we die.
- If we remain with our weapons, we die.

The potential for massive surrenders and a decisive weakening of enemy cohesion also will be greatest when substantial portions of the enemy's food resupply can be successfully interdicted and when U.S. aircraft, missiles, and artillery can keep enemy forces under actual attack or under the threat of immediate attack around the clock for a period of several weeks. Timely U.S. ground attacks will

---

[16]Among other weapons, computer-controlled systems may be vulnerable to attack by high-power microwave, electromagnetic pulse, radio frequency, and antimaterial chemical weapons.

also be necessary to reap the maximum battlefield benefits of such psychological softening.

Sustained attacks have several important effects. They undermine the motivation and morale of enemy troops; they impede the enemy combat leader's ability to bolster or restore morale by forcing enemy personnel to remain constantly under cover and dispersed; and they provide enemy troops the opportunity to desert or surrender by making it difficult for enemy leaders to observe and control troop behavior on the battlefield. (Hosmer, 1996, p. 195.)

**The Gulf War Experience.** Advanced technological systems should magnify the types of psychological effects that were produced by the Coalition air campaign against Iraqi ground forces during the Gulf War. The air campaign intensified the shortcomings in motivation and morale, already present in Iraqi ranks prior to the outbreak of hostilities, by (1) convincing Iraqi officers and enlisted personnel of Coalition air supremacy, (2) proving the inadequacy of Iraqi air defense, (3) confirming the inevitability of Iraqi defeat, (4) intensifying the hardship of the Iraqi troops in the KTO, and (5) increasing the Iraqi soldiers' fears about their personal survival and the safety of their families back home. (Hosmer, 1996, p. 162.)

Iraqi line crossers and prisoners of war testified that they found the following attributes of the Coalition air campaign particularly demoralizing:

- **Ubiquity of Coalition Aircraft.** Iraqi officers and enlisted personnel alike mentioned the omnipresence of the Coalition aircraft as a key factor depressing their morale. They commented on the psychological stress caused by knowing that aircraft were constantly orbiting overhead but not knowing if and when an aircraft might strike their unit. Even Iraqi troops who had not directly experienced actual air attacks reported being demoralized by the persistent threat posed by Coalition aircraft flying overhead.

- **All-Knowing Coalition Intelligence.** The psychological stress was increased by the Iraqi conviction that the Coalition's superior intelligence and target-designation systems enabled Coalition aircraft to respond promptly to any Iraqi vehicular movement; artillery or antiaircraft firing; or the employment of radios, radars, and other emitters. As a consequence, Iraqi troops were often deterred from operating such equipment and were conditioned to abandon their vehicles when Coalition aircraft were about.

- **Intensity of Air Attacks.** The Iraqis also reported being demoralized by both the frequency and magnitude of the Coalition air attacks, including, most particularly, the heavy bombings by B-52s. The round-the-clock attacks some units experienced during the air campaign proved particularly stressful for both Iraqi officers and enlisted personnel because it deprived them of sleep and allowed them little opportunity to perform their duties.

- **Accuracy of Bombardment.** Even though Coalition aircraft actually often missed their targets, Iraqis generally respected and were demoralized by the accuracy of the Coalition bombing.[17] Indeed, in the view of some Iraqis, Coalition aircraft seemed able to hit any target that they could detect on the battlefield.

- **Inadequacy of Iraqi Defenses.** The Iraqi soldiers also were demoralized by the realization that neither the Iraqi air force nor the other active defense measures that they usually relied on could protect them from Coalition air strikes. As the air campaign wore on, some Iraqi air defense units stopped firing on Coalition aircraft because of the perceived futility of the exercise and the danger of being seen and struck in retaliation. (Hosmer, 1996, pp. 160–170.)

Advanced technological systems will undoubtedly enhance the U.S. capability to acquire intelligence, conduct accurate bombardments, and deny an enemy effective air defenses. However, to secure the psychological effects of ubiquity and intensity, the United States will need to acquire and field sufficient air platforms, ground-based attack systems, and munitions to keep enemy troops under attack or the threat of attack 24 hours a day over a several-week period.

Finally, the ability of U.S. forces to inflict decisive psychological damage would be importantly enhanced if U.S. forces were to acquire the capability to deny enemy ground troops sanctuary from effective air, artillery, and missile attack in a broader spectrum of

---

[17]Through most of the air campaign, Coalition aircraft operated at medium altitude so as to minimize losses, which reduced their accuracy.

combat environments. If a sufficient stock of deep-penetrating munitions could be acquired, for example, U.S. forces could attack enemy deployed forces positioned in extensive hardened bunkers and tunnels, something U.S. forces were largely unable to do effectively during the Korean War.[18] Similarly, while the development of the foliage-penetrating radar has increased the U.S. capability to detect some types of targets under heavy overgrowth, even more-effective sensing systems will be needed if U.S. forces are to garner maximum psychological impact from attacks on enemy personnel located in heavily foliaged terrain.

## Implications for Future Enemy-Caused Psychological Effects[19]

**Continued Enemy Attempts to Cause U.S. Combat Casualties.** America's adversaries undoubtedly will continue to view the U.S. public's sensitivity to casualties as their primary lever for forcing the United States to settle conflicts on terms advantageous to their sides. This is almost certainly to be the case, for example, in the event of a renewed outbreak of hostilities in Korea. According to the testimony of North Korean defectors, Pyongyang intends to attempt to maximize U.S. casualties early on in any future conflict partly by conducting chemical and other attacks against on U.S. bases and forces.[20]

Adversary calculations about the leverage that can be derived from the U.S. sensitivity to casualties could prove well-founded in many potential future conflict situations. Except where the lives of U.S.

---

[18]During the last 20 months of the Korean war, intensive U.S. air and artillery attacks had little adverse psychological impact on enemy troops who, except for sporadic sorties at night, were holed up in an elaborate system of bunkers, trenches, and tunnels largely impenetrable to U.S. weapons. (Hosmer, 1996, pp. 182–183.)

[19]Major portions of the following section are drawn from Hosmer (1998).

[20]Such attacks would, of course, also be intended to paralyze U.S. air operations and prevent the deployment of U.S. air and ground reinforcements to South Korea. According to the testimony of Choi Ju-hwal, a North Korean army defector, if war were to break out on the Korean peninsula again, the North's main target would be "the U.S. forces based in the South and Japan, which is the reason that the North has been working furiously on its missile programs." Choi also testified that the North Korean leader, Kim Jong-il, believes that if North Korea can create 20,000 American casualties in the region, "it would win the war." See "North Korean Defectors Warn of Missile Threat" (1996).

forward-deployed forces or other citizens are clearly at risk, the American public is likely to perceive the stakes at issue in most post–Cold War contingencies to be of marginal importance to U.S. national interests. As a consequence, the public and the Congress will have little tolerance for U.S. casualties and protracted combat involvements in such contingencies.

This limited public tolerance for casualties is likely to deter U.S. decisionmakers from intervening in many future conflict situations and lead them to constrain U.S. military objectives and combat behavior once U.S. forces do intervene. The fragility of U.S. domestic support for such involvements will also require that U.S. combatant commanders continue to give priority attention to force protection in future interventions. The propensity of U.S. commanders in Bosnia-Herzegovina to assign highest priority to force protection in their operations and the reluctance they have shown to use U.S. forces in operations (such as the forcible return of refugees) that might promote armed resistance are recent manifestations of an interest in preserving U.S. domestic support for an intervention by avoiding U.S. combat casualties.

**Some Advanced Systems Will Help to Reduce U.S. Casualties.** There are a number of ways that advanced technological systems should enable U.S. forces to operate with reduced casualties and thus undercut an enemy's opportunity to adversely influence U.S. public opinion.

Improved intelligence sensors and platforms, along with improvements in intelligence processing, integration, and connectivity, will make the battlefield more transparent to U.S. commanders, particularly with regard to combat in open terrain. American combat leaders at all echelons should enjoy improved real-time, shared situational awareness about both enemy and friendly forces. This should reduce fratricide and the potential lethality of enemy attacks.

The capability of U.S. air and ground forces to identify and promptly kill enemy targets throughout the entire depth of the battlefield also should reduce the threat to U.S. combat personnel. Military planners from all the U.S. services envisage a future combat environment in which U.S. information dominance, air supremacy, and long-range precision-strike capabilities will permit U.S. forces to destroy enemy aircraft, vessels, armor, and other ground elements before they can engage U.S. forces. In ground confrontations, for example, longer-range fires that can destroy (as opposed to merely delay or disrupt) enemy maneuver units should allow U.S. troops to avoid inherently dangerous close-fire engagements more easily and thereby reduce friendly losses.

The availability of increasingly capable unmanned systems—such as UAVs equipped with multiple sensors—that can provide persistent surveillance over enemy-controlled areas obviously will reduce the risks to U.S. aircrews. The development of microsensors and micro-electromechanical systems may lead eventually to the production and deployment of pocket-sized unmanned aircraft that could scout inside buildings and along streets in support of ground-force operations in urban areas. (Evers, 1996.) Larger UAVs, in time, may acquire the capability to drop leaflets and broadcast PSYOP messages over enemy territory and even to conduct air strikes against enemy targets.

The acquisition and deployment of other advanced technological systems now under development should also help to hold down U.S. casualties; these include through-the-wall detection devices for urban combat, rifle munitions that can kill targets behind obstacles, countersniper sensors that will facilitate immediate and accurate responses to sniping attacks, combat identification systems that will lower the risks of fratricide, and effective mine-detection systems that will reduce the ubiquitous mine threat to U.S. ground forces. (Seffers, 1998.)

Finally, improvements in the U.S. capability to provide intelligence support to friendly indigenous troops or third-country intervention forces without a large U.S. ground presence should increase U.S. options for influencing the outcomes of future conflicts without risking U.S. casualties.

**But Adversaries Can Also Exploit Advanced Technological Systems.** The exploitation of the information revolution, however, is unlikely to be a one-way affair. Future adversaries also can be expected to use advanced technological information systems to make U.S. military interventions more costly and difficult.

Since much of the advanced information technology is expected to emerge from the private sector, we must expect the proliferation of more-accurate and lethal weapon systems based on that technology. Such countries as Russia, which already has a well-established capacity to produce advanced technological systems, and China, which is working assiduously to acquire such a capacity, are likely to field future forces with "finder," "controller," and "shooter" capabilities that will rival some of those possessed by the United States.

Moreover, even minor rogue states are likely to be able to acquire niche capabilities that would threaten U.S. forces.[21] Future enemies will likely have access to advanced technological information systems that will improve their own situational awareness and deny U.S. forces surprise. The widespread availability of high-resolution imagery from commercial and military satellites will make future U.S. operations more difficult and risky. (Nix, 1998.) It seems highly unlikely, for example, that the United States could repeat without enemy discovery the massive vehicle and troop movements that the Iraqis failed to detect during the Gulf War.

The availability of advanced man-portable air-defense systems, equipped with a spectrum of sensors, could pose significant threats to U.S. aircrews during peace operations (which typically depend heavily on U.S. fixed-wing airlift and helicopter assets) and during opposed entry operations. A future attempt to insert American forces by airdrop or helicopter could prove costly if met by an alerted enemy equipped with such advanced man-portable air-defense systems.

A combination of technologies could enable some Third World adversaries to threaten large numbers of U.S. troops, even in rear areas. A rogue state could develop the capability to attack airfields, ports, and other sites of U.S. troop concentration with weapons of mass destruction. This might be accomplished, for example, by a cruise missile armed with biological agents guided by Global Positioning System updates to a site occupied by U.S. forces identified by satellite imagery.[22]

---

[21]Some of the technologies that have been "available to the just and unjust alike" for several years are listed in Livingstone (1995).

[22]The Global Positioning System–derived coordinates of the troop location sites would be known ahead.

The information revolution also is likely to provide future adversaries with communication options that could degrade important U.S. intelligence-collection capabilities. Potential enemies may be able to use high-capacity, landline communication links and hard-to-break encryption and scrambling systems to make their communications more secure from U.S. disruption and compromise. This could increase the risks to future U.S. assault forces, in that the denial of enemy command, control, and communications has been an important element of U.S. force protection in U.S. entry and other offensive operations.

Cyberspace technologies may provide even low-tech states the opportunity to disrupt U.S. military operations, including force deployments, and to attack important targets in the U.S. homeland. Computer hackers in the employ of an enemy might be able to disrupt temporarily the operations of one or more computer-dependent infrastructures in the United States, such as the U.S. banking networks, stock exchanges, and the distribution systems for natural gas and electric power. Whether such attacks would prove successful would depend on the extent to which vital infrastructures had been hardened against cyber threats. The severity of the disruption also might be increased if the cyber attacks were cued by inside agents and accompanied by coordinated physical sabotage. (Molander, Riddile, and Wilson, 1996; GAO, 1996.)

Finally, additional states eventually are likely to exploit advanced information technologies to acquire the capability to attack the United States directly with ballistic or cruise missiles armed with weapons of mass destruction.[23] This would threaten U.S. civilian populations with potential costs not experienced in virtually all previous U.S. wars with foreign powers.[24] Should U.S. forces engage an enemy equipped with such capabilities, the threat of a possible attack on the American homeland is likely to have a significant psychological impact on the U.S. body politic and could constrain severely U.S. war-fighting objectives and military options.

---

[23]Equipment and information that might assist a foreign state to "build long-range missiles are readily available through the Internet and from military surplus dealers." (See Gertz, 1997a.)

[24]America has not fought a foreign power with meaningful strategic strike capabilities since the War of 1812.

**Adversaries Also Can Limit Effects of U.S. Advanced Technologies.** When confrontations with U.S. forces are unavoidable, enemies may choose to employ fighting styles and engage U.S. troops in settings in which the U.S. advantages in maneuver and firepower will be less potent and in which the U.S. commander's situational awareness will be greatly reduced. American forces encountered such tactics both in Vietnam, where the Viet Cong employed close-in fighting tactics in brief combat forays from their heavily foliaged jungle base areas, and in Somalia, where Aideed's militia mounted ambushes against UN and U.S. troops in the warrens of Mogadishu.

By choosing to confront U.S. forces in urban and rural terrain that provides hard-to-penetrate cover and requires close-in fighting, adversaries can both husband their manpower resources and exact U.S. casualties. The U.S. experience with urban warfare in World War II (Aachen and Manila), Korea (Seoul), Vietnam (Hue), and Somalia (Mogadishu) demonstrates that fighting in built-up areas typically generates large numbers of U.S. dead and wounded.[25]

Future adversaries can also be expected to make greater use of camouflage, concealment, dispersion, deception, and human intelligence when confronting U.S. forces. The abortive U.S. attempts to capture Aideed and suppress hostile SNA military activities in Somalia provided numerous examples of how a low-tech adversary can use tactics and local resources that limit the utility of U.S. technological systems. The SNA's militia used shoot-and-hide mortar attacks; small-unit infiltration tactics; and low-technology, hard-to-disrupt communication instruments that reduced their exposure to U.S. countermeasures.[26] Because of their excellent human-intelligence nets, the SNA commanders probably enjoyed a situational awareness in their area of operations that was superior to that of their opposing U.S. and UN commanders.

Finally, adversaries may also attempt to use civilian populations and facilities as a shield against U.S. attacks. American forces frequently encountered such tactics in Bosnia and Somalia, where women and

---

[25]For a discussion of the fighting and losses in Aachen, see Ambrose (1997), pp. 146–154.

[26]The SNA's communication instruments included walkie-talkies, couriers, fires, streetlights, and sounds.

children were often in the forefront of confrontations with U.S. forces.  In Somalia, American troops occasionally came under fire from women and found it difficult to distinguish combatants from noncombatants and to determine the size, disposition, and movement of enemy forces.[27]  By causing civilians to confront U.S. troops, enemies hope to provoke incidents and stimulate media coverage that will both win sympathy for their cause and undermine the legitimacy of U.S. military actions in the eyes of domestic and international publics.

## THE NEED TO MANAGE FUTURE PSYCHOLOGICAL EFFECTS

### Managing Psychological Effects in a Changing Information Environment

Advanced technological systems will facilitate increased media coverage of conflicts and will allow information to be disseminated instantaneously throughout the world:

- The U.S. and foreign news media will become an increasingly ubiquitous presence on the future battlefield.  The media will have an independent capability to gain access to future conflict arenas and to provide real-time visual and audio coverage of battlefield events.  Thus, media will be able to report promptly the human costs of U.S. combat involvements to both U.S. domestic and international audiences.  As the U.S. experience in Vietnam and Somalia demonstrated, media news coverage and commentary will help shape U.S. domestic perceptions about whether a U.S. military involvement is effective or not and, most importantly, whether it merits continued public support. (Hosmer, 1998.)

- Advanced technological information systems will allow state and substate actors, including news services, nongovernmental organizations, and even individual citizens, to make voice, video, and written information instantly available to audiences located

_____

[27]For accounts of the tactics used by Somali men and women in combat, see Bowden (1997a).

in the remotest areas of the globe. Indeed, satellite communication systems and enlarged fiber-optic networks soon will allow cellular-type phone calls from "essentially anywhere on the planet" and, within a decade, will probably make it possible to

> live in a remote area and yet be connected to the worlds of commerce and entertainment via the Internet and other sources of multimedia at rates high enough to support movies-on-demand. The world will soon be a place where not just communications but also torrents of information will be available just about everywhere. (Evans, 1998.)

These changes in the information environment will make it imperative that potential psychological effects be given priority attention in U.S. statecraft, particularly with respect to the design and conduct of U.S. public diplomacy, public affairs, and military operations.

First, both the United States and its future adversaries will have new channels for penetrating previously hard-to-reach audiences with their public affairs and PSYOP messages. Even more importantly, the reporting of the world's independent television and print media will also be able to penetrate previously denied areas. Internet access and content, for example, are likely to prove difficult to monitor and censor even in states where the local print and television media are tightly controlled.[28] At the same time, foreign actors, including those who may oppose future U.S. peace and other military operations, also will be able to exploit the Internet to influence international and U.S. domestic public opinion. The Zapatista rebels in Chiapas and their outside supporters made extensive use of the Internet to

---

[28]According to a Central Intelligence Agency report on China's print and broadcasting outlets, Chinese

> government officials are worried that as the number of Chinese homes with telephone lines grows from the present level of less than 4 percent, the state will become totally unable to monitor Internet access at residences. (See Gertz, 1997b, p. 5; also see Laris, 1997.)

PSYOP specialists may also find opportunities to reach foreign audiences by exploiting satellite-linked television broadcasts. However, the companies planning direct broadcast and interactive links from both low-earth and geosynchronous orbit satellites stress that the sovereignty of the countries receiving such broadcasts would be strictly observed, which suggests that the local government will retain a veto on what could be shown to its population.

publicize the Zapatista cause both within Mexico and to the world at large. (Robberson, 1995.)

The inherent power of the Internet was also manifest in the successful campaign various nongovernmental organizations and individuals have waged around the world to prod their governments to negotiate and sign the treaty banning antipersonnel land mines. Even though the Internet's potential for mobilizing world opinion is likely to be diluted by the increasingly large number of issue-oriented groups contending for attention in cyberspace, it still will remain a potent instrument for rallying like-minded persons to support or oppose particular actions and causes. (Mburjo, 1997.) The bombing of the Al Firdos bunker in Baghdad, in which several hundred Iraqi civilians were inadvertently killed, is the type of contingency an enemy could effectively exploit on the Internet to mobilize anti-American demonstrations throughout the world. The Internet is potentially a potent tool for inflammatory rumor, as well as "black" and "gray" propaganda, in that the actual affiliation of the provider of information can be masked easily and any visual "news" materials that are put on the Web can be transformed so as to make faked events appear true.

Second, the rapidity with which news and propaganda will travel will require U.S. public diplomacy and public affairs officials to be prepared to react promptly to counteract any adverse spin put on stories concerning U.S. military operations. It is particularly important that U.S. officials publicly explain and justify promptly and candidly U.S. actions that cause civilian casualties or collateral damage. As the U.S. experience in Vietnam, Bosnia, and Somalia has demonstrated, even supposedly "unsophisticated" adversaries can be adept at exploiting errant U.S. military operations or at staging military and political events to manipulate public opinion. For example, Aideed, who assumed the public posture of a Somali "David" confronting a U.S. "Goliath," proved to be both a highly skilled propagandist and a master at handling the press. (Hirsch and Oakley, 1995, p. 123.) He and his allies "learned very quickly how to play the CNN [Cable News Network] factor, appearing on CNN in one form or another some 29 times between June and December 1993." (Strobel, 1997, p. 173.)

Third, senior U.S. civilian and military leaders must formulate and articulate intervention objectives that can be supported by the public and the Congress. Should objectives change and the U.S. combat involvement increase during the course of an intervention, it is vital that the reasons for such a change of mission and its possible costs be explained to the public.  The failure of U.S. officials to explain adequately the changes of mission that occurred in Lebanon (1982–1983) and Somalia (1993) fueled confusion and skepticism about the purposes and merits of those interventions in the minds of the U.S. public and Congress.[29]

Finally, the expanding options for reaching audiences in countries and groups that could become future U.S. adversaries make it important that the United States begin its psychological conditioning in peacetime.  The United States needs to advertise its military prowess and commitment to defending U.S. interests prior to the outbreak of hostilities.  Shows of force, exercises, firepower demonstrations, and the like should be used both (1) to deter the potential adversary from attacking U.S. interests and (2) to begin to soften the fighting will of the potential adversary's armed forces in the event conflict does occur.

One reason for the low morale large numbers of Iraqi officers and enlisted personnel suffered prior to the start of hostilities in the Gulf War was the widespread awareness among the Iraqi military that U.S. aircraft, tanks, and other weapons were far superior to their own obsolete military equipment.  Many Iraqis were convinced that the technological superiority of U.S. weapons foreordained Iraq's defeat in any military contest with the United States.  The subsequent Coalition air campaign strongly reinforced the Iraqi view that resistance was futile.  (Hosmer, 1996, pp. 204–205.)

## Managing the Psychological Effects of Future Military Operations

Because the psychological impact of military actions can prove so decisive to conflict cost and outcome, U.S. civilian leaders and military commanders will need to give priority attention to the psychological dimension of warfare in the planning and conduct of future U.S. operations.  It is particularly important that U.S. leaders consult

---

[29]For a discussion of the effects of the public-information failure with respect to the second United Nations Operation in Somalia, see Hirsch and Oakley (1995), n. 9, pp. 158–159. Also, see Strobel (1997), pp. 204, 208, and Hosmer (1998).

with and heed the advice of area experts and persons conversant with psychological effects about the likely psychological impact of a proposed military strategy or concept of operation. Area experts— who may include persons both inside and outside the U.S. government—must be knowledgeable about local political, military, and cultural conditions and with the objectives, likely strategy, and political-military strengths and weaknesses of adversaries. Such knowledge is important because a military strategy or concept of operation aimed at producing beneficial psychological effects is likely to prove counterproductive if the assumptions underlying U.S. military actions are incongruent with prevailing cultural, political, and military realities. (Hosmer, 1998.)

This is particularly true in smaller-scale contingencies, in which even relatively minor military acts can produce major psychological effects. Military operations designed to "send a message" to an adversary about U.S. resolve and capability can have the unwanted effect of enhancing the adversary's popular support and resolution to resist.

Such was the case in Mogadishu during June and July 1993, when U.S. helicopter and AC-130 gunships and ground forces attacked Aideed's weapon caches, radio station, and headquarters sites. While militarily effective in reducing Aideed's immediate weapon inventories and neutralizing his radio, the cumulative effect of these attacks was politically and psychologically counterproductive. Designed to destroy Aideed's power base and command structure, the attacks instead increased support for Aideed among his Habr Gidir subclan and intensified Somali opposition to U.S. and UN forces.[30] The attacks so animated Somali opposition that an estimated 1,500 Somalis proved willing to suffer death or injury in their attacks on U.S. troops during the firefight in Mogadishu on October 3–4, 1993. (Bowden, 1997b.)

In larger-scale contingencies, it is also important that U.S. combatant commanders seek to exploit systematically the potential psychological effects of U.S. military operations. When the battlefield situa-

---

[30]For accounts of the counterproductive effects of these U.S. and UN attacks, see Hirsch and Oakley (1995), pp. 121–122; Maren (1996); Drysdale (1994), pp. 190, 192–193, 197; and Lorch (1993a, b).

tion permits, U.S. theater and joint task force commanders should pursue strategies that will force enemy ground units to react in a manner that will expose them to protracted and effective aerial and other standoff attack.  Systematic efforts also should be made to interdict the resupply of food to forward-deployed enemy troops.  Air and ground component commanders should make the destruction of enemy morale an explicit and priority objective of their campaigns, and personnel expert in psychological effects should be included on component commander planning staffs.  (Hosmer, 1996, pp. 192–194.)  PSYOP should support and closely integrate with all air and ground operations.

## CONCLUSION

There is every reason to believe that the psychological battle will continue to have an important influence on the outcome of conflicts involving U.S. forces.  Future U.S. interventions will be conducted in an ever more-ubiquitous information environment, in which U.S. foreign policy decisions and military operations will become increasingly subject to the instantaneous scrutiny and criticism of U.S. domestic and international audiences.

Enemy leaders will almost certainly continue to perceive casualty aversion to be America's Achilles' heel and will attempt to shape their political-military strategies and tactics to exploit this vulnerability.  The proliferation of more accurate and lethal weapon systems and the access virtually all states will have to advanced technological information systems will provide adversaries with the potential means to raise the human costs of U.S. military interventions and, thereby, to undermine U.S. domestic support for such operations. American leaders may be able to mitigate this threat, however, by giving priority attention to U.S. force protection and by developing and deploying advanced sensors, platforms, and weapon systems that can help to reduce U.S. casualties.

At the same time, the advanced technological systems emerging from the information revolution will increase the U.S. ability to mount psychologically effective attacks on enemy strategic targets and deployed forces.  In particular, anticipated improvements in the capabilities of U.S. "finders," "controllers," and "shooters" should provide U.S. forces the opportunity in many battlefield situations to undermine decisively the motivation and morale of opposing enemy troops. However, to exploit this opportunity to its fullest, U.S. forces will need to acquire the capability to deny enemy troops sanctuary from effective air, artillery, and missile attacks in a broader spectrum of combat environments than is now possible, and U.S. commanders will need to place greater emphasis on the psychological dimension of warfare in the planning and conduct of their operations.

War-fighters in all the U.S. services must recognize that inducing enemy troops to desert, surrender, and abandon their equipment can be just as important to a favorable battlefield outcome as the destruction of enemy armor and artillery. And as the Gulf War experience demonstrated, collapsing an enemy's will to fight can significantly reduce U.S. casualties and thereby vitiate the enemy's most important leverage in the psychological battle.

## REFERENCES

Adelman, Howard, and Astri Suhrke, *The International Response to Conflict and Genocide: Lessons from the Rwanda Experience, Study 2, Early Warning and Conflict Management*, Steering Committee of the Joint Evaluation of Emergency Assistance to Rwanda, March 1996.

Ambrose, Stephen E., *Citizen Soldiers*, New York: Simon & Schuster, 1997.

Blair, Clay, *The Forgotten War: America in Korea 1950–1953*, New York: Times Books, 1987.

Bowden, Mark, "Blackhawk Down, An American War Story," *The Philadelphia Enquirer*, November 16–December 14, 1997a.

_____, "The Final Chapter: Freeing a Pilot, Ending a Mission," *The Philadelphia Enquirer*, December 14, 1997b.

Burkhalter, Holly, "U.S. Might Have Avoided Rwanda Tragedy," *The Christian Science Monitor*, August 9, 1994, p. 19.

Davidson, Philip B. (MG, USA, Ret.), *Vietnam at War*, Novato, Calif.: Presidio Press, 1988.

Drysdale, John, *Whatever Happened in Somalia?* London: HAAN Associates, 1994.

Evans, John V., "New Satellites for Personal Communications," *Scientific American*, April 1998, p. 77.

Evers, Stacey, "ARPA Pursues Pocket-Sized Pilotless Vehicles," *Jane's Defence Weekly*, March 20, 1996, p. 3.

"Excerpts from Iraqi Transcripts of Meeting with U.S. Envoy," *The New York Times*, September 23, 1990, p. 19.

Foreign Broadcast Information Service, *Trends*, FB TM 90-035, August 29, 1990.

_____, *Trends*, FB TM 91-002, January 10, 1991.

GAO—*see* U.S. General Accounting Office.

Gertz, Bill, "Ballistic Missiles Within Easy Reach of Many Nations," *The Washington Times*, September 23, 1997a, p. A9.

_____, "CIA Sees Chinese Media as Catalysts," *The Washington Times*, October 17, 1997b, p. 5.

Hirsch, John L., and Robert B. Oakley, *Somalia and Operation RESTORE HOPE*, Washington, D.C.: U.S. Institute of Peace Press, 1995.

Hosmer, Stephen T., *Constraints on U.S. Strategy in Third World Conflicts*, New York: Crane Russak & Company, 1987.

_____, Psychological Effects of U.S. Air Operations in Four Wars 1941–1991: Lessons for U.S. Commanders, Santa Monica, Calif.: RAND, MR-576-AF, 1996.

_____, *Information-Related Operations in Smaller-Scale Contingencies*, Santa Monica, Calif.: RAND, DB-214-A, 1998. Not cleared for public release

Hunt, Michael H., "Beijing and the Korean Crisis, June 1950–June 1951," *Political Science Quarterly*, Vol. 107, No. 3, 1992, pp. 453–478.

Hussein, Saddam, Open letter to George Bush, *FBIS Trends*, FB TM 91-002, January 10, 1991, p. 2, and FB TM 90-035, August 29, 1990, p. 2.

Kemp, Geoffrey, "The American Peacekeeping Role in Lebanon," in Anthony McDermott and Kjell Skjelsbaek, eds., *The Multinational Force in Beirut 1982–1984*, Miami, Fla.: Florida International University Press, 1991, pp. 139–140.

Laris, Michael, "Beijing Launches a New Offensive to Squelch Dissent on Internet," *The Washington Post*, December 31, 1997, p. A16.

Livingstone, Neil C., "Arms Bizarre," *Sea Power*, December 1995, pp. 45–46.

Lorch, Donatella, "U.N. Says It Will Press Effort to Disarm Somalis," *The New York Times*, July 14, 1993a, p. A6.

_____, "U.N. Finds Peace Elusive with Somali Leader at Large," *The New York Times*, July 15, 1993b, p. A10.

Maren, Michael, "Somalia: Whose Failure?" *Current History*, May 1996, p. 203.

Mburjo, Judith, "Web Makes 'Virtual Diplomacy' Real," *The Washington Times*, June 23, 1997, p. A10.

Molander, Roger C., Andrew S. Riddile, and Peter A. Wilson, *Strategic Information Warfare: A New Face of War*, Santa Monica, Calif.: RAND, MR-661-OSD, 1996.

Moore, Molly, "Schwarzkopf: War Intelligence Flawed," *The Washington Post*, June 13, 1991, p. A40.

Nix, Maj. William I., "GPS's Threat to American Forces," *Marine Corps Gazette*, January 1998, pp. 25–27.

"North Korean Defectors Warn of Missile Threat," *Aerospace Daily*, October 22, 1996, p. 115B.

Parks, W. Hayes, "Rolling Thunder and the Law of War," *Air University Review*, January–February 1983, pp. 19–26.

Pike, Douglas, *PAVN: People's Army of Vietnam*, Novato, Calif.: Presidio Press, 1986.

Richburg, Keith B., "In War on Aideed, UN Battled Itself," *The Washington Post*, December 6, 1993, p. 1.

Robberson, Tod, "Mexican Rebels Using a High-Tech Weapon," *The Washington Post*, February 20, 1995, pp. A1, A21.

Sandler, Stanley, *"Cease Resistance: It's Good for You": A History of U.S. Army Combat PSYOP*, Fort Bragg, N.C.: U.S. Army Special Operations Command, Directorate of History and Museums, 1996.

Seffers, George L., "Pentagon Tests Systems to Battle Sniper Threat" and "Next U.S. Army Rifle Will Attack Around Obstacles," *Defense News*, January 12–18, 1998, pp. 12–13.

Simic, Predrag, "The Former Yugoslavia: The Media and Violence," *RFE/RL Research Report*, Vol. 3, No. 5, February 4, 1994, pp. 40–47.

Strobel, Warren P., *Late-Breaking Foreign Policy: The News Media's Influence on Peace Operations*, Washington, D.C.: U.S. Institute for Peace, 1997.

Truong Nhu Tang, *A Vietcong Memoir*, New York: Harcourt Brace Jovanovich Publishers, 1985.

U.S. General Accounting Office, Information Security, *Computer Attacks at the Department of Defense Pose Increasing Risks*, Washington, D.C.: GAO/AIMD-96-84, May 22, 1996.

U.S. Strategic Bombing Survey, *Summary Report (Pacific War)*, Pacific Report No. 1, Washington, D.C.: U.S. Government Printing Office, July 1, 1945, in David MacIsaac, ed., *The United States Strategic Bombing Survey*, Volume VII, New York: Garland Publishing, Inc., 1976a.

_____, *Japan's Struggle to End the War*, Pacific Report No. 2, Washington, D.C.: U.S. Government Printing Office, July 1, 1945, in David MacIsaac, ed., *The United States Strategic Bombing Survey*, Volume VII, New York: Garland Publishing, Inc., 1976b.

# Chapter Nine

# U.S. STRATEGIC VULNERABILITIES:
# THREATS AGAINST SOCIETY

*Roger C. Molander, Peter A. Wilson, and Robert H. Anderson*

Previous chapters have discussed military opportunities and vulnerabilities arising from information operations and information warfare. But do information operations and warfare constitute a strategic threat to U.S. society? What, indeed, would constitute "strategic information warfare" (SIW)? In this chapter, we address these questions and present a framework for thinking about SIW issues.[1]

## WHAT IS SIW?

In the future, the possibility exists that adversaries might exploit the tools and techniques of the information revolution to hold at risk (not of destruction, but of large-scale or massive disruption) key national strategic assets, such as elements of various key national infrastructure sectors (energy, telecommunications, transportation, financial, etc.). This potential danger constitutes the principal fact of the SIW environment as conceptualized here.

Both regional adversaries and peer competitors may find SIW tools and techniques of use to them in challenging the United States, its allies, and/or its interests. In the near term, SIW weapons may be most useful to regional adversaries applying *asymmetric strategies* (See Figure 9.1) as a way to avoid directly challenging U.S. conventional battlefield superiority. Such strategies involve using some combination of nuclear, chemical, biological, highly advanced conventional, and SIW instruments.

---

[1]This chapter is adapted primarily from Molander, Wilson, Mussington, and Mesic (1998).

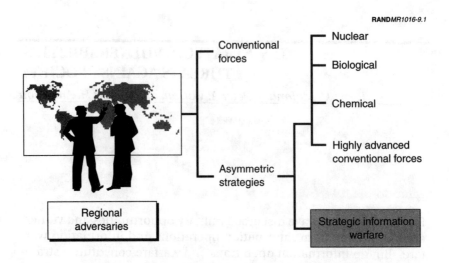

RAND*MR1016-9.1*

**Figure 9.1—Future U.S. Regional Adversaries Might Seek
Asymmetric Strategies**

SIW tools and techniques present a two-pronged threat to U.S. security:

1. **A Threat to U.S. National Economic Security**:  the holding at risk to massive disruption of infrastructure targets critical to the U.S. economy.  A successful SIW attack on one or more infrastructures could produce a strategically significant result, including public loss of confidence in the delivery of services from those infrastructures with a resulting loss in confidence in the government.

2. **A Threat Against the U.S. National Military Strategy**:  the possibility that a regional adversary might use SIW threats or attacks to deter or disrupt U.S. power-projection plans in a regional crisis. Targets of concern include infrastructures in the United States that are vital to overseas force deployment and comparable targets in allied countries.  A key ally or coalition member under such attack might refuse to join a coalition—or worse, quit one in the middle of a war.

In the history of strategic warfare, it is hard to find a conflict worthy of the label *strategic* that did not manifest some important information component. Sun Tzu, for example, recommended the creative use of information to achieve strategic objectives while avoiding conflict. It is also noteworthy that one could undoubtedly produce a list of historical instances in which fundamental changes in technology produced fundamental changes in the information component of strategic warfare.

Yet the potential impact of the information revolution on strategic warfare may be unprecedented. Whereas SIW may have largely played a subordinate role in strategic warfare in the past—in early times, to the strategic impact of conventional armies and navies, and later, to the likes of airplanes, rockets, and/or nuclear weapons—it might play a much greater role in such warfare in the wake of the information revolution. Furthermore, the potential impact of the information revolution on the vulnerability of key national infrastructures and other strategic assets may, over time, give rise to a wholly new kind of information-centric strategic warfare on wholly different time lines (more like the time lines associated with economic embargoes), worthy of consideration independent of other potential facets of strategic warfare, such as those portrayed in Figure 9.1.

Under normal circumstances, SIW might develop in something like the following stages (Figure 9.2):

RANDMR1016-9.2

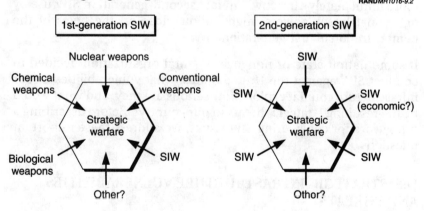

Figure 9.2—Two Concepts of SIW

1. **First-Generation SIW:** SIW as one of several facets or components of future strategic warfare, the latter broadly conceptualized as being carried forward through the orchestration of a number of strategic warfare instruments (as indicated in Figure 9.1)

2. **Second-Generation SIW:** SIW as a freestanding, fundamentally new type of strategic warfare spawned by the information revolution, possibly being carried out in newly prominent strategic warfare arenas (e.g., economic) and on time lines (e.g., years versus days, weeks, or months) longer than those generally, or at least recently, ascribed to strategic warfare.

For established powers, such as the United States, and emerging regional powers, such as Iran, the authors tend to believe that first-generation SIW is the more likely form to be initially manifest. This, however, is an arguable proposition. The United States, for example, might find itself in a situation in the near future where it chooses to exploit its current information-technology advantages and employ second-generation SIW to prevail in an international situation that otherwise would have led to troop deployments, a long campaign, and almost certain high casualties.

For less-developed nations—which may not possess any other effective strategic warfare instruments—second-generation SIW may be more immediately attractive. In fact second-generation SIW use by or against lesser powers might follow close on the heels of the demonstration of first-generation SIW.

If some nation-state or nongovernmental organization decided to conduct SIW against the United States, what vulnerabilities in our infrastructure could it exploit, how serious are they, and what would be the resulting strategic threats to our country? Before describing a framework for considering SIW issues, we address these important questions.

## U.S. STRATEGIC INFRASTRUCTURE VULNERABILITIES AND THREATS

Vulnerabilities of essential U.S. infrastructures to attack, and possible threats against those infrastructures, have been the subject of substantial recent study by the President's Commission on Critical

Infrastructure Protection (PCCIP). We present here a synopsis of the threats and vulnerabilities for five U.S. infrastructure sectors, abstracted primarily from Appendix A of the commission's final report (PCCIP, 1997)—with special attention to the information and communications sector on which so many other sectors' services depend. Interested readers should consult the full PCCIP final report for additional details and discussion of these issues.

What, in fact, are the essential U.S. infrastructures, whose incapacity or destruction would have a debilitating impact on our defense or economic security?[2] The commissioners compressed an initial list of eight sectors into these five, for which they discussed both vulnerabilities and threats:

- *Information and Communications*—the public telephone network; the Internet; and millions of computers in home, commercial, academic, and government use
- *Physical Distribution*—the vast interconnected network of highways, rail lines, ports and inland waterways, pipelines, airports and airways, mass transit, trucking companies, and delivery services that facilitate the movement of goods and people
- *Energy*—the industries that produce and distribute electric power, oil, and natural gas
- *Banking and Finance*—Banks, nonbank financial service companies, payment systems, investment companies and mutual funds, and securities and commodities exchanges
- *Vital Human Services*—water-supply systems, emergency services, and government services.

Before discussing vulnerabilities and threats in each of the above sectors, it is useful to consider an overall assessment spanning the various sectors:

> The threat is real enough. ... Skilled computer operators have demonstrated their ability to gain access to networks without authorization. ... Whatever their motivation, their success in entering networks to alter data, extract financial or proprietary informa-

---

[2]Executive Order 13010 calls infrastructures meeting these criteria "critical." We prefer the terminology "essential."

tion, or introduce viruses demonstrates that it can be done and gives rise to concerns that, in the future, some party wishing to do serious damage to the United States will do so by the same means.

Real vulnerabilities also exist. Infrastructures have always been subject to local or regional outages resulting from earthquakes, storms, and floods. . . . But physical vulnerabilities take on added significance as new capabilities to exploit them emerge, including chemical, biological, and even nuclear weapons. As weapons of mass destruction proliferate, the likelihood of their use by terrorists increases. . . .

Our dependence on the information and communications infrastructure has created new cyber vulnerabilities, which we are only starting to understand. In addition to the disruption of information and communications, we also face the possibility that someone will be able to actually mount an attack against other infrastructures by exploiting their dependence on computers and telecommunications. . . .    (PCCIP, 1997, p. 5.)

Are the vulnerabilities and threats in fact of strategic significance? Many thoughtful analysts agree, and we concur, that a coordinated, repetitive information warfare attack (including perhaps some physical damage to essential nodes) on components of essential U.S. infrastructures could have strategic consequences, especially if conducted in conjunction with other events—e.g., just preceding or during a major deployment of U.S. forces to an overseas theater. This view was reinforced by an exercise conducted by a group led by one of us (Molander) hypothesizing a crisis involving the United States and a peer competitor, in which SIW and other instruments of strategic warfare were brandished and employed against elements of the U.S. infrastructure (Molander and Wilson, forthcoming). We note that such infrastructure attacks might be conducted by nongovernmental organizations loosely networked together. Such coordination is made increasingly possible by the Internet and other new network communication options. See, for example, the writings of our colleagues John Arquilla and David Ronfeldt on the concept of netwar:

an emerging mode of conflict (and crime) at societal levels, involving measures short of war, in which the protagonists use—indeed, depend on using—network forms of organization, doctrine, strategy, and communications. (Arquilla and Ronfeldt, 1997.)

It is important to distinguish different forms of information warfare. Martin Libicki, in a seminal report asking, "What Is Information Warfare?", distinguishes among seven forms: command-and-control warfare, intelligence-based warfare, electronic warfare, psychological warfare, hacker warfare, economic information warfare, and cyber-warfare. (Libicki, 1995.) Although all have importance, the last four are most relevant in considering attacks on essential components of the U.S. infrastructure.

We summarize below the vulnerabilities of, and threats to, the five infrastructure sectors highlighted by the PCCIP.

## Information and Communications

The information and communications infrastructure sector is perhaps the most essential of all, acting as the "nerves" and control for all other sectors. It is also one of the most vulnerable, both to physical attacks on key nodes and switches and to "cyber" attacks through the network itself. The sheer redundancy of the interlinked networks this sector comprises may be reduced somewhat by the new competitive environment launched by the Telecommunications Act of 1996; former cooperators are now competitors.

The public telephone network is extremely complex and interrelated, governed by no single body, and evolving rapidly in time. There is, therefore, no model or simulation that accurately captures its richness; hence, it is difficult to analyze its multifarious failure modes, cascading effects, and the like. As a whole, it has proved quite resilient to periodic natural disasters, but its survivability in a coordinated, repetitive attack by a knowledgeable, determined adversary is unproven and probably unknown.

The vulnerabilities of this sector highlighted in the PCCIP report include *switches* susceptible to software-based disruption (e.g., through remote maintenance dial-in modem ports); a *transport* architecture based on synchronous optical networks, which are remotely managed through packet data network connections that are vulnerable to electronic intrusion; *signaling* systems based on the Signaling System 7 protocol; and *control* signals in an "advanced intelligent network" design that allow changes to be made from remote locations to switch software. Some signals can increasingly be sent from private branch exchanges to control portions of the operation of the network.

As with all other sectors, the threat to these systems may arise from five categories of "bad actors": (1) incompetents, hackers, and disgruntled employees; (2) crooks and organized crime; (3) political dissidents and terrorist groups; (4) adversaries conducting foreign espionage, tactical countermeasures, and orchestrated tactical information warfare; and (5) adversaries seeking to achieve major strategic disruption of the United States. In all sectors, the worst threat comes from the trusted insider, who already possesses physical access, knowledge of systems and procedures, and relevant passwords and system access.

The overall assessment for this sector is not promising. As the PCCIP report concludes:

> The numerous security vulnerabilities in today's I&C [information and communications] infrastructure afford little basis for . . . confidence today, and the trends are not encouraging. In the meantime, the payoff for successful exploitation is increasing rapidly . . .
>
> The second and more critical risk is that presented by cyber and physical attacks intended to disrupt the US I&C infrastructure and the critical societal functions that depend upon it. With network elements increasingly interconnected and reliant on each other, cyber attacks simultaneously targeting multiple network functions would be highly difficult to defend against, particularly if combined with selected physical destruction of key facilities.
>
> The possibility that such disruption could cascade across a substantial part of the PTN [public telephone network] cannot be ruled out.... (PCCIP, 1997, p. A-7).

## Physical Distribution

The physical distribution sector includes roads and highways, trucking companies, personal vehicles, railroads, airline operations, seaports and inland river terminals, oil and natural gas pipelines, and delivery services, including the U.S. Postal Service. At present, this "system" is quite robust because of its geographic dispersion, manual procedures in place to handle problems, and multiple options that are often available for physical transportation between sites.

Within the next five to ten years, however, the picture darkens. By 2010, the Federal Radionavigation Plan calls for the Global Positioning System (GPS) and its augmentations to be this nation's sole radionavigation system. Present GPS signals are quite susceptible to local jamming. Increased use of commercial off-the-shelf software and hardware and shared use of communication networks create additional opportunities for "trap doors" or other implanted devices in software or hardware.

Although attacks against transportation systems account for about 20 percent of all terrorist attacks, the PCCIP found that

> No tested and effective means exist that facilitates reporting and transfer of information between the government and transportation infrastructure stakeholders on threats and attacks. Information-based threats to the physical distribution system are not addressed by DOT [the U.S. Department of Transportation]; private sector concern is on a sector-by-sector and company-by-company basis .... (PCCIP, 1997, p. A-16.)

In addition, one can easily imagine scenarios (e.g., during U.S. troop deployments) when individual railheads, shipping points, or air traffic control centers are crucial for shipment of specific items of ammunition and materiel, or for units being deployed. In those cases, the geographic dispersion and diversity of the transportation system are little consolation, since rerouting and rescheduling—when possible—could involve significant delays.

## Energy

Energy production and distribution systems, including electricity and oil and natural gas systems, are perhaps the second most important and ubiquitous infrastructure, along with information and telecommunications. Recent widespread multistate electric outages in the northeast and on the west coast, illustrating cascading effects during a failure, provide little comfort.

Increasingly, energy industries are introducing

> industry-wide information systems based on open-system architectures, centralized operations, increased communications over public telecommunications networks and remote maintenance. [In

addition,] Supervisory Control and Data Acquisition (SCADA) systems . . . are vulnerable because of use of commercial off-the shelf
(COTS) hardware and software, connections to other company networks, and the reliance on dial-back modems that can be bypassed.
(PCCIP, 1997, p. A-26.)

As a result,

significant disruption would result if an intruder were able to access
a SCADA system and modify the data used for operational decisions, or modify programs that control critical industry equipment
or the data reported to control centers. (PCCIP, 1997, p. A-27.)

With the increasing commercialization and competitiveness mandated in the energy sector, suppliers and distributors are likely to
view implementation of the additional security measures needed as a
deferrable cost.

## Banking and Finance

Anyone wishing to have a strategic impact on the United States need
only tinker with a financial system within which about $3 trillion in
daily payment transactions are transferred among banks and financial institutions. Of all the infrastructure systems, this is clearly the
most protected and the one for which security and sustainability are
extremely high priorities. Nevertheless, as with other sectors, there is
danger from a subverted or disgruntled insider working for a malevo-
lent group or nation-state.

This is also possibly the place to mention a one-time threat, but one
not unique to this sector: the fact that many of the complex information systems serving this sector and its affiliated organizations
must be updated to handle the so-called Year 2000 (Y2K) software
problem associated with the turn of the century. The problem is
widespread enough that source code for these essential systems is
being accessed, viewed, and manipulated by consultants, temporary
employees, and other organizations, since information operations
internal to banks, stock exchanges, etc., may not have sufficient
resources to handle the task in addition to their normal jobs. Other
database and coding changes are needed to handle the conversion to
a common currency in Europe. It is not possible to review and vali-

date every binary file resulting from the necessary recompiling of source code within this entire sector.[3]

## Vital Human Services

This sector includes water-supply systems, emergency services, and government services. These services are highly localized, not forming a strongly interconnected national infrastructure. Failures are therefore likely to be localized. However, because of their importance, failures can have significant psychosocial effects. Communication of vulnerabilities and threats in this sector requires cooperation (largely currently lacking) among thousands of state, county, and city departments, as well as federal agencies. Perhaps the greatest vulnerability in this disparate, decentralized sector comes from increasing reliance on the Internet and the global public telephone network; vulnerabilities and threats to the telecommunications sector were surveyed above.

## THE NEED FOR NEW DECISIONMAKING FRAMEWORKS

The above quick overview of sector threats and vulnerabilities cries out for a framework within which their strategic importance to the United States can be evaluated. What national policies should be instituted to deal with the threat that some nation-state or nongovernmental organization might conduct SIW against the United States? How, indeed, should decisionmaking be conducted in this realm?[4]

We wish to formulate a common U.S. strategy and policy framework for addressing the challenge of SIW. But what is a strategy and policy decisionmaking framework? Its most useful form, a decisionmaking framework, is likely to be a series of relatively simple steps—a process—that presents the strategy and policy (and related) issues that need to be addressed in some particular arena in a logical architecture and along a logical path in a fashion that facilitates decisionmaking on those issues.

---

[3]"Back doors," logic bombs, etc., may be implanted in the binary code by gimmicked compilers, leaving no trace in the corresponding source code; see Thompson (1984) for details.

[4]Adapted from Molander, Wilson, Mussington and Mesic (1998).

New strategy and policy decisionmaking frameworks are born in the crucible of necessity (or perceived possible imminent necessity)—when a specific problem area (1) appears to demand action (or might soon demand action) and (2) is of such a character that no readily applicable decisionmaking framework is available to forge an implementable action plan.

In some situations, there may be an older candidate decisionmaking framework that has been tested for its applicability to the needs of the subject problem area and found wanting. Those who favor formulating the subject area as a rapidly evolving old problem area versus a new problem area may in fact have championed use of such an older framework. Failed attempts to apply an older decisionmaking framework may even have contributed to a delay in the more forthright expression of the need for a new framework.

## AN EVOLVING SERIES OF FRAMEWORKS

An initial search for a single, temporally stable framework to serve the stated function for SIW soon led to the conclusion that the concept of a *single framework* at this stage of development was illusory. Rather, the correct construct for responding to a new strategic warfare component—one truly worthy of the label *strategic* rather than being just another "strategic warfare wannabe"—would have to be dynamic, capable of responding to ongoing changes in both the international security and information-technology environments. The correct construct would in fact have to be (1) *an evolving series of frameworks*, recognizing and accepting the "punctuated equilibrium" realities of convening and executing strategy and policy decisionmaking processes and (2) *a process* that recognizes and supports the dynamic and highly evolutionary character of such a construct (especially in its early stages).

## AN INITIAL FORMULATION

A clear and primary objective in this conceptualization of the SIW decisionmaking framework problem is that the initial formulation of such a framework be one that can in fact evolve in response to changes in its environment—that it have an evolutionary potential rather than being merely a temporary expedient to get decisionmaking going but not have much utility thereafter.

The absence of a precursor framework in this issue area also means that the initial version of the framework will attract attention from stakeholders interested in the future of the information revolution and, of course, from the media. With this perspective in mind, the process of designing an associated inaugural first-generation SIW decisionmaking framework—a generic process that in fact *constitutes* the framework—can be divided into the following distinct steps (see Figure 9.3):

1. **Key Dimensions of the SIW Environment.** Gain an understanding of the key dimensions of the future first-generation SIW "environment" or "battlespace," i.e., the dimensions of that environment that might in principle be shaped or influenced (presumably in some favorable direction) by effective near-term strategy and policy decisionmaking. Achieve this objective by (1) identifying the principal defining features of first-generation SIW within a spectrum of plausible first-generation SIW contexts and (2) selecting from among them the features that might be cast as key dimensions amenable to change as described above.

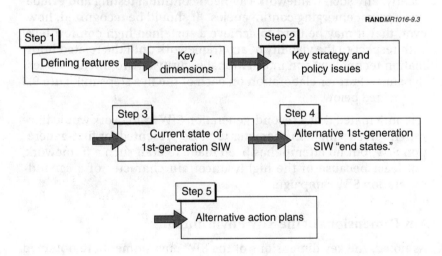

RAND*MR1016-9.3*

Figure 9.3—Designing a First-Generation SIW Strategy and Policy
Decisionmaking Framework

2. **Key Strategy and Policy Issues.** Identify those key strategy and policy issues (and other issues, such as organizational issues) germane to the first-generation SIW problem (i.e., issues on which near-term decisionmaking could shape or influence the above-identified key dimensions of the SIW environment).

3. **Current State of First-Generation SIW.** Assess the current state of first-generation SIW in terms of absolute and relative offensive and defensive SIW capabilities.

4. **Alternative First-Generation SIW "End States."** In the light of the above-cited first-generation SIW contexts and scenarios, craft a set of (plausible and potentially desirable) alternative first-generation SIW "end states"—expressed in terms of the above key dimensions of the first-generation SIW environment.

5. **Alternative Action Plans.** Array the key SIW strategy and policy issues against each of these alternative end states and conceptualize action plans for moving toward one or more of these end states.

Clearly, any such framework will need continual testing and evaluation against emerging contingencies. It should be recognized, however, that it may be hard to achieve a sustained high comfort level with respect to the viability of any framework until the related information technology and international security environments are less dynamic. Further elaboration on each of the five steps in Figure 9.3 is provided below.

It is anticipated that a second-generation SIW framework would have generic steps similar in character to those presented for first-generation SIW, but no attempt has been made to craft such a framework, not least because of the highly uncertain character of a second-generation SIW campaign.

## Key Dimensions of the SIW Environment

As noted, the key dimensions of the SIW environment are obtained by identifying the defining features of the SIW environment and asking which of these can be potentially shaped or influenced in some favorable direction by well-conceived strategy and policy decisionmaking. These dimensions (see Table 9.1) thus constitute the

**Table 9.1**

**From Defining Features to Key Dimensions of the SIW Environment**

| Defining Features | Consequences |
|---|---|
| Entry cost low | May be many actors in the SIW battlespace |
| Strategic intelligence on threat unavailable | Identity and capabilities of potential adversaries may be unclear |
| Tactical warning difficult | May not know attack is under way |
| Attack assessment difficult | May not know perpetrator or targets |
| Damage assessment difficult | May not know full implications of the attack |
| Traditional boundaries blurred | May not know who has various responsibilities before, during, or after an attack |
| Weapon effects uncertain | Both attacker and defender may be uncertain as to weapon effects |
| Infrastructure vulnerabilities uncertain but suspect | U.S. homeland may not be a sanctuary; vulnerable partners could make sustaining coalitions more difficult |

basic factors in the SIW setting that influence attainable objectives relating to SIW and the relationships between purposive action by states (and other actors) and changes in the shape of the SIW environment itself.

## Key Strategy and Policy Issues

SIW presents a broad and complex spectrum of issues and challenges to existing decisionmaking processes. As a consequence, it is clear that some sequencing is appropriate in taking up these issues nationally and internationally. To this end, the key strategy and policy issues identified in this chapter can be roughly characterized in terms of three categories:

1. **Low-Hanging Fruit.** This category encompasses issues that could be moved to closure nationally (and, in some cases, possibly internationally) without undue difficulty once suitable processes are identified or established. Issues that lie in this category (with illustrative alternatives) are

   • **Locus of Responsibility/Authority.** Who should have the lead responsibility—government (and, if so, who within the government?) and/or industry (and, if so, who within the key infrastructures)—in the U.S. national response to the SIW threat?

- — federal government leadership with a national security focus

- — federal government leadership with a law-enforcement focus (e.g., Department of Justice leadership)

- — joint international government leadership—national security focus

- — joint international government leadership—law-enforcement focus

- — international industry leadership—government support.

- • **Tactical Warning, Attack Assessment, and Emergency Response.** How should the United States (and the planet)— its governments and its industry—organize to develop and implement capabilities and procedures to sense and respond to SIW threats?

  - — a government-led, national security–oriented model— labeled a National Infrastructure Condition (NICON) model

  - — a government-led, law enforcement–oriented model— labeled a counterterrorism model

  - — a Centers for Disease Control and Prevention (CDC) model

  - — an industry-led model.

- • **Vulnerability Assessments.** By what means and mechanisms of government and industry cooperation should a vulnerability assessment of key U.S. national infrastructures be undertaken?

  - — a government-led (e.g., Department of Defense–led) assessment of U.S. vulnerabilities

  - — a joint public-private sector effort involving the United States and other key nations (e.g., G-7 and/or potential SIW peer competitors)

  - — an international public-private partnership along the lines of the U.S. CDC or the United Nations World Health Organization (WHO)

  - — an industry-led and government-assisted assessment.

- **Declaratory Policy on SIW Use.** What should the U.S. government declaratory policy be on the use of SIW and the relationship between the use of SIW and the use of other strategic military and economic instruments?

  — retaliation principally in kind for any SIW attack

  — retaliation principally by non-SIW military means in response to such an attack

  — retaliation by economic means, including possibly economically oriented SIW means, in response to such an attack

  — complete ambiguity as to how the United States would respond to such an attack.

2. **Tough Issues to Be Faced Now.** These are urgent but contentious issues related to the inaugural charting of long-term SIW-related national goals and strategy. Examples of these issues (with alternatives) include:

- **R&D Investment Strategy.** Many experts on SIW believe that there is going to be some R&D needed in this area that industry will not do. Handling this R&D (not least because offensive and defensive R&D in this domain is so intertwined) will be tricky. What investment strategy should the U.S. pursue with respect to the likes of monitoring, identification, and traceback techniques; attack assessment techniques; defense and reconstitution techniques; and damage assessment techniques?

  — no significant international SIW cooperation

  — limited international cooperation focused on defensive techniques (e.g., G-7 model)

  — broad international cooperation organized through existing multinational security arrangements (e.g., NATO model)

  — broad international cooperation organized through global arrangements (e.g., WHO model)

  — broad voluntary international cooperation.

- **International Information Sharing and Cooperation**. What principles should guide international collaboration (in particular with allies and coalition partners) in the SIW domain? Is there an SIW parallel to extended deterrence? extended defense?

  — national security-oriented network protection goals

  — coordinated defensive R&D with allies

  — international proscriptions on offensive SIW R&D

  — private-sector, market-driven focus.

3. **Deferred Issues.**  These issues, for one reason or another (e.g., technical uncertainties), are not yet ready to be taken to closure— or, worse, that taking them to closure prematurely might produce "bad" strategy or policy decisions that would be hard to undo. Issues in this category include

   - **Intra- and Intergovernmental Cooperation on Politically Sensitive Privacy Issues.** This subject clearly needs to be included in any discussion of SIW, but more detail is needed on how privacy rights would be protected under specific strategies and policies.

   - **Minimum Essential Information Infrastructure (MEII).** More analytical and conceptual work is needed to determine whether the MEII concept (a system, or more precisely, a process that can produce the wherewithal to provide some minimal level of communications access and services to critical governmental and societal user communities) is at all feasible from both the technical and cost standpoints.

   - **Encryption Policy.**  SIW is just one of the many issue areas that need to be brought to the table when the United States and the international community chart long-term  goals and strategies related to encryption.

Each of these areas requires sensitive treatment.  In turn, each of them overlaps with other elements of a comprehensive approach to addressing SIW policy concerns.  This notion, that an action plan for addressing SIW vulnerabilities requires that trade-offs be made among and between different factors, is central to the unprecedented uncertainties of the cyberspace environment.  The next section addresses defensive and offensive SIW issues that have significance for SIW action plans and policy implementation.

## Current State of First-Generation SIW

Clearly, a macroassessment of the current state of first-generation SIW in terms of absolute and relative offensive and defensive SIW capabilities of the United States and other nations (or other parties) would be difficult to do even at a classified level. The current dynamic character of the information revolution and the embryonic character of SIW as a potential political-military instrument both argue for caution in making such an assessment—classified or unclassified—now and for the foreseeable future.

The following are the principal SIW assessment issues from the U.S. perspective:

1. the extent to which hostile SIW powers already exist and the degree to which they can seriously harm the United States with SIW attacks
2. the extent of current U.S. offensive SIW capability vis-à-vis other states (foe, neutral, or friend)—whether overt or covert—in preventive, preemptive, or retaliatory SIW actions.

To address these issues, the difficult task of evaluating offensive and defensive SIW capabilities must be broached.

The United States, as the global leader in the development and exploitation of information systems, surely has the potential to be an offensive SIW "superpower" if any nation does. Any lesser assessment of U.S. SIW potential vis-à-vis that of others would be judged as laughable by nations that are just beginning to speculate about the significance that SIW instruments may have in future conflicts. The United States, not least because of its global military and economic role, is also likely, at this stage, to have more precise information on the basic architecture and key nodes of a potential adversary's strategic infrastructures—a vital factor in a conceptual SIW campaign (where decisionmakers are bound to ask challenging questions about collateral effects). How far has the inherent U.S. SIW potential been exploited? How fast could it be exploited if the United States

were to make a strong national commitment to the urgent development of offensive SIW capabilities?

On the offensive side, the current U.S. experience with information
operations is as a supporting but relatively low-profile element of
U.S. military strategy and doctrine. The United States has well-
developed and successful offensive command and control, electronic, and other information warfare capabilities (e.g., U.S. Southern Command is a master of psychological operations, and the
military services develop and operate electronic warfare systems—
manifest in the large-scale use of command and control warfare and
the suppression of enemy air defenses in the Persian Gulf War), but
these could hardly be characterized as "strategic" in the sense of this
chapter. Offensive first-generation SIW, which by definition has the
potential to hold at risk a country's central nervous system (its critical infrastructure networks), is a much more-sensitive undertaking
than are "information operations" as supporting missions in conventional warfare. It is one thing to target military leadership, communications, and radar; it is quite another to target public utilities
that, among other things, provide power to hospitals.

The sensitivities of our friends and allies and the political-military
capital that might accrue to possible adversaries from an increasingly
open emphasis on U.S. offensive SIW initiatives have largely kept
more definitive information on these capabilities from being
revealed. While some U.S. SIW offensive capability clearly exists, its
full potential is politically and militarily sensitive. A full debate on
the role of offensive SIW in U.S. national security strategy would
likely have to deal with strong arguments from U.S. information systems and infrastructure equipment suppliers that a U.S. strategic
emphasis on—and possible demonstration of—such a capability
could profoundly and adversely affect their overseas sales.

Beyond being a leading contender to augment its existing arsenal
with offensive SIW capabilities, the United States, again by virtue of
its role in the world, is also a natural target for SIW attack. The
United States leads the world in the development and application of
information technologies and has a complex society and economy
critically dependent on information systems. It is geographically
protected and currently has the world's most formidable conventional military capabilities. If the United States is to be defeated or
thwarted militarily in the near future, it will most likely be because of

the successful use of an "asymmetric" strategy by an enemy seeking to avoid a direct military confrontation.

The first logical step in understanding SIW defensive implications is to conduct a review of potential U.S. vulnerabilities to conceivable SIW attacks across a broad threat and scenario spectrum. Unfortunately (or fortunately), we have very little real-world experience on which to base such an assessment. There have been a number of natural events (storms, earthquakes), human errors (software, control), and purposeful mischief (hobbyist hackers, criminals) that suggest that things can go wrong in various national infrastructures, occasionally on an impressive scale. But none of these past events has been "strategic" in its impact, and none appears to have been strategic in its intent.

One obvious problem with this paucity of defensive SIW-related experience is in relating cause and effect: Have we escaped SIW attacks because certain undetected attempts were not successful or because no one has tried yet?

While a great deal of uncertainty surrounds the future vulnerability of information infrastructures, it can be observed that a number of trends seem to point toward an expanded dependence on inherently less-secure networking concepts. In particular, the widespread adoption of open network standards and technologies means that the industries and applications delivered via cyberspace may become more vulnerable to single-point failures. The growth of electronic commerce, the prospective expansion of electronic stored value (Cyberpayment) payment systems, and plans for the delivery of critical services (e.g., telemedicine, government communications) over the global information infrastructure all present potential targets for an SIW attack.

The defensive SIW assessment thus comes down to an assessment of information-infrastructure vulnerability, threat potential, and vulnerability consequences. These assessments also have problems. Existing information infrastructure systems are complex, dynamic, flexible, and interdependent. They are public and private, military and commercial. Some (e.g., banking) have been "hardened" by design because of the potential risk and cost of compromise. Others have evolved in a more benign environment with nonthreat forcing functions (e.g., cost, accessibility, and interoperability).

Standard risk assessment methodologies (fault-tree analyses, simulations, red teams) have uncertain applicability and future analysis potential because information systems are very complex and because threats can be very diabolical. Information security responsibilities are decentralized, and specific system vulnerabilities that are discovered are very sensitive and tightly held (for obvious very good reasons).

Undiscovered risks may continue to be the greatest concern. This suggests that continuing vigilance is required so that known problems can be fixed as they are discovered (if costs to fix are "reasonable"). If known problems are hidden but not fixed, threats can be monitored and contingency plans can be developed, but associated risks may be impossible to measure in terms of direct (immediate) loss potential (human lives, repair and replacement costs, opportunity costs while equipment is down, etc.).

With the above caveats properly lowering expectations about the precision achievable, a preliminary assessment of the current state of first-generation SIW in terms of the key dimensions listed above is as follows:

1. **Number of Offensive SIW Players**: *Unknown* (but probably between 0 and a few)

2. **Tactical Warning** (Is attack under way?) and **Attack Assessment** (By whom, how big, and what?): Issues are uncertainty in perpetrator identity and the potential value and timeliness of warning indicators; all are *unknown* but perpetrator uncertainties will likely be small in first-generation SIW in which information warfare is only one element of the conflict (but it could be *large* if the perpetrator desires)

3. **Damage Assessment** (size and scope of damage): Significant damage will speak for itself; most critical damage-assessment issues are related to the potential for, and implications of, further damage

4. **Uncertainty in Weapons Effects**: Large

5. **Degree of SIW Vulnerability**: *Unknown* (but there are worrisome trends and real concerns).

Although we do not know with confidence what the current situation with respect to offensive and defensive SIW capabilities is, people with informed *opinions* tend to fall into one of two polar groups: (1) those who see the historical glitches in information infrastructures as indicative of potential vulnerabilities that could be exploited by future adversaries, possibly with significant strategic advantage and (2) those who see this experience as strong evidence that the exploitable effects of whatever vulnerabilities might exist would be relatively modest and that the systems are evolving in a Darwinian mode that will continue to assure appropriate defense mechanisms—that there is no such thing as SIW. Determining the correct view between these two positions is less important than how we should proceed given current (and likely future) uncertainties.

## Alternative First-Generation SIW End States

The fourth step in the SIW framework design process is the crafting of a set of *plausible and potentially desirable* alternative first-generation SIW asymptotic end states—taking into account the nature of the first-generation SIW threats that have been identified and expressed in terms of the previously cited key dimensions of the first-generation SIW environment. Note the criterion "plausible and potentially desirable," which eliminates such possible end states as a very large number of nations with major-league offensive SIW capability alongside generally poor defensive SIW capabilities.

This end state–crafting process is in effect likely to be an aggregation of assessments of the impact and possible future evolution (shaped or not shaped by related targeted strategy and policy decisions) of a set of threats identified in various SIW scenarios—expressed to the degree possible in terms of the key dimensions.

On the basis of the above approach, the following might be an initial array of possible alternative first-generation SIW asymptotic end states:

**U.S. Supremacy in Offensive and Defensive SIW.** The United States overwhelmingly dominates the SIW environment by virtue of possessing

1. far and away the world's best offensive SIW tools and techniques, capable of penetrating any other country's SIW defenses

2. highly effective SIW defenses and reconstitution and recovery capabilities that effectively reduce the vulnerability of potential SIW targets in the United States (e.g., key U.S. infrastructures) to strategically insignificant levels—capabilities that it *selectively* shares with allies

3. traceback capabilities that give very high confidence of perpetrator identification—whereas no other nation has traceback capabilities good enough to identify the United States as the source if it launches SIW attacks.

**Club of SIW Elites.** Through a combination of technical capability and resource allocation, an international condominium of a handful of highly competent SIW nations emerges (e.g., on the order of 5 to 10) with the United States almost certain to be the most competent of the group. Mutual deterrence of SIW use is the norm among club members. This handful of SIW "major leaguers" collaborates with each other to some degree to

1. constrain the spread of major-league SIW capability to other nation-states and nonstate actors

2. de-emphasize SIW and establish a norm of no first use of SIW

3. set international technical standards for cyberspace that help to perpetuate the exclusivity of the club.

**Global "Defense Dominance" in SIW.** As a consequence of broad global cooperation in the fielding of very high quality SIW defenses, the vulnerability of key potential SIW targets (e.g., key infrastructures) in most nations is reduced to strategically insignificant levels. This end state is further bolstered in some measure by international cooperation in the global dissemination of

1. high-quality traceback capabilities (and/or a commitment to provide "Whodunit?" traceback information in the event of a serious SIW attack)

2. high-quality tactical warning and attack assessment capabilities.

This end state would also be bolstered by establishment of an SIW "arms control" regime, along the lines of the biological and chemical weapon arms-control regimes, which would establish international information operation norms, standards, legal restrictions, and enforcement mechanisms. Like currency counterfeiting, software piracy, and other threats to world economic order, SIW becomes something responsible states do not do. SIW rogues are dealt with as the UN dealt with Saddam: Deny them their goals and punish them.

**Market-Based Diversity.** The extent of damage or disruption achievable in an SIW attack is modest, and reconstitution and recovery are fast as a consequence of

1. the natural strength of diversity in the globalization and standardization of cyberspace reducing overall vulnerability to SIW attack to moderate levels

2. global cooperation in providing high-quality damage assessment tools

3. market-reinforced ("good neighbor") cooperation on reconstitution and recovery.

## Alternative Action Plans

The fifth step is applying the methodology to develop alternative action plans. The analytical and conceptual framework described here has application to concrete decisions affecting many areas of public policy. In the context of government actions designed to address SIW vulnerabilities, the framework provides a step-by-step means of addressing the relationship between strategy and policy questions in the SIW domain and the net—or relative—impact of different policy choices on achieving overall SIW-related strategic objectives.

The process of developing a set of alternative action plans is thus one of

1. choosing a set of illustrative alternative SIW end states

2. coming to judgment on a selected set of key SIW strategy, policy, and related issues (such as cited above) with an eye to moving in the direction of a specified end state.

Table 9.2 provides an illustrative set of alternative action plans for navigating toward the four illustrative end states cited above, based on decisions on those SIW issues in the "Low-Hanging Fruit" and

Table 9.2
Alternative Action Plans

| | Competition | Mixed (Competition and Cooperation) | Cooperation | |
| --- | --- | --- | --- | --- |
| | A | B | C | D |
| Key strategy and policy issues | U.S. Supremacy in SIW | Club of SIW elites | Global "defense dominance" in SIW | Market-based diversity |
| Locus of responsibility and authority | Federal government leads<br>National security focus<br>Joint leadership | Federal government leads<br>National security focus<br>Joint leadership | Federal government leads<br>Law enforcement focus<br>Joint leadership | Industry leads |
| Tactical warning and alert structure | Government-led NICON model<br>Counterterrorism model | Government-led NICON model<br>Counterterrorism model<br>CDC model | CDC model<br>Industry-led model | Industry-led model |
| Declaratory policy (links with other military instruments) | Strong retaliation threat (SIW retaliation emphasis)<br>Reassurance on invulnerability of key infrastructure | Moderate retaliation threat v.s nonclub actors<br>Some reassurance on invulnerability of club infrastructures | No retaliation threat<br>Reassurance on resilience of GII | Moderate retaliation threat (emphasis on economic instrumen*s) |

## Table 9.2—Continued

| | Competition | Mixed (Competition and Cooperation) | Cooperation | Cooperation |
| | A | B | C | D |
|---|---|---|---|---|
| International information sharing and cooperation | SIW programs compartmentalized | High degree of cooperation within club (G-7/FATF model) | High degree of cooperation<br><br>Institutional links through NATO, FATF, etc. | High degree of voluntary cooperation |
| Vulnerability assessments | Government-led (NICON organizational model) | Government-led (G-7/FATF model) | Public/private U.S. (WHO Model) | Public/private U.S. (CDC Model) |
| R&d/investment strategy priorities | National security-oriented protection goals | Coordinate defensive R&D with allies | Coordinate defensive R&D with allies | Proscriptions on offensive SIW R&D |
| | Some coordinated defensive R&D with allies | Some proscriptions on offensive SIW R&D | Proscriptions on offensive SIW R&D | Private-sector focus |

"Tough Issues" categories (see above). Note that, in some instances, more than one issue alternative is compatible with the indicated end state. (More detailed descriptions of some of the more cryptic entries in Table 9.2 are provided in Molander, Wilson, Mussington, and Mesic, 1998.)

## CONCLUSIONS

The above-described strategy and policy decisionmaking framework and process—an evolving series of frameworks—would appear to offer a useful means of organizing thinking about the emerging SIW problem and achieving an inaugural action plan in this arena. As such, it should contribute to the ongoing effort to identify the SIW-related issues on which decisions need to be made at this time in the United States and the appropriate forum(s) in which to take up these issues.

This framework and process, though oriented to U.S. national decisionmaking, should also contribute to preparations for the imperative and even more challenging international decisionmaking process on this subject, for which the issue of the appropriate forum(s) for such an undertaking also remains to be resolved.

## REFERENCES

Arquilla, J., and D. Ronfeldt, *In Athena's Camp: Preparing for Conflict in the Information Age,* Santa Monica, Calif.: RAND, MR-880-OSD/RC, 1997.

Libicki, M., *What Is Information Warfare?* Washington, D.C.: National Defense University, Institute for National Strategic Studies, ACIS Paper 3, 1995. Available at http://www.ndu.edu/inss/actpubs/act003/a003cont.html (last accessed February 18, 1999).

Molander, R., and P. Wilson, *The Day After . . . in the American Strategic Infrastructure,* Santa Monica, Calif.: RAND, MR-963-OSD, forthcoming.

Molander, R., P. Wilson, D. Mussington, and R. Mesic, *Strategic Information Warfare Rising,* Santa Monica, Calif.: RAND, MR-964-OSD, 1998.

PCCIP—*see* President's Commission on Critical Infrastructure Protection.

President's Commission on Critical Infrastructure Protection, *Critical Foundations: Protecting America's Infrastructures*, Washington, D.C., 1997.   Also available at http://www.pccip.gov/report_index.html (last accessed February 18, 1999).

Thompson, K., "Reflections on Trusting Trust," *Communications of the ACM*, Vol. 27, No. 8, August 1984.   Reprinted in L. Hoffman, ed., *Rogue Programs: Viruses, Worms, and Trojan Horses.* New York: Van Nostrand Reinhold, 1990.

# Chapter Ten

# IMPLICATIONS OF INFORMATION VULNERABILITIES
# FOR MILITARY OPERATIONS

*Glenn C. Buchan*

Can more effective use of information provide the leverage necessary to offset reductions in military force structure? Can new information systems lead to fundamental changes in the ways the United States uses force or otherwise coerces adversaries? These possibilities, which RAND and others have been analyzing for several years, are certainly extremely attractive, particularly for the United States, which seems to be well-positioned to exploit the new technologies. However, success is by no means preordained. The force has a dark side. One of the potential problems is that relying on the new information-related technologies that appear so powerful could also introduce vulnerabilities an enemy could exploit, or that would allow Mother Nature—or plain bad luck—to render the systems impotent or seriously degrade them. This chapter focuses on these vulnerabilities and their operational consequences and explores possibilities for managing the associated risks.

Recent RAND research has tried to address some of those problems, particularly the problems confronting the Air Force.[1] Some of the problems are common to all of the services. Others are unique, at least to a degree, to particular services, based either on the specific kinds of operations that they conduct (e.g., land versus air, "tactical" versus "strategic"), the kind of equipment they use, and the opera-

---

[1]This discussion is derived primarily from a "sanitized" version of the analysis presented in Buchan et al. (forthcoming a, b). The author gratefully acknowledges the work of all his colleagues that is reflected here. I want to thank Keith Henry, in particular, for producing more appropriate versions of several figures for use in this chapter.

tional and organizational culture that has evolved within each. Joint operations complicate matters even further. Thus, while our discussion and specific analysis focus on Air Force operations, some of the general findings are likely to be more broadly applicable, but the details could vary considerably.

## AN OVERVIEW OF AIR FORCE OPERATIONS AND THEIR DEPENDENCE ON INFORMATION: PRESENT AND FUTURE

Our analysis has focused primarily on operations—war and other lesser operations—as opposed to day-to-day peacetime activities. That means our analysis did not pay much attention to casual or even malicious computer hacking attacks, say, on Air Force computers involved in routine, day-to-day support activities, even though those are by far the most prevalent kind of "computer attacks" that are known to have occurred. It is not that we consider such information vulnerabilities unimportant. Indeed, interference with personnel, medical, and payroll databases, for example, could have annoying—even serious—consequences even in peacetime. However, we believe that protecting information-related systems that support Air Force operations, which are its stock-in-trade, should receive first priority. Moreover, many of the actions required to protect Air Force information systems during operations would be applicable in peacetime as well, *but the converse is not necessarily true.*

Two major sets of systems and processes are central to the Air Force's ability to conduct operations. The first includes all the systems that actually collect the basic intelligence data necessary to support operations, plan the operations, and execute them. Figure 10.1 shows some of the critical systems that the Air Force currently relies on and how they are wired together. The most important elements include the following:

- The whole array of intelligence-collection sensors, platforms, processors, and analysts that collect and analyze the information necessary to provide planners a sense of what is going on, warn them of attacks, allow them to target weapons (if that is appropriate) or otherwise conduct operations, and allow them to assess the effects of earlier operations

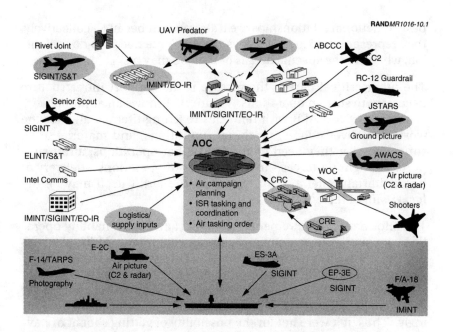

**Figure 10.1—Air Force Combat Operations**

- The planning and command center(s) where information is integrated, plans are constructed, orders are given, and progress of operations is monitored[2]

- The forces that execute the operations

- The communications systems that wire all of the critical systems together

- Systems that provide other critical information to planners and operators (e.g., Global Positioning Systems [GPS] satellites that provide navigational data and location information).

The details of future systems and architectures will change, of course, as technology evolves, operational procedures and organizational relationships change, and the new replaces the old. Physical and electronic "hubs" may not always coincide. Nevertheless, the

---

[2]Currently, the hub of Air Force planning activity is the Air Operations Center (AOC).

basic functional relationships are transcendent because, collectively, they represent the kinds of things the Air Force needs to do to do its job, whatever the specific details of that job may be.

The other critical part of the picture is the support infrastructure necessary to sustain operations. Figure 10.2 shows an airlift network centered at Scott AFB with tentacles reaching literally all over the world to deliver people, machines, munitions, and materiel of all sorts wherever they need to go. In combat operations, airlift supports the fighting forces. In other kinds of operations—delivery of humanitarian relief aid, for example—the airlift itself may be the focal point of the operation.

The information requirements for support and sustainability operations are similar to those of any shipping company. Airlift planners need to know who needs what material, in what quantities and by when, and where the goods need to be delivered. They also need to know what they have available to send, where it is stored, how to get it, and so on. Then, they have to allocate their airlift assets accordingly. Thus, if it were not for the possibility of getting shot at or hav-

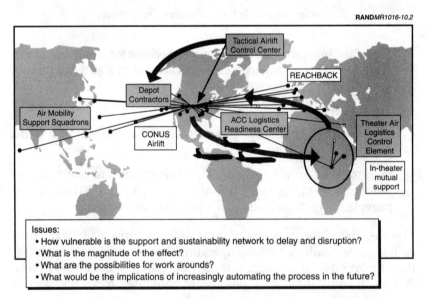

RANDMR1016-10.2

Tactical Airlift
Control Center

REACHBACK

Depot
Contractors

Air Mobility
Support Squadrons

ACC Logistics
Readiness Center

CONUS
Airlift

Theater Air
Logistics
Control
Element

In-theater
mutual
support

Issues:
• How vulnerable is the support and sustainability network to delay and disruption?
• What is the magnitude of the effect?
• What are the possibilities for work arounds?
• What would be the implications of increasingly automating the process in the future?

Figure 10.2—Supporting the Forces and Sustaining Operations

ing someone actively trying to disrupt their operations in other ways, their job would not be that different from that of Federal Express. In fact, current plans are to make military airlift operate more like Federal Express in the future.

An enemy might try to disrupt, distort, or destroy the information necessary to support the Air Force's ability to fight, to support and sustain its operations, or both. As we will show later in this chapter, the potential vulnerabilities of the information systems that support combat operations and sustainability efforts are quite different, as are the consequences of disrupting those systems.

## DISRUPTING AIR FORCE OPERATIONS

### Potential Threats

There are all manner of possibilities for disrupting information systems and information-related operations. Accordingly, we took a broad and comprehensive view of possible threats. Figure 10.3 shows some of those potential threats. They range from the sublime to the ridiculous, the well-understood to the ethereal, and the straightforward to the very challenging. For example, many critical information-related facilities remain vulnerable to direct attack by high explosives delivered any number of ways (e.g., by aircraft, missile, truck bomb, or command attack). Alternatively, an entire base could be cut off from landline communications for a time, or a key warning system could be disrupted deliberately or inadvertently if a critical cable were cut. Other familiar threats, such as jamming, spoofing, or deceiving information systems, could continue to be problems in the future. Futuristic weapons, such as high-power microwave (HPM) devices, could increase the vulnerability of some electronic systems unless they could be effectively shielded. Then, there is the master computer hacker (Kevin Mitnick, in the photo) who looks like—and might even be—the kid next door. Finally, there are natural events and even "Acts of God" (ask any computer user) that can disrupt information systems as thoroughly as any deliberate attack. Information systems have to be resilient to this kind of natural disruption regardless of any concern about "enemy action." Thus, while most of the current topical interest has focused on the newer, trendier threats to information systems, particularly com-

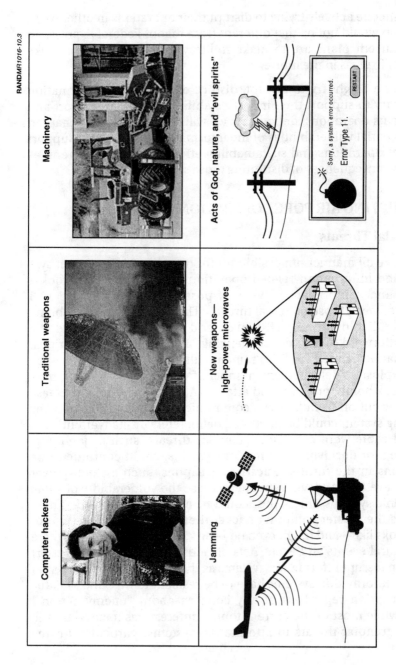

Figure 10.3—Potential Threats to Air Force Information Systems

puter hacking and associated information disruption and manipulation, the possible range of threats is much broader. Indeed, our analysis showed that some of the "old fashioned" threats appear to pose a greater danger to Air Force operations.

The character of the potential threats also has implications for the kinds of opponents that might be able to mount them and the prospects for the intelligence community's being able to help in coping with them. In particular,

- At least some, even most, options for threatening Air Force information systems are within the capabilities of virtually any potential adversary, including non–nation-states. For example, physical attacks with high explosives against vulnerable facilities are within the capabilities of any attacker, although some will have more-effective delivery options available than others. As noted in the first part of this chapter, computer hacking skills are essentially universal. Similarly, effective jammers against unprotected communication systems and GPS satellites are cheap and readily available. Even "high end" futuristic weapons, such as HPM generators, are likely to be available on the international arms market to anyone with money once they become available at all. Thus, intelligence assessments may be of less use than usual in filtering the list of possible enemies who could interfere with U.S. information systems, and traditional notions of "strategic warning" of threats developing may be of little use, barring dumb luck in collecting intelligence.

- While the weapons to attack Air Force information systems appear to be cheap and readily available, *the requisite information to make those attacks effective may be difficult to obtain.* For example, many computer hacking attacks require knowledge that only insiders are likely to possess. Similarly, some physical vulnerabilities may be difficult to identify even if the basic information is unclassified.

- Because of the speed and ambiguity of computer hacking attacks, the prospects for receiving useful "tactical warning" in the traditional sense (i.e., receiving warning in time to respond, identifying the attacker) are remote.

This is going to complicate the defender's problem in trying to protect against attacks on its key information systems.

## Potential Vulnerabilities

The idea that the information systems on which the Air Force relies have numerous potential vulnerabilities is hardly a surprise. The issue is assessing the severity and possible operational impacts of those vulnerabilities.

**Computer Vulnerabilities.** The potential vulnerabilities of the computer networks directly involved in combat operations are strikingly different from those used for support and sustainability functions. Figures 10.4 and 10.5 illustrate the contrast.

Figure 10.4 shows the major groups of computer systems that are used in the AOC's planning process and indicates the critical information flows into and out of the AOC. Figure 10.4 shows the information flows in and out of the AOC and, as the shading in the figure suggests, we found that the computer systems used to plan and execute Air Force combat operations are relatively secure, absent a corrupted insider, in spite of the fact that they are UNIX-based systems that have well-known weaknesses. The intelligence-related systems, in particular, are as secure as technology and good operational procedures can make them. The reason is that the Air Force basically does everything right operationally:

- The databases and information flows among the various computers are encrypted.
- The computer networks are all isolated electronically from non-secure systems (e.g., none of these computers is connected to the Internet).
- All computer disks entering the AOC are checked for viruses.

Thus, there is basically no way to "hack" into the system from the outside if everyone does his job properly. Even a corrupted insider would have trouble because of a couple of artifacts of the design of the AOC. First, the AOC is not fully automated; as a result, information passes through several sets of hands and is scrutinized by many eyes, partly to catch innocent errors that occur routinely in inputting data to computers. Deliberate distortion of data is likely to be caught at roughly the same rate as innocent errors. Second, much planning is still done by hand, at least as a backup to the automated systems.

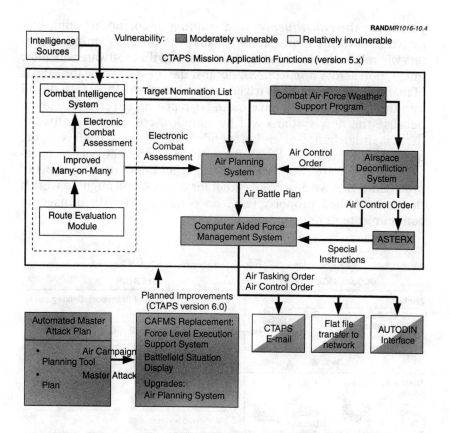

**Figure 10.4—Potential Computer Vulnerabilities in the AOC**

Ironically, *the "inefficient" human involvement in the planning process provides an important hedge against computer hacking attacks,* limiting the likely effect of such attacks to modest delays in generating and disseminating directions to the forces. Interestingly, maintaining enough skilled human planners to take over in an emergency would appear to be a prudent measure simply to protect against computers going down from natural causes.

If the AOC and similar military command centers evolve along the lines presently planned—the introduction of the Global Command and Control System and the Global Command and Support System, for example—the basic vulnerabilities could get somewhat worse. In particular, the *consequences* of disrupting or corrupting computer networks could be more severe because the various command centers will rely on more-common software, and that software will allow integration across *applications*, not just databases. Thus, the effects of malicious code, perhaps triggered by a virus somehow introduced into the network, could have more far-reaching effects. Moreover, because the new systems will be standard commercial software, there is little chance of an independent check on the safety of the code. The burden will be on the software manufacturers to make sure the codes are "bug free." On the other hand, the same sort of protections that we described earlier for the AOC still ought to work if they are applied properly (e.g., no connections with nonsecure communications or computer networks).

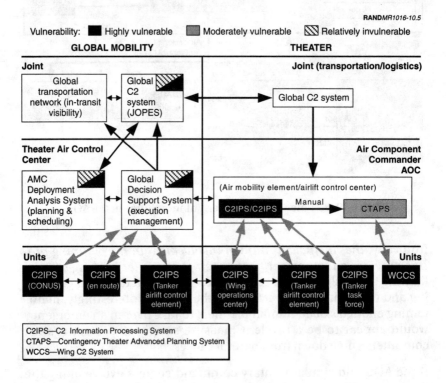

**Figure 10.5—Potential Computer Vulnerabilities in the Support and Sustainability Network**

If there is a danger from computer attacks, it is more likely to be at the Wing level, where controls could be looser. In the meantime, the best way to attack an AOC appears to be the direct way: Blow it up.

The story is quite different on the support and sustainability side. Figure 10.5 shows that some of the computers in that part of the system, particularly the Command and Control Information Processing System (C2IPS), which is widely used throughout the Air Force, are potentially very vulnerable to attack. The main difference is that the C2IPS computers are not always isolated electronically from outside nonsecure networks, and the data are not always encrypted. As a result, the system is potentially vulnerable to the whole array of hacker tricks. Even worse, other computer systems that would otherwise be considered secure are linked to C2IPS and could be corrupted accordingly. Thus, the entire computer network that services support and sustainability operations could be compromised, with key portions degraded or out of service.

However, that need not be as catastrophic as it sounds: In fact, it is not all that different from what actually occurred during Operation Desert Shield when Air Mobility Command's (AMC) computers went down for benign reasons. AMC planners and users in the field planned operations manually, working together closely, and made do. The operations were successful, and delays were minimal. Again, the key was having skilled human backups available. *Only if AMC goes to a highly automated, Federal Express–like system and drastically cuts manpower would computer vulnerabilities appear to pose a serious threat.*

**Communication System Vulnerabilities.** Future Air Force communication networks will be very different from those of the past (i.e., the Cold War years), when the Air Force and the Department of Defense in general invested heavily in dedicated, secure, resilient communications. In the future, while its demands for communication capacity are likely to increase dramatically, the Air Force will be obliged to rely primarily on commercial communication systems. The danger is that commercial systems are not typically configured to withstand jamming, physical attacks against critical facilities, or other standard tricks of the electronic warfare trade. Unless the collective set of future commercial systems can be configured into an adaptive network that is robust against most forms of interference, the Air Force is likely to face critical shortfalls in communication capacity in all but the most benign environments.

Our analysis identified two major types of communication vulnerabilities. The first applies primarily to combat forces operating in a particular theater. Figure 10.6 shows the kinds of communication links used in current theater air operations. Some of the critical links are vulnerable to cheap, mobile, low-power jammers that would be easy for an enemy to obtain and use and difficult and expensive for the United States to suppress or otherwise counter. The result could be a substantial reduction in communication throughput rates. *Moreover, this problem is likely to get worse in the future.* The primary problem is *intratheater* communications because that is where mobile jammers are likely to be most effective. If that problem can be solved, more robust networks of commercial landlines and satellites can take over to move information over long distances if need be.

The second kind of problem relates primarily to the larger set of communication systems that the Air Force relies on to support sus-

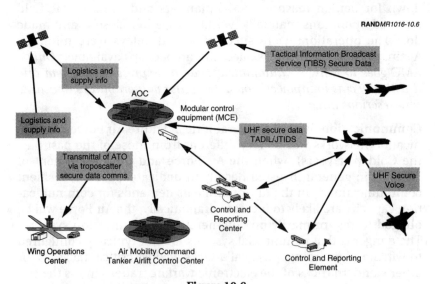

RAND*MR1016-10.6*

**Figure 10.6**
**Figure 10.6—Some Typical Theater Air Communication Links**

tainment operations. One key system is the Public Switched Network (PSN), which—as Figure 10.7 shows—is important to many other users as well. The PSN has a number of potential vulnerabilities.[3] The two sorts of attacks that appear most threatening are physical attacks (e.g., high explosives) against the end office, trunk lines, or base point of presence for the PSN and computer hacking attacks on a switch or digital cross-connect. Of the two types of attacks, the physical attack appears easier to execute, harder to defend against, and more effective in a range of circumstances. The result could be a PSN communication outage for a particular military base or entire region of the country for some period of time.

**Other Types of Vulnerabilities.** Other types of systems are potentially vulnerable to attack as well. One of the most important is GPS. GPS, in its current form, is highly vulnerable to small, cheap, low-power jammers. Denying or degrading navigation data to various users could have diverse and wide-ranging effects. One of the most

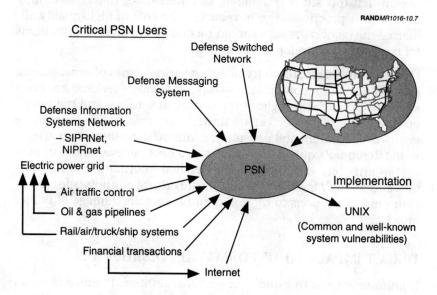

Figure 10.7—Air Force Systems Rely Heavily on Defense and
Public Information Infrastructure

---

[3]See Feldman (1997) for a detailed discussion.

obvious and potentially important is degrading the accuracy of precision-guided weapons that rely on GPS. Figure 10.8 shows how
GPS-guided weapon accuracy could degrade depending on the
power of the jammer, the quality of the weapon's guidance system,
and the quality of its GPS receiver. In the particular example highlighted, a jammer that could fit in the back of a jeep could reduce the
accuracy of a missile equipped with a relatively high-quality GPS
receiver and an affordable inertial measurement system by hundreds
of meters, which would certainly remove it from the "precision-
guided" category of weapons.

Identifying the most cost-effective solution to the GPS jamming
problem involves exploring the trades that Figure 10.8 suggests in
more detail. The issue, obviously, is balancing the effectiveness of
better inertial systems and/or more jam-resistant GPS components
against their cost. Intensive work on this problem is under way
throughout the defense community. Resolving these issues is the
reason that this study concluded, as others have, that determining
how far it is practical to go in reducing the cost of high-quality all-
inertial navigation systems should be one of the high-priority items
for research and development funding.

Using countermeasures to try to defeat various types of sensors (e.g.,
surveillance and reconnaissance systems, weapon seekers) has been
standard practice throughout the history of warfare, and the never-
ending game of "hider versus finder" continues with even more
vigor. Concealment and deception continue to be important arrows
in the defender's quiver and are likely to become even more important as attackers seek increasingly detailed information to find targets and identify them accurately, locate critical aimpoints for precision-guided weapons to try to hit, and assess the damage of earlier
attacks.

## DIRECT IMPACTS OF INFORMATION DISRUPTION

If an enemy were to exploit these vulnerabilities, the effects could
manifest themselves in a number of ways:

- loss or distortion of information
- delays of various sorts
- reduced weapon effectiveness

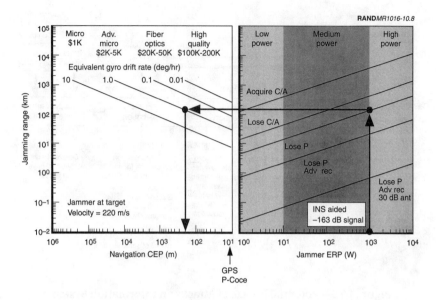

RAND*MR1016-10.8*

**Figure 10.8—GPS Jamming Can Reduce Weapon Accuracy Substantially**

- reduced sortie rates
- reduced target discrimination capability.

All aspects of air operations—force planning, force direction, force execution, and support and sustainability—could be affected.

Figure 10.9 briefly summarizes the immediate effects of the spectrum of possible attacks on information systems on the various processes involved in managing and conducting Air Force operations. The magnitudes of the effects are based on the detailed analysis presented in the RAND study described earlier (Buchan et al., forthcoming), and more-detailed results and the supporting analysis are available there. Note that these results assume that the Air Force continues to operate more or less the way it does today and is likely to in the reasonably near future. Some kinds of changes (e.g., drastic reductions in the number or skill levels of personnel in the AOC, logistics planning cells, or field stations) *could dramatically increase the magnitude of some of the adverse effects of information attacks* (e.g., some delays could be much longer because recovery would be much more difficult).

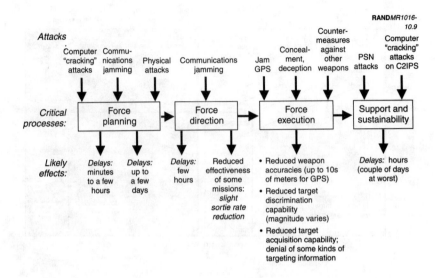

**Figure 10.9—Potential Effects of Attacks on Information Systems**

## OPERATIONAL IMPLICATIONS

What really matters, though, is what effect this array of delays, disruptions, or outright loss of information might have on the outcome—success, failure, and cost—of a range of Air Force operations. In our analysis, the operational world appeared to divide into two major categories (excluding large-scale nuclear conflict): major conventional campaigns and everything else, where "everything else" includes a large spectrum of possibilities (e.g., peacekeeping, humanitarian assistance, hostage rescue). Interestingly, our analysis suggested that—unlike in the traditional force planning world, in which major campaigns are the stressing cases and other types of operations tend to be "lesser-included" cases, in terms of information vulnerabilities—*some kinds of lesser operations are actually more likely to be the stressing cases.*

### Major Conflicts

The reason that the kinds of effects of information disruption described in Figure 10.9 have little impact on the outcome of major campaigns is that, if one accepts the size, effectiveness, and deployment rates projected for future U.S. military forces, the U.S. should be able to bring so much high-quality firepower to bear quickly that its sheer mass simply overwhelms all other factors in the military equation. The delays and imprecision introduced by interfering with U.S. information-related systems generally appear to be mere "speed bumps": They hardly even slow the U.S. forces down.

Figures 10.10 and 10.11 are typical of the results that we found and illustrate the insensitivity of campaign outcomes to even dramatic information disruptions. Figure 10.10 shows the effects of delays in introducing U.S. air forces into a major campaign and the reduced sortie rates that might result from delays in shipping spare parts to the theater. In this particular example, the U.S. objective is to prevent invading enemy forces from reaching a certain point on the ground. In the first case, even a two-week delay in introducing air forces would not have been sufficient to change the outcome, and the delays associated with information attacks are likely to be on the order of hours to a very few days at most. Similarly, sortie-rate reductions would have to be massive—much greater than disruption of the information systems supporting the logistics network would be likely to cause—to have much discernible effect on the overall campaign. The reason is that there is enough firepower available from other sources (e.g., Army forces, in this case) to take up the slack.[4]

Similarly, Figure 10.11 shows the effect of disrupting the planning process. It shows the number of targets killed in a specified amount of time as a function of how frequently a new targeting plan can be generated. We varied the Air Tasking Order generation rate from daily, which reflects current practice, to "infinite" (i.e., the "static" case in the figure), which essentially means that the United States begins the campaign with a single set of targets and a battle plan and never adjusts them over the course of the campaign. Note that, even

---

[4]That, of course, begs the question of what would happen if the Army forces were also delayed and/or disrupted by information attacks. The results then became very sensitive to metaphysics (e.g., How tough are the attackers and the indigenous defenders?) and model artifacts (e.g., How well does the model handle maneuver warfare? Answer: Not very).

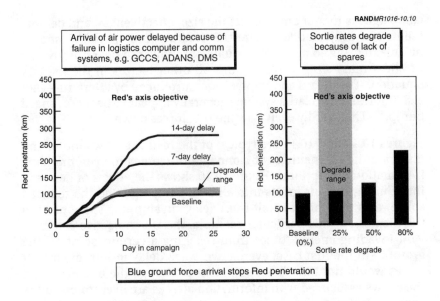

Figure 10.10—Arrival Delays Have Little Effect

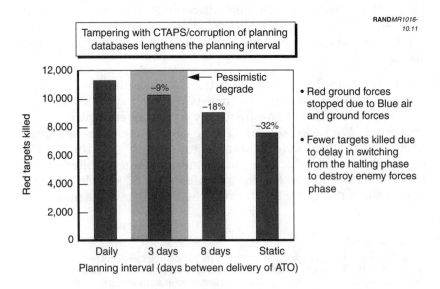

Figure 10.11—Planning Cycle Delays Have Only Minor Effect

in the latter extreme case, the number of targets killed in a fixed amount of time only drops by about 30 percent. In a less extreme but still pessimistic case, the reduction in targets killed is less than 10 percent.[5] Thus, even severe degradation of the planning process would have only a modest impact on the outcome of the campaign. Examining why the effects of information disruption are no greater than they are provides useful insight into more general problems of the value of information in military campaigns and helps put the information vulnerability problem in perspective.

Interestingly, these results are probably "real" and *not simply model artifacts.* Instead, they are *consequences of the nature of large-scale campaigns* and, as noted earlier, *scenario assumptions* (e.g., weapon system effectiveness, force deployment rates, campaign objectives for both sides). In the first place, the postulated campaign is relatively straightforward (and typical). The aggressor's objective is to seize territory in a neighboring country, so it launches an invasion. Accordingly, it needs to overcome the defender's military forces and perhaps also be able to destroy or coerce its government by threatening selected national infrastructure or political leadership targets. The objective of the defenders (the victim country and its U.S. allies) is similarly straightforward: Halt the enemy invasion and prevent the aggressor from being able to damage or coerce its neighbors, preferably at minimum cost (i.e., in lost lives and equipment) to the United States and its allies. Thus, to win, the defenders basically have to destroy enough of the right kinds of targets in a timely manner.

That means that, if the defenders can bring enough effective firepower to bear against the right targets, they win, and that is exactly what is happening in these scenarios. Based on current Department of Defense planning guidance, the U.S. forces are assumed to be so capable and so large that they simply overwhelm the attackers. Moreover, assuming the United States has had the foresight to prepare for this potential conflict well enough in advance (a criterion that the United States barely met vis-à-vis Iraq in the Gulf War), it should have a reasonable list of the aggressor's major fixed installa-

---

[5]In this example, the AOC is assumed to be destroyed on the first day of the war and reconstituted in three days. It then continues to operate at drastically reduced efficiency (or, conceivably, is periodically destroyed and reconstituted again) for the duration of the campaign.

tions, a pretty good picture of the enemy's military forces, and an *a priori* understanding of possible invasion routes at the start of the war. That should provide a major leg up on the targeting problem. Missing are likely to be

- individual mobile targets, particularly those that employ concealment and deception techniques[6]
- fixed targets whose function can be effectively disguised
- detailed knowledge of vulnerable points on some classes of targets.

Thus, the reason that the United States does so well in the cases shown in Figure 10.11 is that its forces are large and capable and already have most of the information that they need to conduct the campaign effectively. Delays in getting materiel to the theater do not matter much because there is so much materiel either available or on the way. Reducing sortie rates does not matter much for the same reason. Not even a failure to be able to adjust battle plays rapidly would have much effect as long as the initial plan was well-constructed. There is some lack of efficiency due to "overkilling" high-priority targets if the defenders cannot assess the effectiveness of their earlier attacks accurately and adjust the allocation of their forces accordingly. That is why the number of targets killed in Figure 10.11 can drop by 10 to 30 percent, depending on how frequently battle plans can be "tweaked." Thus, in this example, even massive interference with U.S. information systems can reduce the efficiency of the campaign, lengthen it somewhat, and raise its cost, but the final outcome is never in doubt.

Reassuring as that result might be from the U.S. point of view, even if the analysis is correct, it raises a couple of key questions:

- What if U.S. forces are not so large and robust?
- Could the cost of "victory" become excessive?

The first is likely to come about in any case as the defense budget continues to shrink but is particularly reasonable to consider if

---

[6]Note, however, that a massive mobile force, such as an invading armor force, is hard to conceal when it launches an attack. That is why the most effective countermeasure for an invading armored force is still likely to be the classical approach: Develop countermeasures to reduce the accuracy of the enemy's weapon guidance systems.

analyses continue to show that the services are buying more fire-power than they need. The second could occur not so much because the U.S. populace is perceived to be casualty-averse, which is probably a myth, but because, in the post–Cold War world, few potential quarrels are likely to be viewed as important enough to vital American interests to justify spilling much American blood.

To address these questions, we parametrically reduced both the size and complexity (i.e., the availability of alternative weapon systems using different technology to take up the slack if an enemy counters one type of system) of U.S. forces and assessed the cost of the campaign in terms of estimated U.S. casualties. To assess the likely impact of increases in U.S. casualties, we drew on the work of one of our colleagues (Larson, 1996) who had done a historical analysis of U.S. public support for past wars as a function of the level of U.S. casualties. We then tried to identify combinations of force reductions and changes in composition that could make them vulnerable enough in terms of increased U.S. casualties for information vulnerabilities to matter.

Figures 10.12 and 10.13 show some examples of the results of that analysis and suggest combinations of conditions under which information vulnerabilities could become important. Both cases show the effect of GPS jamming as forces are reduced. In the first case, alternative precision-guided weapons are available (e.g., laser-guided bombs in this particular case) that could partially replace GPS-guided weapons if someone were to jam GPS. In the second, there are not. Campaign duration is plotted as a surrogate for casualty levels. (We estimated casualties as a function of the length of the campaign to make the correlation). The shading on the figure is based on the casualty levels derived in the Larson analysis.

Figure 10.12 suggests that, absent interference with U.S. information systems, the war is unlikely to last long enough for casualties to become an issue until U.S. forces are reduced by at least 25 percent.[7] In a severe GPS jamming environment (i.e., where GPS essentially

---

[7]For the purposes of this example, cuts were assumed to be uniform across all Air Force systems to get a rough idea of how large force cuts had to be (e.g., 1 percent versus 10 percent versus 50 percent) before they started to matter. In practice, of course, force cuts are likely to vary widely, some types of systems being largely untouched while others are eliminated entirely.

does nothing to improve the accuracy of weapons in the vicinity of the target), the forces could only shrink a few percent (10 percent) before casualties might become a matter of concern, and a 25 percent cut in forces could cause real problems.

The reason that the results shown in Figure 10.12 are not worse than they are is that other precision-guided weapons in the inventory based on different technology—and, therefore, not vulnerable to the same countermeasures—are partially offsetting the loss of the GPS-guided weapons. In the absence of these alternative weapons, the effects of the GPS degradation are much more severe, as Figure 10.13 shows. The force can tolerate only a slight degradation in GPS effectiveness before U.S. casualties could become a concern. In fact, while the analysis shows that a combination of force reductions and a less diverse weapons stockpile would have to occur before information vulnerabilities become a serious concern, comparing Figures 10.12 and 10.13 suggests that the results are more sensitive to the nature of the weapon inventory than to the size of the force. Thus, *maintaining a diverse inventory of weapons that rely on different technologies appears to be particularly important in reducing the impact of weapon vulnerabilities.*

Table 10.1 summarizes some of the impacts of several specific kinds of information vulnerabilities on large-scale campaigns. In general, in analyzing the possible effects of information vulnerabilities on major campaigns, we came to several general conclusions, some of which we were able to quantify to a degree and all of which seemed to pass the "common sense" test:

- If the U.S. maintains the kind of large, capable conventional forces that it currently plans and if they generally operate the way they are supposed to, the United States will have so much high-quality firepower available that potential information vulnerabilities will have little effect on a major conventional campaign.

- Only if U.S. forces are reduced substantially in size (i.e., more than 25 percent or so) and if technical diversity and U.S. policymakers are particularly concerned about casualties will information vulnerabilities have a major impact on U.S. capability to fight and win major conventional wars.

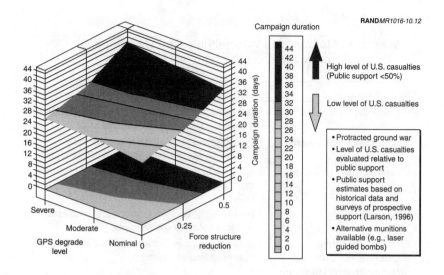

**Figure 10.12—Maintaining Multiple Types of Munitions May Reduce
the Impact of the Vulnerability of Specific Types of Systems**

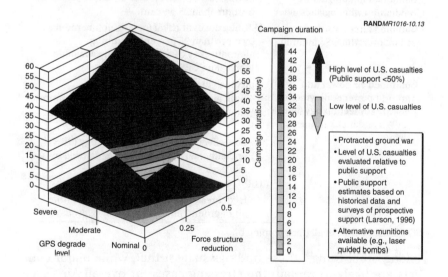

**Figure 10.13—The Combination of Reduced Force Structure and
Simplified Weapon Mix Can Substantially Increase the Impact of
Information Vulnerabilities**

Table 10.1

**Summary of Information Vulnerabilities and Their Impact on the Outcome of Major Conventional Campaigns**

| Vulnerability | Impact |
|---|---|
| Air power deployment | U.S. objectives at risk if delay much greater than 2 weeks, if adversary's break rate high. |
| Ground power deployment | U.S. objectives at risk if delay greater than about 2 weeks, if adversary's break rate high. |
| Air Tasking Order planning | Reduces killing capability and slightly lengthens campaign, but does not put U.S. objectives at risk. |
| GPS jamming | May add high risk to operations unless alternative technologies are available. |
| Denial and deception (hindering battle damage assessment, target discrimination) | Waste resources (munitions and sorties) and may lengthen campaign. |
| Combined logistics delay and GPS jamming | No significant impact if alternatives to GPS munitions are available. |
| Combined force structure reduction with logistics delay | U.S. objectives at risk if force structure reduced by more than 25 percent. |
| Combined force structure reduction with GPS jamming | U.S. objectives at risk if force structure reduced by more than 25 percent, assuming alternatives to GPS munitions are available. Worse if no GPS alternatives. |
| Combined air power and ground power deployment delays, key technology failure (SFW), and break rate sensitivity | Objectives at risk if: 1. Both air and ground power delayed by more than about 7 days. OR 2. Low effectiveness of key technology (SFW) and either air or ground power delayed by a few days. OR 3. High break rate of enemy forces and either air or ground power delayed by a few days. |

SOURCE: Buchan et al. (forthcoming b).

Among other things, these findings suggest that, while major conflicts are likely to remain the stressing cases for overall Air Force combat forces and, therefore, remain the basis for structuring the overall force, *other types of operations and situations may represent the stressing case for information-related systems.*

## Lesser Operations

If information vulnerabilities are ever going to be critical, our analysis suggested that it is most likely to occur in some kinds of smaller-scale operations rather than all-out war. Large-scale conflict has never been the only function of the military or the only external security concern of major powers, but in the post–Cold War world, lower-level military operations have become both much more common and a more important part of U.S. foreign policy (e.g., Bosnia, Somalia, postwar Iraq). Moreover, since some of them can be relatively open-ended, and several may be going on simultaneously, they can collectively tax U.S. military resources considerably.

The problem with characterizing low-intensity conflicts and lesser operations is that they represent such a diverse set of possibilities, as Table 10.2 suggests. The possible problems to be solved are enormously diverse, as are the tasks that need to be performed to deal with them. Some are relatively straightforward. Others are extremely complex. Many are quite benign—unopposed humanitarian relief, for example—although even that is not a foregone conclusion. Still others, while not necessarily benign, are not terribly challenging either. However, as Table 10.2 suggests, some such "lesser" operations share common characteristics that could make them stressing cases from an information-planning point of view and, therefore, potentially sensitive to potential vulnerabilities in information-related systems:

- Sensitivities can be greater than in major campaigns:
  - Time delays sometimes matter more.
  - Political sensitivities are likely to be higher, so the consequences of any miscue are likely to be greater.
- There may be no analog to overwhelming force.
- Information demands are likely to be out of proportion to the other dimensions of the conflict:
  - A considerable amount of information is likely to be required even for a "small" operation.
  - Much of that information may be of an unusual nature (e.g., refugee numbers and locations), involve unfamiliar areas (e.g., Rwanda), and/or be hard to come by (e.g., which way doors open in a foreign embassy).

## Table 10.2

### Characteristics of Some Generic Types of Low-Intensity Conflicts and Lesser Operations—Implications for Information Sensitivities

| Type of Operation | Examples | Characteristics |
|---|---|---|
| Moderate-scale direct action | Panama, Grenada, Haiti | Involves a substantial force and at least some level of combat |
| | | Has limited military operational objectives (e.g., capture Noriega; free "hostage" students and protect selected political figures), but may have broad political objectives (e.g., topple a government) |
| | | Typically involves short time commitment for the bulk of U.S. forces |
| Raids: | | |
| Punitive | Libya, parts of Operation Southern Watch in Iraq | • Limited forces involved, but force is used |
| | | • Timely information on targets and defenses required |
| Preemptive | Israeli attack on the Iraqi nuclear reactor at Osirak | Collateral damage and a spectrum of political sensitivities are typically involved (*potentially high cost of either military or political "failure"*) |
| Rescue missions: | | |
| Hostages or prisoners | Iran, Entebbe, Son Tay | • Information usually at a premium |
| | | • Time lines can be very tight |
| | | • Rescuers probably "outgunned" |
| | | • Reaching hostages and escaping likely to be difficult |
| | | • Politics may be extremely delicate |
| Combat search and rescue | Gulf War search and rescue | Routine (and difficult) operations during combat—opposed, generally behind enemy lines, may or may not have good information on location of personnel to be rescued |

Table 10.2—Continued

| Type of Operation | Examples | Characteristics |
|---|---|---|
| U.S. personnel in combat zones or other dangerous situations | Liberia | • May or may not face opposition<br>• Information is important and may be difficult to get<br>• Usually relatively short duration; timeliness likely to be important |
| Noncombatants of various sorts (e.g., threatened indigenous populations) | Notable special operations during the Cold War | Similar to the above:<br>• operation may be larger scale<br>• politics likely to be more complicated |
| Disaster relief | Earthquakes in Soviet Union during later stages of Cold War | • Generally benign environment<br>• Premium on information for efficiency |
| Humanitarian assistance<br>Normal | Rwanda, early stages of Somalia operation | • Could be opposed (e.g., early days of Somalia)<br>• Identifying, locating, and reaching those in need can be a challenge<br>• Timeliness generally matters<br>• Operation can be large scale<br>• Politics can be complicated |
| With "mission creep" | Later stages of Somalia operation | Can combine the most challenging features of humanitarian assistance and raids or hostage rescue<br>• environment, time-lines, and opposition all can be very demanding<br>• premium on information<br>• politics extremely delicate |

Table 10.2—Continued

| Type of Operation | Examples | Characteristics |
|---|---|---|
| Peacekeeping Normal "Information as a weapon" | Bosnia, post-war Iraq Bosnia | Combines complex and delicate politics with difficult military problems Information, implicitly backed by force, can provide powerful negotiating leverage |
| Peacemaking | Northern Ireland | • Peacekeeping with "attitude"; peacemaking is more proactive <br> • Usually involves a heavier element of coercive military force |
| Insurgency | Kurdish areas of Northern Iraq, U.S. support of Afghan rebels, support for the Contras in Nicaragua | • Long-term commitment <br> • Generally, militarily weaker than dominant force or government <br> • Politics central <br> • Information central |
| Counterinsurgency | Early operations in Vietnam and Laos | The flip side of insurgency; most of the same features except there is a presumption of superior forces available |
| Nation building | Haiti | Combines features of counterinsurgency, peacemaking, and peacekeeping |
| Counterterrorism | Continuing operations of various sorts | • Shares many of the characteristics of raids, hostage rescue, even counterinsurgency <br> • Information critical and hard to collect <br> • Force usually has to be measured <br> • Legal and political constraints <br> • Timeliness usually critical |
| Counternarcotics/interdiction of contraband (e.g., nuclear materials or weapons) | Narcotics interdiction operations | Similar in many ways to counterterrorism; has similar sensitivities |

Table 10.2—Continued

| Type of Operation | Examples | Characteristics |
|---|---|---|
| Counternarcotics/ interdiction of contraband (e.g., nuclear materials or weapons) | Narcotics interdiction operations | Similar in many ways to counterterrorism; has similar sensitivities |
| | Hypothetical raids against the sources | Has both "offensive" and "defensive" components |
| Critical missions within larger campaigns | Scud hunting during Operation Desert Storm | • Missions take on a life and importance of their own; separate "scorekeeping"<br>• Timeliness is frequently important<br>• Can be information intensive<br>• Overwhelming force may not be an option<br>• Frequently have political dimensions |

SOURCE: Adapted from Buchan et al., forthcoming (b).

— As a result, for many classes of operations, success is likely to be extremely sensitive to the quality, quantity, and timeliness of information. Accordingly, enemy interference with information systems is likely to have a much greater impact than it would on large-scale conflicts.

• Defining and deciding what constitutes "victory" and how to measure success and failure can be much more difficult.

In large campaigns, the very scale of events tends to wash out nuances. In lesser operations, the reverse can be true: The smaller scale of events can *accentuate* nuances. Thus, even minor failures and modest casualties can take on disproportionate importance, and many of the problems that barely mattered in large-scale campaigns can be central to the success or failure of lesser operations. A useful analogy might be the comparison between mission-level and campaign-level analysis. Lesser operations frequently may be likened to missions; indeed, as Table 10.2 suggested, particular classes of missions within a larger campaign (e.g., Scud hunting in Desert Storm) may take on a life and political significance of their own independent of their contribution to the overall military campaign. In fact, the Scud example illustrates the larger point about information sensitivity. The failure of the Scud hunt had virtually no effect on the outcome of the military campaign but received considerable attention because of its political implications and, under other circumstances, *could* have been important. Thus, the Iraqis' routine operational practices (e.g., mobility, concealment, deception) to deny the U.S. information about the locations of its mobile missiles was certainly successful.

Similar tactics or other countermeasures might be equally effective in the future, particularly since some of the tactical problems in Table 10.2 probably fall in the "too hard" category for purely technical solutions anyway (e.g., sorting out urban guerrillas from the rest of the population, locating concealed nuclear weapons, differentiating refugees from bandits). Accordingly, these kinds of situations might provide more stressing cases to test the effectiveness and robustness of U.S. information-related systems. Unfortunately, they are necessarily less tidy and well-defined than more traditional campaigns, but that is part of the challenge of planning in the post–Cold War world.

## REDUCING VULNERABILITIES AND COPING WITH THEIR EFFECTS

Deciding what to do about all this is obviously a very complex, multi-faceted problem.  To establish priorities in reducing or eliminating information vulnerabilities, one has to decide how serious the problems are, how severe the threats are likely to be, whether adequate technical and operational solutions are available, and whether those solutions are affordable.  In examining the problem, we found several general trends that affected the way we approached choosing solutions:

- No single set of vulnerabilities was so overwhelmingly important that they demanded top priority, and no threats were so compelling that they dominated the analysis.

- Costs fell into three "bins":  cheap (and, therefore, potentially attractive enough on first principles to require little additional analysis), very expensive (and, as a result, probably too expensive in an austere fiscal environment absent a really compelling need), and somewhere in between (and perhaps worth a more detailed cost analysis for particular options that satisfied the other criteria).

More fundamentally, we found that traditional concepts of relying on intelligence to define threats and provide strategic and tactical warning of "information attacks" and then trying to deter or defeat such attacks by threats of retaliation are particularly inappropriate for coping with attacks on information systems.  Thus, Cold War nuclear metaphors in particular do not apply to this sort of combat. Instead, we found that the most effective general approach to information attacks appears to be to *defend as well as one can afford to and be prepared to adapt and recover as quickly as possible if the defenses fail.*

### Why Intelligence Assessments and Warning Concepts Are Largely Irrelevant

There are several reasons why intelligence assessments to identify potential threats to Air Force information systems and attempts to provide strategic or tactical warning of such attacks are likely to be inadequate and, therefore, why relying on such intelligence support to protect operations would be very risky. Most of them fall into one of two general categories: *ambiguity* and *timeliness*.

**Ambiguity.** Capabilities to disrupt information systems are so widespread that virtually any potential enemy, be it a nation-state, a subnational group (e.g., a terrorist or criminal organization), or even an individual malcontent, could mount some kind of information attack. For example, computer hacking is virtually universal, particularly since there are no geographic limits to its "reach." Moreover, there are undoubtedly "hackers for hire" on the world market who will work for anyone willing to pay for their services. Thus, threat assessments cannot narrow the field of potential enemies much. Neither can the actual source of an attack be identified with confidence, since the national origin, or even the actual identity, of an individual hacker might not tell much about who was behind the attack, and the attack itself could be launched from any geographic point that turned out to be convenient.

The same is true of other kinds of attacks as well. The ability to launch some kinds of physical attacks, either overt or covert, on critical information nodes is virtually universal. Similarly, access to jammers of various sorts is quite widespread. Even more-exotic weapons, such as HPM devices, may become widely available on the international arms market to "upscale" adversaries, once the weapons are available at all.

One of the reasons that the ability to attack information systems is so universal is that the tools are so cheap. Developing or employing a cadre of computer hackers or a commando squad capable of blowing up key installations is cheap. On the other hand, gathering the information to make such attacks truly effective is not necessarily either easy or cheap; indeed, it may be easy to overestimate the danger of really focused, militarily effective information attacks.

Complicating intelligence assessment and warning still further is the fact that both the capabilities and actual preparations to launch attacks on information systems are likely to be virtually invisible. There will probably be no visible indicators. There is no "information equivalent" to a buildup of missiles, for example, or specialized observable activity (e.g., the equivalent of a nuclear test) to observe. Thus, a competent adversary that was trying to be covert might be able to cover his tracks completely, particularly in view of the competing demands on the U.S. intelligence community. As the cliché goes, "The absence of evidence is not evidence of absence."

On the other hand, remaining covert does pose some risks for a potential attacker. It cannot really test its capability to disrupt U.S. information systems without risking tipping its hand and compromising its own capability. That is particularly true if its strategy relies, as it would have to if the United States is taking prudent protective measures, on "perishable" chinks in the U.S. armor, such as a corrupted insider or laxity in enforcing good security procedures. Ironically (and significantly), even a test of offensive capabilities that could be disguised to look like a natural failure is likely to prompt the victim to take corrective action. Even intelligence-collection efforts to identify exploitable weaknesses might get the U.S.' attention and risk compromising future offensive operations against U.S. information systems. Such collection efforts can be difficult and expensive in any case, so the added risk of compromise just increases the burden on the attack planner. Ironically, the defense has an easier time in this regard. It really does not require a detailed assessment of who is threatening its systems or why. All it needs is a "wake-up call" to remind it that implementing reasonable protective measures for its information systems is a prudent thing to do in a hostile world. Even relatively imprecise intelligence is good enough to do that. Conversely, very detailed intelligence information would not provide that much more information that was operationally useful.

**Timeliness.** The time scale of attacks on information systems, particularly electronic attacks (e.g., computer hacking attacks), is another serious problem in developing a response strategy based on reacting to tactical warning. The attacks can simply happen too fast. The damage is done before the defense can react. Notice that that situation contrasts sharply with the Cold War nuclear standoff between the Soviet Union and the United States, in which either side might have as much as a half hour's warning of a missile attack in which to launch its vulnerable intercontinental ballistic missiles, bombers, tankers, and mobile command and control assets. There is no analog for information attacks.

Time scale is also an issue for Air Force operations themselves. Depending on what kind of operation it is, times of hours, days, or weeks can be important even for operations that last much longer. That means that events can move rather rapidly, and responses to information attacks must keep pace. That is why responses to information attacks that may be appropriate for peacetime are likely to be inadequate in an operational situation. For example, the Air Force and others currently place considerable emphasis on tracking down and arresting computer hackers who try to break into sensitive computer systems. That is perfectly appropriate for peacetime, when time and resources favor the victim of the attack, but is going to be of limited value in wartime. In the first place, any wartime hacker who is incompetent enough to get caught in spite of all his inherent advantages—e.g., mobility, anonymity, choice of geographic locations, resources at his disposal—deserves what he gets. Moreover, even in peacetime, tracking down highly skilled hackers has often taken months. That is too long to be useful in most operational situations. The same is true of other kinds of situations, such as fixing the blame for—or even determining the cause of—bombings and airline disasters. Thus, attackers are likely to be neither defeated nor deterred.

**Implications.** These factors all suggest several general conclusions about the role of intelligence and warning in defeating attacks on Air Force information systems:

- Neither intelligence threat assessments nor various warning concepts are likely to be of much use in defending against attacks on information systems if the opponent is competent.

- Because there is likely to be little or no useful warning of an attack on information systems, the first thing to do is protect important information systems as well as one can afford to.

- Because defenses are inherently imperfect and information systems are subject to various kinds of natural failures in any case, having the capacity to recover from an information system disruption is necessary *even in the absence of an information attack "threat."* Thus, once a disruption occurs, the cause does not matter. Repairing the damage is what counts. Also, in most operations, except for relatively bizarre "catalytic war" scenarios,[8] there is likely to be little ambiguity about the source of

---

[8]The "catalytic war" concept was discussed periodically during the early days of nuclear weapons and became a staple of Cold War melodramas. It involves a third

attacks on information systems, since these attacks are very unlikely to occur in a political and military vacuum.

The real test of intelligence and warning is identifying what investments in other types of systems and capabilities one can afford to forgo if one has good intelligence and warning. In the case of information system vulnerability, the answer is, "more." The Air Force cannot afford *not* to defend its critical information systems and be prepared to recover from disruptions that do occur based on the possibility of getting more accurate threat assessment or warning information. Conversely, if it defends adequately and makes plans to recover from problems, better intelligence may not matter much.

In summary, the most reasonable view of the role for intelligence in reducing the vulnerability of Air Force information systems is probably something like the following. One should be prepared to make use of any intelligence about enemy information operations that one gets either routinely (e.g., the "luck of the draw") on either human or communication intelligence, say, or relatively inexpensively by adjusting collection priorities. However, relying on getting this kind of intelligence is very risky, and significant investments in improved collection capability to protect against information attacks on Air Force systems are hard to justify.

## How to Defend and Recover

That means the emphasis has to be on defense and recovery. Our analysis identified a number of potential steps that the Air Force could take to reduce the vulnerability of information systems on which it relies and to minimize the impact of problems that do occur. In prioritizing the protective measures, we concluded that various combinations of steps fit logically together into "packages" of options. The most attractive of those are discussed below. We also identified some areas where more analysis will be required to select the best option.

---

party—usually, but not necessarily, another country—trying to start a war between other countries by creating an incident of some sort and trying to place the blame on others. The reason this subject has come up again recently in the information war context is that it could be much easier to disguise the true source of a computer hacking attack, say, than to disguise more traditional kinds of military attacks.

**The Basic Options.** We derived two basic sets of options that together appeared to represent the basic minimum package necessary to keep the risks associated with Air Force information vulnerabilities within tolerable bounds. The details of the options are described in Buchan, et al. (forthcoming) and summarized below.

*The "No Brainer."* The first package includes a set of options that appear to be relatively cheap and easy to implement, effective for reducing some obvious vulnerabilities, and logical in combination against modest threats. The details are summarized in Table 10.3. This package emphasizes protecting computers against hacking attacks, reducing the vulnerability of the PSN, and taking some basic steps to protect key installations against physical attack. A couple of noteworthy items include improving the career paths of Air Force computer system administrators, either by enhancing the career field inside the Air Force or by contracting out these services, and making much broader use of software encryption on a variety of Air Force computer systems. The second point is particularly important. Very secure Air Force classified computers already use high-quality encryption. However, many sensitive, but unclassified, computers that might be targets for hackers do not. Cheap, effective, readily

**Table 10.3**

**Low-Cost Package to Reduce Obvious Vulnerabilities**

| Problem | Security Measures |
|---|---|
| Vulnerability of computer networks to "cracking" attacks | • Fix AFCERT-identified holes<br>• Use software encryption<br>• Isolate critical systems and eliminate unencrypted links into secure computers<br>• Improve career paths for system administrators<br>• Monitor network activity<br>• Map all U.S. Air Force computers |
| Vulnerability of PSN | • Maximizing the effectiveness of the Telecommunications Service Priority program<br>• Increased physical diversity in military leased-line networks<br>• Better protection for connections between bases and end offices |
| Vulnerability to physical attack | • Extended defensive perimeters around key installations |

available commercial encryption software could give those computers a considerable degree of protection. Implementing this package is an admission price to get "into the game." Thus, we consider adopting it to be a "no brainer."

*A More Expensive Package.* The second package involves a more serious, although probably modest, investment. Table 10.4 describes individual items in more detail. This set of options takes steps to begin to deal with the communication jamming problem, includes exercising seriously with degraded information systems, adds some more-expensive fixes to computer and communication vulnerability problems, and limits reductions in force size and complexity that could exacerbate information vulnerability problems. This package offers significant operational payoffs. It does come at a cost, however. Some of the technical improvements will require making a modest investment. Exercise costs could increase as well. The more serious costs, though, are the opportunity costs associated with having to forgo some of the options for cost savings associated with dramatic force and manpower reductions. That is the real essence of the problem: the trade between achieving possibly dramatic cost reductions by cutting forces and manpower substantially and the attendant risks of substantially increasing the vulnerability of Air Force operations to attacks on or simple failure of major elements of its information support network.

The combination of these two packages of defensive options appears adequate to reduce the overall risk associated with potential vulnerabilities of Air Force information systems to attack or disruption to a manageable level. Moreover, many of these measures would be needed to cope with normal equipment failures, even absent a direct enemy threat.

**Some Unresolved Issues.** There are several problems that are important to solve and for which technical solutions are available but that require more analysis to select the best solution. Reducing GPS vulnerability is an example of such a problem. A number of solutions are available. Identifying the most cost-effective approach will require more-detailed analysis. There are other problems, such as the potential vulnerability of various U.S. systems to HPM, that require more research to resolve. Other problems—the physical vulnerability of command centers, for example—will have to be

**Table 10.4**

**Supplementary Package to Enhance Security Against All Levels of Threats Substantially**

| Problem | Security Measures |
|---|---|
| Vulnerability of computer networks to "cracking" attacks | • Enhance user identification<br>• Alternative communication access<br>• Maintain skilled "backup" personnel<br>• Exercise seriously with degraded systems |
| Vulnerability of tactical communication systems to jamming | • Transition from FLTSATCOM to either MILSTAR or DSCS for Rivet Joint–TIBS Link<br>• Increase AWACS output power and available bandwidth for JTIDS/TADIL–J link<br>• Solve the problems of some existing systems<br>• Retain the option for theater line-of-sight links in GBS and theater-based processing and analysis capability<br>• Develop adaptive networks of redundant components that are collectively resistant to jamming[a] |
| Vulnerability of PSN | • More-extensive implementation of automatic reconfiguration procedures |
| Vulnerability to physical attack | • Expanded ground security forces, perhaps enhanced by additional sensors of various sorts |
| Vulnerability of communication systems to HPM weapons | • Installation of fast-response limiters<br>• Proper shielding during manufacture |
| Vulnerability of GPS to jamming | • Development of high-quality, low-cost IMUs for weapons<br>• Maintenance of alternative approaches to achieving weapon accuracy |
| Sensitivity of force effectiveness to combined vulnerability effects | • Avoiding excessive additional force reductions (>25 percent) in the cases we examined, particularly if the forces are simplified as well |

[a]We have analyzed this possibility for several years. So far, the results are not encouraging, but the final chapter has yet to be written, so the work continues.

addressed in a larger context with information vulnerability as only one element of the problem. Still other problems appear to have no good solutions. One of these is providing assured jam resistant, high-bandwidth communications. Well-known technical solutions are available, but they tend to be overly expensive in the current climate (e.g., MILSTAR-like communication satellites). Finding cheaper alternatives is extremely important. Failing that, the services will have to make operational adjustments (e.g., not rely on operational concepts that require such "heroic" communications capability). *That could have major implications for the viability of many of the heavily information-dependent "Third Wave" military operational concepts currently being discussed.*

## CONCLUSIONS

We found that most vulnerabilities of U.S. Air Force information-related systems appear to be more nuisances than serious problems at present and are likely to stay that way in the future if the United States takes prudent measures to manage the risks. Particularly important is resisting the urge to reduce force levels or technical diversity too much in an attempt to save money. Equally important is maintaining sufficient skilled manpower as "backups" to automated systems if they should fail and exercising with degraded systems to allow operators to maintain their skills.

The value of information—and the effects of information vulnerabilities—could be much more pronounced in some kinds of lesser operations than in major conflicts because the outcomes of lesser operations might be more sensitive to information-related factors (e.g., time delays, collateral damage). As a result, major conflicts may no longer be the appropriate paradigms to emphasize for planning purposes where information-related systems are concerned.

Detailed threat assessments are not going to be of much use as a practical matter in preparing to deal with attacks on critical information systems, because the capabilities to conduct such attacks are so widespread. Similarly, traditional notions of strategic and tactical warning of "information attacks" are likely to be of little use because the attacks can be so ambiguous and occur so rapidly. That means the most effective way to deal with attacks on information systems is (1) *defend* important systems as well as one can afford to, and (2) be prepared to *adapt* and *recover* as quickly as possible from attacks that initially succeed. Ironically, that general approach is necessary even absent an external threat, just to deal with natural failures of information systems. Thus, having to defend against deliberate attacks may not impose much of an added burden.

Relatively straightforward technical and operational solutions appear to be available for most information vulnerability problems to at least allow the United States to manage the risks, if not eliminate the problems entirely. A package of options to address many of the problems appears to be both practical and affordable. However, choosing the most cost-effective solutions to some problems will require more-detailed analysis, and some problems may not have good solutions. Some of those problems could be serious enough to call into question the feasibility of more advanced information-intensive operational concepts.

There is a broader aspect to this problem that we have not considered in this chapter. An enemy might be able to disrupt U.S. military operations indirectly by attacking the U.S. civilian information infrastructure and making enough mischief to divert the U.S. public's and political elites' attention away from overseas operations. Thus, there might be a way to "end run" the relatively invulnerable military information systems. These "strategic" information attacks are considered elsewhere in this volume.

## REFERENCES

Buchan, G. C., *One-and-a-Half Cheers for the Revolution in Military Affairs*, Santa Monica, Calif.: RAND, P-8015-AF, 1997.

Buchan, G. C., et al., *Potential Vulnerabilities of U.S. Air Force Information Systems: An Overview Briefing* (U), Santa Monica, Calif.: RAND, DB-227-AF, forthcoming (a). Classified publication; not cleared for public release.

_____, *Potential Vulnerabilities of U.S. Air Force Information Systems: Final Report*, Santa Monica, Calif.: RAND, MR-816-AF, forthcoming (b). Classified publication; not cleared for public release.

Cheswick, W. R., and S. M. Bellovin, *Firewalls and Internet Security: Repelling the Wily Hacker*, Addison-Wesley, 1994.

Defense Science Board, "Report of the Defense Science Board Task Force on Information Warfare-Defense (IW-D)," Office of the Under Secretary of Defense for Acquisition & Technology, Washington, D.C., 1996.

Denning, P. J., *Computers Under Attack: Intruders, Worms, and Viruses*, Addison-Wesley, 1990.

Feldman, P. M., *Vulnerabilities of the Public Switched Network: Potential Implications for the Air Force*, Santa Monica, Calif.: RAND, MR-869-AF, 1997.

Hoffman, L. J. ed., *Rogue Programs: Viruses, Worms, and Trojan Horses*, Van Nostrand Reinhold, 1990.

Hura, M., G. McLeod, K. O'Connell, P.S. Sauer, "Challenges and Issues in Formulating Defensive Information Warfare Policy: Intelligence Community Perspective," Santa Monica, Calif.: RAND, DB-179-CMS, 1996.  Distribution limited to U.S. Government agencies and their contractors.

Larson, E., *Casualties and Consensus*, Santa Monica, Calif.: RAND, MR-726-RC, 1996.

Neumann, P., *Computer Related Risks*, New York: Addison-Wesley, 1994.

Wilson, E., "The Information Revolution and National Security," Draft, Center for International Development and Conflict Management, College Park, Md.: University of Maryland, October 31, 1995.

# Part III

# ISSUES, STRATEGIES, AND LESSONS FOR DECISIONMAKERS

# MILITARY ORGANIZATION IN THE INFORMATION AGE: LESSONS FROM THE WORLD OF BUSINESS

*Francis Fukuyama and Abram N. Shulsky*

## THE IMPORTANCE OF ORGANIZATION IN A TIME OF REVOLUTIONARY CHANGE

Technological advances in the areas of telecommunications and data processing (which, together, are often referred to as "information technology") have given rise to much discussion about "information warfare." The fundamental expectation behind this discussion is that exploitation of advances in information technology will lead to revolutionary changes in the ways in which wars are fought.

Students of such "revolutions in military affairs" (RMAs) have noted that they often involve major changes in the organizational structure of the armed forces, as well as in the weapons they use and the doctrines according to which they fight.[1] Indeed, since organizational structure both influences and reflects the manner in which information flows into and within the organization, one would expect that an RMA based on information technology would have particularly significant effects on military organizational structure.[2]

---

[1]See, for example, Cohen (1996).

[2]The term "organizational structure" refers to the ways in which the parts of an organization relate to each other: It includes, but is not limited to, the "wiring diagram" showing the subordination and superordination of the various individuals and offices. It is, however, only one of several important related areas in organizational design that have received attention in recent years. Other areas include the organizational process (how work is accomplished); monitoring (how work is overseen); incentives (how individuals are rewarded and promoted); and leadership (how work is supervised and directed). This chapter focuses primarily on structure but discusses some of these other issues as they are related to questions of structure.

Even in cases of RMAs which depend critically on new technologies and weapon systems, organizational questions are nevertheless critical; failure to understand the organizational implications may mean that the promise of the new weapons is lost. Thus, while the German *Blitzkrieg* strategy of World War II depended decisively on the technological advances of the previous decades—tanks, aircraft capable of providing close air support, and mobile radios—it also required certain organizational characteristics. In particular, its fast pace implied that lower echelons had to have the authority to take the initiative to exploit battlefield opportunities; they also had to have more direct, and more rapid, communications with headquarters and other military units that could support them. Front-line *Panzer* units, for example, could request air support directly from the *Luftwaffe* without having to go through higher Army echelons. By contrast, the British and French command structures required unit commanders to go through several intermediary headquarters to communicate with supporting units. (Messenger, 1976, p. 143.)

Many of the organizational characteristics of the German army[3]— "mission orders" (*Auftragstaktik*), the assumption of initiative and responsibility by lower echelons, streamlined administrative and reporting systems—predated *Blitzkrieg* but were consonant with it and were, in fact, important elements in contributing to its success. Failure to understand these components of the RMA hampered the ability of Germany's opponents to exploit the new systems as effectively.

Indeed, innovations in organizational structure may themselves be the source of an RMA. For example, Martin Van Creveld has argued that Napoleon's single most important military innovation was the development of a modern command organization, especially the concept of independently operating combined arms corps. This innovation allowed him to control forces far larger than anything fielded in the preceding centuries of warfare.[4]

---

[3]As noted in footnote 2, organizational issues include more than questions of structure or "wiring diagram." A formal depiction of the organizational structure of the German army would not have looked very different from that of the armies of its opponents; the key difference resided in other organizational features, such as those noted in the text.

[4]This discussion of Napoleon relies on Van Creveld (1985), Ch. 3, especially pp. 58–62, 101–102.

In this case, the RMA did not depend on any major technological advances. Although Napoleon's system depended decisively on his ability to communicate with his corps commanders, who could be spread out over large fronts of up to 70 miles or more in width, his only new communication system was the Chappe optical telegraph, which, however, was not useful for tactical communications in the field because it relied on large fixed installations. Instead, Napoleon relied on organizational innovation to solve the problem posed by the inadequacy of available communication technology. Rather than maintaining tight control, Napoleon granted enough autonomy to his corps to allow them to operate independently for limited periods of time. (Van Creveld, 1985, p. 101.)

Issues of organizational structure are also prominent in the business world, which has also been shaken in recent years by a "revolution" in the way in which large corporations conduct their activities: Indeed, the importance of organizational issues is illustrated by the fact that major advances have sometimes been achieved by reorganization *independently* of any technological advances. For example, the development of "lean manufacturing" by Toyota in the 1950s— arguably the "granddaddy" of the current wave of corporate reorganization—was accomplished without any new technology in the areas of computers and telecommunications. This is true even though an important component of the system—"just in time" inventory management—depended on the rapid flow of information back and forth between Toyota and its suppliers.[5]

The business world has a rich literature on organizational change, as well as extensive corporate experience with reorganization and adoption of information technology. With due deference to the difference between military and commercial organizations, this chapter will attempt to mine that literature for ideas on how to structure military organizations to take advantage of new information technology. First, the chapter will examine the current thinking on corporate organizational responses to information technology. Next, it will

---

[5]According to Womack, Jones, and Roos (1991), p. 62,

> [t]he mechanism [for communicating this information] was the containers carrying parts to the next step. As each container was used up, it was sent back to the previous step, and this became the automatic signal to make more parts.

look at some implications for the armed forces of the principles derived from corporate experience.

The business literature is far from conclusive on how to organize to take full advantage of information technology, and even many of the clearest lessons do not apply in a military setting. Nonetheless, a few implications emerge clearly from the discussion that follows. First, the military will need to institutionalize an environment of constant learning, one that includes the freedom to fail. Second, the military will need to redistribute skills toward the bottom of the hierarchy and give more autonomy to lower levels of the military. Finally, and perhaps most importantly, if the military is to benefit from cutting-edge commercial technology, it will need to confront the politically intractable problem of streamlining its unwieldy procurement system.[6]

## THE EFFECTS OF THE "INFORMATION REVOLUTION" ON CORPORATE ORGANIZATION

Recent writing on corporate reorganization discusses many ways in which the "information revolution" has had implications for issues of organizational structure. Although the literature resonates with a myriad of "buzz words," the major concepts can be summarized under three rubrics. The first two are centrally concerned with the question of how information is handled within an organization, while the effectiveness of the third relies on information technology:

- "flattening" organizational structure—to speed up the flow of information within the organization and create the proper incentives for its use

- "informating" (or "digitization")—to facilitate the collection, processing, distribution, and use of more-detailed and more-timely information throughout the organization

- concentrating on "core competencies"—to emphasize one's sources of competitive advantage, while disencumbering oneself of functions that can be performed better by others.

---

[6]This chapter draws heavily (and, at times, verbatim) on Fukuyama and Shulsky (1997).

The ultimate goal is to create an organization that can adapt more quickly and flexibly to new information. As one of the seminal articles of this school of thought explained, a key characteristic of an organization will be the way in which information is handled in it:

> the typical business will be knowledge-based, an organization composed largely of specialists who direct and discipline their own performance through organized feedback from colleagues, customers, and headquarters.
>
> In its central management, the information-based organization needs few, if any, specialists. . . . the knowledge will be primarily at the bottom, in the minds of the specialists who do different work and direct themselves. (Drucker, 1988, p. 45.)

Many of the current developments in this area focus on the flow of information in an organization and seek to adjust its formal structure (i.e., the "wiring diagram" that defines the formal reporting relationships and the division of areas of responsibility) accordingly. The basic premise, as in the citation above, is that organizations are, and increasingly will be, mechanisms for the processing and exploitation of information. As such, their competitive advantage will come from their superior ability to perform these functions with respect to a given area. The relevance of such a perspective for information-age warfare is clear, but the fact that a military organization's tasks are more varied than those of a corporation suggests that this perspective must be applied with caution.

## Flattening: Creating Shorter Data Paths

"Flattening" an organization typically involves reassigning the functions and authority of one or more layers of middle management, either downward, toward the bottom of the organization (to the workers themselves or their first-level supervisors), or upward, toward the senior management. The overall number of management layers decreases as a result. For example, at Franklin Mint, it fell from six to four after a restructuring; at Eastman Kodak, the distance between manufacturing manager and factory floor fell from thirteen levels to four. (Davidow and Malone, 1992, p. 168.)

The main advantage sought in flattening an organization can be understood in terms of information flows. In the design of a traditionally hierarchical organization, the implicit assumptions are that sharing information within the boundaries of the enterprise is cost free and automatic and that information flows rapidly, and without obstruction, along the lines of authority as indicated on the organization chart. In fact, information is costly to generate and transmit; the process takes time and effort and is not free from error and distortion.

Information enters an organization at all points, and a great deal of local information comes in at the bottom. For example, the first person to know that a supplier's door panels are misshapen may be the assembly line worker who tries to install them on the automobile frame. There are obvious advantages for an organization that can process the latter kind of information close to its source and make use of it. A more-hierarchical organization, by contrast, would require that information entering at the bottom be passed up a multilayer managerial hierarchy for processing and decision and then that the result be passed back down again for action.[7]

The movement of information through a hierarchy does not just slow down the process; there is also the risk that the content will be distorted as it is handed off from one level to another. It is common in bureaucracies for each level to pass along only that information it thinks the next level above or below it wants or needs to hear. The result is necessarily an overall loss of precision, as well as time, as the information passes through the hierarchical structure.

In addition, there is an "agency" problem: Each level in a hierarchy has its own bureaucratic interests and therefore may shape the information that it transmits to suit that interest. Thus, although centralized, hierarchical organization creates the appearance of effective and detailed control, this is often an illusion because those at the top may have only a poor or distorted view of what is going on in the organization's depths.

Flattening also contains some risks, however. Since flat corporations retain a hierarchical structure in which senior managers still have

---

[7]Of course, as anyone who has worked within such a hierarchical organization knows, individuals typically develop personal ties with other parts of the organizations that enable them to short-circuit this process; it is generally understood that doing things "by the book" can be unnecessarily slow and cumbersome. Much of the discussion of flattening involves the working out of this common insight.

ultimate authority to control the behavior of their subordinates, the elimination of middle managers implies that the span of control for senior management necessarily increases, decreasing their ability to supervise their subordinates' activities or identify problem areas.

Flattening may also risk the loss of what may be called a "middle perspective," i.e., the perspective on standard operations held by a first-level supervisor, who is intimately familiar with the routine but is not enveloped by it. The observations of such supervisors (the corporate versions of noncommissioned officers) may be crucial for innovations: Higher-level supervisors may lack the detailed knowledge of day-to-day operations, while those engaged in the actual operations may lack the time and ability to reflect on them.

The corporate penchant for flatness obviously raises the question of whether a similar reorganization—extending the span of control and reducing the number of command echelons—makes sense in a military context as well. In the late 1950s, the idea that increased flexibility of command would be required to operate in a tactical nuclear environment led to the Pentomic Army concept, in which the brigade echelon was abolished.[8] To compensate, the span of control at the division and battalion level was increased to five battalions and five companies, respectively. Although the concept was soon abandoned as mistaken, it may be that, from an organizational point of view, it was premature rather than simply wrong.

While the corporate literature suggests that such flattening could be a useful step, it must be kept in mind that it is not a goal in itself, but only a possible means toward the ultimate goal of creating an organization that can react more quickly to events, especially unforeseen ones. Another means of accomplishing the same desired result (the shortening of data paths) would be authorizing the skipping of echelons for certain types of communications. The familiar device of the "directed telescope," whereby a higher-level commander empowers an agent to gather information directly from a unit several layers

---

[8]See Bacevich (1986), Ch. 5, for a discussion of this reorganization. The driving force behind the Pentomic Army concept was the need to prepare to fight on a battlefield on which both sides were prepared to use tactical nuclear weapons. Many of its features are related to the issue of tactical nuclear weapons and are not of interest here. What is of interest here is the attempt to "flatten" the Army by eliminating an echelon below the corps level.

below him in the hierarchy, is such a method for speeding up communications with a subordinate who is involved in a particularly
critical operation. Similarly, if the high-level commander visits a
front-line unit personally, he has effectively shortened the data paths
by skipping the intermediate echelons.

In the military context, data paths are often shortened in a more *ad
hoc* fashion. Such improvisation is often necessary, although it does
run the risk of creating confusion if the bypassed intermediate levels
are not informed of what is going on. An extreme version of this
phenomenon may occur during military operations other than war
(MOOTW), in which individual actions can take on a larger political
significance. For example, the actions of a single squad in a Haitian
city could have significant repercussions for the entire operation,
especially if they were to be captured on tape by the Cable News
Network and broadcast to the world. As a result, the White House
officials might, under extreme circumstances, wish to be in direct
communication with units on the ground, both to receive reports
directly (otherwise, they could find themselves in the uncomfortable
position of receiving press inquiries about events of which they had
not yet been informed) and to direct actions on the ground (to avoid
unwanted incidents).

While this type of political "micromanagement" is typically unwel-
come, it may be on occasion inevitable given the politically sensitive
nature of many MOOTW. As opposed to this type of *ad hoc* echelon-
skipping, in which the challenge is to balance the advantages of
flexibility against the confusion that can be created when intermediate echelons are left in the dark concerning matters about which
both their superiors and subordinates are aware, one could envisage
a policy decision to mandate direct communication between nonad-
jacent echelons with respect to a given function. For example, it
might be possible to mandate that a company or battalion report
certain types of logistics information directly to a theater-level support agency, bypassing the intervening echelons.

In general, a thorough study of future command and control in the
armed forces should involve a review of all the functions performed
by the command hierarchy to see which levels were crucial for each,
and which merely performed relatively mechanical functions of
transmitting, aggregating, and/or processing data on its way from

one echelon to another.  New information technology would enable one to design shorter, more direct communication paths that, with respect to a given function, bypassed the echelons that did not have a substantial role to play.

## "Informating"

Information technology obviously has great potential for speeding up the flow of information and ensuring that it gets to the right place at the right time in the right format.  At the same time, new means of communication can be counterproductive if they lead to information "overload," the swamping of communication circuits with routine reporting that interferes with the transmission and reception of critical information.  Moreover, the additional reporting burden on subordinate units can interfere with their ability to fulfill more-crucial tasks.

One solution to this difficulty goes by the name of "informating," which is the application of automation to information processes to minimize the reporting burden, avoid "information overload," and gain the greatest possible value from the available data.[9]  The key is to automate the required information processes and then tailor the display of the data to the particular needs of the various consumers at different echelons and with different responsibilities.  Automation can be applied to data collection, transmission, aggregation, processing, and presentation.

In such a system, information is collected automatically or as a by-product of other operations.  One of the best-known examples of this is the Wal-Mart system, in which the information that a particular product has been sold, which is obtained at the checkout counter when the bar code is scanned, is used not only to calculate how much the customer owes but is also transmitted to a companywide

---

[9]The word "informate" was coined by Shoshana Zuboff to describe the process by which information about the "underlying productive and administrative processes through which an organization accomplishes its work" is automatically generated, processed, communicated, and displayed.  This provides "a deeper level of transparency to activities that had been either partially or completely opaque," which is intended to facilitate the effective management of those activities." (Zuboff, 1988, pp. 9–10.)

database. Without increasing the workload of the checkout clerk, and without burdening other company employees, timely and detailed sales information is collected for processing and use.

The information is then aggregated and processed to meet the needs of various users within the company. In a retail organization, for example, this information might be aggregated to supply top management with a sense of the immediate trends in the overall business of the company. The same information can also be used in a more detailed and targeted fashion, for example, to order more of a given product that is selling rapidly; in some cases, suppliers could be directly tied into the retailer's data system and receive orders automatically. With less urgency, historical sales data can be analyzed to spot longer-term patterns in consumer preference.

In some cases, the processing is done automatically according to preset algorithms, delivering a predetermined product to designated users. In addition, the processing algorithm could be configured to recognize certain situations as requiring the intervention of management (e.g., sales figures that change rapidly in a short time, wide discrepancies between stores with similar customer bases, etc.) and "alert" the appropriate official. Finally, the database can be interrogated by managers who wish to know more about how a specific product is selling, how one region differs from another, what the seasonal trends are, etc. The manager of a store can compare his own sales figures to those of neighboring stores or of stores situated in neighborhoods that are similar in socioeconomic terms to determine how well he is doing and in which areas he might be able to improve.

Thus, the data are made available to a wide variety of users within the organization in formats specifically tailored to their needs. This avoids the problem of "information overload," the swamping of users with large amounts of routine data, which makes it harder for them to focus on what is of particular importance. In addition, this is accomplished without burdening a large number of employees with the transmission, aggregation, and processing of the data, tasks that can absorb a great deal of time and energy in traditional organizational hierarchies.

A military analog to this system would be one in which transmitters on vehicles automatically report their position (as determined by a Global Positioning System receiver), either to a central database or on a net. This information would then be processed to display the position of a defined set of vehicles when required by a commander. (Similar systems are used in the commercial world to enable trucking companies to track the locations of the vehicles in their fleets.) Similarly, the usage and status of petroleum, oil, lubricants, and ammunition could be determined by sensors and transmitted; the same might be possible for data on the operability of vehicles.

With appropriate processing, this information could be made available to a variety of users in formats tailored to their requirements. For example, higher-level commanders could review the information in a more aggregated form, while those at lower levels might want to see it on a battalion by battalion, company by company, or vehicle by vehicle basis. At the same time, the same information could be aggregated into a form useful for logistics planning; with appropriate security precautions, data that are classified when they deal with specific identified units could be made available, once aggregated and otherwise sanitized, on an unclassified basis.

In designing such a system, a key point to be kept in mind is that, because a vast amount of very specific and "low-level" data is reported from each unit (e.g., the petroleum, oil, and lubricant levels for each and every vehicle), the resulting database contains altogether much more information than any one user could possibly use. Thus, the danger of "information overload" is real; if any user were to receive all, or even a significant fraction, of the total amount of data contained in the system, he would be hopelessly swamped. Thus, the systems for aggregating and processing the data are as crucial as those for collecting them in the first place. If the latter outrun the former, the result is likely to be a system that is less useful than the less sophisticated one it replaces.

"Informating" can be seen as a decentralizing influence, since it enables information to move more flexibly throughout the organization (including laterally), not just in vertical reporting channels. At the same time, informating depends on the existence of standards that are enforced universally. Each part of the system (sensor, communication device, information processor, output device) must be compatible with the other parts. While the various subsystems can be developed independently, they must adhere rigorously to the standards and protocols that will enable them to interact with each other.

For this reason alone, the adoption of such a system cannot be seen as a merely technical issue; rather, it inevitably acquires a "political" dimension, since it requires that different parts of the organization reach some type of agreement. While this might be accomplished on the basis of consensus among the various parts, it is more likely to require the forceful intervention of the leadership.

While informating facilitates decentralization and rapid execution, it can have the opposite effect as well: For example, the availability of more-detailed and current information may tempt superior echelons to "micromanage" decisions that should be left to their subordinates. Similarly, the potential availability of large amounts of data could inhibit rapid decisionmaking, tempting the commander to keep searching for more and more information long after he should have made his decision.

A more subtle danger could arise from the fact that, in the course of structuring the data flow and developing the processing algorithms, one has in a sense incorporated into the information system a certain set of organizational procedures. If members of the organization come to view certain processes as "black boxes" (i.e., they pay attention only to the result of the process, while ignoring how it actually operates), they may be less likely to think about innovative ways of changing them. Thus, while the automating of information processes is the key to reaping the advantages of advances in information technology, it must be balanced by the ability to retain visibility of the entire process, to interrogate it in unconstrained ways, and to make incremental adjustments to it.

## Concentrating on "Core Competencies"

The notion of "core competencies" is a challenge to the more traditional view of a corporation as tending toward an integrated organization that itself performs all the vital functions (and many not so vital ones) that are important for the conduct of its business. For example, a traditional integrated manufacturing corporation might not only design, assemble, and market its product but might also manufacture components; mine, grow, or trade the raw materials it uses; and service the product, to say nothing of managing the pension fund and running the employee cafeteria.

The traditional understanding among economists of why firms tended to integrate a wide variety of functions under a single management structure had to do with transaction costs.[10] Contracting for goods and services through market interactions was frequently costly, particularly when complex, hard-to-evaluate goods and services were involved, so companies tended to bring these functions in house, even though the companies were not able to perform them as efficiently as could others outside the company who specialized in these functions. With the introduction of cheaper, more-sophisticated information technology, many of the costs of dealing across firm boundaries began to decline, becoming less than the costs associated with the inefficiency of producing a good or service in house:

> Increasing market efficiency [made possible by the use of IT [information technology] for linking buyers and sellers] . . . implies that firms should focus more carefully on the few core competencies that give them strategic advantages in the marketplace. They should buy the additional, more peripheral products and services they need instead of making them. (Malone and Rockart, 1991, p. 132.)

The term "virtual corporation" is often used to describe a company that has divested itself of all but a few key functions, its "core competencies"; ideally, these are functions that it can perform better than anyone else and that provide the company its competitive advantage. Although much of the literature emphasizes the importance of information technology in facilitating the coordination with suppliers that a virtual corporation requires, it should be noted that information technology does not suffice: There must be a sufficient degree of trust among the business partners as well. The amount of trust required varies with the type of good or service being purchased: Buying sandwiches for the company cafeteria is one thing; farming out a delicate manufacturing process (as when a "fabless" semiconductor company limits itself to design work, while hiring another firm to actually fabricate the chip) is another matter entirely.

The model of the virtual corporation is of some relevance to the military, particularly in such areas as procurement, logistics, and other

---

[10]The *locus classicus* for this argument is Coase (1937).

forms of noncombat service support. Even in these cases, however, the question of trust is likely to loom larger than in the corporate world. It may be more efficient for the armed forces to farm out maintenance work on certain types of sophisticated weapon systems; however, a key issue would have to be whether the civilian contractor can be relied on to perform the maintenance if it must be done in a combat theater, where its employees or equipment might be at risk. For example, the Civilian Reserve Air Fleet system, by means of which civilian aircraft are made available to the armed forces in time of crisis or war, does not require the airlines to allow their planes to be flown into air bases that have come under enemy fire.

With respect to the combat functions themselves, the logic of the "core competencies" argument suggests a higher degree of specialization among units, with less "organic" support contained in each individual unit. However, the problems of coordination are much greater in combat than in the world of business; each individual commander is likely to try his utmost to retain control of the support functions that he requires to achieve his mission.

## IMPLICATIONS FOR THE U.S. ARMED FORCES

Before discussing the implications of recent corporate developments for the U.S. armed forces, it is worthwhile noting that, in many cases, the corporate changes are in fact imitating military experience, although this dependence is typically not made explicit. For example, much of the corporate literature talks about the importance of "teams" and the advisability of emphasizing social or group incentives, not just individual incentive, to motivate exceptional performance. This mirrors military concern with "group cohesion"; military organizations have long realized that motivational techniques directed at the individual (e.g., promotion, medals) are insufficient in combat and have to be augmented by the inculcation of small-group loyalty.

Similarly, the emphasis in the corporate literature on "empowering" lower levels of the hierarchy recalls a much remarked-upon feature of the Prussian and German armies for well over a century:

> In the final account, the German Army's system of organization reflected a deliberate choice, a conscious determination to main-

tain at all costs that which was believed to be decisive to the conduct of war:  mutual trust, *a willingness to assume responsibility*, and *the right and duty of subordinate commanders at all levels to make independent decisions and carry them out.*

To generate independence, freedom had to be granted.  To train men toward responsibility, authority had to be delegated.  To create trust, reliability and long standing acquaintanceships had to be assured.  A direct outcome of these considerations [was], in the first place, *the German regulations which, as compared to the American ones, did not go into great detail and did not attempt to prescribe solutions in advance.  A decentralized system of administration left much to the discretion, not to say intuition, of individual commanders and men,* but at the same time put complete and undivided responsibility squarely upon their shoulders. (Van Creveld, 1982, p. 165. Emphasis added.)[11]

In general, it may well be that, while armed forces have always been regarded as the prototypical strictly hierarchical organizations, they in fact have always been "flatter" and more flexible than most corporations (especially in wartime).  This may seem paradoxical until one considers the different environments in which the two types of organizations operate.  However hierarchical a military organization may appear on paper, the confusion, uncertainty, urgency, and stress of combat require the implementation of many contemporary corporate nostrums, such as individual initiative at lower levels, lateral communication, and teamwork.  On the other hand, a manufacturing plant operates in an essentially artificial environment (i.e., a factory designed for a specific operation, producing a range of predesignated products, etc.) that can be regulated in a much more detailed fashion.[12]

Thus, while the manifest differences between corporate and military organizations preclude the automatic application of the lessons of the former to the latter, we should not be surprised if some ideas

---

[11]Another example of corporate borrowing would be the adoption of the practice of preparing formal "after action" reports to capture the lessons of the corporation's experience in a given matter.

[12]A further irony is that the army popularly regarded as the most rigidly hierarchical— the Prussian or German army—in fact operated in a manner most consonant with the recent corporate literature.

from the corporate world turn out to make good sense for the U.S. armed forces.

## Organizational Structures

As has been noted, the primary advantage of flattening an organization is to improve the flow of information from those who have it to those who are in a position to act on it. In general, reducing the number of management layers not only speeds up the flow of information from initial acquirer to ultimate user (since it has fewer stops to make along the way) but can also increase its accuracy (since there are fewer opportunities for distortion, either inadvertent or deliberate).

It should be noted, however, that this argument focuses on a single, if very important, function of middle management: the aggregation, filtering, and transmission of information. It is of course precisely with respect to this function that the advances in information technology suggest that flattening is desirable, since information technology facilitates this work and may enable the automation of much of it. On the other hand, middle management serves other functions as well: It provides leadership to subordinates, performs various specialized functions, and serves as a training ground for future high-level leaders. In considering whether a flatter structure is appropriate, the armed forces must look carefully at these functions as well.

Of these, the leadership function is the hardest to analyze. Organizational literature addresses this issue under the rubric "span of control," i.e., the number of subordinates who report to a given superior. As noted above, some corporate reorganizations that follow the recent trends in organization theory have resulted in spans of "control" that run from 20 or 30 to hundreds of subordinates. Obviously, this is only possible because, in these cases, the superiors do not have to "control" their subordinates in any "hands-on" manner; for the same reason, superiors cannot be expected to be responsible for teaching their subordinates necessary skills or for nurturing their growth as potential future supervisors or executives.

In cases such as these, nonprofessional subordinates are regarded as capable of performing their (limited) functions autonomously, while subordinates who are professionals in terms of their training and responsibilities are seen as capable of guiding their own work. In the latter case, "control" comes from the subordinates' sense of the standards of their profession (e.g., doctors in a hospital, who take their bearings from the standards of the medical profession and resist allowing the hospital administrator to tell them which course of treatment to follow).

For the armed forces, the leadership function is much more complicated. In combat, the span of control is important because superior commanders must provide direction to their subordinates. No matter how much initiative the latter are permitted or encouraged to take, and no matter how good the information flow to them, the need for concerted, decisive action will require that, on some occasions at least, superiors actually direct the actions of their subordinates. This places some limits on the feasible span of control, regardless of the use to which information technology may be put, although only experimentation in realistic exercises will provide insight into the question of how large that span of control can be.

Even in peacetime, the armed forces face unique leadership challenges. To a greater extent than in the corporate world, commanders of combat units are expected to provide professional and personal leadership to their subordinates.[13] This also implies a limit on the span of control. Thus, with respect to the leadership function, the corporate experience may not be very revealing.

In some cases, it might be possible to reallocate the various specialized functions performed by a command echelon (whether combat or support functions) to accommodate a flatter organizational structure. In fact, even with the current number of echelons, some functions can be concentrated at higher levels. For example, the centralization of logistics could, in some instances, rely on information technology to achieve efficiencies.

It is with respect to the training function that some of the most difficult dilemmas regarding flattening may be expected. In the corporate world, it has been noted that the elimination of middle man-

---

[13]However, the recent emphasis in the corporate literature on the phenomenon and importance of "mentoring" provides another example of how the corporate world has adopted certain ideas from the military.

agement layers may mean that newly promoted executives are not as well-prepared for their new responsibilities as previously. For example, at Wal-Mart, the introduction of the automated reporting system described above was accompanied by a much flatter organizational structure than in a typical retailing operation; the elimination of local warehouses and subregional centers means that an up-and-coming junior executive goes directly from the position of store manager to being responsible for an entire region.

This problem may be even more severe for the armed forces, since the gradual progression through the ranks is the most important mechanism for training top leadership. If an echelon is removed, some way will have to be found to compensate for the experience that officers would have gained by commanding at that echelon. Indeed, the problem is much more important for the armed forces than for a corporation, since the latter can recruit outsiders to become high-level officers, whereas the armed forces must "grow" their own.

In the corporate world, lateral transfers (as a way of broadening an executive's experience) and formal education have been used to deal with this problem.[14] The armed forces already use these training mechanisms. An additional possibility, also used in business training programs, would be games and simulations; as information technology makes it possible to have more and more realistic simulations (especially of command functions), this may be an important way of compensating for any decrease in "hands on" experience.

## Creating a Learning Institution

The questions of organizational structure discussed so far have concentrated on the issue of facilitating the flow of information through the organization in support of its current activities. The rapid pace of technological change in the commercial world and the increased pressures of global competition have also focused attention on the necessity of making an organization more adaptable, i.e., able to change more rapidly in response to new information about technological advances, market conditions, the competitive environment,

---

[14]For a discussion of this issue, see Weber et al. (1990).

etc. This problem obviously faces the armed forces as well, especially if we are currently in a period of revolutionary change in military affairs.

The rapid pace of change creates uncertainties with respect to all areas of activity of the armed forces. In addition to procurement decisions, doctrinal questions relating to tactics and organization will be subject to frequent change. As corporations have discovered, major changes in information systems can have wide-ranging effects throughout the organization, many of which come as surprises as the members of the organization learn how to use the new system and exploit more and more of its potential.[15] Hence, since information technology is evolving particularly rapidly, one must expect higher-than-usual degrees of turbulence.

Although the implementation of a new information system often requires a high degree of centralized control (for example, a large amount of "clout" may be required to ensure that the different parts of the organization adopt compatible information technology equipment and systems), the process of refining it and learning how to make optimal use of it requires a great deal of experimentation. For example, while "digitization of the battlefield" may well lead to major changes in the Army's organization, there is probably no way to design an optimal structure now. The information systems that current and evolving information technology will make feasible will have unpredictable effects on how war is fought.

This suggests that a major goal must be making the armed forces a more adaptive organization, especially for the period during which this major transformation will be taking place. There will have to be a great deal of experimentation to discover the best use of the new information systems and to refine them to exploit their full potential. Part of this experimentation will have to involve new organizational forms as well; for example, a major issue would be whether, given the new information systems, it makes sense to institute a greater span of control and hence a flatter organizational structure with fewer echelons.

---

[15]This point is the central thesis of Shoshana Zuboff's discussion of the "informating" of paper mills. (Zuboff, 1988.)

This suggests a major change in the way in which the armed forces prepare for the future. In principle, their behavior in this regard should be characterized by

- constant experimentation with new ideas and methods as the new information systems are absorbed

- pursuit of multiple alternative solutions

- careful analysis of actual operations to extract the maximum amount of information from real-world experience

- willingness to make frequent, small changes in methods and structure as new lessons are learned.

This approach may seem unnecessarily messy. However, a recent study of particularly successful companies noted that, although they invest in R&D in areas that appear promising to them, they often do not have a very clear idea of the precise products in which that technology will be incorporated. The history of successful companies contains many cases in which important products were launched seemingly by accident, although the ground had been prepared by the cultivation of technological expertise and a willingness to innovate "on the fly":

> In examining the history of the visionary companies, we were struck by how often they made some of their best moves not by detailed strategic planning, but rather by experimentation, trial and error, opportunism, and—quite literally—accident. What looks in hindsight like a brilliant strategy was often the residual result of opportunistic experimentation and "purposeful accidents." (Collins and Porras, 1994, p. 141.)

Fostering this type of experimentation imposes a number of requirements. First is the issue of financial resources. Ideally, an experimental unit ought to have some funds available to procure items on a trial basis without having to go through normal procedures. This would be especially true of information-technology equipment, which evolves very rapidly and which is available "off the shelf" in great variety and sophistication. Expertise should be available at the unit level to help in this regard; for example, the XVIII Airborne Corps's "science advisor" provides the components of that unit with information concerning current technological developments that could be of interest. A network of such science advisors could assist units in this regard and serve as a mechanism for disseminating positive experiences from one unit to the rest of the armed forces.

Money is not, however, the only resource that would be necessary; the units must have the time to engage in this type of work. The current high operational tempo of the armed forces, which is due to their involvement in various MOOTW, poses one obstacle in this regard. Beyond that is the issue of readiness levels; to the extent that a unit must maintain a high readiness level, its ability to devote time and effort to experimentation will be limited. It is thus an important question whether a designated experimental unit, such as the Army's Experimental Force,[16] should be required to maintain high readiness as well.

When corporations experiment, they may be able to tell right away whether an idea is a good one or not, since they are involved in their business on a day-to-day basis. For the armed forces, of course, things are different; the real test of a new tactic or organizational structure does not come until it is tried in actual combat. Thus, a great deal of effort must be put into developing methods for trying things out in a test environment that is as close to the real thing— combat—as possible. Such resources as Red Flag and the National Training Center are vital for this effort.

Thus, the third key resource, in addition to money and time, is access to test facilities. At present, for example, units are rotated through the Army's National Training Center for training and evaluation. The goal is to ensure that they are qualified according to current doctrine and to evaluate their capability and readiness. Increasing the adaptiveness of the Army would require that such facilities also be made available for experimentation. However, this goal is not compatible with the training and evaluation goals; the new methods being tested may not require the same skills as those for which the unit is to be qualified, and it would be unfair to evaluate unit or commander competence on the basis of actions taken as experiments, some of which should be expected to fail. Thus, time on current facilities will have to be reallocated, or new facilities will have to be created.

---

[16]Known as EXFOR, it is formally the 1st Brigade, 4th Infantry Division, Mechanized.

Although for this reason (i.e., the advantage of continual testing in the marketplace, as opposed to episodic testing in actual combat) it is inherently easier for corporations to experiment than for the armed forces, other aspects of the issue may be similar. For example, both corporations and the armed forces face the problems of disseminating information and ideas from an experimental unit to the rest of the organization; ensuring that service in the experimental unit is attractive to high-quality personnel and that good performance in it will be appropriately rewarded; and protecting the experimental unit against political pressures emanating from the rest of the organization.

Disseminating information and ideas often turns out to be harder than it might seem. For example, Xerox, in its Palo Alto Research Center skunk works, developed many of the concepts that are basic to personal computer operating systems today. Nevertheless, in part because these ideas were not effectively communicated to the rest of the corporation, Xerox lost out on a potentially lucrative market.

An experimental unit's potential can be limited if the organization's personnel do not see service in it as an attractive career option. This type of problem requires high-level attention to make sure that the organization's promotion system does not favor those who have risen via the traditional stepping stones over those who have served in experimental units.[17]

There may be a tension between these two needs: disseminating information from an experimental or innovative unit versus protecting the career prospects of those who serve in it. The reason is that interchange of personnel between experimental and conventional units is an effective way of disseminating new information and ideas, while one way of achieving the latter goal is to create a separate career track for these personnel, to make sure that their career opportunities are not slighted by members of the larger organization. This however, may tend to isolate them in certain positions, thereby

---

[17]In this regard, it is worth noting that former Chairman of the Joint Chiefs of Staff GEN John M. Shalikashvili, commanded the 9th Infantry Division, the Army's "high-technology test bed" intended to develop a new type of light division, from June 1987 to August 1989. His tenure, however, marked the end of the division's life as an experimental unit. (Mazarr, 1990, p. 25.)

reducing the flow of information. In the Army, for example, the creation of a separate branch for the Special Forces may have helped the promotion prospects of officers with that specialty, but at the cost of limiting their presence in infantry units, thereby hindering the flow of information and ideas.[18]

Finally, the experimental unit must be protected from any political pressures that might emanate from the rest of the organization, either because of competition for resources, because it seems to threaten other parts of the organization, or because of jealousy or any other cause. Essentially, this is a job for the top management, since the experimental unit will not be likely to have its own resources with which to fight. (In the case of the armed forces, it may be that there is congressional interest in the experiment, which could be an important source of support.)

In general, this will mean that the head of the organization must take an interest in the effort. In this regard, a service chief suffers a major disadvantage as compared to a corporate chief executive officer (CEO). A CEO is likely to be in his position for ten years or more, while a chief's tenure is, as a practical matter, limited to four years. It is possible to outwait a service chief, but not the average CEO.

## Personnel Policy: "Freedom to Fail"

The types of changes discussed above will require adjustments in the personnel system to accommodate them. There appear to be two major issues: encouraging risk-taking and improving training and competence at the lower levels of the organization.

Many voices in the armed forces have spoken out against the "zero defects" mentality and in favor of instituting the "freedom to fail."[19] This is particularly important if one wishes to foster an adaptive and

---

[18]This thought was expressed to the authors of the study from which this chapter is adapted (*The "Virtual Corporation" and Army Organization*) by some infantry officers in the XVIII Airborne Corps.

[19]According to GEN Dennis J. Reimer, "we must display positive, creative leadership, *stamp out this zero defects mentality* and create an environment where all soldiers can reach their full potential." (Reimer, 1996, p. 6. Emphasis added.) General Reimer emphasizes throughout the article that the "zero defects mentality" puts tremendous pressure on commanders not to report candidly about problems in their units.

innovative culture, in which individuals are encouraged to try new methods and to attempt unorthodox approaches. Obviously, some of these attempts will fail; if the system is not able to distinguish between failures that are inevitable in the course of reasonable experimentation and those that result from incompetence, innovative behavior will be seen as too risky. For example, the Israeli Army has the reputation for overlooking serious failures when they are seen as resulting from the taking of reasonable risks and when the individual's positive characteristics are considerable. Thus, Ariel Sharon's unauthorized move into the Mitla Pass in the 1956 Sinai Campaign, which resulted in large casualties, did not derail his military career.

Institutionalizing "freedom to fail" is probably particularly difficult to accomplish in an era of downsizing, when there is extra pressure to separate, or not to promote, individuals who would otherwise be considered to meet the standards of the organization. In such an atmosphere, those charged with these difficult decisions are likely to seize on an obvious mistake as an easily defensible justification for a negative evaluation. Unless counteracted, this is likely to induce too much caution into the organization, as everyone comes to fear that a single mistake could be his last. This problem is exacerbated by the overall political climate, which tends to regard every mistake or failure as a scandal.[20]

Concomitant with providing "freedom to fail," the system must be able to adequately reward successful innovation; in particular, to avoid discouraging experimentation, the reward for extraordinary success resulting from "out of the box" thinking must be sufficient to overcome the penalties for failure. Otherwise, trying something new that may or may not work out will appear to be a losing proposition in terms of one's own career.

In this regard, corporations have a major advantage over the armed forces: Their promotion systems are "demand pull" rather than "supply push" in nature. In other words, they promote someone when they have a vacant position to fill, whereas the armed forces promote according to a schedule that is first keyed to the candidate's

---

[20]The same problem exists with respect to procurement, which is discussed below.

length of service and only then looks for a suitable vacancy in which to place the officer. This means that the corporate promotion is tied to a specific position, and the corporation then looks for the eligible candidate who promises, on the basis of prior performance, to be able to do the best job in it. This favors the candidates who have attracted attention to themselves by means of superior performance, as opposed to those whose records are unblemished.

At the same time, the "demand pull" system favors those who have had challenging assignments in the past (since they have a better opportunity of achieving something sufficiently out of the ordinary to attract attention), as well as those whose patrons or "mentors" are in a position to affect the selection (since patrons will have a better sense of the talents of those who have worked under them than of those with whom they have had less contact). For a corporation, this is not too serious a problem, since there is no expectation that its promotion system will be "fair," in the sense of giving everyone an equal chance to rise to the top.

Emphasizing exceptional success, as opposed to the absence of obvious failures, makes the selection process more subjective; there is bound to be a greater difference of opinion as to what constitutes a significant achievement denoting exceptional competence than as to what is a blunder. This implies the risk that "politics" (in the pejorative sense of clientism, the favoring of those in one's own "clique") may play a greater role in the selection process. It also means that it will be harder to operate a servicewide selection process, since a greater familiarity with specific actions will be required to make judgments. Unless Officer Efficiency Reports can be made more informative, it may be harder for board members who do not know those being considered to make decisions about them.

In any case, changes in government personnel systems in this direction will be difficult to attain. This difficulty stems from the necessity of the government to be seen as acting in accordance with certain notions of "fairness" that do not necessarily apply to private organizations, such as corporations. For example, as noted, the promotion system of a corporation can be openly subjective; no one expects every employee to have an equal shot at rising through the ranks, let alone becoming CEO. In governmental organizations, on the other hand, although everyone understands that politics (in both the higher—public policy—and lower—clientism—senses of the term) plays an important role, the overall system must, in principle at least, be seen as being fundamentally fair and objective.

## Personnel Policy:  Distribution of Skills in the Organization

If organizations are to be flatter and more adaptive, they will require a greater distribution of skills throughout their various levels.  Those at the lower echelons will be called on to act more independently than before; many parts of the organization will be expected to engage in some experimentation, and innovation will not be the preserve of a few specialists.  This implies not only the need for more training, a trend already in evidence in the armed forces, but also a recognition that those at lower levels in the hierarchy can play an important role in achieving overall success and can make an important contribution by improving their skills while remaining at their present level in organizational terms.  In other words, promotion need not be regarded as synonymous with career development and "success."

In corporations, for example, specialists may not be "promoted" if that means that they would have to give up exercising their special talent and become managers; an excellent computer programmer may in fact make an indifferent manager.  Instead, the company can reward the specialists by increasing their salaries, giving them more challenging work to do, and assigning them "mentoring" responsibilities by which they impart their knowledge and experience to younger specialists.

Many of these techniques may not be feasible in the armed forces; salary, for example, is set by law and is associated with rank.  Among civilian government employees, grade and, hence, salary level are heavily determined by the number of employees one supervises.  The critical issue, however, is the "up or out" personnel system, which implies, for example, that an excellent commander at the tactical level must either be promoted to a higher level of responsibility or be separated from the service.  The situation may be even worse with respect to one whose specialty (for example, intelligence) tends to lack billets at the higher levels; it may be difficult for the armed forces to retain the services of such specialists over the long term, even though it may be in their interest to do so.  This contradicts the notion of the "flat" organization, in which the retention of skills at the bottom of the hierarchy is crucial.

## "Revolution in Business Affairs": Procurement

The problem of dealing with periods of revolutionary change shows up most dramatically in the area of procurement; especially with respect to major weapon systems, such as a new fighter or tank, the lead time between starting the R&D process and fielding the new system in large numbers is measured in years if not decades. In an era of rapid technological advance, such lead times can seriously hinder the ability of the armed forces to field the most effective weapon systems possible.

While some of this lead time is inevitable, given the complexity of the systems involved, the problem is exacerbated by the regulatory environment in which the procurement takes place. The difficulties involved in procuring information technology have been especially great. This is not surprising, given that technological progress in this area has been particularly rapid; a cumbersome procurement process guarantees that it will be impossible to acquire state-of-the-art equipment. It should be noted that, within the U.S. government, this problem is not unique to the Department of Defense. Other agencies have had similar problems procuring up-to-date information technology and related equipment; for example, the inability of the Federal Aviation Administration to modernize the air traffic control system has led the administration to propose that a government-owned corporation, which could ignore federal procurement regulations, be created to handle this function.[21]

---

[21]Vice President Al Gore has proposed the creation of a "businesslike government-owned corporation, funded by user fees and working outside of traditional governmental constraints." See Gore (1995), pp. 30–31, 123. Of course, it is an open question whether, as a practical political matter, such a corporation could avoid the detailed regulations with which, for example, privately owned defense contractors are burdened. In particular, it is not clear whether the corporation's favored treatment would survive the first scandal that could in any way be traced to its freedom from "traditional governmental constraints." In other words, the more fundamental problem results from the "zero defects" mentality, prevalent in the political system as a whole, for which a clear mistake (moral or intellectual) that costs $1 million is a much more serious matter than an ongoing inefficiency that wastes many times as much money each year. In any case, it is worth noting that corporations, too, often have

Designing a full-scale reform of the government procurement process is far beyond the scope of this study.[22] More importantly, given the amount of energy that has been devoted to this task and the number of studies that have been produced concerning it, one is forced to conclude that the prospects for a thoroughgoing reform are not particularly good. Indeed, there are some constraints (similar to those noted in the discussion of personnel systems) under which government operates that do not apply in the private sector.

For example, the American automobile industry, generally following the Japanese model, has tended to forge closer and longer-term relationships with particular suppliers, moving away from the notion that every contract should be competed among as many suppliers as possible on the basis of price. The underlying view is that a long-term relationship, on the basis of which it is possible to share information and expertise, will produce a better quality-and-price mix in the long run than will an "arm's length" approach that constantly forces suppliers to compete with each other. While the automobile company may not, because of diminished competition, get the best price on every contract, the argument runs, its steady suppliers will, for various reasons,[23] gradually improve in efficiency and hence offer lower prices in the long run.

In general, however, this strategy may not be available to a government agency. The key difference is this: If Ford is satisfied with a supplier, nobody believes, for reasons of "fairness," that Ford nevertheless has an obligation to consider the bid of another potential supplier; it can proceed on a "sole source" basis as it sees fit. The philosophy guiding government contracts, on the other hand, is very different: In principle, they are supposed to be open to all bidders,

---

problems instituting major information systems; even the most flexible procurement system has trouble keeping up with the fast pace of developments in the information technology world.

[22]For a discussion of the problems plaguing the procurement system, especially as it involves information technology, see Kelman (1990).

[23]The supplier will be able to plan his production better, since he will have a better sense of precisely what parts will be needed, when, and in what quantities. By tapping into the automobile company's expertise, he will be able to improve his production processes; working closely with the assembly plant, he will get quicker feedback about the quality of his product and can fix defects sooner. See Womack, Jones, and Roos (1991), pp. 146 ff.

regardless of the costs or benefits involved. (There are, however, some exceptions, which are discussed below.[24])

In addition to the concern for equity, the same "zero defects" mentality is at work here, reflecting the generalized lack of trust affecting the entire political system. This makes it difficult, for example, to relax procurement regulations so as to provide officials with more flexibility; presumably, the detailed rules are designed to make sure that the procurement officials do not play favorites among possible suppliers (or worse).

On the other hand, it might be possible to devise some ways around the procurement system. The purpose of these expedients would be twofold: First, they could facilitate the timely acquisition and utilization of equipment that might not otherwise be available. Second, by showing what is in fact possible, they might serve to change the political climate in ways that would ultimately make a full-scale reform more feasible. In short, instead of attempting a head-on attack against a strongly fortified and heavily defended position, one should seek to infiltrate, undermine, and eventually subvert it.

One possibility would be to make greater use of the skunk works concept, i.e., "umbrella" contracts with a given company, which allow for rapid amendment and modifications that can be negotiated on a sole-source basis. In effect, this short-circuits the government's procurement regulations and makes use of private industry's ability to operate quickly and flexibly. It would also foster a close relationship between the program office and the contractor, which could familiarize the officers and civilian government officials in the program office with commercial practices. This could tend to increase pressures to reform the standard procurement system.[25]

---

[24]Federally funded research and development centers, of which RAND is one, is the exception that comes most readily to mind.

[25]Commercial firms themselves use skunk works, for much the same reason: to provide a venue for technological experimentation and progress unconstrained by the company's own bureaucratic procedures. However, the dissemination of skunk works' experiences to the rest of the corporation cannot be taken for granted: In some cases, such as Xerox's Palo Alto Research Center, the parent company did not absorb advances made by the skunk works. The same forces that necessitate the creation of the skunk works in the first place can, if not countered, negate its usefulness.

Typically, skunk works have been used for secret ("black") programs; the secrecy in which these projects have been shrouded, imposed because of the sensitivity of the technology involved, had the additional benefit of helping them avoid the usual types of controls associated with the defense procurement regime. However, the skunk works format also makes sense for projects that are not particularly sensitive and that, like many information technology initiatives, make use of commercially available technology.

Another possibility would be to use "wartime" procurement procedures during MOOTW. As is well known, a new hard-target penetration bomb, the GBU-28, was developed during the Gulf War in a six-week period, and was used just before the cease-fire to destroy a leadership command, control, and communication bunker.[26] One could search for (or create) other opportunities for doing the same thing. Thus, the political saliency of the current operations in the former Yugoslavia is sufficiently high that it might be possible to procure systems to support it under a "wartime" exception to the rules.

For example, one could argue that air-implanted sensors for surveillance of base perimeters, for convoy security against ambushes, etc., would be sufficiently useful that suspension of the procurement regulations should be authorized to allow rapid procurement: Since such devices have been used in the past, no technological advances would be required to develop and procure a useful system. Given the danger widespread minefields pose for the success of the Bosnian mission, development of new mine-clearing techniques and equipment on an emergency basis could be justified. Similarly, one could search for opportunities to telescope the development process by the deployment of systems that are not yet in the operational inventory, such as the Joint Surveillance and Target Attack Radar System in Operations Desert Storm and Joint Endeavor and Predator in Operation Deliberate Force.

In general, opportunities of this type should be sought out, both to exercise the system so that it will be better able to operate rapidly in case of war and to highlight the cost of the current regulatory regime. One might attempt to institute a system whereby, in the case of any

---

[26]U.S. Department of Defense (1992), p. 148.

ongoing operation, some amount of money would be made available for the development and procurement of equipment under "wartime" rules. A similar procedure might even be adopted for selected major exercises; for example, some funds could be made available early in the planning process for the development and procurement of equipment considered particularly relevant to the exercise.

## ORGANIZATIONAL STRUCTURE MUST REFLECT OBJECTIVES

The study of the corporate reorganization literature can provide many useful insights into questions of organizational structure, process, etc. As noted, the corporate world possesses a major advantage as compared to the military: It engages in its primary activity on a daily basis and can continuously assess, on the basis of real-world experience, whether a given organizational structure, strategy, or procedure is beneficial. The marketplace forces corporations to seek constant improvements in their methods; even a huge corporation, such as General Motors or IBM, can be successfully attacked in the marketplace by a much smaller competitor if the larger company becomes complacent. Thus, one would expect that the corporate world would be the source of a series of organizational innovations, many of which would be worthwhile.

Nevertheless, innovations that are successful in one organization cannot simply be applied to other commercial organizations, let alone to military ones. Rather, they must be thought of as part of the "tool kit" with which one approaches the question of how a given organization should be structured; you would not try to build a house without a hammer, but that does not mean that everything is a nail or that nails are the appropriate fasteners in each case. The objectives of the given organization must be the starting point.

Obviously, military organizations are different from commercial ones. Perhaps less obviously, the variation among military units and missions is such that the same organizational structure will not be appropriate for every situation. The type of structure that is suitable for major theater war may not be what is required for a smaller contingency or for MOOTW. For example, MOOTW make more salient the problem of coordination between military and political decisionmakers: Thus, it may be important to shorten the path between the units on the ground and the National Command Authorities.

Another major distinction would be between the current relatively small volunteer force and the type of force that might be raised by conscription during a general mobilization to fight a major war. With respect to many of its characteristics, the latter force would have to resemble not the "knowledge" organization of current theorists but the more rigid, hierarchical structures of the past. In such a force, it would be hard to reach the levels of training possible in the smaller, longer-term force; thus, less authority could be safely delegated to lower echelons. Instead, the less welltrained personnel either would require closer supervision by superiors or would have to follow more-detailed rules or standard operating procedures. This would imply that spans of control would be smaller and, hence, that there would be more "middle management" layers in the hierarchies.

## EXOGENOUS POLITICAL CONSTRAINTS

Finally, note must be taken of those exogenous political constraints on organizational structure, i.e., the constraints imposed by the larger political system, which can be changed only slowly, if at all. As noted, the pervasive "zero defects" mentality—which tends increasingly to regard every error as a scandal—poses problems for many of the types of organizational innovation discussed above. More generally, it creates a problem for any attempt to disperse authority within an organization and to allow lower levels of the hierarchy to exercise initiative. While a rigid, "top down" method of control will not prevent all problems (and, in fact, it creates many of its own), it at least has the advantage of *appearing* to provide control. This appearance may be illusory, but it has its political uses—when something goes wrong, the existence of a complex set of rules, not all of which, in the nature of things, will have been obeyed, means that it will be possible to find someone to blame. Furthermore, in response to a disaster, one can always add a new layer of regulations or controls to show that one is doing something to prevent the problem's recurrence.

While these tendencies are strong in any bureaucratic setting—there appears to be an ingrained tendency that favors predictability over effectiveness—they are particular strong in government. This will act as a constraint on the degree to which flattening and experimentation can be pursued, at least under peacetime conditions.

However, while these constraints cannot be ignored, they ought not be accepted fatalistically, either. In any attempt to look at organizational questions in the U.S. armed forces, one must keep them in mind. However, the problem of reorganization involves not only designing an improved structure, but figuring out how to implement it as well.

## REFERENCES

Bacevich, A. J., *The Pentomic Era: The U.S. Army Between Korea and Vietnam*, Washington, D.C.: National Defense University Press, 1986.

Coase, Ronald, "The Nature of the Firm," *Economica*, Vol. 6, 1937, pp. 386–405.

Cohen, Eliot, "A Revolution in Warfare," *Foreign Affairs*, Vol. 75, No. 2, March–April 1996, pp. 46–48.

Collins, James C., and Jerry I. Porras, *Built to Last: Successful Habits of Visionary Companies*, New York: HarperBusiness, 1994.

Davidow, William H., and Michael S. Malone, *The Virtual Corporation: Structuring and Revitalizing the Corporation for the 21st Century*, New York: HarperCollins, 1992.

Drucker, Peter F., "The Coming of the New Organization," *Harvard Business Review*, Vol. 66, No. 1, January–February 1988.

Fukuyama, Francis, and Abram N. Shulsky, *The "Virtual Corporation" and Army Organization*, Santa Monica, Calif.: RAND, MR-863-A, 1997.

Gore, Al, *Common Sense Government: Works Better and Costs Less*, New York: Random House, 1995.

Kelman, Steve, *Procurement and Public Management: The Fear of Discretion and the Quality of Government Performance*, Washington:, D.C.: AEI Press/University Press of America, 1990.

Malone, Thomas W., and John F. Rockart, "Computers, Networks and the Corporation," *Scientific American*, September 1991, pp. 128–136.

Mazarr, Michael J., *Light Forces & the Future of U.S. Military Strategy*, Washington, D.C.: Brassey's (US), Inc., 1990.

Messenger, Charles, *The Blitzkrieg Story*, New York: Scribners', 1976.

Reimer, General Dennis J., "Leadership for the 21st Century: Empowerment, Environment and the Golden Rule," *Military Review*, Vol. LXXVI, No. 1, January–February 1996.

U.S. Department of Defense, *Conduct of the Persian Gulf War*, Report to Congress, April 1992.

Van Creveld, Martin, *Fighting Power: German and U.S. Army Performance, 1939–1945*, Westport, Conn.: Greenwood Press, 1982.

_____, *Command in War*, Cambridge, Mass.: Harvard University Press, 1985.

Weber, Joseph, et al., "Farewell, Fast Track: Promotions and Raises Are Scarcer—So What Will Energize Managers?" *Business Week*, December 10, 1990, pp. 192–200.

Womack, James P., Daniel T. Jones, and Daniel Roos, *The Machine That Changed the World: The Story of Lean Production*, New York: HarperCollins, 1991.

Zuboff, Shoshana, *In the Age of the Smart Machine: The Future of Work and Power*, New York: Basic Books, 1988.

# Chapter Twelve

# ARMS CONTROL, EXPORT REGIMES, AND MULTILATERAL COOPERATION

*Lynn E. Davis*

In the past, arms control, export regimes, and multilateral cooperation have promoted U.S. security as well as global stability. Vast stockpiles of weapons have been eliminated. Destabilizing nuclear systems have been banned. Confidence-building measures have enhanced security in Europe. Various treaties and export-control regimes have prevented the spread of weapons of mass destruction and sophisticated conventional weapons. Multilateral cooperation agreements have been used to prevent common threats, such as nuclear smuggling.

The question is whether any of these approaches—arms control, export regimes, multilateral cooperation—can serve U.S. security and global stability in the future in connection with the development and deployment of information-warfare systems. The obvious problem, which other chapters in this book describe, is that so much uncertainty still surrounds this whole subject. Many of the information systems and technologies are just beginning to be designed. Still unclear is an understanding of the kinds of threats that will emerge both to American society or to the U.S. ability to employ its military forces. No one knows who will be able to develop or acquire these new systems and in what time frame. So the strategic assumptions that will guide U.S. policies and strategies cannot be defined. Nevertheless, it is not too soon to begin to consider this question, and this is the purpose of this chapter.

This chapter begins with a description of some of the past accomplishments of arms control, export regimes, and multilateral cooperation. It then turns to what this history suggests for the role that each of these might play in the age of information warfare. Important to future decisions will be one's strategic assumptions about whether the United States will be able to maintain superiority in information warfare and how widely disseminated information-warfare capabilities will be.  The chapter considers various possibilities and then defines some of the issues that will need to be addressed, if any of these three approaches were to be pursued.  The chapter concludes by defining the tasks the United States should undertake during this time of uncertainty, so as to prepare for the possibility that arms control, export regimes, and multilateral cooperation might play a critical role in the age of information warfare.[1]

## PAST ACCOMPLISHMENTS

### Arms Control

During the Cold War, the United States and Soviet governments viewed arms control as a way to promote strategic stability and reduce the threat posed by the accumulation of strategic nuclear arms; with European governments, they saw arms control as the means to ameliorate the threat arising from the massing of conventional armaments in Central Europe.  In the 1970s, arms control had some limited success in promoting these goals.  The Antiballistic Missile Treaty banned nationwide strategic defenses, and the Strategic Arms Limitation Treaty agreements capped the overall levels of Soviet and American strategic nuclear delivery vehicles.  The Helsinki Final Act of the Conference on Security and Cooperation in Europe (CSCE) included principles upon which to conduct relations, as well as some rudimentary confidence-building measures.

As cooperation began to replace confrontation, with the fall of the Berlin Wall and the dissolution of the Soviet Union, arms-control negotiations made more-significant progress.  The CSCE countries agreed in the Stockholm Document to confidence and security-building measures that were designed to reduce the risks of war through surprise attack and misunderstanding in a crisis.  The Strategic Arms Reduction Talks (START) treaties mandated major reductions in the number of strategic nuclear missiles and bombers.

---

[1]The author wishes particularly to thank Jeremy Shapiro for the many ways in which he supported the writing of this chapter, and especially his wise counsel. Thanks as well to Robert Nurick, whose very thoughtful and insightful review improved the argument.

The Conference on Forces in Europe (CFE) Treaty produced equality between the North Atlantic Treaty Organization (NATO) and the Warsaw Pact in the most-dangerous conventional weapons, tanks, artillery, and armored personnel carriers.  Confidence-building measures were expanded and improved through the 1988 Charter of Paris and the 1994 Vienna Document.

In 1997, the United States and Russia agreed to guidelines for a START III treaty, which will lower further the overall number of strategic missiles and bomber weapons and provide for new measures that will increase the transparency of their strategic nuclear warhead inventories and require the actual destruction of the nuclear warheads themselves.  The CFE Treaty will be adapted over the next few years based on a framework, agreed to in the summer of 1997, that calls for further reductions in conventional weapons, as well as measures to prevent any threatening buildup of conventional forces in Central Europe.  The NATO Founding Act of May 1997 envisions a role for arms control in enhancing security in Europe as NATO expands, through confidence-building measures built on exchanges of information on military infrastructures throughout Europe.

In 1995, the Nuclear Non-Proliferation Treaty, in which some 170 countries have agreed not to acquire nuclear weapons, was extended indefinitely and unconditionally.  One of the ways that the nuclear powers gained the support of the nonnuclear states to the extension of the Non-Proliferation Treaty was to commit, through arms control, to further reductions in their own nuclear weapons.  They also provided "security assurances" to the nonnuclear states relating to the circumstances when they would and would not use nuclear weapons in the future.  Arms control has also produced agreement for the destruction of all stockpiles of chemical and biological weapons and the prohibition of any future development.  The Chemical Weapons Convention and the Biological Weapons Convention became possible once the parties recognized that these weapons were not very useful militarily and posed a serious threat if used by others.

This brief history demonstrates that arms-control negotiations can achieve a variety of different goals and that governments have been extremely creative in tailoring various measures to respond to the specific characteristics of the threats and the individual weapon systems. The parties to these arms-control agreements have been nation-states, given their responsibility for deploying and operating the weapon systems. The ability of governments to verify the limits confidently has been a critical element, although the standards of verification have been somewhat relaxed as the threats have diminished.

Measures to build confidence and security proved to be possible, even when only the most minimal cooperation existed among the parties. As cooperation expanded, governments found arms control a useful way to move mutually to lower levels of armaments and even to eliminate reciprocally whole classes of weapons: intermediate-range missiles in Europe and strategic missiles with multiple warheads. They were also prepared to undertake reductions, through reciprocal—but unilateral—steps, and thereby forgo intrusive verification procedures, as in the case of theater nuclear weapons in Europe.

But there have been important limits to what arms control has been able to accomplish. The newest weapon systems have not been banned, even in the case of antisatellite systems, when neither side saw any advantage in their actual deployment. To retain their own military flexibility in a crisis, governments have resisted strict limits on their military activities and deployments, even though limits might have eliminated the threat of surprise attack.

## Export Control Regimes

Historically, the industrialized nations have taken a variety of steps to keep dangerous weapons, as well as the means to develop such weapons, out of the hands of enemies, especially rogue states and terrorists. During the Cold War, the NATO countries, joined by the neutral countries in western Europe, restricted the transfer of all conventional weapons and related technologies to the Soviet Union, China, and North Korea, through the Coordinating Committee for Multilateral Export Controls regime. In this case, the threat was unambiguous and extremely serious.

With the end of the Cold War, the security threats became more diffuse. But governments saw dangers in the spread of dangerous weapons and undertook to establish international norms against the proliferation of weapons of mass destruction, long-range missiles, and sophisticated conventional weapons. To reinforce these norms, multilateral export regimes were established to control transfers of each of these weapons and their related technologies.

The Nuclear Suppliers Group, composed of 30 suppliers, has established guidelines and controls for exports of nuclear materials, equipment, and technologies. The Australia Group is an informal arrangement among most of the industrial countries that reinforces the Chemical and Biological Weapons Conventions by preventing transfers of certain kinds of chemical and biological weapon material and dual-use technologies.

The Missile Technology Control Regime (MTCR), established in 1987, seeks to control exports of equipment and technology, both military and dual-use, that could contribute to missile development, production, and operations. To prevent buildups of destabilizing conventional weapons, as occurred in Iraq, over 30 of the major suppliers of conventional weapons have joined together in the Wassenaar Arrangement to promote transparency and restraint in sales of conventional weapons and related dual-use goods and technologies.

These regimes control exports to both nation-states and nongovernmental groups. They cover weapons and the equipment and technologies that are necessary to develop the weapons. Each of the regimes includes a list of the weapons, equipment, and technologies that are to be controlled; rules governing their transfer; and a commitment to report on licenses that have been approved and denied.

These regimes have been designed in light of the unique characteristics of the weapons they cover. Given the extremely serious threat posed by weapons of mass destruction, these export regimes include rules that generally "ban" any transfers of the listed equipment and technologies. The MTCR members view the long-range missile proliferation threat as sufficiently serious to warrant rules that presume that all transfers of the listed items will be denied to non-MTCR countries.

Conventional weapons are different, for all nations consider them essential to their own defense. A threat arises only in specific circumstances, when weapons are acquired by rogue states and terrorists, or when the introduction of new weapons upsets a regional balance. So members of the Wassenaar Arrangement have been reluctant to coordinate their policies on conventional arms sales or to commit to specific rules governing their transfer. They do, however, each have national policies prohibiting transfers of conventional weapons and military-related technology to Iran, Iraq, Libya, and North Korea.

Even when the political will exists among governments to prevent the spread of dangerous weapons, many obstacles exist. The United States, Japan, and western European countries have fairly sophisticated systems for implementing export controls, but other countries are just beginning to put theirs in place. Most of the goods on the control lists have legitimate civil, as well as military, uses. So governments must create licensing procedures that permit legitimate sales but prohibit dual-use goods from being diverted to dangerous military uses. This is especially difficult in the face of an adversary determined to circumvent the controls.

Strong commercial interests exist in every country for expanding trade in dual-use equipment and technologies, leading to pressures on individual governments to remove items from the control lists. Countries strike different balances between their commercial and nonproliferation objectives. The United States liberalized its trade in supercomputers, over the objections of the Japanese. The Germans expanded their sales of machine tools, notwithstanding U.S. opposition. As a result, it has been difficult historically to achieve agreement on a multilateral approach to controlling the various kinds of dual-use equipment and technologies that could contribute to the development of dangerous weapons.

## Multilateral Cooperation

The difficulties associated with achieving arms-control agreements and putting in place effective export regimes have led to the design of another approach, known as multilateral cooperation. This approach generally focuses on preventive activities, including information sharing and crisis-management planning, and on expanding links among countries between their domestic agencies involved in law enforcement and customs, their intelligence agencies, and their foreign ministries and embassies.

The United States, Russia, and the other G-7 countries designed such an approach in response to the potential threat posed by the large amounts of nuclear fissile materials becoming available with the elimination of the vast superpower weapon stockpiles. Reports of smuggling attempts in Germany in the summer of 1994 sparked the effort. By the Moscow Summit in 1996, Russia had stopped denying the existence of the problem and agreed to a multilateral effort, the centerpiece of which was a program for preventing and combating illicit trafficking in nuclear materials. Focal points were named in each government to be responsible for gathering and evaluating information on nuclear smuggling incidents, communicating among all government agencies, and coordinating a response. International cooperation among law enforcement, intelligence, and national laboratory experts was expanded, including efforts to improve forensic analysis techniques for seized nuclear material. In this case, these steps complemented efforts to improve Russia's system for controlling nuclear exports.

More recently, the United States, Russia, and five other countries agreed to cooperate in defeating computer crime by pledging to coordinate efforts to combat industrial espionage, money laundering, and other wrongdoing in cyberspace; develop new crime-fighting techniques; and search for and prosecute high-technology criminals, even when extradition laws do not apply. (Krauss, 1997.) The key to a successful multilateral approach is a common perception of the potential threats and vulnerabilities.

## INFORMATION SYSTEMS AND TECHNOLOGIES

What does this history suggest for the role that arms control, export regimes, and multilateral cooperation might play, individually or collectively, in the age of information warfare? Critical to answering this question will be how the opportunities and threats of information-warfare systems and technologies will evolve.

### Arms Control

The attractiveness of arms control will depend importantly on who the potential adversaries will be and on what their goals and calculations are. If the main threat is assumed to arise from nongovernmental groups, or from isolated rogue countries, arms control would not be very effective, for they would not be expected to participate. But if the future threat arises, even in part, from nation-states, the possibilities for arms control need to be considered.

The United States has established maintaining superiority, or dominance, in information warfare into the 21st century as its strategic goal . Arms control in this strategy could become a potential liability, because it would be premised on the United States accepting some constraints on its information-warfare capabilities and potential military operations. Most arms-control agreements also assume that the negotiating outcome will be equal limits, not superiority for one party. Equality is often difficult to quantify, and arms control has at times resulted in advantages to one side or the other. But politically, it remains extremely difficult for another party to accept inferiority to the United States in a formal arms-control treaty.

Nevertheless, even when the United States is able to sustain a strategy of superiority, one possibility for arms control would be to ban information-warfare weapons, which the United States and other parties would view as to no one's advantage to develop and deploy. A possible candidate might be a widely discussed future weapon known as the electronic pulse system, which would be designed to attack computer-based systems.

The U.S. military can be expected to resist banning any "new" weapon system before understanding the capabilities it could provide. Potential adversaries may not be willing to give up any potential information-warfare capability. But the United States would have some leverage if it were to determine that a ban would be useful, since the United States would be willing to forgo a weapon that it could certainly be expected to produce. At the same time, the United States could not agree, until it was confident that all countries capable of making the weapons were parties to the agreement and that nongovernmental groups would not be able to acquire them.

If a ban is sought, a key issue would be the choice of an approach to verification. One would be for individual countries to make unilateral commitments that others would reciprocate. Another would be to proceed as in the case of the Biological Weapons Convention, in which the parties formally committed simply to destroy their biological weapons but without any provisions for verification. At that time, the parties judged that no one could expect to achieve an advantage from any use of biological weapons, so relying on the self-interests of the parties to carry out their commitment was sufficient. Still another approach would be to negotiate a detailed agreement with extensive verification requirements and inspections to deter cheating and win congressional support. The problem is that such an agreement would be technically difficult and very time-consuming to negotiate.

The risk of not pursuing any arms control is that the abilities of potential adversaries to acquire information-warfare capabilities would not be constrained in any way. Over time, this could threaten the U.S. ability to maintain superiority.

If superiority is unlikely to be sustained, arms control could usefully be employed to limit the threats to the United States posed by the information-warfare capabilities of potential adversaries against both its military forces and domestic infrastructure.

One possibility would be for the United States to pursue formal measures with countries developing information-warfare capabilities, to build confidence and to reduce the risk of surprise attack and misunderstanding in a future crisis. In the past, such measures focused on reporting on the size and characteristics of military forces and equipment, as well as on different kinds of movements of military forces, including alerts. In the case of information warfare, agreements could be structured calling for exchanges about the characteristics of the various components of future systems and for notifications and observation of activities that would be necessary to prepare for an attack.

The first issue is whether governments would be prepared to share information about their systems, especially their newest systems. It will also be difficult to define precisely which activities would constitute preparations for an attack and whether they could be observed. Another issue is whether any of the governments would judge that such measures would actually build confidence and enhance their security, rather than unacceptably constraining their military capabilities and operational requirements. But more importantly, these measures presume that governments not only perceive a potential threat but also share an interest in building confidence. One could imagine such a possibility. The Russians, and perhaps even the

Chinese, could be concerned about the U.S. lead in these information-warfare capabilities. The U.S. interest would be in trying to avoid surprise or miscalculated attacks against its potentially more vulnerable domestic infrastructure.

Another possible means of building some confidence would be for the United States and others with information-warfare capabilities to provide "security assurances" with respect to the conduct of future information warfare, to reduce the risks of preemptive attacks against U.S. operational systems or the U.S. homeland. For example, governments could pledge not to be the first to attack domestic infrastructures with computer viruses, or in future wars to forgo attacks using information warfare against domestic infrastructures.

Security assurances, however, raise many problems. Such assurances could constrain the use of one's own information-warfare systems unacceptably. Assurances will reduce the deterrent effect of such systems by suggesting that certain conditions would need to apply before they would be used. Such pledges only represent political commitments. So it is uncertain how much confidence assurances provide, given that they may or may not be carried out in times of actual crises or war. Countries with capabilities inferior to those of the United States are unlikely to perceive any advantage in forgoing at least the threat of such future attacks. Nevertheless, the United States, whose domestic infrastructure is the most vulnerable, could potentially benefit from security assurances to which all potential adversaries agree.

Arms control offers the further possibility of achieving limits on future information-warfare systems. The issue for the United States would be whether the prospect of an uncontrolled competition in information-warfare capabilities would be sufficiently dangerous as to warrant both agreeing to limits on its own systems and, more importantly, accepting equality as the legally binding outcome of the negotiations. Other parties would need to judge whether their own security would be served by gaining equal limits with the United States in return for constraints on their own capabilities. And it is not easy to predict the outcome. The parties would have to balance the fact that the United States will be able to retain, in the absence of arms control, superior military capabilities, though not necessarily the prospect of dominance, with the fact that the United States also has serious domestic vulnerabilities, which they could exploit if their own systems were not limited.

If pursued, arms-control negotiations would confront an incredibly complex set of issues involving, for example, how to define equality or equivalence in information systems; which systems, components, and technologies would be limited; and what standard and measures of verification would be required. While it is very difficult to see the value today of pursuing any arms-control approach, a world in which information-warfare capabilities are not controlled could be very dangerous.

## Export Controls

Preventing the transfer of critical components of information systems and technologies would appear to be useful, regardless of how U.S. strategy evolves or what threats may emerge. Controlling systems and technologies that have purely "military" applications, such as certain kinds of sensors, is reasonably straightforward. They could be included on the U.S. Munitions List, thereby requiring a license and approval before any sale.

If the United States alone is capable of developing such systems and technologies, unilateral controls would be sufficient. More likely, at least a few other countries will be able to acquire these capabilities. So the United States would have an interest in ensuring that these countries put in place similar controls. This could be achieved through formal restraint agreements, as in the U.S.-Japan Super-computer Agreement, or through informal understandings.

Much more difficult will be controlling the information systems and technologies (the communication technologies, computers, and software) that have both military and commercial applications. U.S. multinational corporations will wish to use such technologies in their international networks and operations, and U.S. companies will seek to market the technologies internationally. Moreover, as technologies evolve, they will also become more affordable. So, these information systems and technologies will become easily available to potential adversaries, unless they are specifically controlled by all potential manufacturers.

If the United States assumes that it can expect to maintain superiority in information warfare, through its own technological advances and management skills, preventing the dispersion of dual-use information systems and technologies would not be especially critical. If these could be used by others to challenge U.S. superiority, or if superiority is not going to be sustainable, export controls would be more important. This would be the case even if all they could be expected to accomplish would be to delay, rather than prevent, potential adversaries from acquiring certain information-warfare capabilities.

For example, the argument is made that superiority in information warfare will depend on the development of a "knowledge system" that will synthesize existing and new information systems and thereby permit the introduction of technologies into military capability more quickly than the competitors can. In this case, the dispersion of the individual information components and technologies might not be particularly risky. But keeping other countries from obtaining the means of synthesizing all of these would be very important. The issue then would arise as to whether controls could be effectively designed and implemented for the knowledge or method by which a synthesis will occur.

Putting an export-control regime in place for information systems and technologies would not be an easy task, but experience suggests that it is possible. Supercomputers and commercial encryption, which are key components of information-warfare systems, are already controlled as a means of achieving other nonproliferation goals, by the United States and other members of the Wassenaar Arrangement.

U.S. policy calls for a ban on the transfer of the most sophisticated supercomputers and technologies to all countries and prevents certain other supercomputer systems and technologies from being transferred either to nuclear-weapon–related facilities in such countries as Russia, China, and Israel, or to countries that pose a nonproliferation risk, such as India and Pakistan. Difficulties have arisen in ensuring that such controls are observed; witness the recent cases of sales to Russian and Chinese nuclear facilities. And the effectiveness of these controls can be somewhat muted by the linking of computing systems of lesser capability. But U.S. nonproliferation policies are being served by these controls.

Today, the United States also strictly controls transfers of encryption used for military purposes and limits international sales of commercial encryption above certain thresholds.  The policy is extremely controversial, because the knowledge underlying these encryption technologies easily diffuses across national boundaries.  And many do not share the Clinton administration's view that the dissemination of advanced encryption systems poses a threat to U.S. intelligence capabilities and law enforcement.  But the controversy focuses primarily on the utility and effectiveness of the encryption policy, not the ability of the U.S. government to implement its controls, even though they are technically complex.

Designing an export-control system will raise a number of difficult issues.  One would involve decisions about which information systems and technologies to control.  Another would be whether effective controls require that all the critical components of an information-warfare system be covered, or only a few of the most critical.

Take the example of computer software agents (viruses) that could automatically find and destroy certain kinds of instructions in an adversary's surveillance system.  Such agents would be extremely useful in U.S. military operations but would be very dangerous in the hands of terrorists or rogue states.  So controlling their export would seem to be a high priority.  But would it be technically feasible to control such agents? Absent such controls, would the overall export regime be effective?

Export-control regimes are attractive because their focus on individual sales ensures that governments, nongovernmental groups, and individuals are covered.  So another issue that will arise is whether the controls should be global, to avoid any loopholes, or targeted on individual countries or groups, to interfere less with commercial trade.

A large number of countries will have the ability to produce and sell dual-use information systems and technologies, so a successful export-control strategy would require a multilateral approach. Gaining the support of other potential suppliers would be a real challenge.  The Wassenaar Arrangement could provide a forum for assessing the character of the potential threat and its control lists could include specific information systems and technologies.

History suggests that these suppliers will continue to resist any loss of their national sovereignty and will not be prepared to coordinate their export policies, unless an extremely serious threat emerged. But if this were to occur, they might be prepared to coordinate their export-control policies by defining lists of items to be licensed, establishing rules of restraint on transfers, and committing to sharing information on their licensing decisions.

## Multilateral Cooperation

Arms control and export regimes are not only constrained in the kinds of threats they can address but are also extremely difficult to design for the age of information warfare. So the United States is going to need to find other ways to ensure a credible military strategy while reducing its domestic vulnerabilities. One possibility would be to launch an effort involving multilateral cooperation with countries that face similar potential threats. The recent President's Commission on Critical Infrastructure Protection recommended a number of steps that could form the initial elements of such an effort. The commission called for

- an assessment of the characteristics of the risks of information warfare, to reach a common understanding of the potential threats

- the design of protective measures and practices to reduce the vulnerability of the information systems and networks

- the sharing of information and analysis in a timely way on the activities of potential adversaries and unusual happenings in their infrastructures, to be able to respond to potential threats

- steps to deter an attack on critical infrastructures and, should deterrence fail, to cause the attacker to cease and desist

- ways to respond to the basic needs of the populace following a disaster and to restore and reconstitute the infrastructures.[2]

Each country would need to tailor the specific steps to its own particular vulnerabilities. But these steps provide a good agenda for a

---

[2]President's Commission on Critical Infrastructure Protection (1997).

multilateral approach that would prepare for joint actions to respond to the threats if they materialize in the future.

## A STRATEGY DURING THIS TIME OF UNCERTAINTY

Too many uncertainties exist today to be able to decide definitively what role, if any, arms control, export regimes, and multilateral cooperation will play in the age of information warfare. The United States needs, nevertheless, to set the stage for these decisions by taking steps now to reduce the uncertainties, achieve basic understandings about its strategic assumptions, and ensure that, as the systems and technologies are developed, they do not produce instabilities or vulnerabilities.

The first task involves intelligence and analysis. The United States needs to understand more precisely the characteristics and capabilities of future information-warfare systems and the technologies and management skills that will be critical to their development. This would provide a basis for determining who will be able to develop information-warfare systems: only a few governments with an advanced technological base and managerial skills, or any dedicated group anywhere in the world. Under what circumstances and in what time frame will others achieve information-warfare capabilities?

The second task should be for the United States to come to basic understandings about its strategic goals and assumptions with respect to information warfare. What will the characteristics of the threats be? What will U.S. operational military requirements and vulnerabilities in the age of information warfare be? Is superiority a sustainable strategy for the long term? Could the United States be sufficiently confident in the future to base its security on the existence of information-warfare superiority? What risks can be expected to arise for American society?

The United States has an interest in ensuring that the development of information-warfare systems does not lead to global instabilities. So the third task should be for the United States to take steps to ensure that other countries understand U.S. goals and the characteristics of the information-warfare systems that it is developing. Confidence could best be built by early and extensive sharing of information. Engaging the Russians will be particularly important, so that they do not view U.S. programs as a threat to them. This could be done bilaterally or within the framework of exchanges between NATO and Russia. In return, the United States would gain greater understanding of the plans and capabilities of others. Such discussions could also set the stage for more-formal arms-control negotiations and measures, if such a decision is taken in the future.

Export regimes would appear to have a role in preventing the transfer of certain information systems and technologies, irrespective of the specific ways in which the threats will emerge. So the fourth task should be to address how the systems and technologies might be controlled effectively as they are being developed. Among the basic questions that will need to be answered are the following: What critical components in information-warfare systems would need to be controlled: systems, technologies, or management expertise? Can any or all of these be controlled effectively? If so, what is the prospect that the controls would successfully prevent, or at least significantly delay, the development of information-warfare systems by others?

Answering these questions will require cooperation within the United States between the military, which is developing the actual systems; the companies that will be producing and marketing them; and the government officials who will be responsible for their licensing. As success will require support from other countries that will be developing information-warfare systems and technologies, informal discussions focused on these same questions should begin soon.

While the future evolution of information technologies is uncertain, the potential risks to the United States are clear. So the final task should be for the United States to begin to work with other friends and allies to find ways to cooperate in preventing potential threats to their domestic infrastructures.

Carrying out these tasks will prepare the United States for the possibility that arms control, export regimes, and multilateral cooperation will have an important, perhaps even critical, role to play in promoting global peace and stability in the age of information warfare, as they have done in the past.

# REFERENCES

Krauss, Clifford, "8 Countries Join in an Effort to Catch Computer Criminals," *New York Times*, December 11, 1997, p. A12.

President's Commission on Critical Infrastructure Protection (PCCIP), *Critical Foundations: Protecting America's Infrastructures*, October 1997.

# Chapter Thirteen

# ETHICS AND INFORMATION WARFARE

*John Arquilla*

War forms an integral part of the history of mankind, alternately driving civilization forward, then imperiling it. A natural ambivalence toward war has thus developed, with its acceptance as a necessary evil tempered by vigorous, sustained efforts to control its frequency and intensity. Thus, from the dawn of the recorded history of conflict, attempts have been made to craft an ethical approach to war. They break down into two categories: a set of guidelines regarding going to war at all and a set of strictures by which combatants, should they adhere to them, might fight during a war in a just manner. These dimensions of the ethical approach to war have received searching scrutiny. In this early period of the information age, the time has come to revisit these ethical concepts, as new forms of conflict are emerging to test existing understanding of "just wars"—much as advanced information technologies are already requiring a rethinking of a wide range of commercial and criminal laws.

Another reason to devote some attention to ethical issues and future conflict is that, in the mountainous sea of literature on information warfare, little attention has been given thus far to its ethical dimensions.[1] Part of the problem is that information warfare is itself a multifaceted concept—in Martin Libicki's phrase, "a mosaic of forms." (Libicki, 1996, p. 6.) Information warfare is a concept that ranges from the use of cyberspace to attack communication nodes

---

[1] A very thoughtful early discussion of the legal dimensions of information warfare can be found in Aldrich (1996). Also, see Schwartau (1996).

and infrastructures to the use of information media in the service of psychological influence techniques. Because it constitutes such a variety of conflict modes, information warfare poses problems for those who seek out ethical guidelines for its waging.

This subject is of importance to Americans, from civilian and military leaders to the mass public. Information warfare, as it evolves, is demonstrating a growing disruptive capacity, both against classic military command and control nodes and against many elements of the national information infrastructure. Quite simply, the United States, whose society has grown dependent upon advanced information technologies, has the most to lose from a wide-ranging information war—and thus has an interest in preventing its outbreak. A well-informed ethical approach to the burgeoning problem of information warfare may even demonstrate that it is possible, in this case, to do good and to do well. Indeed, an ethical approach to conflict in the information realm may swiftly prove as practically useful and valuable—even when the opponent is a nonstate criminal or terrorist organization—as it is morally desirable.

This chapter draws from historical notions of ethics and war and applies them to the phenomenon of information warfare. First, the key concepts of just war theory are explained, and a functional definition of information warfare is developed. Next, the various ethical formulations are appraised in light of information-age effects on the conduct of warfare. Last, insights are drawn from this analysis, and guidelines for "just" information warfare are advanced.

## CONCEPTS AND DEFINITIONS

A remarkable consistency characterizes thinking about just wars, from ancient to modern times. Thus, nearly three millennia ago, concerns were advanced about the need for an ethical approach to going to war, as well as to waging war. For example, the ancient Greek geographer, Strabo, observed that, in the War of the Lelantine Plain (circa 700 BCE), all parties agreed to ban the use of "projectile missiles" because they constituted an ethically repugnant form of war. The Greeks were also concerned about honoring treaties and conventions and about avoiding undue brutality. (Ober, 1994.) These notions track very closely with the Thomist paradigm, developed in the Middle Ages, which still dominates thinking about ethics and conflict.[2]

## The Concepts of Just War Theory

The key concepts of just war theory fall into the categories of criteria for going to war *(jus ad bellum)* and fighting justly during war *(jus in bello)*:

### Tenets of Just War *(Jus ad Bellum)*

A.  *Right Purpose.* Justifiable reasons for going to war revolve around the concept of self-defense.  Notions of right purpose generally include such ideas as preemption (i.e., striking in anticipation of an oncoming attack), but are less open to the idea that preventive war (i.e., striking at a propitious time) is just.[3]   Also, this category excludes wars of conquest or annexation.

B.  *Duly Constituted Authority.* It is clear from all the literature on ethics and war that a necessary condition for having a just war is that the decision to fight must come from a government—not from an individual.  Wars waged by individuals have always fallen outside the law, the best example being provided by 19th-century prohibitions on the practice of private wars, or "filibusters," as they were then known.

C.  *Last Resort.*  Simply put, war cannot be considered just unless it follows exhaustive pursuit of negotiations and other means of conflict resolution.  A good example of this is given in Thucydides' depiction of the extended crisis-bargaining between Athens and Sparta as both sides sought in vain to

---

[2]See Thomas Aquinas, *Summa Theologica*, especially Book II, Part II.  Ramsey (1961) remains a classic exposition of the Thomist view of just war.  On just war theory during this period, see also Russell (1975).

[3]It should be noted that ideas about "right purpose" in the nuclear era have retained self-defense as an ethical construct, while preemption is viewed as unacceptable— though not without some dissent.  Preventive nuclear war, though seriously contemplated in the late 1940s and early 1950s to preserve the U.S. monopoly on atomic weapons, is very nearly unanimously considered ethically unacceptable.  On these issues, see Rosenberg (1994).

head off the oncoming Peloponnesian War.[4]  The run-up to the Gulf War sounded many echoes of these ancient events.

### Concepts of Just Warfighting (*Jus in Bello*)

D.  *Noncombatant Immunity.*  Wherever and whenever possible, according to just war theory, those waging the war must strive to avoid harming civilians or enemy troops that have surrendered.  Fleeing troops that have no ability to fight (e.g., the Iraqi troops retreating along the "highway of death") fall into a gray area ethically, attacks upon them being allowed— but not encouraged.[5]  Conventional aerial bombing and, later, nuclear war, have posed problems for the notion of noncombatant immunity that remain unresolved.  One attempt to cope with this was by considering air and nuclear attacks on strategic targets as permissible, with civilian losses treated as "collateral." (Walzer, 1977, pp. 255–260.)[6]

E.  *Proportionality.*  There are several aspects to this notion.[7] First, and best known, is the issue of using force in a manner avoiding excessive application.  A second facet, though,

---

[4]Thucydides, *The History of the Peloponnesian War*, Book I, Chs. 1–4. See also Kagan (1994).

[5]On this point, Walzer (1977), p. 129, notes that the rule of thumb is to limit "excessive harm." Yet, he observes that many have argued that this restriction can be relaxed if such action contributes clearly and materially to victory.

[6]Also, it should be noted that strategic aerial bombardment has just as often been used deliberately to terrorize civilians, being considered a key element of deterrence stability and coercive diplomacy. See Quester (1966) and Pape (1995). The willingness of nuclear strategists to accept the likelihood of some "collateral" civilian losses grows, in part, out of the perceived need to strike an adversary in time to disrupt his own oncoming attack (preemption), or to strike early enough that the enemy will not be able even to develop a threatening capability of his own (prevention)—as in the case of the 1981 Israeli raid on the Iraqi nuclear weapon program at Osiraq.

[7]Johnson (1981), pp. xxii–xxiii, observes that the concept of proportionality falls under both *jus ad bellum* and *jus in bello*. In the former case, the author argues that proportionality refers to "doing more harm than good." In the latter, he suggests limits on the kinds of weapons that may be used. For purposes of this study, proportionality is considered as described in E, above, because this captures much of both of Johnson's notions. Further, the idea of doing more harm than good has been considered part of the notion of *jus in bello*, as this is a calculation more possible to make during, rather than prior, to a war—save perhaps with the exception of nuclear war, whose catastrophic consequences for all were never doubted.

might be that this concept requires ensuring that a sufficient proportion of one's forces, relative to the adversary, are employed, so as to enhance the probability of winning. Thus there is a built-in tension between the need for "enough," but not "too much," force. Finally, the term is often used to mean response in kind, or in a tit-for-tat fashion.[8]

F.  *More Good Than Harm.*  This is a concept from the Thomist paradigm. This notion implies, of warfighting, that ethical conduct requires calculation of the net good to be achieved by a particular use of force. An example of such a calculation, though clouded by violation of notions of noncombatant immunity, is Truman's decision to drop the atomic bomb on Hiroshima to avoid a more costly conventional invasion of Japan.

As one considers these ethical constructs, it appears that ideas about the second broad category, just warfighting, might also form part of the calculations for going to war in the first place. Thus, they should all be seen as interrelated aspects of just war theory. However, from an ethical perspective, it seems clear that responding to the *ad bellum* factors must be considered a primary duty of those who would make decisions about war and peace. The *in bello* factors, while related to decisions regarding conflict initiation, should be seen, in ethical terms, as lying within the realm of decisionmakers' secondary duties.[9]

The six facets described above cover most of the conceptual ground, and they should allow for analysis of any latent tensions between duty- and utility-based ethics; the potential for escalation from information warfare to conventional, or even nuclear, war; and the

---

[8]For a modern perspective on the concept of proportionality, see Schelling (1966), who makes the important point that a proportional retaliation for an attack need not use means that are identical to those employed by an aggressor.

[9]The author is grateful to Tora Bikson for pointing out that just war theory, as subdivided above, may be categorized in terms of the classical ethical notions of primary and secondary duty. This notion is apparent in the essays on ethics of Bentham, Kant, and others and is examined in detail in Moore (1993). The notion of duty is also an element in Rawls (1971). However, the conflicts inherent in striving to reconcile sometimes conflicting duties to "fairness" can be considerable, as argued in Alejandro (1997).

prospects for some form of operational arms control.[10]   The need now, though, is to consider how this multidimensional definition of just war theory fits with current notions of information warfare.

## Defining Information Warfare

To consider the ethical dimensions of information warfare, it is first crucial that the phenomenon be classifiable as a true form of war, as opposed to being just a manifestation of criminal or terrorist activity—or an extension of covert psychological operations or intelligence-oriented activities.  With this in mind, it is useful to note that, in the several years since the introduction of information warfare, the concept has evolved and broadened to include activities that, while information-driven, are not considered warfare and therefore do not invoke the ethical concepts of just war theory.

To separate these two classes of activities, a broad view has emerged, in which the term *information operations* refers to the entire range of information-intensive interactions across a spectrum that includes psychological operations; perception management; information security; and, of course, information warfare.  Use of "information operations" thus allows us to reserve the term information warfare for a specific subset of warlike activities, all of which invoke just war theory.

Of what, then, does information warfare consist?  Principally, this form of war concerns striking at communication nodes and infrastructures.  The weapons used in such attacks are generally thought to be those employable via cyberspace (e.g., logic bombs, computer viruses).  However, information warfare also includes the use of a variety of other offensive tools, from conventional explosives to high-power microwave weapons, that can also be used to strike at information-rich targets.

---

[10]Operational arms control consists of constraints on behavior (e.g., on the movement or exercise of troops at certain times and places or the agreement not to use certain types of weapons, such as chemicals, land mines, or dumdum bullets).  Structural arms control refers to limiting, reducing, or eliminating the actual quantities of weapons and, for the present, seems to lie beyond the ability to control in this fashion—given the ease of production and diffusion of information weapons. Yet, technological advances do hold out the prospect for improving surveillance to a point where structural arms control of weapons of information warfare may become feasible.

Attacks on information-rich targets using conventional weapons, while undoubtedly an integral part of information warfare, present few ethical novelties because they have long been a part of warfare. Therefore, this chapter will focus on the ethical implications of the new forms of warfare implicit in information warfare, particularly the weapons employable via cyberspace.

The range of operations that might make use of information warfare extends broadly, from the battlefield to the enemy home front. Thus, information warfare may serve as a form of close-support for military forces during active operations. It may also be employed in strategic campaigns designed to strike directly at the will and logistical support of an opponent. The last notion of information warfare, in which it may be pursued without a prior need to defeat an adversary's armed forces, is an area of particular interest.[11]  In many respects, it resembles notions of the strategic uses of airpower that emerged in the 1920s and 1930s and merits, therefore, close scrutiny from an ethical perspective—much as air warfare was the focus of serious ethical debate prior to and during World War II.[12]

Although it may bear a strategic resemblance to airpower, information warfare has a quite different set of effects and properties. While airpower can generally perform much destruction on fixed points (e.g., in World War II, on U-boat pens and ball-bearing plants),[13] information attacks, even using conventional weapons, inflict far less destruction.[14]  Rather, the effects of information attacks are disruptive, and may occur over wide areas (e.g., knocking out a geographic power grid), even in the face of defensive redundancies emplaced in

---

[11]For an exposition of this view, see Molander, Wilson, and Riddile (1996).

[12]Garrett (1993) provides an excellent summary of the debate about the ethics of airpower. For a good discussion of strategic aerial bombardment as an autonomous tool of war, including skeptical French and cautious British views, see Quester (1966), pp. 50–70.

[13]The discussion here is limited to the effects of airpower using conventional explosives, as opposed to weapons of mass destruction.

[14]"Destruction" should be considered a multidimensional concept. First, there is the physical "burnout" of computers, power lines, system controls, etc. Then there is the erasure or corruption of data. Finally, there is loss of life (e.g., crash of an airliner due to a disrupted air traffic control system) and environmental damage (e.g., an oil pipeline spill resulting from disruption of automated system controls) to round out the concept of destruction.

anticipation of information-warfare attacks. Another difference is that, while strategic aerial bombardment inevitably causes civilian losses, even with today's guided weapons, information weapons will lead to far fewer deaths—despite the widespread disruptive effects. This lower lethality and destructiveness may make the damage done by information-warfare attacks somewhat harder to assess accurately—and may complicate calculations designed to craft a proportional response.

Thus, strategic information weapons have area effects that, in some respects, extend quite a bit further than even weapons of mass destruction—but with "mass disruption" being their hallmark. And it is just this prospect of having wide effects without causing very many deaths or dire environmental consequences that makes information warfare such a potentially attractive form of conflict. Although the existence of these capabilities is the subject of some debate, it is assumed for the purposes of this study that such capabilities either already exist or soon will.

Finally, it is important to note the inherent blurriness with regard to defining "combatants" and "acts of war." In strategic aerial bombardment, it is quite clear who is making the attacks. It is also clear that the enemy combatants are its military forces. This latter notion is relaxed a bit in guerrilla warfare, in which civilians often engage in the fighting. But in information warfare, almost anyone can engage in the fighting. Thus, it is important, from an ethical perspective, to make a distinction between those with access to advanced information technology and those using it for purposes of waging information warfare. Further, the nature of cyberspace-based attacks is such that there may often be an observational equivalence between criminal, terrorist, and military actions. The ethical imperative that attaches to these concerns is the need to determine the identity of the perpetrators of information-warfare attacks and to make a distinction between sporadic depredations and actions that form part of a recognizable campaign in pursuit of discernible aims.

## JUST WAR THEORY AND INFORMATION WARFARE

Armed with the six tenets of just war theory and the pared-down definition of information warfare described above, one may now relate them to each other to determine the extent to which information warfare can be said to be just or can be waged justly. This form of analysis allows for a survey of the ethical issues—and elicits some surprising results.

## Jus ad Bellum

In the realm of going to war ethically, the concept of "right purpose" does not appear to be put under much stress. Self-defense and pre-emption, both allowed under classical just war theory, may have new dimensions because of information warfare, as they may be applied more promptly with disruptive information weapons. The one area that may change is that of the use of force in preventive ways. Under existing just war theory, prevention (i.e., striking to prevent the rise of a threat, like the Israelis at Osirak in 1981) lies on tenuous ground. But information warfare might prove especially useful in derailing the rise of a threatening power—particularly the forms of information attack that might be useful in slowing down a potential adversary's process of proliferation of weapons of mass destruction.

With regard to the second concept, "duly constituted authority," the very nature of information weaponry may introduce new stresses for this long-established ethical concept. For the types of capabilities needed to field an information-warfare campaign—particularly one that is waged principally in cyberspace—there is little need for the levels of forces required in other forms of war. Therefore, the state monopoly on war reflected in the concept of duly constituted authority will likely be shaken, as nonstate actors rise in their ability to wage information warfare. This may be part of an overall phenomenon in which the information revolution is causing a diffusion of power away from states and toward nonstate actors—both peaceful, civil society elements and the new "uncivil society" of information-age terrorists and transnational criminal organizations.[15] Finally, this rise of new nonstate actors capable of waging information warfare may also encourage states to employ them. Indeed, nonstate actors will likely prove useful cutouts that help to maintain deniability, or ambiguity, about the ultimate identity of an adversary. This suggests the possibility that quite weak states may

---

[15]On these issues, see Hoffman (1997) and Williams (1994).

thus be allowed to strike at the strong, given the lessened likelihood that they will be discovered and subjected to retaliation. However, this problem might be mitigated by improvements in cyberspace-based detection, surveillance, and tracking technologies.

This ease of entry into the realm of information warfare not only erodes the strictures against acting without duly constituted authority. It also suggests that the convention regarding going to war only as a last resort will come under strain. For information warfare, though it may disrupt much, at great cost to the target, does little actual destruction—and will likely prove a form of warfare that results in only incidental loss of life. In this respect, information warfare can be viewed as somewhat akin to economic sanctions as a tool of coercion (though probably less blunt an instrument than an embargo). This similarity should also contribute to the erosion of the last-resort principle. However, as with economic sanctions, certain nonlethal parts of information warfare may not be considered acts of war and thus may be exempt from just war considerations—a status that would increase the likelihood of their use but would preserve the integrity of the last-resort principle for actions deemed acts of war.

Finally, in the case that all information-warfare actions are considered acts of war, if information warfare's low destructiveness is coupled with a situation that features self-defensive "right purpose"—say, in a crisis where skillful preemption might head off a general war—the normative inhibition against early uses of force will erode even further.

## Jus in Bello

With regard to the issue of waging information warfare justly, there are also many ways in which the classical concepts will come under pressure. First, one approach to information warfare concentrates on striking an adversary's transportation, power, communication, and financial infrastructures. This must be seen as a kind of war that targets noncombatants in a deliberate manner—because they will suffer from such attacks inevitably and seriously. The purpose of this type of information warfare is to undermine the enemy's will to resist, or to persist, in a particular fight; in this respect, strategic information warfare is very similar to early notions of strategic aerial bombardment that targeted noncombatants.[16]

In the realm of information warfare, it should be noted that, even as planners may be driven to wage a form of war whose effects will be most felt by noncombatants, there is another aspect to strategic attack—one strictly aimed at disrupting the movements and operations of military forces. Information warfare is a sufficiently discriminate tool that making this distinction is possible—and just war theory implies eschewing the targeting of noncombatants and focusing instead upon purely military targets and effects. Thus, an apparently quite attractive coercive tool of force (strategic information warfare) runs hard up against the enduring ethical constraints against attacking noncombatants. This dimension of just war theory may, therefore, pose the most nettlesome policy dilemma—and may require the most creative solution.

Another thorny issue is posed by the just warfighting concept of proportionality, whose major concern is with avoiding the use of excessive force during a conflict. In one respect, the discriminate use of information warfare should make it possible to wage war quite proportionately. That is, it should be possible to respond to information-warfare strikes by some adversary in a very precise, tit-for-tat fashion, neatly calculated and calibrated. However, two problems might emerge that put notions of proportionality under some stress. First, information-warfare attackers might strike at an opponent's critical infrastructures, but have few of their own that could be retaliated against by means of information warfare. This prompts the question of when more traditional military measures—including some amount of lethal force—might be used in response to information-warfare attacks without violating notions of proportionality.

Another problem might arise if the defender, or target, were struck by information-warfare attack and had little or no means of responding

---

[16]See Douhet (1942) and De Seversky (1942). Warden (1989) is a clear throwback to Douhet and De Seversky. On the other hand, nuclear strategists did strive hard to limit noncombatant losses, by developing the concept of counterforce targeting. But this palliative was seen as still allowing massive, civilization-endangering casualties. On this point, see Ball and Richelson (1986).

with information weaponry. Russian strategic thinkers have considered this last issue, with some of their analysts ending up recommending forceful responses—even to the extent of threatening a renewed form of "massive retaliation" with weapons of mass destruction against information-warfare attackers. In this respect, Schelling's suggestion that varied responses can solve one dilemma of proportionality may engender a new dilemma: the asymmetrical retaliatory response may tend toward escalation. A prime example of the sort of problem that can arise is Russian declaratory policy toward information-warfare attacks. As one Russian defense analyst put it recently:

> From a military point of view, the use of information warfare means against Russia or its armed forces will categorically not be considered a non-military phase of conflict, whether there were casualties or not.... considering the possible catastrophic consequences of the use of strategic information warfare means by an enemy, whether on economic or state command and control systems, or on the combat potential of the armed forces. Russia retains the right to use nuclear weapons first against the means and forces of information warfare, and then against the aggressor state itself. (Tsymbal, 1995.)[17]

Thus, Thomas Schelling should be seen as providing some guidance in these issue areas, but his solution poses difficulties and risks. He has noted that proportionality is a reasonable principle, one that need not be considered to require the use of identical weaponry when one is engaging in retaliation. He also implicitly argues that the risk escalatory threats pose is not necessarily credible. See, for example, his assessment of the 1950s U.S. policy of massive nuclear retaliation as a concept that "was in decline almost from its enunciation." (Schelling, 1966, p. 190.) Yet the massive retaliatory threat may be the only credible deterrent that a potential victim of information warfare may be able to pose. Aside from deliberately disproportionate responses, there is also the problem that gauging the comparability of damage done by radically differing weapon systems (e.g., exploding smart bombs versus computer logic bombs) is going

---

[17]Thomas (1997), pp. 76–77, reinforces the point that the Russians see the information-warfare threat as "real, and intensifying" and that one perspective is indeed that "Moscow's only retaliatory capability at this time is the nuclear response."

to prove quite difficult. Finally, the problem of perpetrator ambiguity further weakens proportionate response, because one may simply not have enough data to determine just who is responsible for a particular attack.

The last of the just warfighting issues that must be considered is even more nebulous than notions of proportionality. It consists of the admonition to engage in operations that do more good than harm.[18] However, even if difficult to measure or define, this requirement for ethical calculation of costs versus benefits may be eased by the idea that information warfare requires, and effects, but little destruction and will likely lead to scant loss of life. Unlike the terrible dilemma that faced President Truman—a choice between massive immediate casualties inflicted upon the enemy in the near term, versus perhaps greater long-term losses for Japanese and Americans—information warfare may afford the prospect of a use of force that causes little destruction but that might, used properly, help to head off a potentially bloody war.

## SOME GUIDELINES FOR POLICY

Based on the foregoing description and analysis of the ways in which notions of information warfare interact with just war concepts, it is now possible to think about establishing a general set of guidelines that will help decisionmakers and information warriors behave as ethically as circumstances allow—or at least to recognize and strive to resolve the apparent tension that arises here between utility- and duty-based ethical guidelines. Rectitude aside, it must also be recognized that war is about winning. Therefore, guidance for policy or doctrine must cope with the dilemmas that may emerge as a result of striving to act properly and taking the pragmatic actions that are likely to lead to victory.

A good example of this sort of problem is provided by the ancient Israelites in their (2nd century, BCE) efforts to break free from domination by the Seleucids, the inheritors of one part of Alexander's empire. The Hebrew scripture forbade fighting on the Sabbath—so the Greeks soon learned to attack on this day. The slaughters of the

---

[18]Again, it should be noted that some see this as a *jus ad bellum* issue. See Johnson (1981), p. xxii.

rebellious, but observant, Jews that ensued are poignantly lamented: "Let us all die in our innocence. Leaves and earth testify for us that you are killing us unjustly." As the uprising faltered, one of the wise Jewish leaders, Mattathias, perceived the problem and provided an ethical adjustment, in the nick of time, that allowed them at least to defend themselves without violating God's law: "They will quickly destroy us from the earth. Therefore, let us fight against every man who comes to attack us on the Sabbath day." Thus, just warfighting was allowed on the Sabbath—but only *defensive* operations.[19] Soon, the Maccabees won their freedom.

## Policy Toward Going to War

The first issue engaged, regarding "right purpose," basically boils down to the question of whether the improved capacity for preventive strikes granted by information warfare can overcome the ethical problems posed by offensive war initiation. The ethical problem deepens when it is recognized that preventive war—striking forcefully before an adversary has serious, threatening capabilities—will generally mean going to war before diplomatic options have been exhausted, that is, not as a "last resort."[20] On the other hand, the basically disruptive rather than destructive nature of information warfare suggests the possibility of a "just warfighting" approach to prevention that eases the ethical dilemma.

Simply put, prevention by means of information warfare might be allowable if (1) strikes were aimed strictly at military targets (e.g., command and control nodes), to avoid or generally limit damage to noncombatants; (2) the amount of suasion employed was enough to deter or substantially slow an attacker, without being so excessive as to have dire economic or social effects; and (3) the good done by preventing an adversary from being able to start a particular conflict, or type of conflict, could be said to outweigh the wrong of using force

---

[19]Quotes from 1 Maccabees 2:37–41. This issue was also considered by later Talmudic scholars, notably Gersonides, in his *The Wars of the Lord* (as excerpted in Steinsaltz, 1976). See also the discussion in Steinsaltz (1976), p. 20.

[20]Indeed, the most serious ethical problem with prevention is that the adversary may not even be contemplating going to war, yet he is struck. This dilemma was but one of the considerations—albeit an important one—that led policymakers to decide against striking preventively against either Russia's or, later, China's nascent nuclear capabilities.

beyond the realm of clearly definable self-defense.[21] Thus, *jus in bello* considerations may be seen as mitigating a serious *jus ad bellum* constraint on information warfare.

The second policy concern, that of remaining within the bounds of notions of duly constituted authority, poses little difficulty from the U.S. perspective, or for any state, for that matter—so long as a state actor refrains from employing a nonstate cutout to wage information warfare on its behalf. The problem goes deeper, though, as the very nature of information warfare implies that the ability to engage in this form of conflict rests now in the hands of small groups and individuals—no longer being the monopoly of state actors. This offers up the prospect of potentially quite large numbers of information warfare–capable combatants emerging, often pursuing their own, as opposed to some state's, policies.

Finally, the just war admonition to engage in conflict only as a last resort must also be examined. Here, the previous discussion of prevention is useful, in that early uses of information warfare may, overall, have some beneficial effects and may not do serious damage to noncombatants. Weighed against this, though, are long-standing normative inhibitions against "going first" in war. For policymakers, the answer is most likely that, as in the nettlesome case of duly constituted authority, so with last resort, there is no easily accepted answer. The rise of nonstate actors implies a serious, perhaps fatal, weakening of this just war constraint; likewise, the ease with which use of information warfare may be contemplated suggests that a sea change will occur with regard to notions of "justice" requiring that war always be undertaken as a last resort. Finally, it may prove possible to relax the ethical strictures about last resort if information-warmakers engaging in early use emphasize disruptive acts—avoiding actions that engender significant destruction.

In summary, it appears that policy perspectives on the just initiation of an information war have left a good part of just war theory in tat-

---

[21]In this regard, the oft-stated rationales of war initiators, that they were simply starting the war to "defend" their countries against threats that would soon appear, must be viewed with some skepticism. This is the sort of argument Napoleon advanced, feeling he had to conquer all of Europe to defend France, as did German leaders in the first half of this century.

ters.  Information warfare now makes preventive war far more thinkable (and practical), straining the limits of the concept of "right purpose."  And the manner in which the information revolution empowers small groups and individuals to wage information warfare suggests that the notion of duly constituted authority may also have lost
meaning.  Finally, the ease in undertaking information-warfare
operations, and the fact that they are disruptive, but not very
destructive, weakens the notion that justice requires that war be
started only as a last resort.

## On Just Warfighting

Given the ease with which entry may be made into the ranks of
information warfare–capable states and nonstate actors and the
attractiveness of targets that primarily serve civilian commercial,
transportation, financial, resource, and power infrastructures, the
greatest *jus in bello* concern for information warfare may be the
problem of maintaining "noncombatant immunity."  The number of
actors will be (perhaps already is) large and is hardly subject to centralized control.  The civilian-oriented target set is huge and is likely
to be more vulnerable than the related set of military infrastructures—except to the extent that the infrastructures simultaneously
serve both the military and civilian sectors.  Thus, the urge to strike at
targets that will damage civilians (mostly in the economic and environmental senses, but including some incidental losses of life) may
prove irresistible.  In many ways, information warfare affords the
opportunity to achieve the coercive goals that Douhet and De
Seversky associated with strategic air bombardment—minus the
bloodshed.  Indeed, strategic information warfare appears to lie
somewhere between airpower and economic sanctions on the spectrum of tools of suasion.  It can be far more disruptive and costly to
an adversary than an economic embargo but is less destructive than
bombing—characteristics that may make it a very attractive policy
option.

But the ease of engaging in and the attractiveness of information
warfare must be weighed, for the purpose of policy analysis, against
both the ethical and practical concerns.  The ethical problem is clear:
A significant aspect of information warfare aims at civilian and civilian-oriented targets; also, despite its negligible lethality, it nonetheless violates the principle of noncombatant immunity, given that

civilian economic or other assets are deliberately targeted. In addition to the ethical dilemma posed by information warfare, there is the practical problem that whoever might begin the business of striking at civilian-oriented targets would be inviting retaliation in kind—both from nation-states and from individuals or small groups that are armed with advanced information technology.

The problem is akin to that of the issue of the aerial bombing of cities, as conceived of in the 1920s and 1930s. The air powers of the day were in general agreement—once it grew clear that many would have this capability—that they would avoid striking at each others' cities. Indeed, with only a few exceptions, the warring states at the outset of World War II strove to refrain from deliberately bombing civilian targets.[22]  Indeed the circumstances that sparked a shift, leading to the London Blitz and the Royal Air Force's retaliatory fire bombings of German cities were accidental.[23]  However, once the shift was made, all combatants went about the business of civilian targeting with a will, culminating in the nuclear attacks on Hiroshima and Nagasaki. The trend of targeting civilians deepened, if anything, in the Korean War, at the end of which only one undamaged building stood in all Pyongyang.[24]  But today's technologies are refining the accuracy of air bombardment, making it possible to craft campaigns that do far less damage to civilians or civilian-oriented targets.

No such technological solution appears imminent in the realm of information warfare. There is rather the problem of a diffusion of attack capabilities to many actors who may have the capability to

---

[22]The German *Luftwaffe's* bombings of Warsaw and Rotterdam, the early exceptions, were nevertheless circumstances in which both cities formed part of active enemy resistance to advancing German forces, and held substantial military assets within their boundaries. On these bombings, see Bekker (1968), pp. 55–57, 100–114. On the accidental end of the "no-capital-cities" bombing convention in World War II, see Legro (1995), pp. 134–141.

[23]This had do with a German pilot inadvertently jettisoning his bombs over London when he thought he was elsewhere. Although this "accident" spurred the Germans to begin bombing British cities, senior *Luftwaffe* leaders had been arguing for this expansion of the campaign as a means of forcing the British Royal Air Force to come out and grapple with German fighters. On this, see Keegan (1989), p. 96.

[24]Hastings (1987), p. 268, notes: "Installations in Pyongyang were hit again by massed bomber raids in July and August [1952]. . . . Pyongyang had been flattened, hundreds of thousands of North Korean civilians killed."

mount precise attacks, but perhaps have little incentive to limit their aggression. This implies a practical need to find ways to discourage attacks on civilian-oriented targets. From a policy perspective, there is an initiative that a leading information power, such as the United States, might take: adopting a declaratory doctrine of "no first use" of information warfare against largely civilian targets. It is a simple, straightforward step, but one that nevertheless still allows for information-warfare strikes against military-oriented targets (e.g., operations centers, logistics, and command and control nodes).[25] Further, it allows retaliation in the event that one's own civilian targets have been hit (presuming that the attacker's identity can be ascertained).

The problem of ambiguity regarding information-warfare perpetrators is indeed difficult but is not insurmountable. In the context of war, there is always some purpose to such attacks, and one may add logical inference to the pool of other detection resources in parsing out just who is behind the attacks in question. This may mitigate the problem of ambiguity, which existed in earlier eras—and has been coped with effectively. A good example of dealing with ambiguity is the "phantom" submarine attacks on merchant ships bringing aid to the Loyalists during the Spanish Civil War (1936–1939). Britain quickly inferred that the Italians, supporters of the Fascists, were likely suspects behind these attacks; a retaliatory threat was soon made, despite Italian denials of culpability. The British remained firm, asserting that the Italians would be struck unless the attacks were halted. The "phantom pirate" attacks stopped immediately and never resumed.[26]

---

[25]It is the same, in many respects, as the notion of no first use in the nuclear context. However, in the nuclear setting, this type of restraint was thought to increase the risk of the outbreak of conventional war. Because U.S. power today is preponderant, it is hard to conceive of a no-first-use pledge for information warfare as having the effect of undermining the deterrence of conventional war. The nuclear no-first-use debate is neatly exposited in two short essays. For the view in favor of no first use, see Bundy et al. (1982). The rebuttal soon followed, from Kaiser et al.(1982).

[26]See Thomas (1961), pp. 475–476, who notes that the British retaliatory threat went beyond attacking phantom submarines in Spanish waters, to include all international waters, even Italian territorial waters. The Italian Foreign Minister, Count Galeazzo Ciano, in his *Diaries* (1952), pp. 7–8, observed that this threat, along with skillful British diplomatic maneuvering at the Nyon Conference, put an end to the secret Italian campaign.

The other potential problem with a no-first-use pledge is that it takes away an attractive coercive tool—the use of information-warfare strikes against a potential aggressor's many infrastructures as a means of signaling or deterring attack in some politico-military crisis. Against this benefit, however, one must weigh the cost of participating in a behavioral regime in which such attacks are tolerated—and that would likely do enormous disruptive harm to the richest set of information targets in the world, which are to be found in the United States. Even with a pledge of no first use against civilian-oriented targets, the option of using information warfare against enemy militaries remains—and, properly employed, might prove to be a good deterrent.

Compared to the problems with crafting policy approaches that will cope with the new dilemmas for noncombatant immunity, which are difficult but not unduly so, the policy alternatives in the realms of "proportionality" and acting in a way that does "more good than harm" seem much less daunting. With regard to proportionality, a number of very straightforward options seem available.

First, a good declaratory position on proportionality might extend to a policy by which information-warfare attacks would engender identical retaliatory response—subject, of course, to proper identification of the perpetrator. However, when the attacker does not have a set of information targets large enough for a proportionate response, or has no information-oriented targets, the retaliation might have to take the form of the use of more-traditional military force against strategic targets of the perpetrator. In this case, proportionality may prove complex in the operational phase.

With regard to doing more good than harm, this aspect of just war theory seems still both useful and feasible. The discriminate nature of information warfare should allow a very careful calibration of effects. The only likely difficulty could ensue in situations in which information-warfare attacks do not have the coercive results envisioned. Indeed, it may prove very difficult to predict the psychological effects of such attacks on either elite decisionmakers or mass publics. In this case, if information warfare were used preventively or preemptively and failed in its purpose, it might even be said that an escalation to general war was the fault of taking the information-warfare action in the first place. Therefore, the risks of escalation versus the likelihood that information warfare will head off a conflict must be very carefully assessed before relaxing any notions of "right purpose," "last resort" or "noncombatant immunity."

## CLOSING THOUGHTS

The key points to be drawn from this chapter begin with the insight that information warfare may seriously attenuate the ethics of going to war (*jus ad bellum*).  Secondarily, though, just warfighting (*jus in bello*) issues seem to retain their currency and value.

Policy toward and doctrinal development of information warfare thus need to focus on the latter area, taking special care to avoid encouraging strikes against civilian-oriented targets but giving less consideration—relatively—to proportionality and doing more good than harm.  The last two issues are simply less nettlesome than the burgeoning problem of civilian vulnerability to strategic information warfare.

Information warfare makes war more thinkable.  This seems inescapable—and quite troubling.  Yet it does not require that waging information warfare be either destructive or unjust.  To the contrary, ethical notions of just warfighting will likely continue to provide a useful guide to behavior well into the information age.  This poses the possibility of giving an affirmative answer to James Turner Johnson's question (Johnson, 1984) about whether modern war, replete with all its emerging technologies, can ever be just.

## REFERENCES

Aldrich, Richard W., *The International Legal Implications of Information Warfare*, Colorado Springs:  Institute for National Security Studies, 1996.

Alejandro, Roberto, *The Limits of Rawlsian Justice*, Chicago:  University of Chicago Press, 1997.

Aquinas, Thomas, *Summa Theologica*, Chicago:  University of Chicago Press, 1952.

Ball, Desmond, and Jeffrey Richelson, eds., *Strategic Nuclear Targeting*, Ithaca, N.Y.:  Cornell University Press, 1986.

Bekker, Cajus, *The Luftwaffe War Diaries*, New York: Doubleday, 1968.

Bundy, McGeorge, George F. Kennan, Robert S. McNamara, and Gerard Smith, "Nuclear Weapons and the Atlantic Alliance," *Foreign Affairs*, Spring 1982, pp. 753–768.

Ciano, Count Galeazzo, *Diaries*, London: Methuen and Company, 1952.

De Seversky, Alexander, *Victory Through Air Power*, New York: Simon and Schuster, 1942.

Douhet, Giulio, *The Command of the Air*, Ferrari trans., New York: Coward-McCann, 1942.

Gersonides, Levi, *The Wars of the Lord*, as excerpted in Adam Steinsaltz, ed., *The Essential Talmud*, New York: Basic Books, 1976.

Garrett, Stephen, *Ethics and Airpower in World War II*, New York: St. Martin's Press, 1993.

Hastings, Max, *The Korean War*, New York: Simon and Schuster, 1987.

Hoffman, Bruce, "Responding to Terrorism Across the Technological Spectrum," in John Arquilla and David Ronfeldt, eds., *In Athena's Camp: Preparing for Conflict in the Information Age*, Santa Monica, Calif.: RAND, 1997, pp. 339–367

Johnson, James Turner, *Just War Tradition and the Restraint of War*, Princeton, N.J.: Princeton University Press, 1981.

Johnson, James Turner, *Can Modern War Be Just?* New Haven: Yale University Press, 1984.

Kagan, Donald, *On the Origins of War*, New York: Doubleday Anchor, 1994.

Kaiser, Karl, Georg Leber, Alois Mertes, and Franz-Josef Schulze, "Nuclear Weapons and the Preservation of Peace," *Europa-Archiv*, Vol. 7, Summer 1982, pp. 157–171.

Keegan, John, *The Second World War*, New York: Viking, 1989.

Legro, Jeffrey W., *Cooperation Under Fire: Anglo-German Restraint During World War II*, Ithaca, N.Y.: Cornell University Press, 1995.

Libicki, Martin, *What is Information Warfare?* Washington, D.C.: National Defense University Press, 1996.

Molander, Roger, Peter Wilson, and Andrew Riddile, *Strategic Information Warfare: A New Face of War*, Santa Monica, Calif.: RAND, 1996.

Moore, G. E., *Principia Ethica*, London: Cambridge University Press, [1903] 1993.

Ober, Josiah, "Classical Greek Times," in Michael Howard, Geo. Andreopoulos, and Mark R. Shulman, eds., *The Laws of War: Constraints on Warfare in the Western World*, New Haven: Yale University Press, 1994, pp. 12–26.

Pape, Robert A., *Bombing to Win: Airpower and Coercion in War*, Ithaca, N.Y.: Cornell University Press, 1995.

Quester, George, *Deterrence Before Hiroshima*, New York: John Wiley & Sons, 1966.

Ramsey, Paul, *War and the Christian Conscience: How Shall Modern War Be Conducted Justly?* Durham, N.C.: Duke University Press, 1961.

Rawls, John, *A Theory of Justice*, Cambridge, Mass.: Belknap Press, 1971.

Rosenberg, David Alan, "Nuclear War Planning," in Michael Howard, Geo. Andreopoulos, and Mark R. Shulman, eds., *The Laws of War: Constraints on Warfare in the Western World*, New Haven, Conn.: Yale University Press, 1994, pp. 160–190.

Russell, Frederick H., *The Just War in the Middle Ages*, Cambridge, England: Cambridge University Press, 1975.

Schelling, Thomas C., *Arms and Influence*, New Haven, Conn.: Yale University Press, 1966.

Schwartau, Winn, "Ethical Conundra of Information Warfare," in Alan D. Campen, Douglas H. Dearth, and R. Thomas Goodden, eds., *Cyberwar: Security, Strategy and Conflict in the Information Age*, Fairfax, Va.: AFCEA International Press, 1996, pp. 243–249.

Steinsaltz, Adam, *The Essential Talmud*, New York:  Basic Books, 1976.

Thomas, Hugh, *The Spanish Civil War*, New York:  Harper & Brothers, 1961.

Thomas, Tim, "The Threat of Information Operations:  A Russian Perspective," in Robert Pfaltzgraff and Richard Shultz, eds., *War in the Information Age:  New Challenges for U.S. Security*, London: Brassey's, 1997.

Thucydides, *The History of the Peloponnesian War*, New York: Everyman's Library, 1938.

Tsymbal, V. I., "Concepts of Information Warfare," a speech presented at the conference on Evolving Post–Cold War National Security Issues, held in Moscow, September 12–14, 1995.

Walzer, Michael, *Just and Unjust Wars*, New York:  Basic Books, 1977.

Warden, John, *The Air Campaign*, London:  Brassey's, 1989.

Williams, Phil, "Transnational Criminal Organisations and International Security," *Survival*, Vol. 36, No. 1, Spring 1994, pp. 96–113.

# Chapter Fourteen

# DEFENSE IN A WIRED WORLD: PROTECTION, DETERRENCE, AND PREVENTION

*Zalmay Khalilzad*

The effects of new information technology are all around us. Change is abundant in everything from the computers on our desks to the cell phones in our pockets. For the most part, we welcome these changes and the improvements that they herald in our lives. These changes offer many advantages for the United States, which leads the world in the civilian and military application of information technology. Our civilian sectors already bristle with a dense information infrastructure that offers unprecedented wealth and convenience. Our armed forces lead all other militaries in applying new information technologies to the problem of national defense.[1]

But technical advances are not unmixed blessings. Already, the increasing interdependence of our societal infrastructure and its concentration at unique nodes has created considerable vulnerabilities. Truck bombs against power plants, handheld surface-to-air missiles against civil aircraft, and biological agents distributed over urban complexes are all examples of ways in which terrorists, non-national groups, small rogue states, or peer competitors can directly attack the United States and cause significant damage.

As we wire the world and our lives, we add new vulnerabilities that will be exploited. As a country and a society, we have no desire to stop, or even slow down, the dramatic technological improvements that the information revolution offers. Nonetheless, as we incorpo

---

[1] I am grateful to Jeremy Shapiro for his research support. I would like to thank Harold Brown, John White, Robert Preston, Abram Shulsky, Alan Vick, and David Orletsky for their reviews of earlier versions of this chapter.

rate new systems into our lives and as we become increasingly dependent upon them, we must be prepared to protect ourselves.

The new information infrastructure achieves its economic and social potential through its interconnections. These interconnections may ultimately create a single system wiring together the entire national information infrastructure. Everyone and everything might be wired to everything else. Despite its enormous advantages, the prospect of a single system has brought to the fore the inherent defensive advantages of isolation. The previous isolation of systems meant that it was difficult to attack them remotely and that it was even more difficult to disrupt them all at the same time.

Interconnections create vulnerabilities because they create the potential for attacks, launched from afar, to threaten the U.S. economy, society, and national security. Using information tools, adversaries can threaten to disrupt U.S. economic well-being by attacking key national infrastructures or U.S. military operations and power projection at multiple levels. However, increased reliance on cyberspace is unlikely to make war bloodless. Disrupting our information systems can create physical damage indirectly. But attacks against our information systems need not be used alone; they can be even more effective and damaging if used in combination with some physical attacks—whether by conventional forces and/or with weapons of mass destruction.

The single system is far in the future, but even the current level of interconnection exposes us to potential disruptions that would almost certainly have been impossible a few years ago. U.S. vulnerabilities to disruption may dramatically increase the costs of our military operations and impose important new constraints on U.S. foreign policy. In some cases, the recognition that taking action could involve significant new risks not only to U.S. forces but to the U.S. homeland may undermine U.S. resolve. Had the United States been vulnerable to large-scale disruption by the Serbs or the Iraqis, and given the widespread ambivalence about getting involved in these conflicts, would the U.S. government have taken the action it did in Bosnia and Kuwait? The vulnerability of U.S. allies can make the building and maintenance of coalitions more difficult.

The possibility of massive disruption and more-effective destruction—both economic and military—and the resulting constraints on the U.S. power may embolden hostile actors to challenge U.S. interests. They may offer opportunities for all types of adversaries. Individual hackers or terrorists, substate actors (such as criminal gangs, insurgent groups, or transitional political organizations), rogue states, and peer competitors can use these techniques against the United States in the hope of advancing their various aims.

The persistence and perhaps increase in U.S. vulnerability to disruption is likely to require us to rethink our current definition of national security—defenses against threats mounted from abroad. Dealing with information attacks can result in some merger of the internal and external threats. This in turn will raise many fundamental organizational and legal issues, including ones about relations between the U.S. government and nongovernmental entities, such as our financial institutions. It might well increase tensions between domestic law enforcement and security against external threats. Similarly, there is likely to be increased tension between concerns about privacy and civil rights and concerns about national and personal security. It may also create new missions for the U.S. armed forces. The military already has the task of protecting its own information systems. Might our armed forces also be expected to defend the systems in the civil infrastructure that they rely upon but do not own? What role might they be given in the defense of vital sectors of the national information infrastructure? Will the Department of Defense eventually be responsible for defending U.S. society from information attacks, much as it is currently responsible for defending it from air attacks?

There are a variety of ways for hostile forces to attack our information systems and new methods for such attacks are being developed. Techniques for information attack includes physical destruction, electromagnetic pulse (high-altitude electromagnetic pulse or high-energy radio frequency guns), corruption of insiders and computer intrusion attacks. This chapter focuses on computer intrusion attacks. It begins with an assessment of the threat and the types of attacks that our information system is facing now and might face in the future. It then focuses on the roles that protection, deterrence, and prevention can play in dealing with computer intrusion attacks. At the end, we sketch a comprehensive national strategy for dealing with the changing threat of disruption to our military and society.

## THE THREAT

The information-warfare threat is increasingly real.  Extremely sophisticated information-warfare tools have become freely available over the Internet.  Books have been published around the world on how to use information-warfare techniques.  Now even novice hackers can easily find system vulnerabilities that it once took years of experience and sophisticated training to detect.  While countermeasures to these tools do exist, they require great expertise and awareness to implement.  Indeed, machines with inadequately trained system administrators often exhibit security holes that have been widely known for years.  Given the increased reliance on computer networks in recent years, this disparity between the ease of attacks and the difficulty and delay in adopting countermeasures has led to a dramatic increase in computer crime in recent years.[2]

The global context in which these vulnerabilities reside is very complex.  In contrast with the bipolar situation of the Cold War, now there are many different possible enemies in the form of individual terrorists, various coordinated subnational groups or networks, small (usually rogue) states, and potential peer competitors.  Table 14.1 summarizes the types of actors that might perpetrate information-warfare attacks.

First, there are the individuals who break into computer systems. These fall into two types.  There are those who break in for pure pleasure, for the challenge.  Although illegal, this so-called "gray hat" hacking is quite different from that carried out by "black hats," who threaten to damage for purposes of blackmail or theft of funds or information.  Gray hats are criminals, but they are more akin to vandals than to thieves.  Both gray and black hats can be trusted insiders who gain access through privileged information.

Even though these gray and black hats are motivated by very different incentives, they share an important characteristic: They generally do not have ideological motives and have little interest in upsetting national security.  (Hundley and Anderson, 1995–1996.)  How-

---

[2]See the Testimony of L0pht Heavy Industries in U.S. Senate Committee on Governmental Affairs (1998) for a description of the ease with which current computer security can be penetrated.

**Table 14.1**

**Information-Warfare Actors**

| Type | Subtype | Goal |
|---|---|---|
| Individuals | Gray hats | Mayhem, joyride, minor vandalism |
| | Black hats | Money, revenge |
| Coordinated subnational groups or networks | Ad hoc groups | Mayhem, vendettas |
| | Criminal groups | Money, power |
| | Terrorist (political) | Gaining support for and deterring opposition to a political issue or cause |
| | Terrorist (millennial) | Fear, pain, and disruption |
| | Insurgent group | Overthrow of a government or separation of a province |
| | Commercial organization | Industrial espionage, sale of information |
| States | Rogue state | Deterring, defeating, or raising the cost of U.S. involvement in regional disputes; espionage |
| | Peer competitor | Deterring or defeating the U.S. in a major confrontation, espionage, economic advantage[a] |

[a]Espionage and using information-warfare techniques for economic advantage also apply to many friendly and even some allied governments.

ever, such attackers can directly affect national security if they target national security agencies or critical infrastructure. An individual can create a "virtual mass" with widely distributed, diversely targeted and synchronized attacks. Individual attackers can indirectly threaten national security if they act as "inventors" or pathfinders of disruptive measures that are expanded and adapted by others, including groups with hostile intent against the United States.[3]

---

[3]They also can be helpful through their actions, making systems aware of vulnerabilities and allowing them to be fixed before someone with more malicious intent can break in.

When led by a cause to join together for some purpose, organized gray hats may also be able to cause damage that could have more-serious military consequences. Coordinated groups, therefore, present an altogether different type of threat.

The threat picture becomes more complex when one includes not only small, ad hoc groups but also dedicated organizations that gain information-warfare expertise to attain specific goals. The (possibly apocryphal) Dutch hackers who volunteered to help Saddam Hussein during the Gulf War by mounting information-warfare attacks on the U.S. military would certainly have been engaged in a military action on behalf of a nation-state (albeit as cyberspace guns for hire). Such groups could also be developed or employed by terrorist groups, transnational criminal organizations, or insurgent groups. These groups or other hostile actors might hire cybermercenaries.

Traditional states could develop and use information-warfare techniques. It is not hard to envision, for example, that a country's secret service would have a group of intelligence officers whose goal was to employ information-warfare techniques to gather intelligence on potential opponents (including current allies), for commercial, political and military purposes. An adversary could use the approach in preparation for a possible attack using either physical or information-warfare means. Certainly, many of the attacks on DoD computer systems, documented in a recent General Accounting Office report (GAO, 1996), could indicate an intelligence preparation of the battlefield whose purpose is to map the defense information infrastructure for future exploitation. A foreign intelligence organization might employ skilled individuals, whether gray or black hats, for assisting in using information-warfare techniques for intelligence purposes. Alternatively, it might recruit an insider with knowledge of U.S. military networks.

Coordinated groups and states will likely not use solitary hackers. Rather, they will rely on coordinated and repeated attacks of different agents or massed attacks. They may also demonstrate the capacity to attack several sites simultaneously, denying the defender the ability to concentrate defensive resources. It is important to recognize that the coordination can be done some time in advance and then carried out by autonomously operating attack cells. Decapitating such an organization will therefore not eliminate its capacity to do damage.

In sum, the possibility of damage from multiple, coordinated attacks exceeds the potential damage from individual attackers focused on single targets. (Hundley and Anderson, 1995–1996.) Multiple and coordinated information-warfare attacks would have a greater chance of overwhelming local security measures than lone individuals, unless, perhaps, an insider is involved.

Coordinated groups and states could disrupt U.S. military operations and threaten parts of the U.S. civilian infrastructure. Hostile states may use computer technology to electronically shut down, degrade, corrupt, or destroy the U.S. systems critical for carrying out a particular military operation. The result may be only to delay the operation, but in many scenarios such a delay could have a strategic impact.

States may also attack or threaten to attack U.S. information infrastructure in retaliation for U.S. actions or to deter future operations. As we will discuss in a subsequent section, the "weapons" and tools used could be very diverse and include viruses and logic bombs. A state could use such weapons directly via the Internet or could use agents residing in the United States or a third state. Many of the tools required for information attacks are within the means of groups and even smaller developing countries.

Finally, major regional powers or a putative peer competitor—that is, powers with a substantial information technology expertise—could eventually develop the capacity to attack a large part of, if not the entire, military and civilian national information infrastructures simultaneously. Some might emphasize military targets or civilian targets or both. It is possible that regional powers lacking nuclear weapons and missiles that can reach the United States may place greater emphasis on targeting U.S. civil society with information warfare.

The possibility of a massive information-warfare attack against the United States has been termed "an electronic Pearl Harbor." (Munro, 1995; Graham, 1998.) While that is probably far-fetched at the moment, information weapons in the hands of major regional powers or potential global rivals could eventually become weapons of disruption capable of having a strategic impact on U.S. national security. (Molander, Riddile, and Wilson, 1996.) For example, China might consider the use of information attacks to disrupt U.S. power projection in a U.S.-China military confrontation over Taiwan. The Chinese might believe that such attacks against the U.S. logistics system would delay and perhaps preclude timely American assistance to defend Taiwan in case of a Chinese attack. Other powers may also consider the use of information technology to disrupt U.S. military power projection.

## THE ATTACKS

Conceptually, every information system consists of four types of components: physical systems, transmission systems, software, and data. Each component is critical to the functioning of the information system and is potentially vulnerable to either corruption or disruption. Table 14.2 lists a few types of attacks on each component, although it does not pretend to exhaust the possibilities.

Computer intrusion—the focus of this chapter—can be used to attack the data, software, and even transmission components of an information system. Only the physical components are generally invulnerable to such attacks, and there are exceptions to this rule.

Computer intrusions have gained prominence in recent years because the connection of so many systems to public networks, particularly the Internet, has greatly expanded the available targets and the importance of the data and control functions these systems contain. Such attacks are novel because they can be perpetrated remotely and often covertly. Attackers can use a variety of means to intrude into networked computers. A few common examples from the Internet world follow, but this list is far from exhaustive:

- **Password Attacks**—This is the simple expedient of guessing, or cracking through brute-force techniques, the passwords needed for entry into a computer system. Public-domain programs exist that automatically try all possible combinations or quickly test for words using the entire dictionary. This type of attack is relatively simple to defeat, mostly by ensuring that users choose their passwords carefully. Nonetheless, this is probably still the most common type of attack and is quite often successful in achieving entry into even sensitive computers.

Table 14.2

Information-Warfare Attacks

| Information-System Component | Purpose of Attack | Types of Attacks |
|---|---|---|
| Physical component | Disable or corrupt computer hardware | Prepositioned hardware logic bombs, disruption of power supply |
| Transmission system | Intercept or disrupt communications | Tapping, spoofing, overloading or jamming, computer intrusion |
| Software | Disable, corrupt, or establish control of software functions | Prepositioned software logic bombs, exploitation of bugs, viruses, computer intrusion |
| Data | Destroy, steal, or corrupt computer data | Viruses, computer intrusion |

- **Packet Sniffing**—Internet transmissions travel in small data packets through several intermediate hosts before arriving at their ultimate destinations. Each data packet contains the address of the sender and recipient, as well as the data being sent, which might include credit card information, personal data, or even passwords. Packet sniffers are programs placed on intermediate hosts that intercept and examine passing data packets for interesting bits of information. Packet data can be protected by encryption. However, the hacker can still use the address of the sender and recipient as a precursor to Internet Protocol (IP) spoofing. Packet sniffing is technically difficult to accomplish but is also quite difficult to protect against entirely.

- **IP Spoofing**—Each computer on the Internet is identified by an IP address. IP spoofing essentially means fooling another computer about your computer's identity by sending a fake IP address. False identification may allow the hacker to gain privileged access because the server will falsely believe the hacker to be coming from within the internal network or from another trusted network. False identification may also allow a hacker to hijack a user's communication with the server, intercepting outgoing messages and substituting his own responses. Well-configured systems can guard against most types of IP spoofing, but many fail even to try. Some types of IP spoofing, particularly session hijacking from within trusted networks, are extremely difficult to protect against.

- **Confidence Games**—Hackers often exploit user naiveté to gain system access. Such confidence games usually involve getting users to reveal their passwords or other personal data by claiming to be the system administrator or by providing a false log-in prompt or false Web site. Strict operating procedures and user education will protect against many such con games, but humans, being fallible, will always remain vulnerable to such deceptions.

- **Exploiting Software Bugs**—When two computers communicate for any purpose (to exchange e-mail, to allow Web browsing, etc.), they do so through software programs designed to allow a limited exchange of data but, at the same time, to prevent either user from performing inappropriate operations on the other's machine. However, because data interchanges and allowed operations can be quite complex, many of the software programs controlling intercomputer communications have contained serious bugs. Hackers that discover these bugs can often use them to disrupt operations, steal data, or gain control of machines with which they are legitimately entitled to communicate.

  Such bugs, once discovered, can usually be easily fixed. However, the fixes are often not implemented at particular sites. Moreover, because software evolves so rapidly, new problems are always emerging. Many of the most publicized hacker attacks, including the Internet Worm of 1988, have exploited these types of bugs. Internet browsers, because of their great complexity, widespread use, and rapid development, have proved, and will no doubt continue to prove, to be a rich source of such bugs.

As even this cursory review has indicated, the likelihood of closing off all major avenues of attack is slim. The next section will discuss how a combination of defensive strategies can reduce and manage the threat that these various information warfare actors and attack methods imply.

## STRATEGIES OF DEFENSE: PROTECTION, DETERRENCE, AND PREVENTION

There are three basic strategies for defense against information warfare: protection, deterrence, and prevention. *Protection* seeks to reduce vulnerability by hardening possible targets against attack, minimizing the damage that such attacks can do, and increasing the ability to recover quickly. *Deterrence* implies reducing the incentive of other actors to engage in information-warfare attacks through credible threats of retaliation. Finally, *prevention* means hindering the ability of enemies to acquire, deploy, or successfully use information-warfare weapons and techniques. Protection, deterrence, and prevention are all related. For example, the kind of protection needed will depend to a degree on how well one has succeeded at prevention. Protection is the preferred strategy because, if successful, it permits the psychological and political benefit of living without vulnerability. After protection, deterrence is preferred because it does not require offensive action, except after great provocation. To hinder the acquisition of undesirable capabilities, prevention must also be considered, even though it has some offensive components. To meet all threats, a successful information-warfare defense is likely to need to use all three strategies.

## Protection

Protection measures against information-warfare attack can be taken at both local and national levels.

**Local Protection.** At the local level, protection would involve steps that each potential target, military or civilian infrastructure, must take for its own security. Protection, in this context, means local defense—that is, hardening particular nodes in the information infrastructures in an effort to reduce and perhaps even eliminate vulnerabilities.

Protection involves implementing both technical and nontechnical measures. Technical measures are tools used to secure information systems, akin to a lock on a door. Such tools are numerous and varied but the most common are authentication, firewalls, encryption, audit logging, intrusion detection and monitoring, virus protection, and vulnerability assessment tools. (Denning, 1996.) Rapid advances are being made in all of these areas, spurred by the desire of private-sector computer users to guard against crime and protect privacy. This has had the desirable side effect of enhancing the protection of national security assets. In this way, small-scale intrusions have served to spur an immune system–like response in the infrastructure that can help protect it against larger attacks.

Technical protection measures get the most attention, but they are only as good as the nontechnical measures that support them. Nontechnical measures refer to standard operating procedures adopted to implement technical security measures, akin to a regulation requiring everyone to lock the door behind them when they leave. Most intrusions into computer systems are not traceable to faulty technical means but rather to faulty implementations and procedures. Well-known security holes and improper password procedures persist in many computer systems despite frequent warnings. Individual computer users bear the cost of increased security measures in terms of decreased usability. They consequently tend to resist or ignore cumbersome security procedures until they have personally suffered from lax security.

Issues of procedures, behavior, personnel selection, and monitoring as in counterespionage can help alleviate this problem. Procedures designed to prevent and detect suspicious activity by trusted insiders are the most critical element in any protection scheme. Good technical and nontechnical local security measures are probably sufficient to defend against most potential individual attackers—especially if they are not very skilled.

In theory, perfect protection is possible. In reality, it is unlikely. Local security measures by themselves may not be sufficient against determined and skilled individual attackers, organized groups, and states. Protection may not be sufficient because so many different programs and systems are involved in today's computer implementations that, even given exhaustive security engineering, an unforeseen interaction will eventually occur. Such interactions are, in fact, so common that they have been termed "normal accidents" in other, simpler, domains. (Perrow, 1984.) However, these systems are likely to grow even more complex as they evolve, decreasing prospects for achieving perfect security.

Individual vulnerabilities therefore will persist even with relatively good efforts at local defense. In cyberspace, moreover, individual vulnerabilities can create systemic ones. Just one poorly guarded point of entry can threaten the entire network because, having broken into one system, the intruder can have the security credentials to enter all other similar installations.

**National Protection.** The U.S. government recently initiated a national protection program whose intent is to secure the nation's critical infrastructure from serious attack by 2003. (White House, 1998.) The program emphasizes interagency cooperation for planning, sharing information, and coordinating a government response to infrastructure attacks. It also attempts to establish a public-private partnership to allow coordinated protection of the over 90 percent of critical infrastructure in private hands.

Within the government, a newly created National Coordinator for Security, Infrastructure Protection, and Counterterrorism will chair four separate interagency groups tasked to deal with various aspects of protecting critical infrastructure. Among them, the Critical Infrastructure Coordination Group will coordinate the creation of a sector-by-sector National Infrastructure Assurance Plan. The plan will include a vulnerability assessment, a strategy for mitigating the vulnerabilities, identification of the most critical systems, and a design for the immediate restoration of essential systems.

For operational purposes, the interagency National Infrastructure Protection Center at the Federal Bureau of Investigation (FBI) will gather vulnerability information from all sources, government and private sector; disseminate analyses; and coordinate the governmental response to any information-warfare attack.

The kernel of the government's program is to create what has been termed elsewhere a minimum essential information infrastructure (MEII) that is nearly invulnerable against attack and is easily reconstituted. (Molander, Riddile, and Wilson, 1996.) This means identifying and protecting the minimum mixture of information systems necessary to ensure the nation's continued functioning in the face of an information-warfare attack. The MEII could include the systems that DoD uses for essential activities but does not own, as well as other networks that are vital for the nation. MEII components would be required to take extraordinary measures, both technical and nontechnical, to ensure their security and ability to recover quickly from attacks.[4]

---

[4]An alternative to a protected self and an unprotected "other" is a series of different levels of protection.

The MEII would simplify the problem of systemic defense by nailing down specifically which elements of the vast information infrastructure merit defending. Protecting this smaller target should be easier than attempting to defend all systems nationwide.

The idea of an MEII implies that the essential elements of the information infrastructure, be they in public or private hands, can be identified, hardened against attack, or isolated from possible contamination by the rest by having, for example, a separate communication network for them. Unfortunately, separating the MEII from the rest of the domestic systems presents some inherent problems and difficult choices.

The information infrastructure achieves its economic potential through vast interconnections. These connections create interdependencies between elements of the infrastructure—interdependencies that are not always apparent. As the interconnections grow exponentially, as they have done recently, defining these cascading dependencies becomes ever more difficult. It seems likely that, having traced through all of the interconnections and dependencies in the infrastructure, the MEII might not be so minimal after all. An MEII that encompasses the majority of the information infrastructure would not have greatly simplified the task of defense.

Without separation, the MEII can be hardened against attack through stringent local defense, perhaps involving some government role. The government could affect the local defenses by means of rules and regulations intended to encourage owners to reduce their infrastructure's vulnerability. In addition, the government could periodically test the security system of essential infrastructure by red team–type exercises.[5] When weaknesses are identified, Washington could insist on solutions. The government could also insist that essential systems have the ability to recover quickly from attack should defenses be defeated.

Even if an MEII is created, it must be understood that protection measures are not one-time events; they must be updated frequently as both the threat environment and the underlying infrastructure

---

[5]The Joint Chiefs of Staff and the National Security Agency recently conducted one such red team operation, code-named Operation Eligible Receiver. It revealed substantial vulnerability in both the civilian and military infrastructure. See Gertz (1998).

change.  In recent years, information systems have demonstrated an extraordinary level of dynamism.  In effect, they are continually undergoing a process of change, making them quite difficult to protect or attack.  The offense-defense race for advantage in these dynamic information systems will continue without end.  Windows of vulnerability will inevitably emerge; the key is to adapt faster and safer.[6]

**Beyond Protection.**  Despite their limitations, measures of protection can reduce vulnerability.  Protection must be emphasized as a central pillar of any national strategy.  Defensive measures would have to be updated, because the race between efforts at protection and offensive measures is likely to continue.  However, even adaptive, local, and national protective measures are unlikely to be adequate, especially for defending against major powers and even skilled nonstate organizations.  In this sense, then, the situation may ultimately resemble the one the United States faced in the late 1940s and 1950s, when the Soviet Union developed nuclear weapons and intercontinental delivery vehicles:  a vulnerability against which no protection seemed good enough.

At that time, we responded by developing a strategy that focused on the threat rather than the vulnerability.  That is to say, we focused on deterring the Soviet Union from using these weapons, rather than foreclosing our vulnerability to them.  This approach resulted in the doctrine of nuclear deterrence.  Although we could not protect ourselves, we could build a retaliatory force that would be capable, even if we suffered a surprise all-out attack, of surviving the attack and being able to deliver a devastating blow against the Soviet Union successfully.  In addition, we could make it credible that, if attacked, we would indeed respond in such a manner; if nothing else, we could convey the sense that, once the Soviets had attacked our country with nuclear weapons, the President would have no choice but to respond in kind.  The result was a deterrence strategy considered so robust that, for most of the Cold War, it was a matter of national policy not even to *try* to build defenses against ballistic-missile attack.

---

[6]A trend toward safer adaptation can be observed in the growth of antivirus software and in corporate security services.

However, the analogy with nuclear weapons and mutual assured destruction is imperfect. The effects of a massive nuclear attack, at least the primary effects in terms of blast, thermal damage, and fallout, were fairly calculable and therefore fairly predictable. The effects of information attacks are much more complex. As a result, the kinds of calculations that were involved in theories of deterrence, mutual assured destruction, and counterforce are considerably more difficult in the case of information warfare. Also, calculations about how a strategic nuclear exchange would unfold were rather similar in the United States and the Soviet Union. Some military and even political leaders on both sides might have talked about prevailing, but in the end, the political leaders knew better. The outcome of all-out information warfare is much less obvious. In the case of nuclear war between the United States and the Soviet Union, both sides had enormous overkill capabilities against urban industrial targets and, in the end, completely inadequate counterforce capabilities. The People's Republic of China claimed at one point to be less vulnerable because it was much less an urban-industrial society. How all of this is likely to play out in terms of information warfare, with respect to both relative vulnerability and relative capability, is much less clear

## Deterrence

Despite the differences between nuclear weapons with mutual assured destruction and information warfare, should a deterrence strategy become a major component of our approach against strategic information-warfare threats? Given the differences between the information-warfare and nuclear threats, how useful is the nuclear deterrence paradigm? (Thomas, 1997; Harknett, 1996.)

Some Russian military analysts, who see the Russian defense establishment as far behind in both information-warfare technology and techniques, have hinted that Russia would retaliate against a strategic information-warfare attack with nuclear weapons. (Thomas, 1996.) Essentially, such a policy demonstrates a belief that information-warfare attacks can be deterred, as nuclear attacks were during the Cold War, by threats of massive retaliation. Whether such a linkage is credible is another question.

Deterrence requires several elements that are quite difficult to achieve in an information-warfare context. First, there must be a clear declaratory policy that specifies what punishment an aggressor can expect if he carries out a particular unacceptable behavior or attack. Next, we must have the ability to identify an attack and the attacker and the ability and willingness to respond in ways that cause unacceptable damage to the attacker. Finally, deterrence requires establishing the credibility to retaliate in the eyes of the prospective adversary.

Given these elements, a deterrence strategy might work. But we are not there yet with regard to information attacks. The threat is evolving, and a broad understanding of it has not yet jelled. Not surprisingly, the United States lacks a declaratory policy about information attacks. It is not clear whether one is even seriously under consideration. Would we adopt a strategy of "mutually assured disruption"? A deterrence strategy in the information-warfare context has serious limitations but might be useful, especially against a major power or a peer competitor capable of launching a massively disruptive information attack on the United States.

**Identification of an Attack.** During the Cold War, much effort went into developing the ability to identify a Soviet nuclear attack correctly. Early-warning systems were built to detect the launch of Soviet missiles and the trajectory of delivery vehicles heading toward the United States. Systems were also put in place to confirm or deny that an attack had taken place. Nevertheless, there always was some danger of false warning caused, for example, by equipment failure, sunspots and other natural electromagnetic phenomena, or human error. There was also a concern that a Soviet attack might begin with destruction of U.S. early warning systems or bypass them by use of certain exotic possibilities, such as "suitcase" bombs brought into the United States and used against our command and control centers.

At present, the situation with respect to information attack is very different. Indeed, determining whether a malfunction is an attack or a "glitch" is a major problem. For example, if the problem is traced back to a programmer's error, we would have to try to determine, using the entire panoply of intelligence and investigatory techniques, whether the error had been intentional or not; it might never be possible to come to a definitive conclusion. Even where it is possible to determine malicious intent (e.g., one can demonstrate that a virus has been transmitted to a machine from the outside), it may be difficult to determine whether the hacker was trying to cause major damage or was just fooling around. For example, a November 1988 attack on the Internet, mounted by a computer science graduate student at Cornell, caused major slowdowns but was apparently intended as a harmless experiment that went awry due to a miscalculation. (Markoff, 1990.)

The important point here is that glitches of various sorts are daily occurrences, some are more serious than others.[7] For a deterrence strategy to work, we would have to be able to identify which attacks were deliberate and which were mere mistakes.

**Identification of the Attacker.** Even after an incident is identified as an attack, one must determine its source before one can retaliate. For a good part of the Cold War, this was not a major problem, since there was only one hostile country that possessed nuclear weapons. China's nuclear program complicated the problem somewhat, although as long as the threat was limited to intercontinental ballistic missiles, that problem was expected to be resolved by technical intelligence means that could identify the missile trajectory. A submarine-based threat could make things more difficult, requiring that one maintain a constant awareness of the locations of all potentially hostile ballistic-missile submarines (SSBNs).[8] Indeed, in contemplating the "N-country" problem, some theorists felt that it would be necessary to develop "signatures" that could determine, once a nuclear detonation had occurred, which country's device it had been.

In the case of information warfare, this is likely to be a much greater problem. It is often very difficult to determine the source of an attack. A clever attacker can use a series of intermediate machines, which makes it hard to trace the attack back to its ultimate source. The problem might become easier if the attack is massive and sustained—the kind that is likely to do the most damage. However, a hostile country could complicate things for the United States by

---

[7]An example is the AT&T programming error that closed down most of its long-distance telephone capacity for ten hours on January 15, 1990. This malfunction cost AT&T more than $75 million. (Lee, 1991.)

[8]It would not be enough to know a hostile country's habitual SSBN patrol areas, since the attacking SSBN could try to infiltrate another country's area precisely to deceive us.

basing its information warriors on someone else's territory or even in the United States itself; similarly, it could employ foreign nationals to conduct the attacks. Software production is now a global industry; parts of the computer code that control the flight systems of a new airliner being built in Washington State or Toulouse, France, may be written in India. If, several years later, a plane crashes because of a logic bomb, tracing its source may be well-nigh impossible. Although, as will be discussed below, the potential for improving the ability to trace information-warfare attacks exists, the situation is quite bad today and is likely to present large problems for some time to come. More importantly, deterrence depends on the attacker perceiving that he can be identified.

Identifying all attacks in a timely and accurate fashion is likely to remain a major problem both for deterrence and defense. Identifying smaller attacks is likely to be particularly difficult. This problem is likely to remain similar to tracing the source of terrorist attacks. This is the one area in which the problems of applying a deterrence strategy are fairly easily managed, although there may be some difficulties here as well. If we identify a state as the source—direct or indirect—of an information-warfare attack, we could easily retaliate using physical or information attacks of our own or both. While proportionality of response will always be a concern, the United States could certainly justify and carry out physical destruction of enemy information-warfare sites, such as headquarters.

If the source of the attack were a state capable of delivering a nuclear strike against us, we might limit our retaliation to information-warfare means, to avoid dangerous escalation. This might be adequate, although, as the society most dependent on information technology, we probably have more at stake in information-warfare attacks than any other country. Therefore, an adversary that is not as dependent as we on information systems may not be deterred from attacking us with information warfare if it believes that our response will be only to attack its information systems. Such an adversary may judge that the result would be advantageous to it. On the other hand, we might be able to put our technological lead to use by mounting more disruptive attacks on others than they can mount on us or by taking steps to blunt the effects of their attacks. These possibilities could reinforce deterrence against a power that is less dependent than the United States on information systems.

Against nonstate actors, we might be affected by legal constraints, especially if the individuals operate from the territory of allied or friendly nations (or from our own). If we were forced to proceed against individuals by means of criminal prosecutions, there would be a danger in some cases of having to divulge the sources and methods by means of which we identified the source of the attack. This is part of the more general and difficult issue of law enforcement and national security.

**Will to Retaliate.** Deterrence requires a potential attacker to be convinced that, if he attacks, retaliation will follow. In response to anything but the most massive disruptive attacks, there are likely to be significant problems in conveying this belief.

First, there is the credibility problem. As noted, information warfare–like situations occur every day. Computers mysteriously fail; air traffic control systems seize; and new viruses appear. Many of these situations result from malicious activity rather than accident, although attaining complete knowledge about which is which is essentially impossible. Thus, even if we were determined to respond to every identified attack, there would still be many cases in which we did not respond, either because we regarded the situation as an accident, were not sure whether it was an accident or an attack, or could not identify the attacker.

To put the matter as starkly as possible, there are likely to be hundreds of cases a year—especially minor ones—of information-warfare attacks not leading to retaliation; during the entire Cold War, there was no nuclear attack to test this proposition. Related to that distinction, it was possible to establish in people's minds (whether or not the idea was true) that the nuclear "threshold" was an awesome one; cross it, and there is no telling what will happen next. The information-warfare threshold is crossed every day; so far at least, very few people are the worse for having violated it.

In most cases, the situation is more similar to crime and terrorism than to nuclear confrontation. Crimes are committed every day; some perpetrators are caught and punished, but many others are not. Partly as a result, terrorists can easily believe that they, too, will get away with their criminal activities. However, if the attackers can be identified, the threat of getting identified, caught, and punished can work as a deterrent.

The longer it takes to identify the attacker and to administer the resulting punishment, the less the deterrent effect, both psychologically and practically. As a psychological matter, criminologists tend to agree that swiftness of punishment is crucial. As a practical matter, the perpetrator could have reason to hope that intervening events might dull the impulse toward retaliation. Political circumstances can change. For example, if we now found out that Yasser Arafat were responsible for a terrorist act that had long gone unsolved, we would not retaliate against him. The attacker can hope to "counterdeter" the retaliation: Having shown his ability to mount an information-warfare attack, he can credibly claim that he will mount another if we retaliate for the first one. If a long-enough period has transpired since the initial attack, this might have some political effect.

Finally, there is the issue of the will to retaliate effectively. During the Cold War, it was hard to imagine that the Soviet Union would attack us with nuclear weapons unless it meant business. Thus, it was plausible to say that any nuclear attack would be met with a nuclear retaliation.[9] Of course, there were serious questions whether we would attack the Soviet homeland with nuclear weapons in case of a limited Soviet nuclear attack against a military target on some U.S. ally. With information attacks, the factors affecting the U.S. response might get both easier and more difficult. Unlike nuclear attacks, information attacks may not be regarded as tantamount to all-out war and therefore the threat of a massive response may not be taken seriously.[10]

On the positive side, in case of an information attack, except against a peer competitor, the balance of power should favor the United States. This should lend credibility to any U.S. declaration that it would respond to an information attack on its homeland. With regard to a peer competitor, the response strategy would have to be

---

[9]Although even in this case, the inherent weakness of deterrence strategy led to the development of "war fighting" variants, etc.

[10]Whether we would have actually responded—or whether it would have made sense for us to respond—massively against Soviet industrial and population centers in case of a limited Soviet nuclear attack was hotly debated among deterrence theorists. Some argued that a mutually assured destruction posture lacked credibility because our response would have resulted in our own destruction, as well as the destruction of the Soviet Union.

informed by the dangers of escalation to an all-out war including the use of nuclear weapons.

**Credibility and Certainty.** For deterrence to be a viable strategy, therefore, the potential attacker must have strong reason to believe that he is likely to be caught and to be punished with a devastating response. Otherwise, he may blunder into an attack that brings down a devastating retaliation on his head. For effective deterrence, we must be able to convince a potential attacker that, if he were to attack us, we would know that he did it. Improving our ability to the point of high-confidence perfection in identifying the source of attacks is critical. The technical means for tracing the source of attacks are improving. But unless it improves enough that potential attackers can be convinced that they will be identified, deterrence will be problematic.

Similarly, we have to be able to convince potential attackers that we can launch devastating retaliation to information warfare—with our own information-warfare or non–information-warfare attacks. Relying on the threat of information-warfare attacks for our response can involve potentially insurmountable problems. Suppose, for example, that we devise a clever information warfare means of shutting down all communications in a potential adversary's capital. Can we convince that country without providing some indication of how we would go about it? And if we did, would we not be giving the adversary some clues about how to thwart us? No such problem arose with respect to nuclear retaliation; the Soviets already knew we had nuclear-armed bombers and intercontinental and submarine-launched ballistic missiles. This knowledge did not appreciably help them defend themselves—but it did cause them to spend enormous amounts on air defense and anti-ballistic missiles (which almost surely would not have worked).

**Mutually Assured Disruption?** The problem that nuclear deterrence strategy was meant to solve was that a known adversary had a known way to apply a tremendous destructive power against which we could not protect ourselves. We used the fact that we had a similar capability to establish a deterrence relationship, which, whatever its theoretical difficulties, worked.

Although deterrence should play a role in our strategy for dealing with major information-warfare attacks, the analogy with nuclear deterrence is not a perfect fit. In information warfare, deterrence will be particularly useful in defending against a massive attack. A peer competitor or other sophisticated state actor with a large offensive information-warfare capability could threaten a massive disruption of American society. A series of coordinated attacks across the national information infrastructure, from the electrical power grid to the air transport system, might have the effect of paralyzing the nation for a significant period. Because only a very limited number of countries would have both the capability and motivation to mount such an attack in the face of serious U.S. defense efforts, the attacker could probably be identified. Such a nation would, moreover, have many lucrative information-warfare targets of its own. Because this attack would entail massive disruption of U.S. society, the idea that the United States would respond in kind should be credible.

At present, however, there is no peer competitor and probably no state actor capable of launching such an attack. (Deutsch, 1996.) At present, we have an asymmetric dependence on information in comparison with almost everyone in the world—especially with some of the Third World states that are hostile to the United States, such as Iran, Iraq, Libya, and North Korea. In such cases, deterrence could be based on use of conventional military force and could be tailored to specific opponents. The declaratory policy could emphasize the certainty of punishment but could be deliberately somewhat ambiguous with regard to extent and means.

In most other circumstances, especially attacks involving individuals and groups, a better paradigm for thinking about information warfare might be terrorism and crime. Here, the relevant deterrence may be the one practiced by the criminal justice system, rather than deterrence according to the nuclear model. In the latter case, the phrase "if deterrence fails" was ominous indeed, since it implied the need to unleash a retaliatory capability that could destroy civilization.

Nevertheless, the national aim should be to signal to potential information-warfare attackers that there is a serious chance that we will catch them and that they will be punished, especially if they launch a big attack that has significant consequences. At present, with our limited detection capability, there is little possibility that such a concern would deter anything but the extremely large attacks, since we suffer small information-warfare attacks all the time and have almost never retaliated. As our detection capability improves and as we retaliate effectively against an information-warfare attack, we might gain the benefit of some deterrent effect. However, a deterrence strategy will not be fully effective in every case as long as some potential attackers believe

a.  that they can disguise their attacks as accidents

b.  that their attacks can be conducted anonymously

c.  that the level of damage can be kept below our response threshold

d.  that, by the time we identify the source of the attack, other factors will have intervened.

## Prevention

There is an additional concept of information-warfare defense that could be useful against the middle-level threats that coordinated groups and small states can present: prevention. In this context, prevention means hindering the ability of such enemies to acquire, deploy, or successfully use information-warfare weapons and techniques.[11]

In terms of limiting the ability to acquire information-warfare capability, the U.S. government currently restricts the export of some information-warfare–related technologies, such as cryptographic systems and software, and limits the dissemination of information-warfare–related information. However, limiting the spread of capability will be very difficult. Computer and communication technologies have already spread throughout the world. Essential knowledge about computer operating systems and programming is also widely available outside the United States.

However, another important approach can be measures to prevent or limit the deployment and use of information-warfare tools. This approach can involve developing a capability to preempt or thwart an attack against the United States. Preventing the deployment and use of information-warfare weapons requires having

---

[11]This section is based on work by former colleague Douglas Merrill.

1. the ability to identify potential attackers
2. a concept of warning in the information-warfare context to determine when an information-warfare attack is imminent
3. an offensive information-warfare capability both to collect information about potential attackers and to respond in a preemptive manner to warnings of imminent information-warfare attack.

Meeting these requirements will not be easy. Each requirement presents major challenges.

**Identify Potential Attackers.**  We have already discussed the problems with acquiring the ability to identify the attacker.  One possible procedure for identifying attackers is to follow their traces back through cyberspace.  This process involves noticing an attacker on one's system and finding the attacker's entry point into the system.

To track the attacker, the defender needs access to intermediate machines that the attacker might have used while traces of the attacker are still present.[12]  Tracing an attacker back to the initial machine requires expertise on the part of system operators, organizational capacity to respond quickly to an intrusion, and international cooperation. (Johnson and Nissenbaum, 1995.) We could train system operators to perform this backtracking, but this would place a significant new load on them. (Perrow, 1984.)

Another limitation of relying on local system administrators to backtrack is that doing so does not provide a strategic overview of the situation.  Individual system administrators will have difficulty integrating information from the various different sources that would be affected in a broadly based information-warfare attack.

A national intelligence effort can provide this coordination.  However, the idea of such a national intelligence effort raises many difficult legal issues, including privacy and intelligence-oversight issues. Nonetheless, because individual system operators cannot integrate

---

[12]Once a tracer knows the machine from which a particular attack is based, a more complex process of physically locating the hacker can begin.  It is worth noting that, for example, a hacker could use a dial-up long-distance phone line to attach to the first machine.  Thus, knowing the initial machine is not necessarily the same as knowing the physical location of the attacker.

all the different information, a set of procedures would be needed to enable various national and civilian actors to interact so that effective assessments of the breadth of an attack can be made.

The President's decision to expand the FBI's National Infrastructure Protection Center (NIPC) into an interagency focal point for gathering information and coordinating a government response is an important step in this direction. (White House, 1998.) However, the private sector is not participating in the NIPC. Since the private sector owns and operates much of the critical infrastructure, a way needs to be found for it to interact with NIPC.

In the end, however, even national integration of this information, while an important first step, is unlikely to be enough, because cyberspace does not recognize national boundaries. Ultimately, international cooperation akin to the measures being taken at the national level might have to be considered.[13]

**Warning in an Information-warfare Context.** A crucial component of a prevention strategy against information-warfare threats is the warning that an information-warfare attack is imminent. Without warning, there is no possibility of preemption and therefore none of prevention. The location and type of potential trouble are very complex in an information-warfare context. What constitutes an indicator that a concerted information-warfare attack is about to be undertaken? Pinning down a measure that can answer this question effectively is very difficult. One reason this is so very hard to do is that an "attack" by an adversary using information-warfare techniques need not originate from within that country's territorial boundaries. An adversary's information-warfare operatives can launch an attack from a neutral country, an ally, or even from within the United States itself.

Information-warfare warning is especially hard because the basic capability to engage in information-warfare activities is so widespread. Internet access would be the primary barrier to entry to the information-warfare arena, but most of the world now has Internet access, at least to a limited extent. Thus, almost every nation on earth contains potential threats to U.S. interests. It is almost impos-

---

[13]See the Davis, Chapter Twelve in this volume, for a discussion of the possibilities for multilateral cooperation on this issue.

sible to keep watch over every nation using traditional human intelligence-gathering techniques—there is simply too much information to process. Thus, we need to develop automated tools to support the intelligence process.

What would constitute an actual warning signal that an information-warfare attack is under way or imminent? Are there information-warfare–only indicators that could be developed on the analogy of conventional military indicators?

The case of one nation-state attacking another to gain territory with information warfare only is very unlikely. Therefore, preparations for conventional attack can also be taken as a warning of information-warfare attack. Information-warfare operations alone are not good at taking ground—but they can help make opposing forces less effective. However, once a country has taken over the territory it is seeking, it might try to rely on offensive information warfare to deter the victim's powerful friends from getting involved to retake the occupied territory. Iraq, for example, might have tried to stop or disrupt U.S. deployments and operations in the Persian Gulf if it had had the capability for offensive information warfare and had used it by attacking military targets or important civilian targets that the military used, such as the U.S. telephone system.

Nonstate actors may not offer traditional warning. Since such groups are organized differently from nation-states, they have fewer resources for developing traditional military options. These groups therefore are unlikely to coordinate information warfare with (observable) traditional military means but could combine it with physical terrorist acts. The United States could face information-warfare threats without non–information-warfare warning. Can information-warfare–only indicators be developed?

One warning of a conventional attack is the sudden massing of troops, or an increase in the average activity level of a country's troops. Similarly, a sudden change in the amount of network (i.e., Internet) traffic from a country could indicate something is about to happen. For example, an increase in Internet Control and Message Protocol packets[14] coming from a country could indicate that the

---

[14]Machines on the Internet use these packets to determine network structure.

country was trying to gather data about other hosts on the Internet as potential targets. On the other hand, such an increase could indicate the presence of several new hosts and routers on that country's segment of the Internet. Telling the difference requires other sorts of intelligence about the country's intentions. This "other intelligence" would presumably be data on the country's goals and needs—traditional targets of human intelligence-gathering.

A sudden increase in the number of viruses being spread through the Internet could be another indicator of possible information-warfare attack. An opponent could conceivably use viruses to prepare the battlefield by rendering military and key civilian systems inoperable at critical times.

A sudden increase in computer intrusions may provide some warning of an attack. Before such an attack could take place, any country would have to engage in extensive "intelligence preparation of the battlefield" to determine which targets were most valuable and which were most vulnerable. This information-collection process might take place over the course of a long period, but it would undoubtedly intensify after the decision for an attack had been made.

All of these warnings are overly general and not deterministic. In and of themselves, none of these warnings provides sufficient information for definitive action to be taken, because any or all could be symptoms of something besides potentially hostile information-warfare intent. They must be considered in concert by someone capable of assessing the warnings from all sources. The NIPC might eventually become capable of this task, but it will first need to be able to integrate information quickly about attacks on critical infrastructures in both the public and private sectors. Finally, these more- or less-passive warning systems, given their limited precision, must be supplemented by more-intrusive techniques for gathering intelligence and achieving warning.

**Use of Offensive Techniques.** To gain the level of certainty necessary for preemption, passive warnings will need to trigger a series of more-active measures to determine more precisely the likelihood and source of the attack. One such active measure could be the selective use of offensive information warfare.

When a vague warning is received that an entity might be engaged in information-warfare activities, targeted intelligence gathering would be required to verify the information. Some of this will need to be gathered by human intelligence, and some can be gathered by signals or other technical intelligence-gathering methods. However, some information-warfare techniques can serve an intelligence function.

For example, once one suspects that a particular machine might have been used for an attack against the United States, one might be able to insert a code into the suspect group's machine to perform intelligence gathering on line. Such a code, for example, could make a special record of outgoing connections to systems, particularly those within U.S. domains, and periodically send them to a U.S. intelligence officer. This officer then compares them to tactical warnings of break-ins.

Such warning measures will need to be supplemented by sensitizing traditional intelligence-gathering mechanisms, particularly signals intelligence and human intelligence, to information-warfare indicators. The intelligence community will need to understand that indicators of information-warfare activity that come from such covert channels will need to be integrated with these other warning signals, perhaps in a forum outside the intelligence community.

**Offensive Information Warfare Can Be Exercised in Response to Warnings.** The final step in a prevention strategy is to disable the enemy's ability to carry out a planned attack. If intelligence can provide a reasonably accurate mapping of the location and intent of a potential attacker—as we have seen, this is a very demanding task—he can be quite vulnerable to either offensive information warfare or conventional attacks to disable his systems. In information warfare, as in modern conventional warfare, the most difficult problem is finding and identifying the target. Once those tasks are accomplished, most targets can be successfully attacked.

One potential problem in this regard, however, is training. Like all high-tech weapons, extensive training is required to use offensive information-warfare weapons. It matters little how advanced a weapon is if its operator is not trained to use it. Untrained or inadequately trained operators make mistakes; in wartime, this costs lives.

For traditional weapons, military services try to arrange live-fire training whenever possible to ensure that warriors know what will happen when they use a weapon.

Each of the U.S. military services spends many millions of dollars developing skill training and giving military personnel the opportunity to engage in warlike activities. For example, the U.S. Army uses the National Training Center at Fort Irwin, Calif., to train soldiers, and the Air Force uses exercises, such as Red Flag. Part of what made the U.S. forces so dominant in the Persian Gulf war was their training system. (Biddle, 1996.)

These exercises appear to provide great benefits. Field exercises, such as those the Air Force conducts at Hanscom Air Force Base, are also important. But a lot more needs to be done:

1. Exercises bringing together intelligence officers and operators are critical. Field commanders will be a major information-warfare target in any conflict. They must become proficient in operating and responding in an information-warfare environment.

2. Attracting, training, and keeping good technical people with skills relevant for information-warfare operations are also very important. The system does not do this well; because of increased competition from the private sector, this is a growing problem.

3. Our military services need to address directly how information warriors will be trained for both defensive and offensive operations. It is possible that intelligence gathering can provide vital training on the offensive information-warfare techniques.

Prevention strategies can be useful when applied against a reasonably limited set of hostile actors. The reason for this is that prevention is too information intensive to use against the large number of individuals and small groups that could conceivably threaten U.S. computer-based information systems. To be practical, a prevention strategy needs to be focused and applied selectively. Emphasizing prevention as an element of U.S. strategy can also reinforce deterrence. An appreciation by potential adversaries that even the probing of U.S. systems might lead to planting of software to monitor the source computer's activities can complement U.S. efforts at deterrence and defense.

## TOWARD A NATIONAL STRATEGY FOR INFORMATION-WARFARE DEFENSE

National security, by definition, is defense against threats mounted from outside the United States. Dealing with information-warfare threats, like dealing with terrorism, requires a different approach, one that merges the external and internal threats. Table 14.3 summarizes the main strategy to be used against each adversary; it should be emphasized, however, that these strategies supplement each other in all cases and need to be used in combination.

In any serious national defense strategy to deal with the information-warfare threat, local and national protection must be emphasized first. Eliminating vulnerability is always preferable to managing threats. However, protection alone is unlikely to be sufficient. Therefore, it must be accompanied with plans to prevent and deter attacks. Prevention should be emphasized as the primary strategy for the middle-level threats that are most imminent. For the highest end of the threat spectrum, a deterrence strategy to defend against weapons of mass disruption by a major power is likely to become essential.

**Table 14.3**

**Information-Warfare Actors and Strategies**

| Type of Actor | Subtype | Main Strategies |
|---|---|---|
| Individuals | Hacker "gray hats" | Protection, deterrence |
| | Criminal "black hats" | Protection, deterrence, prevention |
| Coordinated substate groups or networks | Ad hoc | Protection, deterrence, prevention |
| | Criminal | Prevention, deterrence, protection |
| | Terrorist (political) | Prevention, protection |
| | Terrorist (millennial) | Prevention, protection |
| | Insurgent | Prevention, protection |
| | Commercial organizations | Prevention, protection |
| States | Small | Prevention, deterrence |
| | Peer | Deterrence |

Developing a comprehensive national strategy requires facing up to some serious legal, strategic, organizational, and policy challenges. Currently, DoD does not have the necessary legal standing to engage domestically in many of the activities that the prevention strategy is likely to require, especially the need to search private computer systems and seize or destroy systems being used for information warfare. As a society, we have not determined whether an information warfare attack on a nonmilitary target—even against systems that DoD relies on but does not own—is a military attack. These issues must be clarified.

Similar clarity is needed about responsibilities for gathering intelligence for effective information-warfare defense. Traditionally, the intelligence services (civilian and military) have divided up their areas of responsibility roughly along geographic lines. If a target was within the United States, the FBI was in charge; outside the United States, either the Central Intelligence Agency or the National Security Agency ran the show, depending on the intelligence goals and methods. Dealing with the information-warfare threat may require some jurisdictional adjustments and increased cooperation across the intelligence, law enforcement, and military communities.

## REFERENCES

Biddle, Stephen, "Victory Misunderstood: What the Gulf War Tells Us About the Future of Conflict," *International Security*, Vol. 21, No. 2, Fall 1996.

Carley, William M., and Timothy L. O'Brien, "How Citicorp's System Was Raided and Funds Moved Around the World," *Wall Street Journal*, September 12, 1995, p. 1.

Denning, Dorothy E., "Protection and Defense of Intrusion," paper presented at the Conference on National Security in the Information Age, U.S. Air Force Academy, February 1996. Last accessed on March 3, 1999 at **http://www.cs.georgetown.edu/~denning/infosec/USAFA.html**

Deutsch, John M., "Foreign Information Warfare Programs and Capabilities," Director of Central Intelligence Testimony to the U.S. Senate, Committee on Governmental Affairs, Permanent Subcommittee on Investigations, June 25, 1996.

GAO—*See* U.S. General Accounting Office.

Gertz, Bill, "Infowar Game Shuts Down U.S. Power Grid, Disabled Pacific Command," *Washington Times,* April 16, 1998, p. 1.

Graham, Bradley, "Lack of Disclosure Impedes Development of Safeguards," *Washington Post,* February 28, 1998, p. A6.

Harknett, Richard J., "Information Warfare and Deterrence," *Parameters,* Autumn 1996, pp. 93–107.

Howard, John D., *An Analysis of Internet Security Incidents, 1989–1995.* unpublished dissertation., Pittsburgh, Penn.: Carnegie Mellon University, 1997.

Hundley, Richard O., and Robert H. Anderson, "Emerging Challenge: Security and Safety in Cyberspace," *IEEE Technology and Society Magazine,* Vol. 14, No. 4, Winter 1995–1996, pp. 19–28.

Johnson, Deborah G., and Helen Nissenbaum, eds., *Computers, Ethics and Social Values,* Englewood Cliffs, N.J.: Prentice Hall, 1995.

Lee, Leonard, *The Day the Phones Stopped: The Computer Crisis,* New York: Donald I. Fine, 1991.

Markoff, John, "Computer Intruder Is Put on Probation and Fined $10,000," *The New York Times,* May 5, 1990, p. 1.

Molander, Roger C., Andrew S. Riddile, and Peter A. Wilson, *Strategic Information Warfare: A New Face of War,* Santa Monica, Calif.: RAND, MR-661-OSD, 1996.

Munro, Neil, "The Pentagon's New Nightmare: An Electronic Pearl Harbor: A Look at the On-Line Frontier," *The Washington Post,* July 16, 1995, p. C3.

Perrow, Charles, *Normal Accidents: Living with High-Risk Technologies,* New York: Basic Books, 1984.

President's Commission on Critical Infrastructure Protection, *Critical Foundations: Protecting America's Infrastructures,* October 1997.

Sandberg, Jared, "Hackers Take Revenge on the Author of a New Book on Cyberspace Wars," *Wall Street Journal,* December 5, 1994, p. B6.

Stout, David, "Pentagon Acknowledges Hacker Intrusion into a Computer System," *New York Times,* April 22, 1998, p. 1

Thomas, Timothy L., "Russian Views on Information-Based Warfare," *Airpower Journal,* Special Edition, 1996, pp. 25–35.

_____, "Deterring Information Warfare," *Parameters,* Winter 1996–1997, pp. 81–91.

U.S. Department of Defense, Joint Chiefs of Staff, *Joint Vision 2010,* 1996.

U.S. General Accounting Office, "Information Security: Computer Attacks at the Department of Defense Pose Increasing Risks," May 1996, GAO/AIMD-96-84.

_____, "Computer Security: Pervasive, Serious Weaknesses Jeopardize State Department Operations," May 1998a, GAO/AIMD-98-145.

_____, "Air Traffic Control: Weak Computer Security Practices Jeopardize Flight Safety," May 1998b, GAO/AIMD-98-155.

U.S. Senate Committee on Governmental Affairs, "Weak Computer Security in Government: Is the Public at Risk?" Public Hearing, May 19, 1998.

The White House, "Protecting America's Critical Infrastructure," Presidential Decision Directive 63, May 1998. Last accessed at http://www.ciao.gov/paper598.html on 18 March 1999.

Wildhorn, Sorrel, Brian Michael Jenkins, and M. M. Lavin, *Intelligence Constraints of the 1970s and Domestic Terrorism, Vol. I: Effects on the Incidence, Investigation, and Prosecution of Terrorists,* Santa Monica, Calif.: RAND, N-1901, 1982.

# Chapter Fifteen

# CONCLUSION: THE CHANGING ROLE OF INFORMATION IN WARFARE

*Martin Libicki and Jeremy Shapiro*

Information achieves value by improving decisions. Thus, the role of information in warfare must be to affect strategic or tactical decisions in one's favor. This role is as old as warfare itself; indeed, it might be said to be the very purpose of warfare. So what is new, or, more precisely, why does information seem to be becoming more important now? In a word: technology. New machines and new processes have recently become integral to collection, processing, and dissemination of information. An increasing percentage of decisionmaking and decision support has been transferred from people to machines. People operate under familiar physical and psychological parameters. Machines operate under unfamiliar and increasingly complex parameters. They and their logical processes are subject to attacks and manipulations that are both novel and difficult to understand intuitively.

In evaluating the effects of these new machines and new processes, the chapters in this volume have covered an extremely diverse set of topics and viewpoints, ranging from the sources of national power and the possibilities for psychological operations to the rise of arcane techniques as the new arm of military decision. These topics are ultimately linked only by their information and national security components. The influence of information in and on warfare appears so pervasive that one may reasonably wonder how "information warfare" differs from warfare itself. Information war fare in this sense is less a distinct topic than an approach—a way of bringing to the fore an aspect of warfare that has always been critical but that we sense is becoming still more important.

At the same time, dramatic changes in the ways we communicate, organize, and work will inevitably mean that wars may be fought for entirely new motives and even by new actors.  David Gompert sees the new technologies as creating a world far more favorable to U.S. interests in which peer competitors and even major theater wars will cease to plague the United States.  By contrast, John Arquilla, David Ronfeldt, and Michele Zanini see a world of new threats, stemming primarily from nonstate actors that may create a very unstable environment and severely tax U.S. defense resources.  Finally, Jeremy Shapiro cautions against accepting either of these claims of wholesale transformation.  Yet, all three contributions warn that those who see only direct military effects may miss the greater change.  According to Carl Builder, the U.S. military has tended to see new technologies in terms of how they can improve mission capabilities, rather than anticipating how their missions will change.

If the future looks foggy, a wait-and-see attitude is easiest to justify. But the Department of Defense (DoD) must be aware of the context in which it operates and know that this context is subject to change by technological and other influences—even if it cannot help but react to changes that it cannot influence.  Inevitably, an awareness of the possibility of a radical social transformation means that the military must strive to maintain both its flexibility and its link to civil society.  A military cut off from civilian influences in a time of social transformation risks becoming dangerously out of touch with the polity it is supposed to protect.

The purpose of this volume has been to prepare the United States for these transformations by revisiting old questions with a new attention to information and emerging information technology.  The chapters probably raise more questions than they answer, but in their diversity they serve to highlight the important areas for attention.  This final chapter will point to several such areas and the implications of all this for the nation and for the U.S. Air Force.

## TREND OR FAD?

One theme that runs through nearly all of the chapters in this volume is the idea that the new technologies herald a new age of warfare. Nonetheless, many maintain that less has changed than we might think.  They hold that the nature of war; the admixture of fear, glory, and survival instincts; the transcendent qualities of leadership (or its failures); and Clausewitzian fog and friction are both persistent and dominant; "information warfare" is just another in a series of failed technological solutions to this permanent feature of war.

Their millenarian counterparts aver that people war as they work. Just as the transition from agriculture to industry was correlated with the industrialization of warfare, so too will the transition from industry to information-based services be correlated with the "informating" of warfare. War waged in cyberspace might be bloodless and even clean, a possibility that has led one high-ranking military officer to see information technology as "America's gift to warfare." (Owens, 1995.) Sun Tzu is an icon in this pantheon, with his observation that the "acme of skill" consists in winning without fighting.

This war of words between those who see war as hopelessly messy and violent and those who foresee bloodless battles belies an important change. For the United States and its allies, people are expensive; stuff is cheap. Silicon is getting cheaper, and casualties are growing prohibitively expensive. Thus, as any economist would argue, it makes sense to substitute what is getting cheaper for what is getting more expensive—that is, to substitute as much silicon for casualties as one can. Throughout the U.S. military, precision weapons are being substituted for simple shot and shell (precision weapons accounted for over 99 percent of all North Atlantic Treaty Organization ordnance dropped in Bosnia in 1995), and networked sensors are illuminating the battlespace to generate aimpoints that give these precision weapons somewhere to go. Information technology is changing the U.S. military, whether it creates a new age of warfare or not. It is changing others as well, albeit more slowly and less completely so far.

No sooner, however, does a military adopt a certain functional architecture then the core of that architecture becomes its center of gravity, the logical target for the enemy, and thus what must be most vigilantly protected. Just as no one today would build a car without brakes and bumpers, so should no one design an information system without due attention to its fault modes, whether accidental or deliberately induced. Deception (dummies, decoys, and ghosts) represents a time-honored way of inducing failure in both man and machine-based information systems. Electronic warriors have thought through the interplay of measure, countermeasure, counter-countermeasure, and so on for years, in part because radar and radio-electronic communications are meant to work "outdoors" where the enemy may lurk. System architects have been somewhat slower to catch on, in large part because computers were designed for indoor work. Only recently, with ubiquitous networking, have they been transformed, with little forethought, into outdoor systems.

The sudden understanding that critical systems are vulnerable to someone operating from a phone booth anywhere in the world has led, and properly so, to great concern. Information security is increasingly a cost of doing business—especially in war, an endeavor whose purpose is to foil others.

## PERFECT SECURITY?

Is perfect information security possible? This issue is probably the most vexing of any in the science of computer security; its answer rests, in large part, on which metaphor we use to describe information warfare: engineering, combat, or disease.

In theory, perfect security is possible. There is no such thing as forced entry in cyberspace. If someone enters a system without authorization, it can only be through a door inadvertently left open. Information security is therefore an engineering problem, akin to making a ship watertight. In that case, it may be misleading to think in terms of "information-warfare weapons" or in terms of second-order considerations, such as arms control or deterrence. Insofar as information weapons exist, their design follows directly from the features and flaws of the system being attacked. Focusing on the weapons rather than on the security flaws has the unfortunate effect of centralizing a problem best dealt with at the local level.

In practice, however, pessimists argue that, as systems grow more complex and continue to evolve rapidly, what is theoretically possible becomes practically impossible. Determining all fault modes with security implications simply cannot be done in any feasible time period. In the real world, then, information security may, like combat, be a continual race between offensive measure and defensive countermeasure.

Combat is marked by a conceptual parity between offense and defense. No wall, however thick, can withstand a battering ram of sufficient size; no battering ram, however large, can knock down a wall of sufficient thickness. It may be thus with information security. One side builds defenses; the other side builds weapons; and the race is never ending. This metaphor implies that invulnerability from information attack is impossible or is at least fleeting. This is the premise that led Zalmay Khalilzad to think beyond local measures of information security to national strategies.

Information-warfare hawks go further by invoking the metaphor of disease. They see a world of big organisms at risk from small germs. Offensive information warfare is cheap; for most tasks, a laptop and a phone line suffice. Not everyone can be a good hacker, but rogue hackers can peddle their expertise worldwide. Disposable jammers can wreak havoc on communication systems. Viruses can propagate endlessly from one machine to another. Tools of intrusion and cover-up flow freely on the Internet. Cyberspace is becoming increasingly plague-ridden, and ever-larger percentages of computer investment must be devoted to protection. In this view, information security is a crisis that threatens us all and demands a centralized public response, much as the urbanization of the 19th century created a requirement for public health.

But the disease metaphor also speaks to a growing facet of information warfare: complexity. On the one hand, the more complex a system is, the harder it is to ensure its integrity. On the other hand, people—the world's most complex information-processing systems—are generally immune to the sorts of attacks that keep system administrators up nights.

A normal person told by a stranger that the world would be a better place when he or she is dead is unlikely to take that information to its logical conclusion. The information makes no sense; there is little a stranger can do to make one believe in such nonsense; and, anyway, such strangers have no authority to so command you. The last two barriers to doing stupid things have analogies in computer security: virus protection (lack of trust in outside sources) and authentication (verifying that a person is known to you). But the first notion of "common sense" is far less effective in securing computers. We expect our machines to do what they are told, but such expectations leave them prey to low-level, but insidious, information-warfare attacks.

With the inevitable (if oft-delayed) advent of artificial intelligence, the practice of generating general mission orders and having the machine determine how and when to carry them out may become more common. Heuristics may prevent them from doing stupid things. Yet, such technologies as knowledge engineering, rule-based logic, and neural nets, while making machines more sophisticated, leave them harder to predict and understand. The price of preventing obvious failure may leave them heir to the subtle manipulations that humans have long been exposed to. (See, for instance, MacKay, 1841.)

## NATIONAL POLICY ISSUES

The policy issues that information warfare raises are, in a sense, a subset of the policy issues that are raised by the entire field of information technology. Some come under the rubric of national public information policy—a shadowy area that often mixes truth and propaganda. Other issues are raised by the increasing importance of network systems to the U.S. economy and the consequent desirability of their protection.

It is only somewhat of an oversimplification to reduce the issue of national public information policy to the blunt question: Should it be the official policy of the U.S. government to lie? Of course not, John Arquilla suggests. Yet, as Brian Nichiporuk argues, DoD may at times want to insert false messages into another nation's communication systems. Moral difficulties aside, as long as the United States is not directly threatened (a condition that, by and large, obtains today), its primary national security strategy consists of inducing other nations to adopt what are considered good and universal norms of conduct. Among them are democracy, rule of law, and freedom of expression. All three must rest on a foundation of truth. If that foundation erodes, the norms get shaky. In any case, as society becomes increasingly networked and as electronic surveillance makes the world increasingly transparent, the art of lying becomes harder and harder.

The issues that relate to protecting the national information infrastructure, as Roger Molander, Peter Wilson, and Robert Anderson outlined, are dense and intertwined. In theory, the government's right and responsibility to protect cyberspace are straightforward, perhaps even more obvious than a comparable aegis over protecting the nation's ships, aircraft, and space satellites. In practice, the government may wish to approach this new task gingerly.

The justifications for the government's diffidence stem from technology. By and large, people play havoc with networks by attacking systems attached to them. Each system has its owner, and each owner is the one to choose the hardware and software, as well as set the parameters and policies that collectively determine how easily an attack takes place. The government can facilitate good choices with both carrots and sticks. It can also prosecute malefactors and seek to dissuade their sponsors—although, as Glenn Buchan points out, this may be very difficult to do. What the government cannot do is to erect a barrier through which bad bytes cannot flow, a continental firewall as it were.

If the government cannot reliably protect systems, should it nevertheless accept the responsibility to do so? The answer is not obvious (replace "systems" with "borders" and most people would answer "yes"). Popular sentiment may leave the government little choice in the matter, especially after the first disaster. Yet accepting such responsibility for itself has a tendency to reduce the responsibility of others, notably system owners—and the latter have the means and tools to protect themselves. Roger Molander et al. speak of a "loss of confidence" in national institutions as a result of strategic information warfare. Would accepting responsibility create a linkage whereby loss of confidence in, say, the telephone system also erodes the confidence that people feel in the government?

As both the Gompert and the Arquilla, Ronfeldt, and Zanini contributions emphasized, realizing the true potential of information technology requires a decentralized market economy and the motivated actions of each of its citizens. Except for providing common infrastructures, the logic of centralization is absent. Indeed, centralization and hierarchy may limit the advantages one can draw from the new technologies.

Not only are owners of the information infrastructure desirous of defending their own systems, but most do not answer to the federal government, and some are highly suspicious of any unsolicited "help" they may get from such quarters. Many suspect that bureaucrats are incapable of understanding or keeping pace with emerging technology. An overemphasis on security at the expense of other features and the bureaucracy's natural tendency to emphasize procedures over outcomes may yield no better security and far less innovation. If nothing else, there is a perceived contradiction between the government's offer of help to the owners of private systems, and its continuing efforts against the market for encryption products, which are one of the better defenses.

If owners bear *all* the costs (including third-party costs) of their own negligence, there is no reason they cannot provide optimal levels of protection in this field as in others. True, some aspects of information security are best done collectively because of economies of scale (e.g., research and development, indicators and warning). Others are inherently matters of state (e.g., criminal prosecution, military retaliation). Nonetheless, they hardly constitute, even collectively, all the tasks necessary for a complete defense of the nation against information warfare. The burden is therefore on the government to demonstrate that the protection of commercial information infrastructure is a national security concern that cannot be discharged any other way. Convincing a population wary of government intervention of the need for such intrusive government action may require a crisis.

Turning from the general to the more specific, the federal government can do many useful things to help matters when the only interesting question is not "whether" but "how much":

- *Protect Its Own Systems:* Not only are national systems of national importance, but the federal government has declared that the security of its information systems would set a standard for the rest of the nation.

- *Enforce the Law:* A thicket of laws already exists against computer hacking, abuse of spectrum (e.g., jamming radio signals), and microwave weapons (as a category of weapons in general). In enforcing such laws, the federal performance has been very efficient, and an unexpectedly high percentage of high-profile attacks has resulted in successful prosecutions.

- *Promote Standards:* Standards are important for interoperability, security, and creating a performance level against which existing systems can be judged.

- *Invest in Research and Development:* The level of federally sponsored research and development in information security has risen at a good clip from the $100 million-per-year level of several years ago (a lightweight secure network operating system remains one crying need). Although the scarcity of skilled researchers puts an upper bound on any funding trajectory, R&D funding today means more graduate students tomorrow and more professionals the day after.

- *Establish an Incident Clearinghouse:* The Computer Emergency Response Team is a well-established clearinghouse for collecting information on Internet security incidents, disseminating warnings, and generating countermeasures for novel attacks. Other industries and the military are starting similar clearinghouses for their own sectors. The Computer Emergency Response Team model represents a compromise between centralized and decentralized control that combines the best features of both. It preserves local responsibility but provides a central repository of expertise that can acquire a global view of any emerging threat.

Some policy instruments are worthwhile, but have some potential for backfiring if broader ramifications are not kept in mind:

- *Generating Indications and Warnings:* In theory, premonitions of an information attack could be broadcast so that system owners can ratchet up their monitoring and review their access procedures. In practice, as Glenn Buchan points out, premonitions may be hard to come by, and establishing the credibility of such indications and warnings may raise difficult issues about sources and methods.

- *Fostering International Norms and Cooperation:* Progress has been made in fostering international cooperation among law enforcement agencies and in persuading other countries to make computer hacking a criminal offense. As Lynn Davis warns, however, beyond some point, other nations will demand that the United States pay comparable heed to violations of what they consider norms in the information age (e.g., violation of data privacy—a nascent issue in Europe). If U.S. military policy is to maintain "information dominance," emerging norms against the use of information weapons may limit the utility of that capability.

Still other policy instruments seem attractive but require a good deal of thought prior to their implementation:

- *Determining a Minimum Essential Information Infrastructure (MEII):* Research to determine candidate members in a national MEII is all well and good, but should policy actually be based on the findings? Two troubling questions present themselves: "essential" for what end, and "essential" for how long (in the face of furious technological change)? An MEII for the military (or the broader national security community) raises fewer difficult issues. DoD's various operational plans answer the question of ends, and its acquisition policies inform near- and medium-term changes in its own MEII. Once the elements of a defense MEII are determined, DoD can use several specific tools (e.g., through clauses in defense contracts) to bolster the security of networks essential to its own missions. Nonetheless, the increasing interconnection of civilian systems with the DoD information infrastructure complicates even this simpler task.

- *Protecting Auditing and Testing:* Honest third-party audits may become more frequent if the auditors can be shielded from having to testify in civil suits about what they find. Red-team testing of critical systems may become more common if owners could be covered from some legal liabilities that accidentally result from such tests. Yet, there is no legal protection that cannot be abused, and extensions of long-standing claims to one area give rise to demands for protection in others (e.g., if computer security specialists, why not safety engineers?).

- *Limiting Legal Indemnity for the Consequences of Attack:* If an attack on a network (e.g., one that controls electrical distribution) causes harm to third parties, can third parties sue network owners and collect damages against them? If the answer is *no*, network owners will underinvest in security (and demand the government step in to cover their failures). A *yes* answer, however, adds one more basis for lawsuits in a very litigious society.

- *Declaring a Retaliatory Policy on Information Attack:* Can the United States deter a strategic information attack by declaring it tantamount to a physical attack (e.g., mass disruption as a subspecies of mass destruction)? Were such a thing possible, deterrence might obtain, but as Zalmay Khalilzad enumerates, practical difficulties abound:   setting a threshold for response, determining the perpetrator, and forcing the United States to react in predetermined ways where wisdom might suggest otherwise.

- *Declaring a No-First-Use Policy on Information Warfare:* It makes sense for residents of glass houses to look askance at stones.  Nevertheless, the case that information warfare has a bad reputation morally that shell and shot lack may be hard to make.  Again, practical difficulties matter.  In nuclear warfare, the event is unmistakable; the perpetrator can often be identified reliably; and the requisite equipment can be placed under secure command and control.  None of this applies to information warfare.

## AIR FORCE POLICY ISSUES

At one level, information warfare presents fewer troubling policy issues for the Air Force than for the nation as a whole.  Understood broadly, information warfare is a collection of operational techniques that are used with greater or lesser efficacy as circumstances and capabilities warrant.  At another level, however, as the Air Force redefines and reorganizes itself, it must necessarily ask whether information warfare is at the heart of its mission or whether it is one of several adjunct competencies necessary to promote the main task of aerospace superiority.

Most of what falls under information warfare, with its many historic components (e.g., command-center targeting, psychological operations, electronic combat, signals intelligence), has been parceled out for action long ago.  However, to many, the mechanization of the world's decision processes has introduced a new medium of warfare, cyberspace.  Conflict in cyberspace, like conflict in predecessor media, must be dealt with in its own terms and may justify entirely new missions and organizations.

The concept of cyberspace as a new medium, of course, cannot help but resonate with the U.S. Air Force. Air forces spent most of the first half of the 20th century arguing that their medium was fundamentally different from those before it.  Mastering the medium of air, they claimed, required new doctrine, new culture, and new people and, as a result, a new home for its masters.  Having won the argument for air, the U.S. Air Force makes a similar argument for space: It too is a new medium, with its own doctrine, culture, and people. However, the argument continues, the link between air and space is strong (e.g., the natural complementarity between space assets and high stratospheric unmanned aerial vehicles to support surveillance; reconnaissance; and, perhaps soon, communications). Thus, those who pioneered the first should be asked to master the second. In its 1996 Corona conference, the Air Force hierarchy concluded that the Air Force should see itself as an Air and Space Force today and perhaps a Space and Air Force in the future.

Airmen have been arguing since Douhet that air operations could, in and of themselves, be an arm of decision. Both the Six-Day War and Desert Storm indicate that, under certain circumstances, winning the air campaign makes the land campaign very easy. Information warfighters, using Desert Storm as an example, now make similar claims for information warfare. Achieving information superiority will make winning the air and land wars much simpler.

Warfare in cyberspace fits a service that has been quick to convert new technological possibilities into new forms of power and quick to see that new media have new rules. The great majority of U.S. "military opportunities" that David Ochmanek and Ted Harshberger document would appear to accrue to the Air Force. But history also suggests that institutions that have mastered one new medium are not automatically assigned the next. After all, the U.S. space program grew out of work undertaken by the *Army* at Redstone Arsenal.

More fundamentally, integrating cyberspace warfare will perhaps, as Carl Builder's contribution suggests, require the Air Force to address "the enterprise question." What are the Air Force's objective, purpose, and comparative advantage as a service? This is the question that bedeviled the Army during the interwar period and, after much acrimony, eventually led to an independent air force. If the Air Force wishes to absorb the cyberspace mission as warfare in a new medium, it must be prepared for the creation of new constituency in its midst, one that will seek its own identity and perhaps independence from the Air Force's pilot culture. This much may be seen from its experience with integrating space operations and the consequent struggles over space assets, people, and organizations. Nevertheless, it is quite likely that the issue of whether to absorb cyberspace as a single medium into the Air Force is less likely to be as defining as were similar issues in earlier media.

First, post–Goldwater Nichols, the various commanders in chief (CINCs) have increasing say and discretion over how they put force packages together—and with ever finer granularity. The Air Force may argue that information operations are so uniquely integral to air and space operations that they belong in the same service. Come wartime, however, a CINC will likely build a force by picking up a squadron here, a vessel there, and a battalion somewhere else based on the logic of time and place. Information operations will need to function in this joint, CINC-determined environment.

Second, once the issue of constructing coherent force packages is left to the CINCs, the service slice of information warfare will consist of training and equipping information warriors. The Air Force may be able to make a case for training information warriors (a subject that the military has only started to come to grips with), but, in contrast with aerospace warfare, equipping them is usually a trivial undertaking that need not be limited to one service.

Third, as widely noted, information warfare spans considerable terrain, whose boundaries are very difficult to distinguish. For this reason, in asking about the relevance and wisdom of making information warfare an Air Force mission, it may be worthwhile to look at individual chunks as Table 15.1 subdivides them.

Information assurance is a broad function with many responsibilities. Intrusion detection and thwarting of attacks on systems is the focus of the Air Force's 609th squadron at Shaw Air Force Base and the impetus for intense activity at the Joint Information Warfare Center at Kelly Air Force Base. But real-time cybercombat is just one

**Table 15.1**

**Information-Warfare Matrix**

|  | Unit Level | Systemic |
|---|---|---|
| Defense | Information assurance | System of systems |
| Offense | Hacker attacks, electronic warfare | Command-and-control warfare |

aspect of information assurance. Vigilance, sound engineering choices, and internal controls are of comparable importance. Responsibility for these functions is best pushed down the hierarchy. Defending networks should be the primary responsibility of those who run them. Complexity and the need to integrate information about attacks offer the counterarguments. The more one must know to defend a network, the more it pays to concentrate the expertise and information within a few people as opposed to forcing everyone to learn everything.

Tactical offensive information warfare (see the contribution by Brian Nichiporuk) has two components: intelligence and operations. If existing intelligence and information functions are a clue, the civilian leadership is not predisposed to assign primary responsibility for information warfare to any one service. A large and growing share of DoD's information functions reside in defense agencies and joint commands, even if Air Force personnel and facilities provide more than proportional support for these missions. Offensive information warfare, especially, is likely to be the province of intelligence agencies because of its elite and clandestine nature.

Offensive electronic warfare, however, is an enterprise that is disproportionately Air Force today (although the Navy has comparable responsibilities in the fleet, and the Army conducts similar operations). Indeed, the mission to suppress enemy air defenses is critical to successful air operations. Extending this mission to encompass information warfare offensive techniques would seem an easy fit for the Air Force.

At the systemic level, information warfare is the organization of information to provide warfighters with what has been termed "dominant battlespace knowledge," an important component of which is the DoD's nascent "system of systems." Insofar as the ability to kill what can be seen makes seeing (locating, identifying, and tracking) the key to war, seeing is increasingly best done by networking sensors and human observers to create a shared ground truth that forms the basis of command, control, and operations. This evolution can be seen in the widely heralded transition from platform-centric warfare (wherein networks exist to enhance platform performance) to network-centric warfare (wherein platforms are the eyes, ears, and fists of a broader entity). If there is to be an entity in charge of building and maintaining this shared ground truth, the Air Force, with its air and space intelligence, surveillance, and reconnaissance assets, is as good a candidate as any. Indeed, some in the Air Force have concluded that the first assets the United States should deploy into a combat zone are not the folks who are "First to Fight" but the illuminators. With today's technology, these illuminators may be represented by a package of the Joint Surveillance and Target Attack Radar System; the Airborne Warning and Control System; Rivet Joint; and, soon, long-range unmanned aerial vehicles. (See Fulghum, 1998.)

Finally, systemic information warfare is a matter of determining how an adversary uses information to inform decisions and then using this knowledge to disrupt or corrupt their decisionmaking processes. Of course, some attack methods may be attacks on information systems themselves, but if critical nodes of an adversary can be discovered, iron bombs are another feasible approach, as Glenn Buchan argues.

Based on what is admittedly an initial assessment of various aspects of information warfare, the best places for the Air Force to build up and defend unique core competencies lie in the area of unit-level operations against enemy information systems and in the care and maintenance of the top-level system of systems. By contrast, the case for centralizing tactical systems defense and understanding adversary decision processes under Air Force control will be harder to make.

## A TIMELESS LESSON OF INFORMATION WARFARE

Deeper consideration of this area, however, suggests that information warfare, in the end, may be less about a discrete set of activities or responsibilities than about a way of thinking about conflict. It forces warfighters to ponder not just each side's physical capabilities, but also the decision processes that govern when, where, and with what effect these physical capabilities are used. These are habits of mind that all warfighters, at all times, should adopt and not simply those of any one service or nation. That new technologies have made us reconsider this timeless piece of wisdom does not mean that everything has changed suddenly. To the contrary, we may simply be rediscovering what we have really known all along.

## REFERENCES

Fulghum, David A., "Info War Fleet Tapped for Fast Deployment," *Aviation Week & Space Technology*, February 9, 1998, pp. 90–91.

MacKay, Charles, *Extraordinarily Popular Delusions and the Madness of Crowds*, New York: Crown Trade Paperbacks, 1995 [1841].

Owens, Admiral William, quoted in Douglas Waller, "Onward Cyber Soldiers," *Time*, Vol. 146, No. 8, August 21, 1995.